Reimagining Nonprofits

What is the nonprofit sector and why does it exist? Collecting the writing of some of the most creative minds in the field of nonprofit studies, this book challenges our traditional understanding of the role and purpose of the nonprofit sector. It reflects on the ways in which new cultural and economic shifts bring existing assumptions into question and offers new conceptualizations of the nonprofit sector that will inform, provoke, and inspire. Nonprofit organization and activity is an enormously important part of social, cultural, and economic life around the world, but our conceptualization of their place in modern society is far from complete. *Reimagining Nonprofits* provides fresh insights that are necessary for understanding nonprofit organizations and sectors in the twenty-first century.

EVA WITESMAN is Professor at the Romney Institute of Public Service and Ethics and Director of the Ballard Center for Social Impact at Brigham Young University. An institutional theorist who studies the nonprofit, public, and private sectors, she serves as chair for the Public and Nonprofit Division of the Academy of Management.

CURTIS CHILD is Associate Professor and Chair of Sociology at Brigham Young University. He has published widely on nonprofit organizations and is a member of the Association for Research on Nonprofit Organizations and Voluntary Action.

Contents

Figures

Tables

Contributors

SEONGHO AN is Assistant Professor in the School of Public Administration at the University of Central Florida

PATRICIA BROMLEY is Associate Professor in the Graduate School of Education and the Doerr School of Sustainability at Stanford University

ELEANOR BROWN is James Irvine Professor in the Department of Economics at Pomona College

ELIZABETH A. CASTILLO is Assistant Professor of Management at California State University San Bernardino

CURTIS CHILD is Associate Professor in Sociology at Brigham Young University

JASON COUPET is Associate Professor in the Andrew Young School of Policy Studies at Georgia State University

KANDYCE FERNANDEZ is Assistant Professor in Public Administration at the University of Texas at San Antonio

RUTH K. HANSEN is Assistant Professor in Management at the University of Wisconsin–Whitewater

MING HU is Assistant Professor in Nonprofit Management at Macau University of Science and Technology, Macau (China)

HEE SOUN JANG is Associate Professor in the Department of Public Administration at the University of North Texas

BOK GYO JEONG is Associate Professor in the College of Business and Public Management at Kean University

IRINA KRASNOPOLSKAYA is Researcher in the Institute for Law and Philanthropy at Tel Aviv University

MEEYOUNG LAMOTHE is Associate Professor in the Department of Political Science at the University of Oklahoma

MISUN LEE is a PhD candidate in the Askew School of Public Administration and Policy at Florida State University

MEGAN LEPERE-SCHLOOP is Assistant Professor in the John Glenn College of Public Affairs at Ohio State University

YUNG-PIN LU is Assistant Professor in the School of International and Public Affairs at Shanghai Jiao Tong University

GEORGE E. MITCHELL is Associate Professor in the Marxe School of Public and International Affairs at Baruch College, City University of New York

LAURIE MOOK is Associate Professor in the School of Community Resources and Development at Arizona State University

REBECCA NESBIT is Professor in the Department of Public Administration and Policy at the University of Georgia

ADA ORDOR is Director and Professor at the Centre for Comparative Law in Africa in the Faculty of Law at the University of Cape Town

ROBERT W. RESSLER is Senior Research Associate in the Institute for Child, Youth and Family Policy at Brandeis University

ANA CLARISSA ROJAS DURAZO is Assistant Professor in Chicana and Chicano Studies at the University of California–Davis

HEITOR SANTOS is a PhD candidate in the Graduate School of Education at Stanford University

SHARIQ SIDDIQUI is Assistant Professor in the Lilly Family School of Philanthropy at Indiana University Indianapolis

YULIA SKOKOVA is an independent scholar

RICHARD STEINBERG is Professor of Economics and Philanthropic Studies at Indiana University Indianapolis

JIWON SUH is Assistant Professor in Public Affairs and Planning at the University of Texas, Arlington

LIZA L. TAYLOR is an independent researcher

ROBBIE WATERS ROBICHAU is Associate Professor in the Bush School of Government and Public Service at Texas A&M University

JOHN R. WHITMAN is an instructor at Harvard University Extension School

CATHERINE E. WILSON is Associate Professor in Public Administration at Villanova University

EVA WITESMAN is Professor in the Romney Institute of Public Service and Ethics at Brigham Young University

GREGORY R. WITKOWSKI is Senior Lecturer of Nonprofit Management in the School of Professional Studies at Columbia University

Acknowledgments

Organizing this volume has been a collaborative effort, from start to finish. Many thanks are in order. First and foremost, we are deeply grateful for our team of contributors who endured multiple rounds of revisions and exerted tremendous imagination and effort to bring this volume to pass.

Colleagues, mentors, and administrators at our home institution, Brigham Young University, provided all the support we could hope for. Our respective departments and colleges (the Department of Sociology; the College of Family, Home, and Social Sciences; the Romney Institute for Public Service and Ethics; and the Marriott School of Business) offered generous financial and student support without which the project would have been impossible.

We are deeply indebted to the in-house copy-editing help we received from Brigham Young University's Faculty Publishing Service. Heather Randall shepherded the process with professionalism and patience. And although we are sure they learned more about sector theory than they ever hoped for, Suzana Dvorak, Emily Furner, Kim Sandoval, and Rebecca Timmons provided much-needed editorial assistance. We simply could not have done this without them.

Research assistants Hannah Lyons and Cassidy Wixom caught the global vision of the project and helped us to bring many of our international chapters from hope to reality.

We express joyful gratitude for colleagues who read drafts, gave advice, celebrated with us, and nudged us along the way. Rob Christensen, Jon Jarvis, Jane Lopez, Laura Padilla-Walker, Brigitte Madrian (and her celebration bell), John Bingham, Jill Piacitelli, and Rick Miller provided kind and unfailing encouragement.

We both feel fortunate to have enjoyed a nurturing professional environment that has sustained us for nearly two decades. From the care we received as graduate students at Indiana University's Paul H. O'Neill School of Public and Environmental Affairs (Nonprofit

Service Corps forever!) to our continued memberships in the ever-supportive Association for Research on Nonprofit Organizations and Voluntary Action, Public and Nonprofit division of the Academy of Management, and Public Management Research Association, we are indebted to colleagues around the world. Thank you for your abundant kindness and perceptive critiques that energized us and saved us from embarrassing errors.

The Cambridge University Press editorial team has been a wonder to work with. Valerie Appleby took our initial vision, which we already felt was ambitious, and pushed us to expand it even more. Carrie Parkinson held our hands along the way, making what might have otherwise seemed like an impossible goal feel within our reach. Veena Ramakrishnan and Eric Christianson were excellent members of the team, professional and kind. Thank you all for empowering our vision.

A very special thanks to our families, who inspire us every day to hope for a better world and work toward it with our whole hearts. Thank you for your support and patience during frustrating days and long nights, and thank you for celebrating our victories along the way. To our respective spouses, Owen and Sage, we are grateful for your sustaining and eternal love – and offer ours in return. To our children, Julia, Amelia, Sophia, William, Afton, Sandor, Jonah, and Remy, any improvement we make in this world is for you.

1 *An Invitation to Rethink the Nonprofit Sector*

CURTIS CHILD AND EVA WITESMAN*

1.1 An Invitation

The chapters in this volume speak to what the nonprofit sector is and why nonprofit organizations exist. As the editors of this volume, we take the opportunity in these introductory pages to describe what we mean by asking these questions, to explain what we believe good explanations of the nonprofit sector should do for us, and perhaps most importantly, to persuade readers that these are issues worth caring about.

Nonprofit activity is an enormously important part of the social, cultural, and economic life of many countries – for good or ill – and for that reason alone demands our attention (Frumkin, 2002; Weisbrod, 1991). This is true whether nonprofits are officially recognized or loose coalitions of individuals operating outside of state purview. By almost any measure, nonprofits (referred to variously as tax-exempt organizations, nongovernmental organizations, civil society organizations, voluntary organizations, third-sector entities, and the like) matter (Salamon, 2015). Formally organized nonprofits are numerically plentiful, employ millions of people throughout the world, and contribute substantially to national economies (Salamon & Sokolowski, 2004), which is to say nothing of their social significance. Worldwide, people associate in the nonprofit space to advocate, resist, celebrate, amuse, elevate, and inspire (Berry & Arons, 2003; Frumkin, 2002). Indeed, whether it be through participation in the arts, sports, the outdoors, politics, religion, education, social movements, or health care, it is hard to imagine a life not touched in some way – and often in a meaningful way – by the nonprofit sector (Salamon, 2015).

Recognizing this, many scholars now engage in the difficult work of classifying nonprofits, documenting their activities, and estimating

* Many thanks to Jon Jarvis, Megan LePere-Schloop, Jane Lopez, and Becky Nesbit for helpful comments on previous versions of this chapter.

their impacts. They do so within and across nations, standardizing measurements over space and time (e.g., Hall & Burke, 2006; Salamon & Sokolowski, 2004; United Nations Department for Economic and Social Affairs, 2018). They profile nonprofits' economic and social contributions (McKeever et al., 2016) and debate the finer points of nonprofit management, strategy, and marketing (e.g., Guo & Saxton, 2020; Renz, 2016). They document the work that sustains civil society through volunteering and philanthropic giving (e.g., Barman, 2017; Bekkers & Wiepking, 2011; Frumkin, 2006; Wilson, 2000) and offer critical perspectives of the sector and its organizations (Eikenberry et al., 2018; INCITE! Women of Color against Violence, 2017). It is demanding work, and all of it is worthy of time and effort.

However, we fear that, in its effort to shine light on the varied aspects of social life shaped by the nonprofit sector, the field of nonprofit studies has collectively turned its attention away from the basic, existential questions about the sector that once animated nonprofit scholarship and that deserve our continued contemplation. The result is that the empirical scrutiny of all things nonprofit has blossomed, while thinking deeply about the *what* and *why* of the nonprofit sector has grown stagnant. We are left dependent on intuitions about the sector's place in modern society that are in some cases decades old and, more problematically, do not represent the fulness of nonprofit organizations' rich diversity.

We have organized this volume on the premise that it is imperative to continue asking deep questions about the existence of the nonprofit sector and how it fits into society. Only in so doing can we begin to understand why (some would say *whether*) it makes sense to distinguish a nonprofit sector from the institutions of business, government, or family. Further, it is worth considering whether a "third" sector should command such significant amounts of privilege and influence. By considering questions about the *what* and *why* of the nonprofit sector, including how it is justified and what makes it unique, we are able to evaluate whether current arrangements are best for a thriving society. We are advocating, in short, for a renewed attention to first-order questions because such questions permit us to reflect on the current state of affairs in new and productive ways.

A simple thought experiment might help to illustrate. Imagine a new settlement in a previously uninhabited and ungoverned land. Eager to create the institutions that will be most likely to advance human flourishing, the settlers must decide on what their world should look like. Surely, there are countless decisions to make, but for our purposes, let us consider how they might *organize* their new world. Quite literally, what will be the nature of the organizations that they create to carry out the work of building and maintaining a society? Based on the contexts from which they came, the settlers would have several templates available to them: government-like entities, owned by the people and supported by a system of taxation; business-like associations, directed by the financial interests of their owners who are free to make decisions accordingly; nonprofit-like organizations that are private but without owners, whose purpose is to produce a benefit to society; and perhaps others still. If our settlers were creating their world anew, would these options and distinctions be obvious? Which organizational types would be desirable, or even necessary? Is it possible that the settlers would construct different arrangements, perhaps experimenting with combinations of existing entities, prohibiting other types, or innovating new forms altogether?

The answer to admittedly hypothetical questions like these have implications for how we regard the realities of today across varying national, cultural, and economic contexts. If we can imagine that our settlers would choose to support a type of nonprofit organization like those that now exist, which specific types of arrangements would they prefer, and what is that decision based on? What is the added value of promoting and protecting a sector of such organizations? What do those organizations have in common, and to what extent are they truly distinct from other types of organizations? If, on the other hand, we find it difficult to imagine our settlers justifying the creation of nonprofit-like organizations, then what are we to make of the actual existence of a nonprofit sector today? Such insights might shape how we reorganize and govern the nonprofit sector that actually exists.

This thought experiment helps us develop an imagination about the organized world. It is an exercise to aid us in considering not only what nonprofits are but why they exist. The experiment locates us in the role of creator, artists before an empty canvas. It is a fiction to be sure, but a fiction that is useful for thinking clearly about reality.

Let's leave that hypothetical world and come back to our own. The social world presents itself to us (Berger & Luckman, 1967), and we are left to navigate it, perhaps making incremental improvements along the way if we are lucky. Does that mean that considering these issues is pointless? No. Even in this real world – a world that is stubborn about change and in which we may never enjoy a fresh start – sector distinctions matter in ways that are not simply academic. For one, policy and managerial decisions could be informed by a more sophisticated understanding of nonprofit organizations' place in the modern economy (Weisbrod, 1991). On the consumption side, buyers regularly make choices between products and services that could be produced by different types of organizations, and these decisions potentially have profound consequences in their lives. Consider the choice of receiving medical care from a nonprofit, for-profit, or government provider, or the choice of receiving an education from a nonprofit, for-profit, or government college. Why these different options exist, and how (and why) the choice of sector matters in the quality of service, if at all, are questions whose answers direct us, again, to reflect on the existence and purpose of a nonprofit sector.

The time is right to reengage in conversations about what the nonprofit sector is, why it is, and what we hope it might do for us. Our traditional understanding of nonprofits has viewed them as a remedy to the failures of business and government to effectively meet the needs of a diverse society. However, as businesses evolve into an increasingly prosocial space (through social enterprise, corporate responsibility efforts, and an increased focus on environmental, social, and governance metrics), the narrative that has long defined nonprofits as fundamentally different from business is shifting. Indeed, the boundaries separating the nonprofit sector from governments and businesses have long been, and continue to be, fuzzy (Powell, 2020; Steinberg & Powell, 2006). We live in a so-called sector-bending era (Dees & Anderson, 2003), in which sector boundaries once thought to be rigid are being crossed by organizations of all types. Nonprofit organizations develop commercial revenue streams (Child, 2011), businesses pursue prosocial missions (Vogel, 2005; Yunus & Weber, 2010), nonprofits and governments are evaluated according to their business-like efficiencies (Box, 1999; Dunleavy et al., 2006), and new legal designations formalize different types of hybrid ventures (Reiser, 2010, 2011). Bromley and Meyer (2017) have argued that such boundary spanning is multidirectional, implying that, with the ascendancy of organization as a social form, sector distinctions may continue to erode until a future day in which they are either nonexistent or functionally meaningless. Although some research suggests that the classification of sector remains important to practitioners' work (Child et al., 2015), it is nevertheless the case that scholars largely consider sector blurring the new normal.

We also now live in a world that is much more globally connected than it once was (Friedman, 2005). Yet our primary ideas about what nonprofits are and why they exist are rooted in a single cultural perspective – primarily a Western, affluent, academic one. Moreover, they are deeply intertwined with the US legal system. Through the greater cultural exchange that has come with the Internet and other improvements in global awareness, it is clear that there are many forms of nongovernment, nonbusiness organizing that differ from country to country, from culture to culture, and even from organization to organization. Explanations for the existence of nonprofits based in American tax law do a poor job, in many cases, of explaining the existence of nonprofits in Asia, Africa, or Latin America (for example); the role of nonprofit organizing among indigenous peoples; or the social organizing that occurs without formalization but creates the glue that holds neighborhoods, movements, and societies together.

These realities – the blurring of sector distinctions, the ascendancy of hybrid forms, increased globalization, and questions about the importance of sector as a defining characteristic of the organized world – render an evaluation like this especially timely. They suggest a need to revisit and revitalize our conversations about the nature and role of nonprofits. The landscape has shifted, and we need a new map.

1.2 A Note about Theory

Scholars often characterize this volume's motivating questions – about the *what* and *why* of the nonprofit sector – as "sector theory." Unfortunately, the word "theory" has developed a rather negative connotation as something inscrutable, cerebral, and, dare we say, boring. We hope to convince you otherwise. Esoteric though it might sound, theory isn't only for eggheads. Rather, theory's abstract quality (even if the abstraction is modest) provides a medium through which we communicate with one another to convey our ideas (Suddaby, 2014). Theory thus understood is the collection of ideas that form an understanding of something we care to know more about. If you are reading this volume because you care about understanding nonprofit organizations, then you are necessarily interested in theories of the nonprofit sector. Contrary to what students in introductory theory classes might conclude, theory is not necessarily the canon of old ideas from (mostly) dead thinkers. It is the collection of living ideas about a particular puzzle, incorporating the best parts of a conversation that has taken place, sometimes for many years.

Still not convinced? Consider trying to make sense of a series of observations – in this case, about the set of all nonprofit organizations – without an overarching theme, guiding questions, or guesses about what you are observing. Without a theory, you would be left, essentially, with an unfiltered pile of empirical observations and one-off conclusions about nonprofit organizations, none of which would be connected to the others in a meaningful way. They would necessarily be disconnected because the thing that connects them into a cohesive statement about this puzzle is, after all, theory. Said differently, it would be difficult to build a body of knowledge about nonprofits if there was not some narrative thread tying observations and insights together, in turn creating, questioning, and revising those explanations. This is the process of developing and refining theory.

Eva Witesman unpacks this more in Chapter 4, but for now we can think of theories of the nonprofit sector simply as explanations for what the nonprofit sector is and why nonprofits exist. These explanations come in many varieties (Abend, 2008), but in all cases, sector theory answers the simple questions of *what* and *why*: What is the sector? Why nonprofits? The chapters in this volume consider these questions in one way or another.

For those wanting a more technical definition, in this volume we'll think of theories as explanations of social phenomena, in which "explanations" are not necessarily statements about causes (Sutton & Staw, 1995; Whetten, 1989) – although they certainly could be – but something more akin to accounts. These accounts come in the form of insights, interpretations, concepts, or frameworks that shed light on a phenomenon, rendering it understandable. The phenomenon in question here is the nonprofit sector. Nonprofit sector theories in this more technical sense are therefore statements that help us account for voluntary, prosocial, and organized action. Accordingly, sector theories have two basic qualities: First, they provide generalized statements, meaning that they do more than account for the idiosyncrasies of one particular place in time. Even if theory is rooted deeply in a particular case or illustration, there is at least some abstraction involved in sector theorizing, which makes the arguments transferable beyond any single context (Lincoln & Guba, 1985). Second, the explanations we're dealing with here focus on voluntary (and organized) action that is not aimed at generating profit. We are not concerned here with why individuals engage in philanthropic (or other) action. Nor are we seeking explanations for government-imposed action (which is involuntary) or business action (which we assume to be focused on generating profit). Nonprofit sector theory deals with nonprofit action, with the term "nonprofit" used in its broadest sense to encompass the range of nonstate, nonbusiness actors and actions, both formal and informal.

Countless others have reflected on or offered more technical definitions of what it means to be nonprofit (e.g., Frumkin, 2002; Hansmann, 1987; Powell, 2020; Salamon, 2015; Steinberg & Powell, 2006; Weisbrod, 1991). We take a decidedly forgiving approach, casting a wide net and not fretting too much about delineating precise sectoral boundaries. This is partly because what it means to be nonprofit is fluid (Child & Witesman, 2022). But it is also because we want to give our contributors as much flexibility as they need to develop their own ideas about sector theory, including where the boundaries of the nonprofit sector might be.

It should be clear that this volume does not focus directly on topics that have recently become the bread and butter of much academic work on nonprofit organizations and related topics, even those that are theoretical in nature. But that does not mean that current empirical work should be seen as disconnected from the theoretical foundations of sector scholarship that we ponder here. Indeed, studies of philanthropic giving, volunteering, nonprofit management, strategic planning, finances, board function and effectiveness, advocacy, capacity, measurement, and the like are mostly outside of the volume's direct scope, but it is our belief that one cannot properly consider any of these subjects if one does not hold an idea of what the nonprofit sector is and why it exists in the first place.

1.3 Looking Ahead

If we have persuaded you that asking first-order questions about the nonprofit sector is worth your time, and if we have likewise succeeded in establishing how we regard theory (including why it is valuable), then join us as we explore perceptive critiques of existing theory and fresh attempts at developing new theory. Our approach here has been to gather a wide array of perspectives, with the purpose of jump-starting a new generation of debates about the role of nonprofit organizations in society. Some of the chapters use past sector theory as a launching point, while others begin with completely new ideas. In all cases, the contributors to the volume have sought to expand our understanding of what nonprofits are and why they exist. We have aimed to include a diversity of authors. While we lament that it is not possible to include all relevant perspectives in a single volume, we have nevertheless sought to provide a wide enough array of them that many more will be inspired to enter the conversation.

The three main parts of this volume proceed in the following way: In the first part, we explore the general idea of sector theory in more depth, reviewing trends in theorizing about nonprofit sectors and priming the exploration of sector theory by defining it more carefully. In Chapter 2, Curtis Child provides an overview of traditional sector theories on which the field of nonprofit studies is currently based. We include this chapter especially for newcomers to the field or for those wanting a refresher. In Chapter 3, Megan LePere-Schloop and Rebecca Nesbit offer an empirical analysis of how nonprofit theory has been used in academic publishing. In Chapter 4, Eva Witesman develops the idea of sector theory more rigorously, reflecting on the characteristics of "good" sector theory. Together, these introductory chapters set the stage for a conversation about sector theory that continues throughout the remainder of the volume.

The chapters in the second part of the volume critique established sector theories. For instance, Ruth K. Hansen and Gregory R. Witkowski show in Chapter 5 how the standard models for making sense of the provision of services by the market, government, and nonprofit sectors systematically fail to account for the needs of the most underprivileged in society. They adapt the Behaviors from Intergroup Affect and Stereotypes (BIAS) model to assess factors that lead to the invisibility of certain populations. Next, Laurie Mook and John R. Whitman offer in Chapter 6 a critique inspired by the social economy perspective for understanding nonprofit and similar activity. This perspective, popular in Europe, Canada, and Latin America, does not start from the premise that there are three distinct sectors of the economy (i.e., for-profit, government, and nonprofit). Rather, the social economy perspective focuses attention on the intersection of the sectors as part of a mixed economy. In Chapter 7, Richard Steinberg, Eleanor Brown, and Liza L. Taylor (re)conceptualize "three-failures" theorizing by proposing the Sectoral Advantage Framework, which revises and generalizes the three-failures approach.

Continuing with critique, in Chapter 8, Ana Clarissa Rojas Durazo invites us to consider the nonprofit sector and its relationship to the state and market. Rojas Durazo warns of a nonprofit industrial complex, which paradoxically works against the interests of the very communities that one could be forgiven for expecting the nonprofit sector to support. Shariq Siddiqui then uses concepts and traditions from Islam, in Chapter 9, to highlight the value of looking at nonprofit action with fresh eyes. In Chapter 10, George E. Mitchell and Jason Coupet reexamine the informational problems that form the basis of contract failure theory. They introduce the idea of an "asymmetry of uninformedness" that restructures our understanding of traditional economic models of the nonprofit. And in Chapter 11, Elizabeth A. Castillo considers what sector theorizing might look like if we draw from different epistemological positions, such as those found in the natural sciences.

Together, these critiques of traditional nonprofit theory prepare us to move to new ground: exploring alternative theories of the nonprofit sector. This is the purpose of the third part of the volume. Patricia Bromley and Heitor Santos start things off in Chapter 12 by situating nonprofit organizations within the broader context of organization itself. They suggest that focusing on sector theory, as traditionally understood, diverts our attention from a more fundamental sociocultural development: the expansion of organization. Moving from sociology to political science, Catherine E. Wilson, in Chapter 13, conceptualizes nonprofits as key components of representation – broadly defined – in democratic societies. Her theory of multilayered representation prevents the reduction of individual and community expression to solely political variables.

The four chapters that follow draw insights from a range of international contexts. In Chapter 14, Ada Ordor suggests that nonprofit law plays a role in creating a legal framework that allows people to participate in the improvement of their own lives and communities through self-development, facilitating the improvement of individuals, institutions, and communities from within. She uses examples from the African continent, and Nigeria and South Africa in particular, to make her point. Meeyoung Lamothe, Jiwon Suh, Misun Lee,

Hee Soun Jang, Bok Gyo Jeong, and Seongho An then use the South Korean context in Chapter 15 to view the nonprofit sector as being intentionally engineered by government. This is different from seeing nonprofits as partners in public service (Salamon, 1995). In their view, states may actively collaborate with nonprofits to direct and shape the sector in measurable ways, with the end goal *not* necessarily being partnership. In Chapter 16, Ming Hu and Yung-pin Lu examine how political parties – particularly, the ruling party – determine the development of the nonprofit sector in a one-party state, such as China. The view is very different from what we would expect if relying primarily on ideas developed in Western, democratic contexts. The same is true when looking at insights gained from theorizing nonprofit sectors that operate under authoritarian regimes like Russia, which is the focus of Chapter 17. In it, Yulia Skokova and Irina Krasnopolskaya suggest that a state's political regime is related to the hierarchy of functions performed by the nonprofit sector in that state, with a focus on the specific function of legitimacy.

The final set of chapters in this part continue to offer visions of nonprofit sectors – and sector theory – through applying interdisciplinary lenses and frameworks. In Chapter 18, Robert W. Ressler introduces a sociological theory of symbolic reality – physically and temporally bounded social contexts that facilitate some human interactions and inhibit others – as the reason nonprofits exist. Eva Witesman, in Chapter 19, distinguishes nonprofit institutions from public and private ones through the voluntary (rather than coercive) assignment of roles and the use of the good or service by nonpayers. And in Chapter 20, Robbie Waters Robichau and Kandyce Fernandez develop a theory of nonprofit*ness* (based in moral authority), which they contrast with publicness (based in political authority) and privateness (based in market authority).

Together, these perspectives on nonprofit organizing demonstrate new directions for thinking about the role – or roles – of nonprofits in society. The diversity of concepts and ideas also opens the door for future theorizing about what the sector is and why it exists. In the final chapter of the volume, we (the editors) synthesize the volume's contributions and suggest directions for future scholarship.

Our aim throughout the volume is to rekindle a curiosity about the nonprofit sector and its many roles in society. How and why do people organize in the nonprofit sector, and what are the defining characteristics of the space we call nonprofit? We hope the chapters in this volume provide ideas to motivate discussion, inform policy and practice, and shape new questions about the ways people organize to influence our world.

References

Abend, G. (2008). The meaning of "theory." *Sociological Theory*, *26*(2), 173–199.

Barman, E. (2017). The social bases of philanthropy. *Annual Review of Sociology*, *43*, 271–290.

Bekkers, R., & Wiepking, P. (2011). A literature review of empirical studies of philanthropy: Eight mechanisms that drive charitable giving. *Nonprofit and Voluntary Sector Quarterly*, *40*(5), 924–973.

Berger, P. L., & Luckman, T. (1967). *The social construction of reality: A treatise in the sociology of knowledge*. Anchor Books.

Berry, J. M., & Arons, D. F. (2003). *A voice for nonprofits*. Brookings Institution Press.

Box, R. C. (1999). Running government like a business: Implications for public administration theory and practice. *The American Review of Public Administration*, *29*(1), 19–43.

Bromley, P., & Meyer, J. W. (2017). "They are all organizations": The cultural roots of blurring between the nonprofit, business, and government sectors. *Administration & Society*, *49*(7), 939–966.

Child, C. (2011). Whither the turn? The ambiguous nature of nonprofits' commercial revenue. *Social Forces*, *89*(1), 145–161.

Child, C., & Witesman, E. (2022). The social meanings of the third sector: How action and purpose shape everyday understandings of "nonprofit". *Nonprofit and Voluntary Sector Quarterly*. Advance online publication. https://doi.org/08997640221081523

Child, C., Witesman, E., & Spencer, R. (2015). The blurring hypothesis reconsidered: How sector still matters to practitioners. *Voluntas*, *27*(4), 1831–1852.

Dees, J. G., & Anderson, B. (2003). Sector-bending: Blurring lines between nonprofit and for-Profit. *Society*, *40*(4), 16–27.

Dunleavy, P., Margetts, H., Bastow, S., & Tinkler, J. (2006). New public management is dead – Long live digital-era governance. *Journal of Public Administration Research and Theory*, *16*(3), 467–494.

Eikenberry, A. M., Mirabella, R. M., & Sandberg, B. (2018). *Reframing nonprofit organizations: Democracy, inclusion, and social change* (1st ed.). Melvin & Leigh.

Friedman, T. L. (2005). *The world is flat: A brief history of the twenty-first century*. Macmillan.
Frumkin, P. (2002). *On being nonprofit: A conceptual and policy primer*. Harvard University Press.
Frumkin, P. (2006). *Strategic giving: The art and science of philanthropy* (illus. ed.). University of Chicago Press.
Guo, C., & Saxton, G. D. (2020). *The quest for attention: Nonprofit advocacy in a social media age* (1st ed.). Stanford Business Books.
Hall, P. D., & Burke, C. B. (2006). Nonprofit, voluntary, and religious entities. In Susan B. Carter, Scott Sigmund Gartner, Michael R. Haines, Alan L. Olmstead, Richard Sutch, & Gavin Wright (Eds.), *Historical statistics of the United States: Earliest times to the present* (mill. ed.) (pp. 837–850). Cambridge University Press.
Hansmann, H. B. (1987). Economic theories of nonprofit organization. In W. W. Powell (Ed.), *The nonprofit sector: A research handbook* (pp. 27–42). Yale University Press.
INCITE! Women of Color against Violence. (2017). *The revolution will not be funded: Beyond the non-profit industrial complex*. Duke University Press.
Lincoln, Y. S., & Guba, E. G. (1985). *Naturalistic inquiry*. Sage.
McKeever, B. S., Dietz, N. E., & Fyffe, S. D. (2016). *The nonprofit almanac: The essential facts and figures for managers, researchers, and volunteers* (3rd ed.). Rowman & Littlefield.
Powell, W. W. (2020). What is the nonprofit sector? In W. W. Powell & P. Bromley (Eds.), *The nonprofit sector: A research handbook* (3rd ed.). Stanford University Press.
Reiser, D. B. (2010). Blended enterprise and the dual mission dilemma. *Vermont Law Review, 35*, 105–116.
Reiser, D. B. (2011). Benefit corporations – A sustainable form of organization. *Wake Forest Law Review, 46*, 591–625.
Renz, D. O. (2016). *The Jossey-Bass handbook of nonprofit leadership and management* (4th ed.). Jossey-Bass.
Salamon, L. M. (1995). *Partners in public service: Government-nonprofit relations in the modern welfare state*. The Johns Hopkins University Press.
Salamon, L. M. (2015). *The resilient sector revisited: The new challenge to nonprofit America*. Brookings Institution Press.
Salamon, L. M., & Sokolowski, S. W. (Eds.). (2004). *Global civil society: Dimensions of the nonprofit sector* (Vol. 2). Kumarian Press.
Steinberg, R., & Powell, W. W. (2006). Introduction. In W. W. Powell & R. Steinberg (Eds.), *The nonprofit sector: A research handbook* (2nd ed.). Yale University Press.
Suddaby, R. (2014). Editor's comments: Why theory? *Academy of Management Review, 39*(4), 407–411.

Sutton, R. I., & Staw, B. M. (1995). What theory is not. *Administrative Science Quarterly*, *40*(3), 371–384.

United Nations Department for Economic and Social Affairs. (2018). *Satellite account on non-profit and related institutions and volunteer work*. United Nations.

Vogel, D. (2005). *The market for virtue: The potential and limits of corporate social responsibility*. Brookings Institution.

Weisbrod, B. A. (1991). *The nonprofit economy*. Harvard University Press.

Whetten, D. A. (1989). What constitutes a theoretical contribution? *Academy of Management Review*, *14*(4), 490–495.

Wilson, J. (2000). Volunteering. *Annual Review of Sociology*, *26*(1), 215–240.

Yunus, M., & Weber, K. (2010). *Building social business: The new kind of capitalism that serves humanity's most pressing needs*. Public Affairs.

PART I

Overviews

2 *An Overview of Nonprofit Sector Theories*

CURTIS CHILD*

We are not the first to puzzle about nonprofit organizations and sectors. In fact, over the last half century, scholars have developed several compelling explanations for *what* and *why* nonprofits are, and these explanations have become the conventional wisdom for people who wonder about such things (see Anheier 2005; Frumkin 2005; Ott & Dicke 2015; Powell & Bromley 2020; Powell & Steinberg 2006). The goal of this volume is to expand the canon, but before critiquing traditional explanations or offering altogether new accounts, it helps to take stock of where we've been. The purpose of this chapter, then, is to briefly review 10 answers to the book's motivating concerns: What is the nonprofit sector? And, Why nonprofits?

As we explained in Chapter 1, our interest is in explaining the existence of voluntary, prosocial, and organized action. As theories, these explanations are generalizable observations, meaning that they are intended to provide ideas that transcend a particular time and place. As statements about the nonprofit sector, the theories deal with voluntary and organized action that is not aimed at self-enrichment. They give insights about the nonprofit sector in part by describing how or why nonprofit action is different from other types of action and organization, such as those that are typically thought of as government or business. These theories are not all origin stories, per se. Rather, some theories provide a description of what the sector is. They describe the role the nonprofit sector plays in society, regardless of how the sector came about in the first place. And some are normative justifications of the sector, advocating for what the sector should be and why a nonprofit sector is desirable.

* Thank you to Rich Clerkin, Kirsten Grønbjerg, Jon Jarvis, Megan LePere-Schloop, Jane Lopez, Becky Nesbit, and Eva Witesman for helpful comments on previous versions of this chapter.

Although the premise of this book is that the portfolio of explanations available to students of the nonprofit sector needs continual revision and expansion, it would be foolish to consider the already existing explanations as entirely problematic. True, the work of theorizing the nonprofit sector is not yet complete, but the authors of these original explanations asked important questions. They contemplated why nonprofits exist and how we should think about their role in political, social, and economic spaces. Those same questions still motivate us. Moreover, those who asked these questions provided compelling and often sophisticated answers, which necessarily shape how we approach the questions today. While understandably imperfect, their writings framed the subsequent conversations that took place in classrooms, hallways, conferences, journals, board rooms, and government offices.

We cannot hope to do justice to the full range of existing explanations, which we differentiate here for expository convenience. Nor can we document exhaustively the trajectory of any one idea. Instead, we provide an overview of what we see as the core explanations that have informed thinking and writing about nonprofits since the 1970s, identifying in the process 10 answers to the questions of what the sector is and why it exists. Some caveats to this approach are necessary. First, sometimes different but related ideas come out of the same writings, from the same authors. We separate those core ideas here because we see them as analytically distinct, able to stand on their own. Second, we recognize that each of these explanations has generated considerable discussion, critique, and refinement. We do not present them here because we necessarily believe they are accurate or incontestable. Rather, we see these as the elemental notions that have since been elaborated upon as the field of nonprofit studies has grown and evolved. In this overview, we stick to the core arguments, as stated by the people who articulated them. We leave the remainder of the volume – and, hopefully, future work – for critiquing and offering new perspectives. Third, in some cases it is nearly impossible to declare authoritatively where an idea began. In such cases, we point to the author(s) whom, in our judgment, scholars of nonprofits commonly reference when repeating the argument.

A note on nomenclature. The explanations reviewed in this chapter come from a variety of historical and disciplinary contexts, each with its own preoccupations and specialized vocabulary. Some authors write about nonprofits, others about voluntary organizations, associations, civil society entities, charities, the commons, and more. Some are explicitly concerned about the creation of a nonprofit sector, while others come at it indirectly. These nuances are important, but the consequence is that scholars of nonprofit studies often, for better or worse, resort to using the terminology of nonprofit organizations and sectors to describe a wide range of types of organizations (grassroots coalitions, associations, foundations, etc.). For instance, although Tocqueville never used the term "nonprofit," scholars who study nonprofit organizations use his ideas to understand nonprofits, and they use terms like "nonprofit" as they do. For ease in providing a high-level overview while moving across multiple traditions, we have done the same. We acknowledge that doing so might be grating to specialists, but we beg forgiveness for a simplified overview such as this.

2.1 Historical Context

The early 1970s to the late 1980s was a rich moment in the history of nonprofit studies. It was during these decades that the "nonprofit sector" started being recognized as such (Barman, 2013; Hall, 1992; Hodgkinson & Painter, 2003; Smith, 1999, 2016). Prior to the late 1960s, nonprofit organizations certainly were operating in varied fields, but they had not yet come to be seen as occupying a distinct sector of the economy vis-à-vis the government and private sectors. This started to change as criticisms of foundations and charities in the US, taking form partially in the Tax Reform Act of 1969 (Hall, 1992), motivated scholarship on the kinds of organizations we now refer to as nonprofit. The result was an emerging notion that foundations, charities, and other entities were in fact part of an interconnected sector (Barman, 2013).

Perhaps the most significant effort to study nonbusiness, nongovernment organizations took place under the auspices of the Filer Commission. The Filer Commission was a private group of prestigious members whose purpose was, in part, to "study the role of both philanthropic giving in the United States and that area through which giving is principally channeled, the voluntary, 'third' sector of American society" (Commission on Private Philanthropy and Public Needs, 1975, p. 1). Notably, the Commission referred to the "third sector" as "one of the least chartered regions" and "something of a terra incognita, barely explored" (p. 31). That would not last long, however, as the Commission's report conveyed a new vision. According to Hall (1992), it "gave substance to what, up to then, had been only an idea that charitable tax-exempt organizations composed a coherent and cohesive 'sector' of American political, economic, and social life" (p. 78; see also Hodgkinson & Painter, 2003).

The development of the so-called nonprofit sector was a result of, and was in turn energized by, research on foundations and charities (Smith, 1999, 2016). The creation of the Association of Voluntary Action Scholars (AVAS), established in 1971 (the precursor to the Association for Research on Nonprofit Organizations and Voluntary Action) and itself built on the work of the Center for a Voluntary Society, was key to establishing an academic field and, arguably, the sector itself (Smith, 1999, 2003, 2016). So was the establishment of a new journal, the *Journal of Voluntary Action Research* (later renamed *Nonprofit and Voluntary Sector Quarterly*), the first scholarly publication dedicated solely to the study of voluntary associations and nonprofit organizations.

Other notable moments shaping the history of the sector also occurred around this time. Partly inspired by the Filer Commission's recommendations (Hodgkinson & Painter, 2003), the Independent Sector was founded in 1980 as the first sector-wide professional association in the US designed to represent the interests of nonprofit organizations of all types. It reflected and no doubt further solidified in the public imagination the notion of a more or less discrete nonprofit sector. The same can be said for the cohorts of graduating students of professional nonprofit management programs (Mirabella, 2007; Mirabella et al., 2019), who were socialized into adopting the emerging view of the nonprofit sector as they came to be employed in it.

Outside of the US, but influenced by developments taking place there (Smith, 2013), scholars in Europe and other parts of the world also started focusing their attention on voluntary, third-sector organizations. For instance, the Association for Research in the Voluntary and Community Sector was formed in the UK in 1978; an AVAS spin-off held its first meeting in Brussels in 1980 (Smith, 2003); and the journal *Voluntas* started publication in 1990, followed two years later by the formation of the International Society for Third Sector Research (ISTR) (Hodgkinson & Painter, 2003). Dozens of centers, networks, programs, and associations were established in these and subsequent decades (Smith, 2013, 2016), which further internationalized the study of nonprofit organizations. Similar to what AVAS had done in the US, these organizations gathered scholars from a variety of disciplines to establish a new field of study, lending further credibility to the idea that the diversity of organizations, from cooperatives and grassroots enterprises to foundations and professional associations, could all be thought of as occupying a single nonprofit sector.

Thus, starting in the US, and then moving abroad, the idea of a nonprofit, independent, or third sector came into being. Its creation was not only the consequence of actual changes among nonprofit and nonprofit-serving organizations (e.g., the establishment of sector-wide advocacy groups) but, importantly, was also the outcome of people – scholars, policy experts, practitioners, and so on – who were starting to think about nonbusiness, nongovernmental organizations in a new way.

With the sector now constructed, it deserved an origin story, or at least an accounting. Scholars therefore turned their attention to questions about *what* the nonprofit sector was and *why* it existed – concerns that would preoccupy the field for decades more to come (Hodgkinson & Painter, 2003). Political scientists, legal scholars, economists, and philosophers had already developed justifications for governments and for-profit firms. But, as Hansmann observed as late as 1980, "The existing literature in law and economics … [had] largely overlooked nonprofit institutions" (p. 836). This is partly attributable to the fact that the idea of a unified sector was only a recent development. And although scholars had long studied nonprofit organizations (see Steinberg, 2006, p. 119 for a partial review), the products of this research were not the kind of broad explanatory accounts upon which the field of nonprofit studies could be built. So, starting in the 1970s, scholars started developing explanations for why nonprofit organizations exist and what their place is or should be in modern society. I present them here in order of thematic relevance, not chronologically.

2.2 Nonprofits as Solutions to Market and Government Failures (Market Failure Theory, Government Failure Theory)

In justifying the existence of nonprofit organizations as part of the organizational, political, and economic landscape, scholars articulated arguments that have come to be known as "failure" explanations. The basic logic of these arguments is always the same: the existence of nonprofits is explainable by some social or economic need that other societal institutions have failed to provide. Explanations focusing on market and government failures came first.

Notwithstanding Hansmann's lament in 1980 that legal scholars and economists had overlooked nonprofit organizations, Burton Weisbrod, an economist at the University of Wisconsin, had already laid out an economic rationale for nonprofits in the early 1970s. He did so first in 1972 (reappearing later in chapter 3 of Weisbrod, 1977). At this point in time, the idea of "market failure" was well established in the economics and public administration literatures (e.g., Bator, 1958), so Weisbrod's contribution was mainly to connect it to the existence of nonprofit organizations. He did so by noting, as others had done, that governments will provide collective goods because markets often do not. However, not everyone is satisfied with government provision, especially when there is excess demand or preferences are heterogenous (James, 1987). Government is a blunt tool, sometimes providing just enough – but often too little or too much – of what people want. Weisbrod argued that when government supply does not match constituent demand, and private sector substitutes are unsatisfying, then consumers may turn to nonprofits (see Steinberg, 2006; Young, 2000). Nonprofits have the flexibility to be prosocial (not just pro-profit), unlike businesses. But they also aren't beholden to the popular will of the people.

Weisbrod understood nonprofit organizations to be a direct response to market failure as well as an indirect response to market failure through government failure. He noted that the voluntary production of collective goods in many ways historically *preceded* the government provision of them, suggesting that nonprofits were responding directly to market failures even before governments were widely seen as responsible for supplying the variety of services expected from them today (Weisbrod, 1977). Although the language of failures and responses to failures implies a certain sequencing (i.e., first market failure, then government failure, and then nonprofits), the temporal ordering was unimportant to Weisbrod (1972, 1977). What *was* important was that nonprofits could be accounted for by unmet demand owing to market and/or government failures.

The result of Weisbrod's scholarship was that it provided a compelling account of why nonprofit organizations operate alongside, and sometimes instead of, businesses and governments in the modern (albeit US) economy: Why do nonprofits exist? Because they provide goods and services that people want but governments and private businesses are unable or unwilling to supply. Why are there nonprofit food banks but not nonprofit fast-food restaurants? Because there is a market for fast food and not for food banks, notwithstanding the need for both. Why are there nonprofit universities and public ones? Because nonprofit universities can cater to the needs of particular groups of constituencies (religious minorities, elites, etc.) in a way that the state cannot. Weisbrod provided a justification for nonprofits' place in the social, political, and economic landscape (Hansmann, 1980).

2.3 Nonprofits as Remedies to Contract Failures (Contract Failure Theory)

Another of the failure theories was developed only shortly after Weisbrod's writing. Its advocate was Henry Hansmann, a young legal scholar at the University of Pennsylvania. Complementary to Weisbrod's view, the theory gave insight specifically to the circumstances under which nonprofits respond to market failures. Whereas for Weisbrod nonprofits arise to solve collective action problems that governments are unable or unwilling to address, for Hansmann the role of nonprofits was to address information asymmetry problems in the marketplace. Nonprofits remedy a problem he called "contract failure," which is a specific type of market failure.

Hansmann developed his "general theory" (Hansmann, 1980) of nonprofit enterprise in a pair of legal essays written in the early 1980s. Building on the insights of Arrow (1963), Weisbrod, and others, he articulated a reason why nonprofit organizations would exist in market societies in which the forces of supply and demand should be sufficient to guide business firms in distributing goods efficiently. In fact, he wrote, there are some goods whose quality consumers are not able to judge, or providers whose credibility is difficult to ascertain (p. 844), and this limits how effectively markets can allocate them. Because of information asymmetries between business firms and consumers, businesses are able – and incentivized – "to charge excessive prices for inferior goods" (p. 835). This market failure – he called it contract failure because the root problem is the inability of consumers to monitor their contracts with providers – is one that the government is suited to address by certifying a type of organization (i.e., the nonprofit enterprise) to operate ostensibly without a profit motive (Salamon, 1987).

Nonprofit organizations help consumers deal with information asymmetries because the law prohibits them from enriching shareholders with profits. This is why nonprofits are in high demand in certain industries – like humanitarian services, in which the consumer of a good is often not the same as the person paying for it (see Hansmann, 1980, p. 846; 1981a, p. 1633) – and, according to Hansmann, why governments should regulate and support them (see Hansmann, 1980, p. 898; 1981b, p. 55). As a theory of consumer expectations (Hansmann, 1987), it assumes that consumers are aware of organizations' nonprofit status and that they will favor nonprofits when purchasing goods whose quality is hard to judge or from organizations whose dependability cannot readily be determined (Handy et al., 2010). Although organizational status does not convey specific details about the good or service in question, it at least assures the consumer that the organization selling the product does not have an incentive to take advantage of the consumer's weak purchasing position. What nonprofits provide is trust (Salamon et al., 2017). Why do they exist? Because they solve information asymmetry problems in the market.

2.4 Nonprofits as Preceding the State and Market (Voluntary Failure Theory)

Lester Salamon, a policy scholar at Johns Hopkins University who had spent a considerable amount of time working in administrative positions at the US Office of Management and Budget and, later, at the Urban Institute, advanced yet another failure theory in the 1980s. Named "voluntary failure" theory (Salamon, 1987, 1995, 2002), it inverted Weisbrod's position that nonprofits "fill the gaps" left by market and then government failures. Salamon proposed instead that government action can be thought of as a response to the failures of volunteerism as nonprofits (and other voluntary initiatives) respond to market failures. Thus, although Weisbrod was insistent that the temporal ordering of failures was unimportant, Salamon viewed things differently. For him, it was voluntary action, not necessarily governments, that stepped in historically when markets failed. Why do nonprofits exist? Because there are needs that the market did not or could not address.

In light of this, the more pressing question for Salamon was, Why do governments ever become involved in addressing social problems? His answer was that they do so when voluntary organizations fail to address social problems in equitable, professional ways. "It is reasonable to expect," he wrote, "that the private, nonprofit sector will typically provide the first line of response to perceived 'market failures,' and that government will be called on only as the voluntary response proves insufficient" (Salamon, 1995, p. 44). Although Salamon was not the first to note the possibility that governments step in when voluntary organizations fail (Commission on Private Philanthropy and Public Needs, 1975, p. 9; Weisbrod, 1977), he was the first to establish the idea as a theory of the role of nonprofit organizations in modern (still US) society.

Much of Salamon's writing on this topic focused on documenting four classes of problems endemic to nonprofit organizations that might make government solutions desirable if not necessary: philanthropic insufficiency (nonprofits sometimes lack the resources necessary to accomplish their missions), philanthropic particularism (nonprofits often have a narrow focus, which can be manifest as favoritism or exclusivity), philanthropic paternalism (nonprofits are necessarily responsive to philanthropic donors, which may be at odds with the needs of the people they are serving), and philanthropic amateurism (nonprofits may be led by well-intentioned individuals who nevertheless lack professional expertise).

2.5 Nonprofits as the Consequence of Entrepreneurship (Entrepreneurship – or Supply-Side – Theory)

Failure explanations, sometimes referred to as demand-side theories, imply that one economic or political institution's inability to provide a needed good or service is useful for explaining the existence of nonprofit organizations. For instance, the availability of nonprofit provision alongside the absence of market or government provision is taken as evidence that nonprofits are filling the needs left unmet by market and government inaction. But as any undergraduate studying economics understands, demand alone is insufficient to explain production. Supply is also needed, and failure explanations do little to account for who is "supplying" nonprofit organizations and what their motivations are for doing so (Salamon et al., 2017; Steinberg, 2006).

Dennis Young was among the first to address this issue by constructing a supply-side theory of the nonprofit sector. Beginning with a paper in 1981, which was developed further in a 1983 monograph, Young developed a theory of entrepreneurship that addressed how entrepreneurs sort themselves into different industries and sectors. (Entrepreneurship was not a new academic focus. But as Frank noted in his foreword to Young's book, scholars had at this point in time focused mostly on entrepreneurship in the business sector [Young, 2013].) The starting point for Young's analysis (1981, 1983) was constructing ideal types of entrepreneurs, who differ according to their experiences, values, interests, and tolerance for risk. These characteristics orient the entrepreneurs to particular industries, which themselves vary according to what they can provide the entrepreneur in terms of the type of service they want to provide (e.g., social versus technical), their desire for professional control, their affinity for prestige, and the like. Once an entrepreneur selects an industry, they might further sort themselves into a sector (e.g., nonprofit, business, government) based on the value they place on things like income potential, the desire for bureaucratic flexibility, and the service ethic that prevails in the sector.

Later in the decade, James (1987) arrived at a similar conclusion about the importance of entrepreneurs when trying to understand the nonprofit sector. Whereas Young was investigating why entrepreneurs establish ventures in the nonprofit versus business or government sectors, James was interested in why some countries had larger nonprofit sectors than others. While paying due attention to demand-side variation, such as the diversity of the population, her theory also explored supply-side variability. Demand might create a market for nonprofit organizations, she reasoned, but it is entrepreneurs who meet that demand, and she argued that religious or ideological entrepreneurs, especially, helped account for nonprofit-sector differences across countries. As evidence that ideological entrepreneurship matters, James pointed to the considerable role that religious organizations played in establishing nonprofit organizations (e.g., in early twentieth-century Holland, religious groups established 95% of its private schools).

Perhaps more important than Young's answer to why some entrepreneurs choose to work in the nonprofit sector, or James's observation that religious movements established large parts of the sector, is that Young and James asked the questions in the first place. Any account of the nonprofit sector, they reminded us, must incorporate questions about the people who populate the sector. Why do we have a nonprofit sector? According to this perspective, because there is a stream of entrepreneurs who, for a variety of reasons (not all of which are monetary), choose the nonprofit form as an outlet for their creative interests.

2.6 Nonprofits as Interdependent with Government (Interdependence Theory)

Salamon's ideas about voluntary failure were embedded in a larger critique of sector theory, not to mention a theory of the US welfare state, both of which moved the conversation in a different direction. Inspired by the observation that nonprofits work in close collaboration with governments in a way that prior theories did not anticipate, Salamon (2002) argued that nonprofits are co-deliverers of the welfare state and that any theoretical statement about the existence of a nonprofit sector must take this into account. Failure theories, which had dominated thinking about the nonprofit sector, portrayed governments and nonprofits as filling in where the other came up short. If Weisbrod had it right, nonprofits would provide needed services when governments would not. But how does that explain why governments and nonprofits so often work collaboratively – not one instead of the other but both together?

A student of the US welfare state, Salamon (1987, 2002; Salamon et al., 2017) observed an empirical fact that did not comport with prevailing explanations of the sector. It was that many nonprofits, particularly those working in human services, relied substantially on governments for their support. This pointed to the possibility of governments and nonprofits working together as complements rather than as substitutes. It was a pattern that had gone largely unnoticed, not because it was unimportant but because theory had prevented scholars from seeing it. "Few facets of the American welfare state," Salamon (1987) wrote, "have been so thoroughly overlooked or so commonly misunderstood as the role of the nonprofit sector and the relationships between nonprofit organizations and government. Yet few facets also are as important" (p. 29). He then exposed the culprit: "The partnership between government and the nonprofit sector has been overlooked, in my view, not because of its novelty or because of a lack of research but because of a weakness in theory" (p. 32).

The solution for Salamon (1987, 2002) was not only to update the received wisdom about nonprofits (i.e., to update the failure theories) but, more, to advance a new theory of "third-party government." The idea, simple but perceptive, was that the US government relied on nonprofits to carry out many of the government's functions. Salamon (1987) speculated that this was a consequence of the federal structure of the government and the nation's pluralism, not to mention concerns about flexibility and economy. Young (2000) added that although governments are typically instrumental in addressing free-rider problems, that does not mean governments will necessarily provide the good or service themselves. Sometimes it is more efficient for the government to coerce people to pay taxes in order to help fund the provision of collective goods while relying on nongovernmental entities (i.e., nonprofit organizations) to deliver them (Coase, 1990; Williamson, 1981; Young, 2000). Whatever the cause, Salamon and others spent the next decades uncovering the extent to which governments relied on nonprofits as "partners in public service" (Salamon, 1995) and as collaborators administering the "tools of government" (Salamon, 2002). Why, then, according to Salamon's ideas about interdependence, do nonprofits exist? Because the government needs them to deliver the welfare state.

2.7 Nonprofits as an Outcome of Class Relations (Social Origins Theory)

Salamon had more ideas yet about the nonprofit sector. Building on his earlier theories, but now drawing on data from around the world, he and his collaborators puzzled over why there was such significant cross-national variation in nonprofit sectors. Their observations led them to develop a new explanation of nonprofits, one that they called the social origins theory of civil society (Salamon & Anheier, 1998). This approach was fundamentally different from those that came before it. Demand-and-supply explanations locate explanatory power in the preferences and sentiments of individuals but, Salamon argued (2017), they fail to acknowledge that the individuals theorized are themselves embedded in broader sociopolitical patterns that shape whatever rational choices people think they are making. Salamon's task, as he saw it, was to uncover those hidden forces so that he could understand their role in shaping the development of civil society.

According to the social origins approach (Salamon & Anheier, 1998; Salamon et al., 2017), the historical development of nation-states is closely tied to the relationships among different classes in society. Although these relationship configurations in some instances took form hundreds of years ago, they did so at critical historical moments, with their impact casting a long shadow on civil society. Relationships among the classes are not wholly determinative, of course, and Salamon and colleagues identified a handful of other factors that likewise shaped the contours of civil society development – for example, the role of governments, political parties, and dominant ideologies. Nevertheless, patterns in power relationships are, to proponents of the theory, the central causal factor. Salamon and colleagues (2017) identified five such patterns, which he called traditional (in which nobility and landowners dominate), liberal (in which the bourgeoisie dominates), welfare partnership (in which landed and industrial elites face pressure from the working class), social democratic (in which worker mobilization is effective, yielding pluralist power-sharing arrangements), and statist (in which "modernizing elites" support militarization and industrialization).

An example is instructive. In a "social democratic" pattern of civil society development, as in Sweden, the power of landed elites was weak and the power of labor strong. As the country industrialized, the resulting power configuration was pluralistic, involving professional and commercial elites as well as support for a large working class. One outcome of the influential working class was that welfare services were seen as a right, and one typically provided by government. Nonprofits, under this regime, were not needed to deliver the welfare state, since there was considerable support for the government's role in doing so. This rendered the service delivery function of nonprofits rather small. Instead, nonprofits operated primarily in expressive fields, like the arts, sports, and advocacy. Compare this to a "traditional" pattern of civil society development, in which the elite class is hegemonic, exploiting a primarily agrarian populace. Wary of threats to their power, the elites impose obstacles to civil society development, leaving the nonprofit sector small and fundamentally dependent. Fourteenth-century southern Italy is a case in point, as was India until recently.

Why do nonprofits exist? According to this perspective, the answer is a historical one. The existence of nonprofits, and how the sectors are organized in contemporary times, is the consequence of broad historical patterns, especially the relationships between classes.

2.8 Nonprofits as the Commons (a Theory of the Commons)

Some sector theories are descriptive explanations of what the nonprofit sector is, including the role that the sector plays in society. One such theory was formulated by Roger Lohmann, who advocated for a positive account of nonprofits. Famously, he complained that describing *non*profits by what they are *not* (they are not government organizations; they are not for-profit businesses) is like calling lettuce a nonanimal (Lohmann, 1989) – a description that is technically accurate but substantively unhelpful. He also took issue with the generally negative portrayal of nonprofits as being important only when businesses and governments fail to provide for goods and services demanded.

Lohmann offered an alternative account of the sector, one that saw it as a unique kind of environment in which groups produce a particular type of good. For him, the sector is a commons – a space of free, uncoerced participation in which people come together with shared resources, to pursue a shared purpose, and in a way that creates a sense of mutuality and fairness (Lohmann, 1992a, pp. 312, 320, 321).[1] Importantly for Lohmann, the commons isn't just filling in where other sectors fail – a negation-based accounting indeed. Rather, the people occupying it actively produce the "purposes, goals, objectives, and outcomes" (p. 320) that they care about. Mass is a common good for Catholics, as is the play of a soccer game in a community sports league.

Crucial to this telling of nonprofits is that each sector is governed by a different imperative, which has implications for why people participate in them. Markets are for producing private goods. Governments are for producing public goods. And the commons are for producing common goods. Whereas people engage in for-profit businesses primarily to secure private financial resources, they come to the commons to produce goods that are often nonpecuniary in nature – language, art, ceremony, myth, contemplation, inquiry, and self-expression, to

[1] Although the Ostroms and Lohmann share an interest in the commons, their work was largely not informed by each other's. Lohmann (2016) noted that "sociologists, social workers, volunteer action coordinators, and voluntary action practitioners who formed the core of the initial membership of AVAS had at the time a seemingly unrelated agenda of interests and were working in an entirely different academic silo from that of Hardin, the Ostroms, and the economists and political theorists interested in collective choice problems" (p. 30S).

name a few (Lohmann, 1992b, pp. 67, 95). Why is there a nonprofit sector? For Lohmann, the answer is that the sector is a setting for gathering and expressing that is neither coerced by government nor compelled by the market.

2.9 Nonprofits as Vehicles for Creating Meaning and Checking Power (a Theory of Mediating Structures)

Related to the notion that the nonprofit sector is a commons is the argument that nonprofit organizations help individuals navigate the complexities of modernity by collecting individual interests and positioning them against large, impersonal bureaucracies. From this perspective, nonprofits are desirable not only because they provide spaces for pursuing shared purpose (which was Lohmann's point) but also because they form a bulwark against the institutions that dominate modern society – such as the welfare state and multinational corporations. Berger and Neuhaus articulated this view in 1977, and scholars of nonprofits often point to their short book when referencing it, but the core idea is repeated throughout the long history of political and social science writing (Edwards & Foley, 2001; Fung, 2003; Tocqueville, 2004; Villa, 2006).

For Berger and Neuhaus, there is a critical tension in modern societies: On the one hand, modern societies are dominated by large and impersonal institutions, vast bureaucracies whose effect on individuals is alienating. "One of the most debilitating results of modernization," they wrote, "is a feeling of powerlessness in the face of institutions controlled by those whom we do not know and whose values we often do not share" (Berger and Neuhaus, 1977, p. 7). On the other hand, paradoxically, members of society want the institutions. As much as they are against big government, they are committed to social security and Medicare. As much as they want to support local businesses, they shop at Walmart. The consequence is that the megastructures are here to stay, for good or ill.

Acknowledging this, Berger and Neuhaus advocated for public policies that would protect and support what they referred to as "mediating structures," such as the neighborhood, the family, the church, and voluntary associations, or what we are referring to here as organizations in the nonprofit sector. As "institutions that mediate between the two spheres" – that is, between individuals and large bureaucracies – mediating structures are thus one solution to a central problem of modern life. According to Berger and Neuhaus (1977), "Such institutions have a private face, giving private life a measure of stability, and they have a public face, transferring meaning and value to the megastructures" (p. 3). Without mediating structures, individuals would be left to confront the megastructures on their own, and they surely would fail. As "value-generating" and "value-maintaining" agencies (p. 6), mediating structures provide spaces to come together and create meaning in an alienating world.

Mediating structures are therefore necessary to the expressive function of the sector (Frumkin, 2005), but they are more than that. Berger and Neauhaus's argument suggests that these islands of expression and meaning also have an instrumental purpose: They push back against state power and other interests (Lechterman & Reich, 2020). They thus have a contestatory function too: raising a collective voice, representing varied interests, and checking entrenched power. "Civil society gives identity and voice to the distinct interests and diverse points of view characteristic of modern society," Edwards and Foley (2001) write (p. 6). "It stimulates public debate and presses government for action on a thousand and one matters of public interest."

Why is there a nonprofit sector? The answer here is a descriptive and normative one. Nonprofits are useful – and desirable – to people who want to find and share meaning *and* are critical for those who want to mobilize and resist according to their shared values.

2.10 Nonprofits as Incubators of Democratic Citizens (a Theory of Associationalism)

Berger and Neuhaus's mediating-structures theory has a strong affinity with some well-known political theories that connect the nonprofit sector to the healthy functioning of democracies. Perhaps the most well known of these is identified with Tocqueville's (2004) writings about associational life in the early United States. In his text *Democracy in America*, Tocqueville observed that "Americans of all ages, all conditions, and all minds are constantly joining together in groups" (p. 595). He wrote memorably that "wherever there is a new undertaking, at the head of which you would expect to see in France the government and in England some great lord, in the United States you are sure to find an association" (p. 595). The reason for joining associations, Tocqueville argued, is that in a context as comparatively equal as America, individuals are relatively weak: "They can do almost nothing by themselves." They therefore form associations to pursue their collective interests. "From that point on," he said, "they cease to be isolated individuals and become a power to be reckoned with...; a power that speaks, and to which people listen" (p. 598).

Tocqueville's ideas feel similar in spirit to Berger and Neuhaus's theory, and there are certainly overlaps. But it is important to note the particular emphasis Tocqueville placed on the effects of association on the individuals who associate. For him, the joiners learn something about how to engage in a democracy. Individuals associate, and "the more of these small joint affairs there are, the more capable men become – perhaps unwittingly – of pursuing large affairs in common" (Tocqueville, 2004, p. 604). They learn "how order is maintained where large numbers of people are involved, and how those large numbers of people can be made to march in step and according to plan toward a common goal. They learn to subject their will to the will of all and to subordinate their individual efforts to the joint venture." Associations, Tocqueville asserted, "can therefore be looked upon as vast free schools to which all citizens come to learn the general theory of associations" (p. 606).

The notion that the sector could help serve an important democratic function captured the imagination of scholars of nonprofits (Clemens, 2006; Edwards & Foley, 2001; Frumkin, 2005; Fung, 2003; Lechterman & Reich, 2020; Putnam, 2000; Putnam et al., 1992). From this view, the nonprofit sector isn't just a place where people unite their interests and represent them to the state and society (the point of the mediating-structures argument). It is also a space where important things happen to the people who associate. Primary among them are that individuals learn the habits and skills necessary for engaging in democratic society. Nonprofits, then, become the so-called schools of democracy. In them, people learn to organize, share ideas, and communicate their interests.[2]

Why is there a nonprofit sector? Normatively, the nonprofit sector exists as an important space for learning to engage with and building the social connections necessary for a thriving democracy.

[2] For an alternative reading of Tocqueville's take on the value of civic associations, see Villa (2006).

2.11 Summary and Conclusions

The 10 theories reviewed here make up, arguably, the canon of sector theory. Scholars refer to them, written introductions to the field cover them, and we suspect that most undergraduate and graduate surveys of the field of nonprofit studies review them. Table 2.1 provides a summary, and Lepere-Schloop and Nesbit offer an empirical assessment in Chapter 3.

I offer here a few observations. Note first that this is not an exhaustive list of all the theories that scholars of nonprofits rely on in their work. I have focused here on sector theories, so the perspectives previously summarized deal primarily with the question of what the sector is and why we have nonprofits. It is also worth observing that I have laid out the theories in elemental form, when in practice they are not often treated in isolation (e.g., James, 1987; Steinberg, 2006). Some of the theories take an economically rational perspective, starting with individuals making choices based on some sort of cost–benefit analysis and resulting in the existence of a sector (e.g., contract failure theory, supply-side theory). Others follow a functionalist logic, in which the existence of the sector is presumed to meet some prior need (e.g., market and government failure theories). Most are US-centric, at least in their development if not in their application. And there is a tendency to equate sector theories with legally delineated nonprofit organizations, which are themselves defined by tax codes (at least in the US).

Nor is this a complete list of all explanations for the nonprofit sector. Others have written about nonprofits as sites of social experimentation (Douglas, 1987) or as critical elements of the public sphere (see Lechterman & Reich, 2020's discussion of Habermas). Still others might see nonprofits as, essentially, a special case of private enterprise (Fram & Withers, 1999). The list could go on, so the point is only that there are certainly other answers to the what and why of nonprofits. That said, I believe the 10 perspectives summarized here provide a sufficient introduction to the prevailing wisdom, making the remainder of the volume more comprehensible.

In the introductory chapter, Witesman and I embraced an expansive approach to theory. Rather than get bogged down in debates about what counts as theory, we reframed the question. Sector theory, we argued, is simply an answer to the questions, What is the nonprofit sector, and Why do we have nonprofits? Some answers can be

Table 2.1 *Summary of sector theories*

Theory	What is the nonprofit sector? Why nonprofit organizations?	Noteworthy
Market failure (nonprofits as solutions to market and government failures)	Nonprofit organizations exist because markets sometimes fail to provide goods and services demanded.	Markets are assumed to be the primary mechanism for producing and distributing goods and services.
Government failure (nonprofits as solutions to market and government failures)	Nonprofit organizations exist because markets and governments sometimes fail to provide goods and services demanded.	Markets are assumed to be the primary mechanism for producing and distributing goods and services. Governments come next. When both fail, nonprofits fill in the gap.
Contract failure (nonprofits as remedies to contract failures)	Nonprofit organizations exist because consumers are sometimes unable to trust contracts with for-profit providers.	A special case of market failure.
Voluntary failure (nonprofits as preceding the state and market)	Nonprofit organizations exist because markets sometimes fail to provide goods and services demanded. Governments help out when nonprofits fail.	Markets are assumed to be the primary mechanism for producing and distributing goods and services. Contrary to the expectations of government failure theory, however, in this account nonprofits respond first to market failure. Governments step in when nonprofits are insufficient.
Entrepreneurship (nonprofits as the consequence of entrepreneurship)	Nonprofit organizations exist because entrepreneurs have an interest in creating them.	Also referred to as supply-side theory. Shifts attention away from unmet demand (a key criterion of failure theories) and focuses instead on the interests of entrepreneurs who supply the sector with nonprofit organizations.

Table 2.1 (*cont.*)

Theory	What is the nonprofit sector? Why nonprofit organizations?	Noteworthy
Interdependence (nonprofits as interdependent with government)	Nonprofit organizations exist partly because governments rely on them to deliver the welfare state.	Whereas government failure theory suggests nonprofits fill in where governments fall short, interdependence theory highlights the complementary relationship between governments and nonprofits.
Social origins (nonprofits as an outcome of class relations)	Nonprofit organizations (their existence and the characteristics of the sector) are shaped by the history of broad sociopolitical patterns, in particular the relationships among classes.	Does not refute the other theories but emphasizes that the nature of the nonprofit sector must be understood through a historical lens.
The commons (nonprofits as the commons)	Nonprofits are spaces of free, uncoerced participation where people come together with shared resources to express and pursue a shared purpose, doing so in a way that creates a sense of mutuality and fairness.	A positive account of nonprofit organizations. Focuses on what nonprofits are instead of what they are not.
Mediating structures (nonprofits as vehicles for creating meaning and checking power)	Nonprofit organizations combine shared interests and push back against entrenched power.	A normative theory, suggesting why members of modern welfare states should want to support nonprofits.
Associationalism (nonprofits as incubators of democratic citizens)	Nonprofit organizations exist to socialize citizens, which has benefits for democracy.	A normative theory, connecting nonprofits to democratic functioning.

understood historically, as authors trace the origins of nonprofit organizations and sectors over time. Salamon's social origins approach is the most historical of the theories listed in Table 2.1. Voluntary failure theory can be understood historically as well. Other theories are descriptive, providing accounts of the role that nonprofits (or the sector broadly) play in society. These are quite common, and virtually all the examples from Table 2.1 have some descriptive component. Lohman's commons approach, especially, contemplates what the nonprofit sector is. Finally, some theories are normative, meaning that the statements are used to suggest a vision for the way society should be, regardless of whether it is already so. Berger and Neuhaus's mediating structures theory and Tocqueville's theory of democracy are often used with a normative bent.

Of course, this is necessarily an overview. Each argument has a life of its own, so to speak, with a history of embellishments, refinements, and critiques. Rather than work through the trajectory of each concept, my purpose here has been to introduce readers to the central idea that the original author(s) was trying to convey. Moreover, aside from pointing out how one of the theories might be based on a criticism of a prior theory, I have not offered much by way of my own critique. The field of nonprofit studies owes a lot to these pioneering ideas, so it seems appropriate first to spend some time understanding them on their own terms before picking at them. Many of the chapters that follow include substantive critiques, and Witesman offers some useful ideas for how to evaluate the quality of sector theories in Chapter 4.

References

Anheier, H. K. (2005). *Nonprofit organizations: Theory, management, policy*. Routledge.

Arrow, K. J. (1963). Uncertainty and the welfare economics of medical care. *The American Economic Review*, *53*(5), 941–973.

Barman, E. (2013). Classificatory struggles in the nonprofit sector: The formation of the national taxonomy of exempt entities, 1969–1987. *Social Science History*, *37*(1), 103–141.

Bator, F. M. (1958). The anatomy of market failure. *The Quarterly Journal of Economics*, *72*(3), 351–379.

Berger, P. L., & Neuhaus, R. J. (1977). *To empower people: The role of mediating structures in public policy*. American Enterprise Institute for Public Policy Research.

Clemens, E. S. (2006). The constitution of citizens: Political theories of nonprofit organizations. In W. W. Powell & R. Steinberg (Eds.), *The nonprofit sector: A research handbook* (2nd ed., pp. 207–220). Yale University Press.

Coase, R. H. (1990). *The firm, the market, and the law*. University of Chicago Press.

Commission on Private Philanthropy and Public Needs. (1975). *Giving in America: Toward a stronger voluntary sector*.

Douglas, J. (1987). Political theories of nonprofit organization. In W. W. Powell (Ed.), *The nonprofit sector: A research handbook* (1st ed., pp. 43–54). Yale University Press.

Edwards, B., & Foley, M. W. (2001). Civil society and social capital. In B. Edwards, M. W. Foley, & M. Diani (Eds.), *Beyond Tocqueville: Civil society and the social capital debate in comparative perspective* (pp. 1–14). Tufts University.

Fram, E. H., & Withers, J. (1999). Conflict of interest in the board room? New research points the way to solutions. *Nonprofit World*, *17*(2), 19–21.

Frumkin, P. (2005). *On being nonprofit: A conceptual and policy primer*. Harvard University Press.

Fung, A. (2003). Associations and democracy: Between theories, hopes, and realities. *Annual Review of Sociology*, *29*, 515–539.

Hall, P. D. (1992). *Inventing the nonprofit sector and other essays on philanthropy, voluntarism, and nonprofit organizations*. Johns Hopkins University Press.

Handy, F., Seto, S., Wakaruk, A., Mersey, B., Mejia, A., & Copeland, L. (2010). The discerning consumer: Is nonprofit status a factor? *Nonprofit and Voluntary Sector Quarterly*, *39*(5), 866–883.

Hansmann, H. B. (1980). The role of nonprofit enterprise. *The Yale Law Journal*, *89*(5), 835–901.

Hansmann, H. B. (1981a). Consumer perceptions of nonprofit enterprise: Reply. *The Yale Law Journal*, *90*(7), 1633–1638.

Hansmann, H. B. (1981b). The rationale for exempting nonprofit organizations from corporate income taxation. *Yale Law Journal*, *91*(1), 54–100.

Hansmann, H. B. (1987). Economic theories of nonprofit organization. In W. W. Powell (Ed.), *The nonprofit sector: A research handbook* (pp. 27–42). Yale University Press.

Hodgkinson, V., & Painter, A. (2003). Third sector research in international perspective: The role of ISTR. *Voluntas: International Journal of Voluntary and Nonprofit Organizations*, *14*(1), 1–14.

James, E. (1987). The nonprofit sector in comparative perspective. In W. W. Powell (Ed.), *The nonprofit sector: A research handbook* (pp. 397–415). Yale University Press.

Lechterman, T., & Reich, R. (2020). Political theory and the nonprofit sector. In W. W. Powell & P. Bromley (Eds.), *The nonprofit sector: A research handbook* (3rd ed., pp. 171–191). Stanford University Press.

Lohmann, R. A. (1989). And lettuce is nonanimal: Toward a positive economics of voluntary action. *Nonprofit and Voluntary Sector Quarterly*, *18*(4), 367–383.

Lohmann, R. A. (1992a). The commons: A multidisciplinary approach to nonprofit organization, voluntary action, and philanthropy. *Nonprofit and Voluntary Sector Quarterly*, *21*(3), 309–324.

Lohmann, R. A. (1992b). *The commons: New perspectives on nonprofit organization, voluntary action and philanthropy*. Jossey-Bass.

Lohmann, R. A. (2016). The Ostroms' commons revisited. *Nonprofit and Voluntary Sector Quarterly*, *45*(4), 27S–42S.

Mirabella, R. M. (2007). University-based educational programs in nonprofit management and philanthropic studies: A 10-year review and projections of future trends [10.1177/0899764007305051]. *Nonprofit and Voluntary Sector Quarterly*, *36*, 11S–27S. http://nvs.sagepub.com/cgi/doi/10.1177/0899764007305051

Mirabella, R. M., Hoffman, T., Teo, T. K., & McDonald, M. (2019). The evolution of nonprofit management and philanthropic studies in the United States: Are we now a disciplinary field? *Journal of Nonprofit Education and Leadership*, *9*(1), 63–84.

Ott, J. S., & Dicke, L. A. (Eds.). (2015). *The nature of the nonprofit sector* (3rd ed.). Westview Press.

Powell, W. W., & Bromley, P. (2020). *The nonprofit sector: A research handbook*. Stanford University Press.

Powell, W. W., & Steinberg, R. (2006). *The nonprofit sector: A research handbook* (2nd ed.). Yale University Press.

Putnam, R. (2000). *Bowling alone: The collapse and revival of American community*. Simon & Schuster.

Putnam, R. D., Leonardi, R., & Nanetti, R. Y. (1992). *Making democracy work: Civic traditions in modern Italy*. Princeton University Press.

Salamon, L. M. (1987). Of market failure, voluntary failure, and third-party government: Toward a theory of government-nonprofit relationship in the modern welfare state. *Journal of Voluntary Action Research*, *16*, 30–48.

Salamon, L. M. (1995). *Partners in public service: Government-nonprofit relations in the modern welfare state*. Johns Hopkins University Press.

Salamon, L. M. (Ed.). (2002). *The tools of government: A guide to the new governance*. Oxford University Press.

Salamon, L. M., & Anheier, H. K. (1998). Social origins of civil society: Exploring the nonprofit sector cross-nationally. *Voluntas*, *9*, 213–248.

Salamon, L. M., Sokolowski, S. W., & Haddock, M. A. (2017). *Explaining civil society development: A social origins approach*. Johns Hopkins University Press.

Smith, D. H. (1999). Researching volunteer associations and other nonprofits: An emergent interdisciplinary field and possible new discipline. *The American Sociologist*, *30*(4), 5–33.

Smith, D. H. (2003). A history of ARNOVA [10.1177/0899764003254841]. *Nonprofit and Voluntary Sector Quarterly*, *32*(3), 458–472. http://nvs.sagepub.com/cgi/content/abstract/32/3/458

Smith, D. H. (2013). Growth of research associations and journals in the emerging discipline of altruistics. *Nonprofit and Voluntary Sector Quarterly*, *42*(4), 638–656.

Smith, D. H. (2016). A survey of voluntaristics: Research on the growth of the global, interdisciplinary, socio-behavioral science field and emergent inter-discipline. *Voluntaristics Review*, *1*(2), 1–81.

Steinberg, R. (2006). Economic theories of nonprofit organizations. In W. W. Powell & R. Steinberg (Eds.), *The nonprofit sector: A research handbook* (2nd ed., pp. 117–139). Yale University Press.

Tocqueville, A. de (2004). *Democracy in America* (A. Goldhammer, Trans.). Library of America.

Villa, D. (2006). Tocqueville and civil society. In C. B. Welch (Ed.), *The Cambridge companion to Tocqueville* (pp. 216–244). Cambridge University Press.

Weisbrod, B. A. (1972). *Toward a theory of the voluntary non-profit sector in a three-sector economy*. Conference on Altruism and Economic Theory, New York.

Weisbrod, B. A. (1977). *The voluntary nonprofit sector: An economic analysis*. Lexington Books.

Williamson, O. E. (1981). The economics of organization: The transaction cost approach. *The American Journal of Sociology*, *87*(3), 548–577.

Young, D. R. (1981). Entrepreneurship and the behavior of nonprofit organizations: Elements of a theory. In M. J. White & G. E. Peterson (Eds.), *Nonprofit firms in a three sector economy* (Vol. 6, pp. 135–162). Urban Institute.

Young, D. R. (1983). *If not for profit, for what? A behavioral theory of the nonprofit sector based on entrepreneurship*. Lexington Books.

Young, D. R. (2000). Alternative models of government–nonprofit sector relations: Theoretical and international perspectives. *Nonprofit and Voluntary Sector Quarterly*, *29*(1), 149–172.

Young, D. R. (2013). *If not for profit, for what?* Originally published by Lexington Books (now open access). http://scholarworks.gsu.edu/facbooks2013/1

3 *The Prevalence of Traditional Nonprofit Sector Theories in Research*

MEGAN LEPERE-SCHLOOP AND REBECCA NESBIT

In the 1970s and 1980s, scholars laid the groundwork for the field of nonprofit studies by developing 10 theoretical explanations of the nonprofit sector, particularly explanations about why the sector exists (see Chapter 2). Contemporary scholars now use these theories in their own work. They collect and analyze data to determine whether the theories match their observations. When there is a mismatch, they revise and build upon the theories to make them more helpful and accurate.

At least that is how things are supposed to work. It is actually difficult to tell if this is happening. To what extent are contemporary scholars in fact using these 10 explanations of the nonprofit sector? We address this question by using scholarship, or published academic articles, as data. Bibliometric studies such as this one use publications to assess patterns in scholarly knowledge production (Wolfram, 2003). Bibliometric studies are popular because they help to assess the state of knowledge in a field of study (Wan Utap et al., 2009). In this chapter, we use a bibliometric analysis to understand use of the 10 nonprofit sector theories in contemporary scholarship.

Other scholars have conducted bibliometric analyses of nonprofit scholarship (Brudney & Durden, 1993; Bushouse & Sowa, 2012; Kang et al., 2021; Ma & Konrath, 2018; Shier & Handy, 2014), but none of these studies focused on understanding nonprofit sector theory. Because of this, it is likely that nonprofit scholars do not know the extent and ways in which nonprofit sector theories have been used over time.

This is problematic because theory plays an important role in the development of scholarly research and is a major determinant of the evolution of knowledge (Darden & Maull, 1977). As other work in this volume posits, the 10 nonprofit sector theories have significant limitations. A systematic understanding of the use of sector theories therefore allows nonprofit scholars to assess their progress as a field, understand the limitations and gaps of the current theories-in-use, and springboard into new theoretical perspectives. We focus on research that uses the 10 theories discussed in Chapter 2: government failure, market failure, contract failure, voluntary sector failure, entrepreneurship, (nonprofit–government) interdependence, social origins, the commons, mediating structures, and associationalism. Specifically, we seek to answer the following questions:

- How has use of the 10 nonprofit sector theories evolved over time? What percentage of research articles in the major nonprofit journals cite each nonprofit sector theory?
- Are scholars using nonprofit sector theories differently depending on the topic of their research? Do scholars cite nonprofit sector theories when doing research on some topics more than others?

To address these descriptive research questions, we examine work published in the three major nonprofit journals that cites an a priori list of seminal works on the 10 nonprofit sector theories described in Chapter 2.

3.1 Data and Methodology

We measure theory use based on citation of one or more seminal works (book, chapter, or article) on one of the 10 nonprofit sector theories. Our data comprises 20 years (1999–2019) of articles published in the top three nonprofit studies journals – *Nonprofit and Voluntary Sector Quarterly* (*NVSQ*), *Nonprofit Management and Leadership* (*NML*), and *Voluntas* – downloaded from the Scopus[1] abstract and citation database (Elsevier, 2021). We screened out articles listed in Scopus that had no references or that had 10 or fewer references[2] to focus our analysis on research articles, thereby excluding editors' notes, remembrances, editorials, responses to critiques of published papers, and so forth. This produced 2,349 Scopus records for our article data set. We used the Natural Language Toolkit package (Loper & Bird, 2002)

[1] Web of Science, an alternative abstract and citation database, does not consistently include information on articles published in *NML* and *Voluntas* until after 2008.

[2] We first checked PDFs of articles with 10 or fewer references and hand-corrected Scopus records that were missing most references.

in the open-source programming language Python (Hügel, 2020) to construct a new data set of the 124,176 references from these articles.

To identify seminal works associated with the 10 nonprofit sector theories, we used the iterative process visualized in Figure 3.1. We began by working with the editors of this volume to generate an initial list of seminal works for each theory.[3] We then searched for the title of each seminal work in our reference data set to identify different editions and republications. Next, we used this start list to mine the reference data set. We matched references based on the name of the lead author, publication year, and title of the seminal works in our start list. This data-mining process allowed us to both identify all articles citing seminal works from our start list and to identify other works commonly co-referenced with works from our start list. We then considered each co-referenced work and decided whether to add it to our list of seminal works. A frequently co-referenced work was added to our list of seminal works based on three criteria: (a) the work made a significant theoretical contribution by developing theory or synthesizing and assessing theory, (b) the focus of the work was not empirical analysis to test theory, and (c) our research team agreed that the work could be assigned to a single sector theory. This iterative process resulted in a list of seminal works associated with each of the 10 nonprofit sector theories presented in Table 3.1. We used our final list of seminal works to identify articles published in *NVSQ*, *NML*, and *Voluntas* over the period of study that cite the 10 nonprofit sector theories.

We used a more traditional hand-coding process to sort articles published in *NVSQ*, *NML*, and *Voluntas* over the study period into broad topics of nonprofit research. Specifically, we used a two-cycle process of provisional and elaborative coding (Saldaña, 2016). First, we developed a start list (Miles et al., 2014) of nonprofit research topics using published research discussing substantive areas of nonprofit research (Brudney & Durden, 1993; Bushouse & Sowa, 2012; Kang et al., 2021; Ma & Konrath, 2018; Shier & Handy, 2014) and coded accordingly. Second, we refined our topic codes using elaborative coding (Auerbach & Silverstein, 2003). This process produced

[3] The four individuals who developed this list have a combined 50+ years of experience conducting research in nonprofit studies. Three of the four regularly teach graduate-level courses that cover nonprofit sector theories.

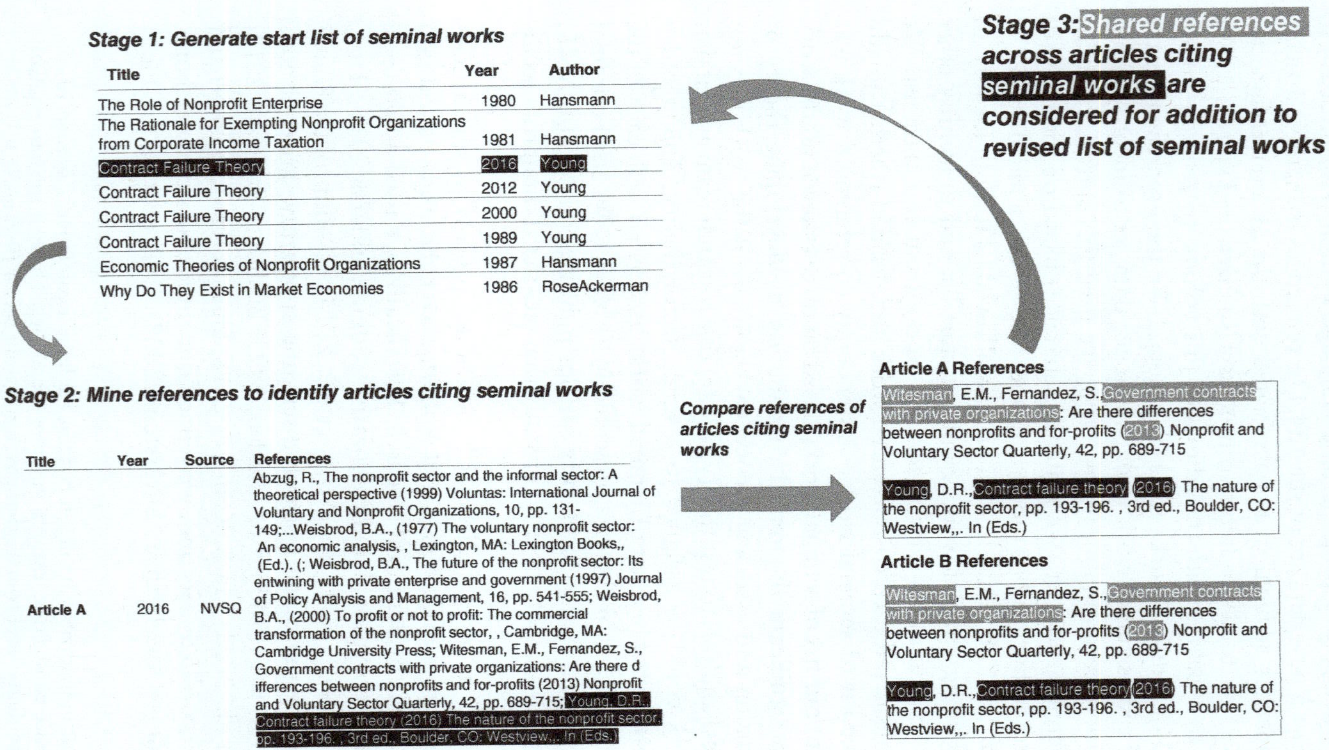

Figure 3.1 Iterative process used to identify seminal theory works

Table 3.1 *Seminal works by nonprofit sector theory*

Theory	Seminal work identified by research team	Seminal work identified through text mining
Government failure	Douglas, 1987; Young, 2016b	James, 1990; Winston, 2007; Young, 1989b
Market failure	Salamon, 2016; Weisbrod, 1977, 1986, 2009	Anheier & Ben-Ner, 2003; Bator, 1958; Ben-Ner & Gui, 2003; Kingma, 2003; Preston, 1988; Stiglitz, 1989
Contract failure	Hansmann, 1979, 1981, 2003; Young, 2016a	Ben-Ner, 1986; Handy, 1997; Hansmann, 2003; Krashinsky, 1984; Ortmann & Schlesinger, 1997, 2003; Rose-Ackerman, 1996; Steinberg, 1997, 2003, 2006; Young, 1989a
Voluntary failure	Salamon, 1987b; Young, 2016c	Salamon, 2003; Young, 1989c
Entrepreneurship	James & Rose-Ackerman, 2013; Young, 1980, 1983	Badelt, 1997; Ben-Ner, 2002; Ben-Ner & Van Hoomissen, 1991; Boschee, 2001; Chaves, 1998; Cordes et al., 2004; Glaeser & Shleifer, 2001
Interdependence	Grønbjerg, 2016; Salamon, 1987a; Salamon, 1995; Salamon & Toepler, 2015; Smith & Grønbjerg, 2006	Brinkerhoff, 2002; Coston, 1998; Lipsky & Smith, 1989; Salamon & Elliott, 2002; Smith & Lipsky, 2009; Van Til, 2008; Wolch, 1990; Young 2000; Young, 2006
Social origins	Anheier, 2006; Badelt, 1990; Salamon & Anheier, 1998	Bode, 2006; DiMaggio & Anheier, 1990; James, 1987, 1989; Kramer, 2000; Kramer et al., 1981; Salamon & Anheier, 1997
The Commons	Lohmann, 1989, 1992a, 1992b, 1995, 2011, 2015	–
Mediating structures	Berger & Neuhaus, 2021	Berry, 2003
Associationalism	Clemens, 2006, 2016; de Tocqueville, 1988; Edwards & Foley, 1998, 2001; Putnam et al., 1992; Putnam, 2000; Skocpol, 2003; Skocpol et al., 2005	Eikenberry, 2009; Eikenberry & Kluver, 2004; Putnam, 1995; Skocpol, 1996, 1997; Skocpol et al., 2000; Skocpol & Fiorina, 2004; Smith, 1994, 1997, 2000; Theiss-Morse & Hibbing, 2005; Tschirhart & Gazley, 2014; Verba et al., 1995; Warren, 2022; Woolcock, 1998; Wuthnow, 1998

15 nonprofit research topics described in more detail in the next section.[4] Every article in our data set was coded to a single topic, allowing us to examine the distribution of articles citing seminal works by research topic.

3.2 Findings: Trends in Citation of Nonprofit Sector Theory

We begin by presenting findings from Figure 3.2, which shows overall trends in articles published in *NVSQ*, *NML*, and *Voluntas* citing any of the seminal works from our list. We find that, during the study period, between 39% and 54% of articles in any given year cite at least one seminal work on one of the 10 nonprofit sector theories. While the percentage of articles citing at least one seminal work fluctuates quite a bit over time, it has a downward trend. Still, the fact that an average of 45% of articles cite at least one seminal work over the

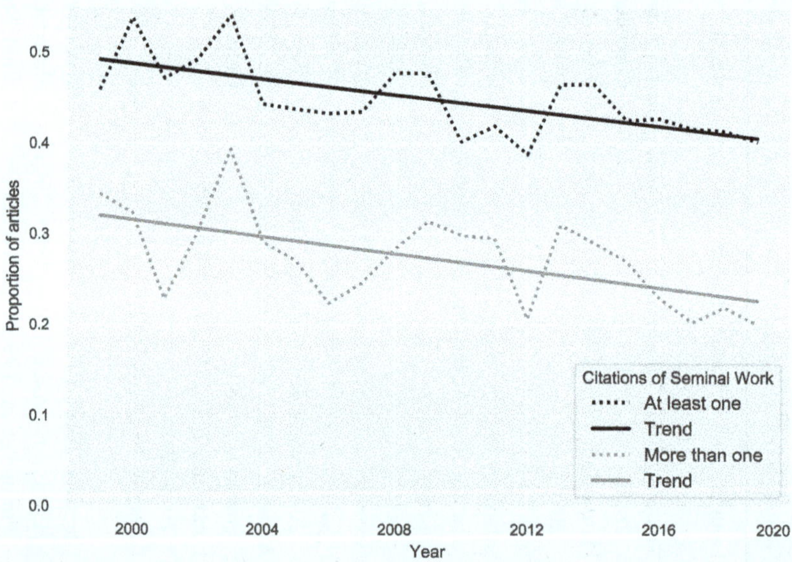

Figure 3.2 Proportion of articles citing any sector theory seminal work by year

[4] Further information about our topic-coding process and final topic codes is available by request and will be published in a different outlet in the near future.

study period shows the overall importance and influence of nonprofit sector theory.

The rate at which articles published in *NVSQ*, *NML*, and *Voluntas* cite more than one of the seminal works from our list, including more than one work on the same nonprofit sector theory, also declines over time. The percentage of articles per year citing more than one seminal work ranges from 20% to 39%, with an average of 27%. This finding seems to indicate that most articles published in *NVSQ*, *NML*, and *Voluntas* are not deeply engaging with seminal works on nonprofit sector theory, perhaps because they are drawing upon other theoretical frameworks.

We now shift our focus to findings on trends in the citation of at least one seminal work across the 10 nonprofit sector theories, as shown in Figures 3.3–3.12. During the study period, seminal work on associationalism had the highest single-year citation rate, peaking at 33% in 2009. Seminal work on associationalism also had the highest average citation rate at 23%. Citation of seminal work on government failure, contract failure, entrepreneurship, social origins, mediating structures, and associationalism was stable over the study

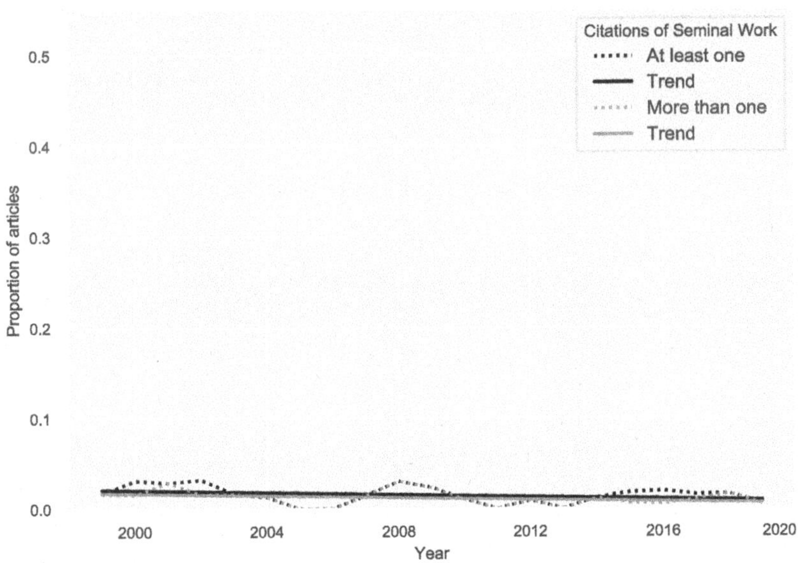

Figure 3.3 Proportion of articles citing government failure seminal work by year

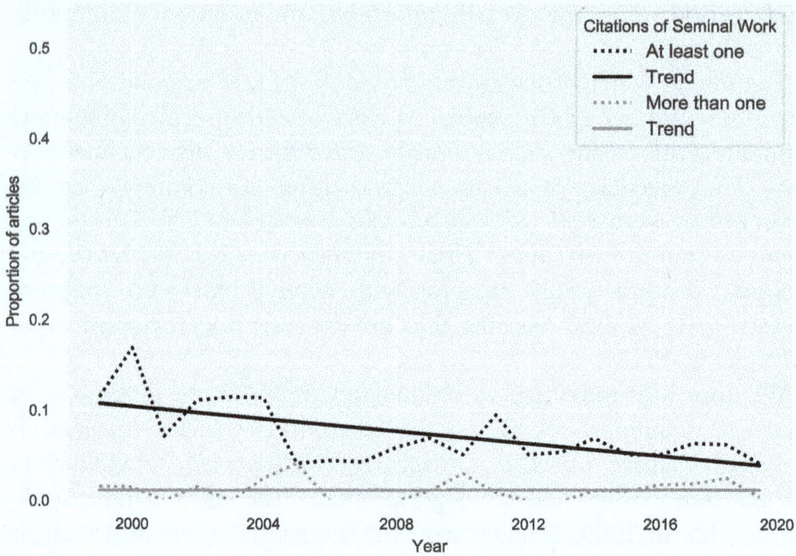

Figure 3.4 Proportion of articles citing market failure seminal work by year

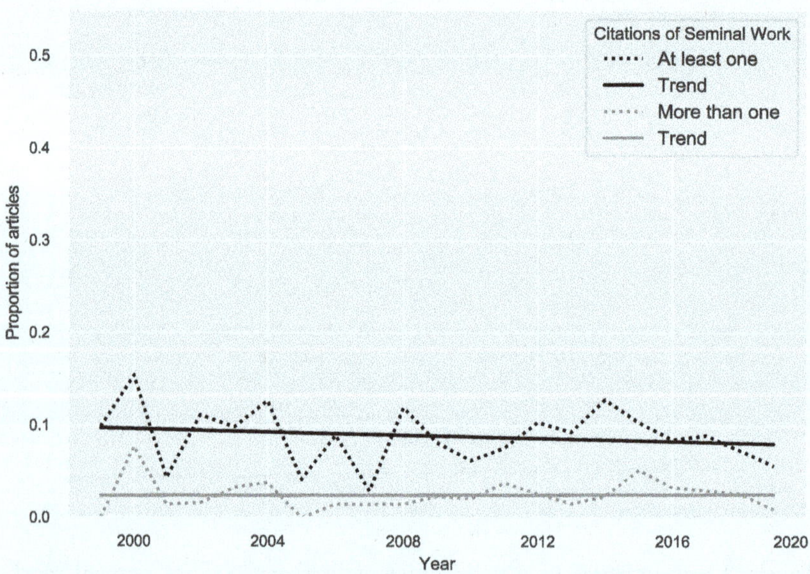

Figure 3.5 Proportion of articles citing contract failure seminal work by year

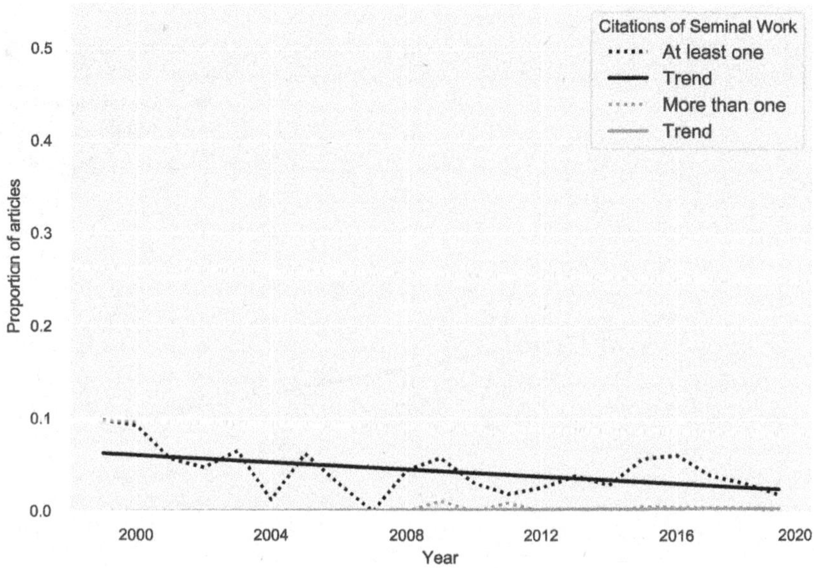

Figure 3.6 Proportion of articles citing voluntary failure seminal work by year

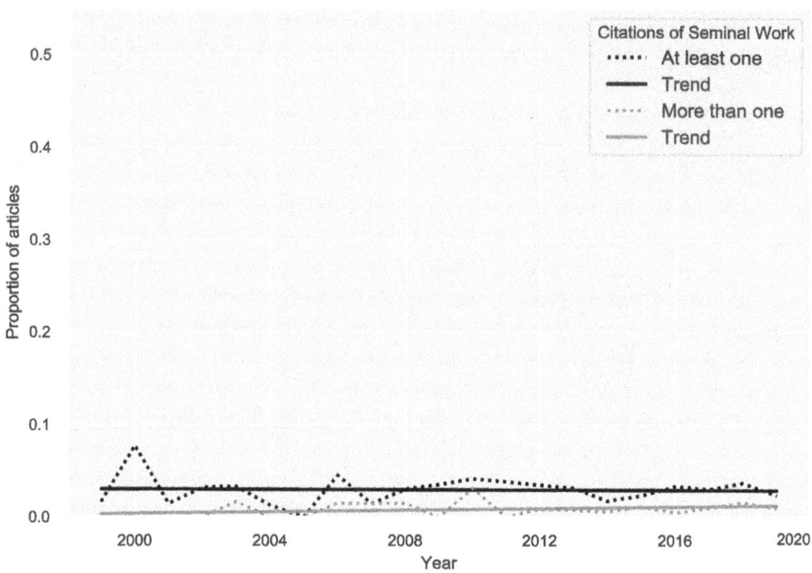

Figure 3.7 Proportion of articles citing entrepreneurship seminal work by year

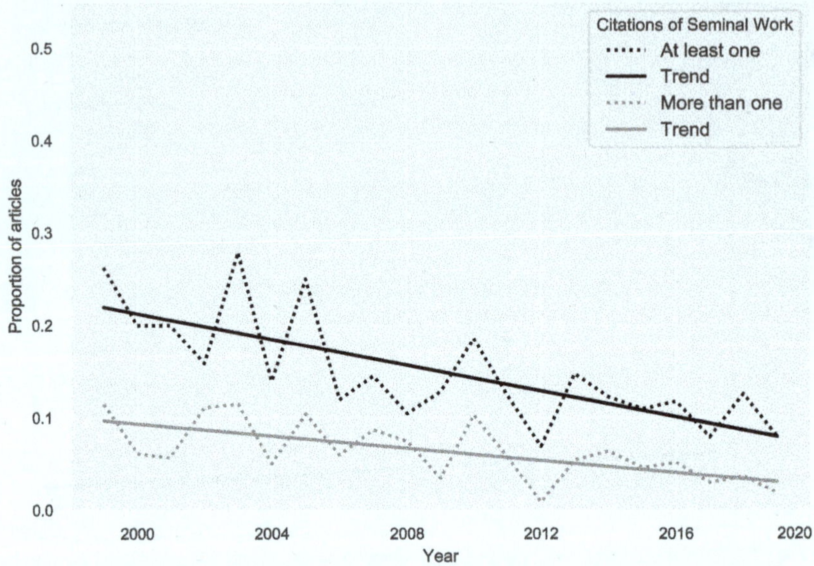

Figure 3.8 Proportion of articles citing interdependence seminal work by year

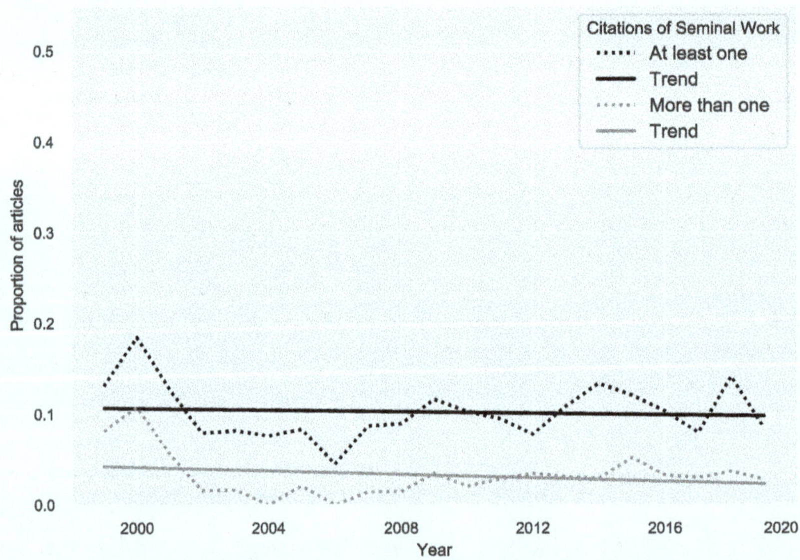

Figure 3.9 Proportion of articles citing social origins seminal work by year

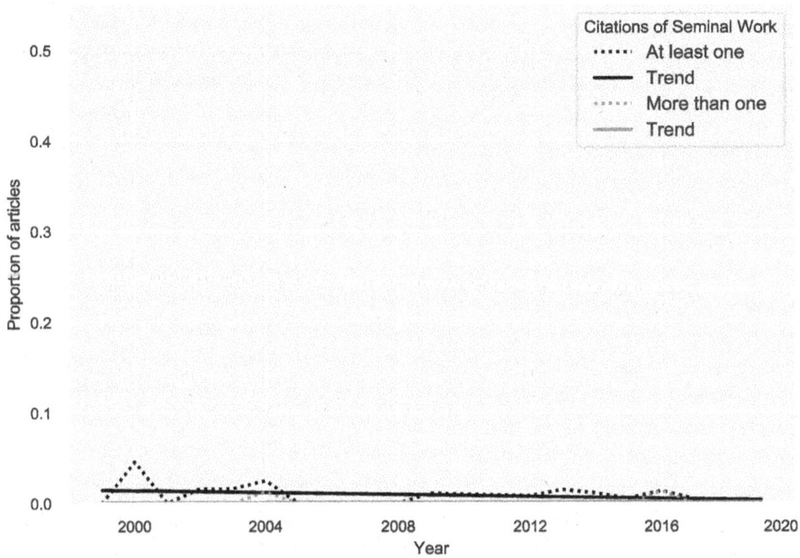

Figure 3.10 Proportion of articles citing the commons seminal work by year

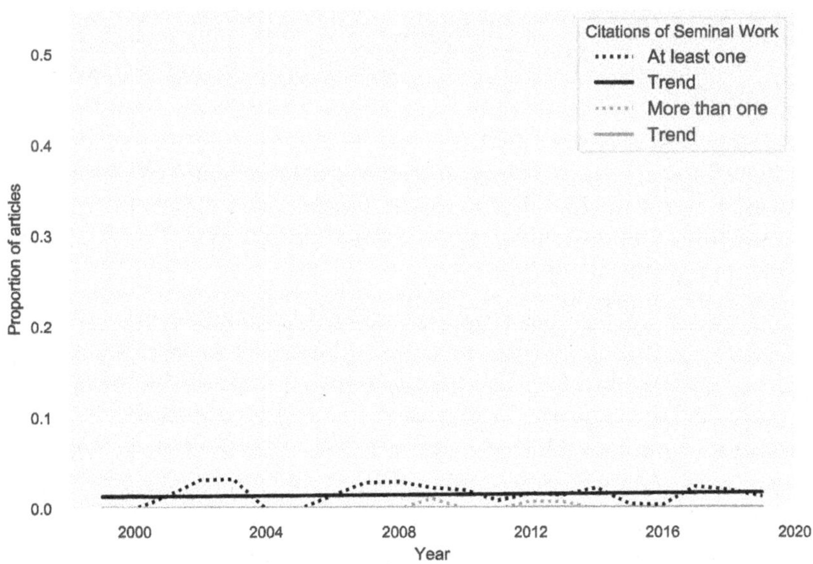

Figure 3.11 Proportion of articles citing mediating structures seminal work by year

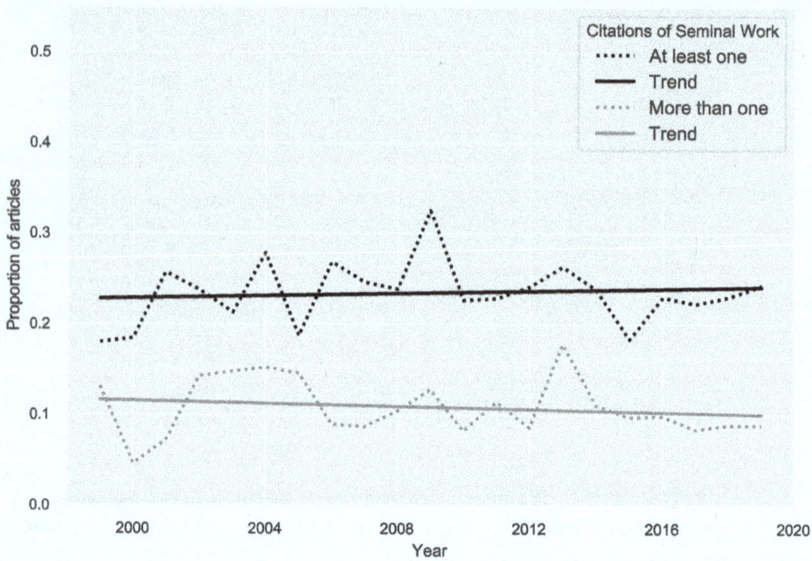

Figure 3.12 Proportion of articles citing associationalism seminal work by year

period. On average, however, work on contract failure (9%), social origins (10%), and associationalism (23%) was cited at higher rates than the other theories with stable citation rates. In contrast, citation of seminal work on market failure, voluntary failure, interdependence, and the commons declined. Together, this trend suggests that interest in each of the 10 nonprofit sector theories may be somewhat independent of interest in the other theories. Finally, it is important to note that most articles that cite a seminal work on any of the 10 nonprofit sector theories cite only one.

The final set of findings we present relates to trends in use of the 10 nonprofit sector theories to contribute to knowledge in specific topical areas. The first column of Table 3.2 lists the 15 nonprofit research topics identified through our hand-coding of articles published in *NVSQ*, *NML*, and *Voluntas*. The topics are listed in order from those with the largest article count to those with the least (see "Article count" column in Table 3.2). For example, 275 articles deal with "Volunteering."

Using Table 3.2, we can consider patterns in articles that cite at least one of the seminal works on our list by topical area. The second-to-last column (>0 seminal work) of Table 3.2 indicates the percentage

Table 3.2 ***Citation of any seminal work by nonprofit research topic***

	Percent of articles citing seminal works on theory		
Nonprofit research topic	Article count	>0 seminal work	>1 seminal work
Volunteering	275	46%	20%
Nonprofit governance, accountability, and performance	269	30%	17%
Philanthropy	243	31%	14%
Organization theory	238	59%	41%
Civil society/nonprofit sector and the domestic/foreign state	194	56%	40%
Prosocial behavior and sociopolitical outcomes	178	69%	50%
Organizational structure, strategy, communication, and innovation	152	31%	19%
Public policy advocacy/formation, social movements, global civil society	125	35%	20%
Organizational behavior	118	35%	22%
Financial management	114	39%	22%
Nonprofit sector distinctiveness	106	68%	55%
Social innovation and impact	103	37%	23%
Organizational collaboration, networks, and partnerships	101	38%	20%
Critical issues for nonprofit mission, values, and roles	75	56%	37%
Nonprofit education and training	58	21%	9%

of articles on each topic that cite at least one seminal work on nonprofit sector theory. Interestingly, excluding "Nonprofit education and training," at least 30% of articles across topical areas cite at least one seminal work on nonprofit sector theory. Some 68% or more of articles on "Prosocial behavior and sociopolitical outcomes" and "Nonprofit sector distinctiveness" cite a seminal work on nonprofit sector theory. Other topical areas that cite seminal work on nonprofit sector theories at high rates include "Organization theory" (59%), "Civil society/nonprofit sector and the domestic/foreign state" (56%), and "Critical issues for nonprofit mission, values, and roles" (56%).

We can also use Table 3.2 to consider patterns across topical areas in the percentage of articles that cite more than one of the seminal works on our list. The last column (>1 seminal work) of Table 3.2 presents the percentage of articles in each topical area that cite more than one of the seminal works on our list. We see that, across all topical areas, a considerably lower percentage of articles cite more than one seminal work. Several topical areas stand out, however, in the percentage of articles that do cite more than one of the seminal works from our list. Specifically, articles on "Nonprofit sector distinctiveness" (55%), "Prosocial behavior and sociopolitical outcomes" (50%), "Organization theory" (41%), "Civil society/nonprofit sector and the domestic/foreign state" (40%), and "Critical issues for nonprofit mission, values, and roles" (37%) engage seminal works in a deeper way. Together, these findings suggest that the topical focus of a nonprofit research article shapes whether, and to what extent, authors cite nonprofit sector theory. Research that seeks to understand the distinguishing features and contributions of the sector and its relationship with other sectors tend to cite work on the 10 theories at higher rates.

Finally, we consider how the topical focus of research is associated with citation of seminal work on specific nonprofit sector theories. Each row of Table 3.3 presents the percentage of articles in a topical area that cite at least one seminal work on the sector theory listed at the top of each column. For example, of the articles in the database focused on "Volunteering," 0% cite work on government failure, 1% cite work on market failure, 1% cite seminal work on contract failure, and so on.

The findings presented in Table 3.3 suggest that the topical focus of research articles shapes *which* of the 10 sector theories authors tend to cite. For example, and as might be expected, work on "Organizational collaboration, networks, and partnerships" that often examines nonprofit contractual and collaborative relationships with government cites seminal work on interdependence more than the other theories. Articles on "Financial management" and "Organization behavior" cite work on contract failure and/or market failure more than other theories. Articles on "Volunteering" and "Prosocial behavior and sociopolitical outcomes" cite work on associationalism at elevated rates. Only four topical areas intensely cite seminal work across multiple nonprofit sector theories: "Nonprofit sector distinctiveness," "Organization theory," "Critical issues for nonprofit mission, values, and roles," and, to a lesser extent, "Civil society/nonprofit sector and the domestic/foreign

Table 3.3 *Citation of seminal work by theory and nonprofit research topic*

	Percent of articles citing seminal work on theory										
Nonprofit research topic	Government failure	Market failure	Contract failure	Voluntary failure	Entrepre-neurship	Inter-dependence	Social origins	The Commons	Mediating Structures	Associa-tionalism	>1 seminal work
Volunteering	0%	1%	1%	1%	1%	1%	3%	0%	0%	42%	20%
Nonprofit governance, accountability, and performance	0%	3%	7%	1%	2%	10%	7%	2%	1%	11%	17%
Philanthropy	2%	5%	7%	2%	1%	8%	4%	0%	0%	14%	14%
Organization theory	4%	14%	15%	11%	8%	26%	25%	1%	2%	26%	41%
Civil society/nonprofit sector and the domestic/foreign state	3%	10%	8%	8%	2%	32%	18%	1%	2%	19%	40%
Prosocial behavior and sociopolitical outcomes	1%	0%	1%	1%	1%	5%	4%	1%	1%	67%	50%
Organizational structure, strategy, communication, and innovation	0%	3%	6%	3%	1%	11%	7%	0%	0%	14%	19%
Public policy advocacy/formation, social movements, global civil society	0%	3%	2%	0%	0%	10%	10%	0%	11%	19%	20%
Organizational behavior	0%	9%	19%	1%	4%	8%	6%	0%	1%	9%	22%
Financial management	3%	13%	23%	4%	1%	9%	9%	0%	0%	5%	22%
Nonprofit sector distinctiveness	6%	25%	31%	17%	11%	25%	28%	6%	3%	27%	55%
Social innovation and impact	0%	7%	10%	4%	14%	6%	16%	1%	2%	14%	23%
Organizational collaboration, networks, and partnerships	0%	3%	4%	6%	2%	27%	5%	0%	1%	12%	20%
Critical issues for nonprofit mission, values, and roles	3%	11%	12%	4%	0%	25%	17%	1%	0%	36%	37%
Nonprofit education and training	0%	0%	0%	2%	0%	2%	7%	0%	0%	14%	9%

state." Together, these findings suggest that scholars are strategically citing the nonprofit sector theories to frame their research and contribute to knowledge creation in specific topical areas.

3.3 Discussion: Improving Nonprofit Sector Theory

These results indicate that the 10 nonprofit sector theories are an important foundation within nonprofit studies research. While use of these theories varies across the body of nonprofit research produced in any given year, the fact that on average 45% of articles published in the three core journals engaged these theories every year indicates that they are an important component of nonprofit inquiry. In fact, it is possible that our data underrepresent the influence of the nonprofit sector theories because scholars might be citing research derived from these seminal works without citing the original works themselves. The consistent use of these theories implies that scholars are still seeking to understand and address foundational questions related to the nonprofit sector, such as why the nonprofit sector exists, how it came into being, and how it differs from and relates to the government and business sectors. We assert that these questions continue to be persistent and important areas of inquiry for nonprofit scholars, even though nonprofit scholars are interested in many more topics and approaches than just sector theory.

That said, our analysis also suggests that use of the nonprofit sector theories in many research articles published in *NVSQ*, *NML*, and *Voluntas* is ceremonial. Scholars are much more likely to cite a single rather than multiple seminal works from our list. A yearly average of 29% of articles cited more than one seminal work during the study period. This suggests that many authors are using these theories (and the scholarly works they are based on) as supporting references rather than attempting to really explain, build upon, or test nonprofit sector theories (Corley & Gioia, 2011). In articles that cite only one seminal work, we suspect that treatment of these theories tends to be ceremonial,[5] with some notable exceptions (Kamerāde et al., 2016). By "ceremonial," we mean that, to contextualize their

[5] To begin to verify this assumption, we examined a random sample of 10 articles that cite one seminal work. In this sample, the average count of in-text citations of each referenced seminal work was 1.7. Further, most of the papers devoted less than a paragraph to discussion of the sector theory related to the seminal work.

own work, scholars make passing references to a well-known theory without deeply engaging its concepts and arguments in a substantive way. This phenomenon is not unique to nonprofit studies or the use of the sector theories. For example, Wry et al. (2013) noted similar citation patterns of Pfeffer and Salancik's (2003) seminal book on resource dependence theory.

Still, nonprofit scholars need to deeply engage with sector theory to address some of the fundamental questions of the field. Many scholars bemoan the lack of theory or weak theorizing in academic research (Blumer, 1954; DiMaggio, 1995; Sutton & Staw, 1995; Weick, 1995). Robust use of these theories necessitates sufficient background information on the theories so the reader understands their major concepts and components; likewise, empirical studies would include measurements of the theories' concepts in their empirical analyses.

The multidisciplinary nature of nonprofit studies, which is a strength in many ways, may create extra challenges for deep engagement with the sector theories. Nonprofit scholars are trained and tenured within a variety of disciplines. Although nonprofit academic programs tend to be housed in public administration and business departments, these programs can be found across a wide range of disciplines (Mirabella, 2007; Mirabella & Wish, 2000). The great variation in background and training of nonprofit scholars means that it is unlikely that a majority of nonprofit scholars have completed PhD-level courses that focus on nonprofit sector theories or provide a systematic overview of the seminal works on our list (Allison et al., 2007; Jackson et al., 2014; Shier & Handy, 2014). This idea is further supported by the variation in nonprofit curricular content at the master's and undergraduate levels (Mirabella & Wish, 2000). Nonprofit scholars' ceremonial engagement of the seminal works – and by extension, the 10 sector theories – could be due to systematic obstacles and deficiencies in nonprofit graduate education.

Another way that the multidisciplinary nature of nonprofit studies informs the interpretation of our findings is that many nonprofit scholars publish their academic research in their home disciplinary journals in addition to the multidisciplinary nonprofit journals that we consider in this chapter. For example, many nonprofit scholars are tenured in public administration departments and are incentivized to publish their research in public administration journals in addition to nonprofit journals. This means that not all nonprofit research, particularly research on the nonprofit sector theories, is captured in our analysis (which focuses on research published in a small set of journals). There is much more nonprofit scholarship out there (LePere-Schloop & Nesbit, 2022a), so it is possible that the use of these sector theories is more widespread than what our analysis implies.

However, the fact that nonprofit sector research is published in other journals is not necessarily negative because it also creates opportunities for nonprofit sector scholars to influence research and thinking in other areas. The fact that nonprofit scholarship is published in a variety of disciplines opens up the possibility for fruitful interdisciplinary knowledge integration that can advance the field. Knowledge integration occurs when the concepts, theories, and methods from one discipline shape and alter the paradigms in another discipline (National Academies, 2005; Porter et al., 2006; Rafols & Meyer, 2010). Our prior research provides evidence of knowledge integration between public administration and nonprofit studies on a variety of research topics, such as collaboration, financial management, and public service provision, and there is great potential for more substantial knowledge integration across a variety of other topics, such as organizational performance, public policy, and critical perspectives on nonprofit distinctiveness (LePere-Schloop & Nesbit, 2022b). Knowledge integration across nonprofit studies and other disciplines will benefit all nonprofit scholars by expanding and honing their paradigms. To the extent that authors intentionally cite research from other disciplines or write articles aimed at helping scholars in other disciplines to see the relevance of nonprofit studies, nonprofit studies will benefit from its multidisciplinary nature.

Our results also indicate that nonprofit scholars' use of the 10 sector theories is uneven. Some theories get a lot more attention than others, specifically, associationalism, contract failure, nonprofit-government interdependence, and social origins. The factors driving use of each of these theories may be different. For example, associationalism may receive relatively more attention due to the popularity of Robert Putnam's (2000) book *Bowling alone*. In contrast, contract failure, developed in the influential discipline of economics, has been well established for decades. Other theories of the nonprofit sector, particularly voluntary failure, entrepreneurship theory, the commons, and mediating structures, seem to have achieved less traction in nonprofit research over the past two decades.

The uneven attention to different nonprofit sector theories may also be connected to the fact that nonprofit studies is still a relatively young field, especially compared to established disciplines like economics, political science, and sociology. In fact, the formal nonprofit sector that we know it today was not formally recognized until the 1970s (Soskis, 2006). The first association for nonprofit scholars was created in 1971 (called the Association of Voluntary Action Scholars), and it reached the 1,000 member mark only in 2000 (Smith, 2003). This was accompanied by a strong growth in university nonprofit programs through the 1990s and 2000s (Mirabella, 2007). Ma and Konrath (2018) referred to the 1970s and 1980s as the "paradigm-building" phase of nonprofit scholarship, and they characterized scholarship during this period as focusing on the foundational theories of the sector, including the original failure theories. In subsequent phases, nonprofit scholars built upon those foundational theories and introduced a host of new research areas (Ma & Konrath, 2018). Some of the sector theories (e.g., social origins and entrepreneurship) emerged as scholars' research showed the limitations of the prior theories and scholars attempted to theorize new reasons for the existence of the nonprofit sector and its relationship with the other sectors. It is also interesting that during this period nonprofit scholars developed their own "homegrown" theories of the sector: voluntary failure and interdependence. All of the other sector theories originated in other disciplines, such as economics and sociology. We suspect that as scholars continue to test and build upon these theories, they will grow in utility and popularity.

Another explanation for uneven attention to these 10 sector theories is that theories are not all equal in their explanatory power or their testability. It requires large data sets with specific information to test the hypotheses and assumptions of a sector theory. Some theories are easier to test than others based on the available data. We speculate that one potential explanation for the uneven use of the sector theories is the lack of multiple, robust data sets from a variety of country contexts that can be used to explore and test these theories of the sector. In the United States, for example, very few sector-level data sets exist. The primary data set used for sector-level explorations of the nonprofit sector is the IRS 990 data, available from the National Center for Charitable Statistics. While these data are helpful, they are subject to several limitations and issues (Froelich & Knoepfle, 1996; Froelich et al., 2000; Gordon et al., 2007) that could limit scholars' ability to empirically test the full range of nonprofit sector theories. Nonprofit scholars and their professional and research associations need to advocate for better and more systematic data about the sector. Scholars can also support and contribute to endeavors like the Nonprofit Open Data Collective to help build stronger data repositories for nonprofit research (Lecy, 2020).

These theories might not be equally useful to help answer big questions about the nonprofit sector, particularly because they often address different research questions. The nonprofit studies field would benefit from more systematic literature reviews that summarize, synthesize, and contextualize the existing theoretical, conceptual, and empirical research related to each of these theories or groups of theories. These reviews would help future researchers to build more systematically on the existing empirical research and to enhance our understanding of the boundary conditions of each theory. The reviews would also help scholars understand where the field is in terms of providing additional definitive answers to questions about how and why the sector exists and its relationship with and difference from the other sectors.

We also found that nonprofit scholars are strategically using the 10 sector theories to investigate different research topics. Scholars view the sector theories as particularly informative when researching phenomena occurring at the level of the sector or large groupings of organizations. It was relatively uncommon for scholars to use the sector theories to understand volunteering and prosocial behaviors. We suggest that there are some missed opportunities here. Researchers could do more to consider how these, or new theories of the sector, help us understand the behavior of individuals and communities, not just organizations. For example, government failure theory could potentially be used to broaden our understanding of why individuals choose to support particular nonprofits with donations of time and money. These questions are particularly pertinent to understanding politically related nonprofits but may also be relevant to understanding support of basic human services and disaster response in the current environment of political polarization (Paarlberg et al., 2019, 2020). The 10 sector theories can possibly be used to understand other important aspects of the nonprofit sector, including how individuals relate to and are influenced by nonprofit organizations.

To summarize, the 10 sector theories are important to nonprofit studies research, particularly research on topics related to sector distinctiveness and other topics highlighting the uniqueness of nonprofit organizations. Scholarly engagement with the sector theories within these topics is more substantial, but, generally speaking, robust scholarly engagement with the sector theories is low. Nonprofit scholars could do much more to question, develop, and refine the existing sector theories – or to develop new ones. Our research highlights the importance of a book like this one to encourage scholars to discuss and question existing sector theories and pose new sector theory contributions to better understand the nonprofit sector.

References

Allison, L., Chen, X., Flanigan, S. T., Keyes-Williams, J., Vasavada, T. S., & Saidel, J. R. (2007). Toward doctoral education in nonprofit and philanthropic studies. *Nonprofit and Voluntary Sector Quarterly*, *36*(4_suppl), 51S–63S. https://doi.org/10.1177/0899764007305054

Anheier, H. K. (2006). Nonprofit sector in comparative perspective. In W. W. Powell & H. K. Anheier (Eds.), *The nonprofit sector: A research handbook* (2nd ed.) (pp. 89–114). Yale University Press.

Anheier, H. K., & Ben-Ner, A. (2003). *The study of nonprofit enterprise: Theories and approaches*. Springer Science & Business Media.

Auerbach, C., & Silverstein, L. B. (2003). *Qualitative data: An introduction to coding and analysis*. New York University Press.

Badelt, C. (1990). Institutional choice and organizational behavior in the third sector. In H. K. Anheier & W. Seibel (Eds.), *The third sector: Comparative studies of nonprofit organizations*. De Gruyter. https://doi.org/10.1515/9783110868401

Badelt, C. (1997). Entrepreneurship theories of the non-profit sector. *Voluntas: International Journal of Voluntary and Nonprofit Organizations*, *8*(2), 162–178. https://doi.org/10.1007/BF02354193

Bator, F. M. (1958). The anatomy of market failure. *The Quarterly Journal of Economics*, *72*(3), 351–379. https://doi.org/10.2307/1882231

Ben-Ner, A. (1986). Nonprofit organizations: Why do they exist in market economies? *The Economics of Nonprofit Institutions: Studies in Structure and Policy*, *1*, 94–113.

Ben-Ner, A. (2002). The shifting boundaries of the mixed economy and the future of the nonprofit sector. *Annals of Public and Cooperative Economics*, *73*(1), 5–40. https://doi.org/10.1111/1467-8292.00184

Ben-Ner, A., & Gui, B. (2003). The theory of nonprofit organizations revisited. In H. K. Anheier & A. Ben-Ner (Eds.), *The study of the nonprofit enterprise: Theories and approaches* (pp. 3–26). Springer US. https://doi.org/10.1007/978-1-4615-0131-2_1

Ben-Ner, A., & Van Hoomissen, T. (1991). Nonprofit organizations in the mixed economy. *Annals of Public and Cooperative Economics*, 62(4), 519–550. https://doi.org/10.1111/j.1467-8292.1991.tb01366.x

Berger, P., & Neuhaus, R. (2021). To empower people: The role of mediating structures in public policy. In J. S. Ott & L. A. Dicke (Eds.), *The nature of the nonprofit sector* (4th ed.) (pp. 350–361). Routledge. https://doi.org/10.4324/9780367696559-32

Berry, J. M. (2003). *A voice for nonprofits*. Brookings Institution Press.

Blumer, H. (1954). What is wrong with social theory? *American Sociological Review*, *19*(1), 3–10. JSTOR. https://doi.org/10.2307/2088165

Bode, I. (2006). Disorganized welfare mixes: Voluntary agencies and new governance regimes in Western Europe. *Journal of European Social Policy*, *16*(4), 346–359. https://doi.org/10.1177/0958928706068273

Boschee, J. (2001). Eight basic principles for nonprofit entrepreneurs. *Nonprofit World*, *19*(4), 15–18.

Brinkerhoff, J. M. (2002). Government–nonprofit partnership: A defining framework. *Public Administration and Development*, 22(1), 19–30. https://doi.org/10.1002/pad.203

Brudney, J. L., & Durden, T. K. (1993). Twenty years of the *Journal of Voluntary Action Research/Nonprofit and Voluntary Sector Quarterly*: An assessment of past trends and future directions. *Nonprofit and Voluntary Sector Quarterly*, 22(3), 207–218. https://doi.org/10.1177/089976409322300

Bushouse, B. K., & Sowa, J. E. (2012). Producing knowledge for practice: Assessing *NVSQ* 2000–2010. *Nonprofit and Voluntary Sector Quarterly*, *41*(3), 497–513. https://doi.org/10.1177/0899764011422116

Chaves, M. (1998). The religious ethic and the spirit of nonprofit entrepreneurship. In W. W. Powell & E. S. Clemens (Eds.), *Private action and the public good*. Yale University Press.

Clemens, E. S. (2006). Constitution of citizens: Political theories of nonprofit organizations. In W. W. Powell & R. Steinberg (Eds.), *The nonprofit sector: A research handbook* (2nd ed.) (pp. 207–220). Yale University Press.

Clemens, E. S. (2016). The constitution of citizens: Political theories of nonprofit organizations. In J. S. Ott & L. A. Dicke (Eds.), *The nature of the nonprofit sector* (pp. 261–275). Routledge.

Cordes, J. J., Steuerle, C. E., & Twombly, E. (2004). Dimensions of nonprofit entrepreneurship: An exploratory essay. In D. Holtz-Eakin & H.S. Rosen (Eds.). *Public Policy and the Economics of Entrepreneurship* (pp. 115–148). MIT Press.

Corley, K. G., & Gioia, D. A. (2011). Building theory about theory building: What constitutes a theoretical contribution? *Academy of Management Review*, *36*(1), 12–32. https://doi.org/10.5465/amr.2009.0486

Coston, J. M. (1998). A model and typology of government–NGO relationships. *Nonprofit and Voluntary Sector Quarterly*, *27*(3), 358–382. https://doi.org/10.1177/0899764098273006

Darden, L., & Maull, N. (1977). Interfield theories. *Philosophy of Science*, *44*(1), 43–64. https://doi.org/10.1086/288723

de Tocqueville, A. (1988). *Democracy in America: And two essays on America*. Penguin UK.

DiMaggio, P. J. (1995). Comments on "What theory is not." *Administrative Science Quarterly*, *40*(3), 391–397. JSTOR. https://doi.org/10.2307/2393790

DiMaggio, P. J., & Anheier, H. K. (1990). The sociology of nonprofit organizations and sectors. *Annual Review of Sociology*, *16*, 137–159. www.jstor.org/stable/2393790

Douglas, J. (1987). Political theories of nonprofit organization. In W. W. Powell & R. Steinberg (Eds.), *The nonprofit sector: A research handbook* (1st ed.) (Vol. 43, p. 45). Yale University Press.

Edwards, B., & Foley, M. W. (1998). Civil society and social capital beyond Putnam. *American Behavioral Scientist*, *42*(1), 124–139. https://doi.org/10.1177/0002764298042001010

Edwards, B., & Foley, M. W. (2001). Civil society and social capital: A primer. In *Beyond Tocqueville: Civil society and the social capital debate in comparative perspective* (pp. 1–14). University Press of New England Hanover.

Eikenberry, A. M. (2009). Refusing the market: A democratic discourse for voluntary and nonprofit organizations. *Nonprofit and Voluntary Sector Quarterly*, *38*(4), 582–596. https://doi.org/10.1177/0899764009333686

Eikenberry, A. M., & Kluver, J. D. (2004). The marketization of the nonprofit sector: Civil society at risk? *Public Administration Review*, *64*(2), 132–140. https://doi.org/10.1111/j.1540-6210.2004.00355.x

Elsevier. (2021). *About Scopus – Abstract and citation database*. Scopus. www.elsevier.com/solutions/scopus

Froelich, K. A., & Knoepfle, T. W. (1996). Internal Revenue Service 990 data: Fact or fiction? *Nonprofit and Voluntary Sector Quarterly*, *25*(1), 40–52. https://doi.org/10.1177/0899764096251004

Froelich, K. A., Knoepfle, T. W., & Pollak, T. H. (2000). Financial measures in nonprofit organization research: Comparing IRS 990 return and audited financial statement data. *Nonprofit and Voluntary Sector Quarterly*, *29*(2), 232–254. https://doi.org/10.1177/0899764000292002

Glaeser, E. L., & Shleifer, A. (2001). Not-for-profit entrepreneurs. *Journal of Public Economics*, *81*(1), 99–115. doi.org/10.1016/S0047-2727(00)00130-4

Gordon, T., Khumawala, S. B., Kraut, M. A., & Meade, J. A. (2007). The quality and reliability of Form 990 data: Are users being misled? *Academy of Accounting and Financial Studies Journal; Arden*, *11*, 27.

Grønbjerg, K. A. (2016). Changing shape of government-nonprofit relations. In J. S. Ott & L. A. Dicke (Eds.), *Nature of the nonprofit sector* (pp. 235–237). Routledge. https://doi.org/10.4324/9780367696559-22

Handy, F. (1997). Coexistence of nonprofit, for-profit and public sector institutions. *Annals of Public and Cooperative Economics*, *68*(2), 201–223. https://doi.org/10.1111/1467-8292.00043

Hansmann, H. (1979). The role of nonprofit enterprise. *Yale Law Journal*, *89*(5), 835–902.

Hansmann, H. (1981). The rationale for exempting nonprofit organizations from corporate income taxation. *Yale Law Journal*, *91*(1), 54–101.

Hansmann, H. (2003). The role of trust in nonprofit enterprise. In H. K. Anheier & A. Ben-Ner (Eds.), *The study of the nonprofit enterprise: Theories and approaches* (pp. 115–122). Springer US. https://doi.org/10.1007/978-1-4615-0131-2_6

Hügel, S. (2020). *PyZotero* (1.4.10). http://doi.org/10.5281/zenodo.2917290

Jackson, S. K., Guerrero, S., & Appe, S. (2014). The state of nonprofit and philanthropic studies doctoral education. *Nonprofit and Voluntary Sector Quarterly*, *43*(5), 795–811. https://doi.org/10.1177/0899764014549056

James, E. (1987). Nonprofit sector in comparative perspective. In W. Powell & R. Steinberg (Eds.), *The nonprofit sector: A research handbook* (1st ed.) (Vol. 43, p. 45). Yale University Press.

James, E. (1989). *The nonprofit sector in international perspective: Studies in comparative culture and policy*. Oxford University Press.

James, E. (1990). Economic theories of the nonprofit sector: A comparative perspective. In H. K. Anheier & W. Seibel (Eds.), *The third sector: Comparative studies of nonprofit organizations*. De Gruyter. https://doi.org/10.1515/9783110868401.21

James, E., & Rose-Ackerman, S. (2013). *The non-profit enterprise in market economics*. Taylor & Francis. https://doi.org/10.4324/9781315015163

Kamerāde, D., Crotty, J., & Ljubownikow, S. (2016). Civil liberties and volunteering in six former Soviet Union countries. *Nonprofit and Voluntary Sector Quarterly*, *45*(6), 1150–1168. https://doi.org/10.1177/089976401664968

Kang, C. H., Baek, Y. M., & Kim, E. H.-J. (2021). Half a century of NVSQ: Thematic stability across years and editors. *Nonprofit and Voluntary Sector Quarterly*, 08997640211017676. https://doi.org/10.1177/08997640211017676

Kingma, B. R. (2003). Public good theories of the nonprofit sector. In H. K. Anheier & A. Ben-Ner (Eds.), *The study of the nonprofit enterprise: Theories and approaches* (pp. 53–65). Springer US. https://doi.org/10.1007/978-1-4615-0131-2_3

Kramer, R. M. (2000). A third sector in the third millennium? *Voluntas: International Journal of Voluntary and Nonprofit Organizations*, *11*(1), 1–23. https://doi.org/10.1023/A:1008914531485

Kramer, R. M., Kramer, R. M., & Wilensky, H. L. (1981). *Voluntary agencies in the welfare state*. University of California Press.

Krashinsky, M. (1984). *Transactions costs and a theory of the non-profit organization*. (Working Paper #84). Program on Non-Profit Organizations, Institution for Social and Policy Studies, Yale University.

Lecy, J. (2020). *Nonprofit open data collective*. Nonprofit Open Data Collective. https://nonprofit-open-data-collective.github.io//

LePere-Schloop, M., & Nesbit, R. (2022a). Disciplinary contributions to nonprofit studies: A 20-year empirical mapping of journals publishing nonprofit research and journal citations by nonprofit scholars. *Nonprofit and Voluntary Sector Quarterly*, *52*(1_suppl), 68S–101S. https://doi.org/10.1177/08997640221119728

LePere-Schloop, M., & Nesbit, R. (2022b) The nexus of public administration, public policy, and nonprofit studies: An empirical mapping of research topics and knowledge integration. *Public Administration Review*, *83*(3), 486–502. https://doi.org/10.1111/puar.13587

Lipsky, M., & Smith, S. R. (1989). Nonprofit organizations, government, and the welfare state. *Political Science Quarterly*, *104*(4), 625–648. https://doi.org/10.2307/2151102

Lohmann, R. A. (1989). And lettuce is nonanimal: Toward a positive economics of voluntary action. *Nonprofit and Voluntary Sector Quarterly*, *18*(4), 367–383.

Lohmann, R. A. (1992a). The commons: A multidisciplinary approach to nonprofit organization, voluntary action, and philanthropy. *Nonprofit and Voluntary Sector Quarterly*, *21*(3), 309–324. https://doi.org/10.1177/089976409202100030

Lohmann, R. A. (1992b). The commons: New perspectives on nonprofit organization, voluntary action and philanthropy. *Faculty Scholarship*, 754. https://researchrepository.wvu.edu/faculty_publications/754

Lohmann, R. A. (1995). Commons: Can this be the name of "thirdness"? *Nonprofit and Voluntary Sector Quarterly*, *24*(1), 25–29.

Lohmann, R. A. (2011). 14. Deliberation and dialogue and commons theory. In *Resolving community conflicts and problems* (pp. 264–276). Columbia University Press.

Lohmann, R. A. (2015). Voluntary action in new commons. *Faculty Scholarship*, 760. https://researchrepository.wvu.edu/faculty_publications/760

Loper, E., & Bird, S. (2002). NLTK: The Natural Language Toolkit. *ArXiv*. http://arxiv.org/abs/cs/0205028

Ma, J., & Konrath, S. (2018). A century of nonprofit studies: Scaling the knowledge of the field. *Voluntas: International Journal of Voluntary and*

Nonprofit Organizations, *29*(6), 1139–1158. https://doi.org/10.1007/s11266-018-00057-5

Miles, M., Huberman, A., & Saldaña, J. (2014). *Qualitative data analysis: A methods sourcebook* (4th ed.). Sage.

Mirabella, R. M. (2007). University-based educational programs in nonprofit management and philanthropic studies: A 10-year review and projections of future trends. *Nonprofit and Voluntary Sector Quarterly*, *36*(4_suppl), 11S–27S. https://doi.org/10.1177/0899764007305051

Mirabella, R. M., & Wish, N. B. (2000). The "best place" debate: A comparison of graduate education programs for nonprofit managers. *Public Administration Review*, *60*(3), 219–229. https://doi.org/10.1111/0033-3352.00082

National Academies. (2005). *Facilitating interdisciplinary research*. National Academies Press. https://doi.org/10.17226/11153

Ortmann, A., & Schlesinger, M. (1997). Trust, repute and the role of nonprofit enterprise. *Voluntas: International Journal of Voluntary and Nonprofit Organizations*, *8*(2), 97–119. https://doi.org/10.1007/BF02354189

Ortmann, A., & Schlesinger, M. (2003). Trust, repute, and the role of nonprofit enterprise. In H. K. Anheier & A. Ben-Ner (Eds.), *The study of the nonprofit enterprise: Theories and approaches* (pp. 77–114). Springer US. https://doi.org/10.1007/978-1-4615-0131-2_5

Paarlberg, L. E., LePere-Schloop, M., Walk, M., Ai, J., & Ming, Y. (2020). Activating community resilience: The emergence of COVID-19 funds across the United States. *Nonprofit and Voluntary Sector Quarterly*, *49*(6), 1119–1128. https://doi.org/10.1177/0899764020968155

Paarlberg, L. E., Nesbit, R., Clerkin, R. M., & Christensen, R. K. (2019). The politics of donations: Are red counties more donative than blue counties? *Nonprofit and Voluntary Sector Quarterly*, *48*(2), 283–308. https://doi.org/10.1177/0899764018804088

Pfeffer, J., & Salancik, G. (2003). *The external control of organizations: A resource dependence perspective*. Stanford University Press.

Porter, A. L., Roessner, J. D., Cohen, A. S., & Perreault, M. (2006). Interdisciplinary research: Meaning, metrics and nurture. *Research Evaluation*, *15*(3), 187–196. https://doi.org/10.3152/147154406781775841

Preston, A. E. (1988). The nonprofit firm: A potential solution to inherent market failures. *Economic Inquiry*, *26*(3), 493–506. https://doi.org/10.1111/j.1465-7295.1988.tb01511.x

Putnam, R. D. (1995). Tuning in, tuning out: The strange disappearance of social capital in America. *PS: Political Science & Politics*, *28*(4), 664–683. https://doi.org/10.2307/420517

Putnam, R. D. (2000). *Bowling alone: The collapse and revival of American community*. Simon and Schuster.

Putnam, R. D., Leonardi, R., & Nanetti, R. Y. (1992). *Making democracy work: Civic traditions in modern Italy*. Princeton University Press.

Rafols, I., & Meyer, M. (2010). Diversity and network coherence as indicators of interdisciplinarity: Case studies in bionanoscience. *Scientometrics*, *82*(2), 263–287. https://doi.org/10.1007/s11192-009-0041-y

Rose-Ackerman, S. (1996). Altruism, nonprofits, and economic theory. *Journal of Economic Literature*, *34*(2), 701–728. www.jstor.org/stable/2729219

Salamon, L. M. (1987a). Partners in public service. In W. W. Powell & R. Steinberg (Eds.), *The nonprofit sector: A research handbook* (1st ed., Vol. 43, p. 45). Yale University Press.

Salamon, L. M. (1987b). Of market failure, voluntary failure, and third-party government: Toward a theory of government-nonprofit relations in the modern welfare state. *Journal of Voluntary Action Research*, *16*(1–2), 29–49. https://doi.org/10.1177/089976408701600104

Salamon, L. M. (1995). *Partners in public service: Government-nonprofit relations in the modern welfare state*. Johns Hopkins University Press.

Salamon, L. M. (2003). Voluntary failure theory correctly viewed. In H. K. Anheier & A. Ben-Ner (Eds.), *The study of the nonprofit enterprise: Theories and approaches* (pp. 183–186). Springer US. https://doi.org/10.1007/978-1-4615-0131-2_11

Salamon, L. M. (2016). Market failure. In J. S. Ott & L. A. Dicke (Eds.), *Nature of the nonprofit sector* (pp. 230–234). Routledge. https://doi.org/10.4324/9780367696559-21

Salamon, L. M., & Anheier, H. K. (1997). *Defining the nonprofit sector: A cross-national analysis*. Manchester University Press.

Salamon, L. M., & Anheier, H. K. (1998). Social origins of civil society: Explaining the nonprofit sector cross-nationally. *Voluntas: International Journal of Voluntary and Nonprofit Organizations*, 9(3), 213–248. https://doi.org/10.1023/A:1022058200985

Salamon, L. M., & Elliott, O. V. (2002). *The tools of government: A guide to the new governance*. Oxford University Press.

Salamon, L. M., & Toepler, S. (2015). Government–nonprofit cooperation: Anomaly or necessity? *Voluntas: International Journal of Voluntary and Nonprofit Organizations*, 26(6), 2155–2177. https://doi.org/10.1007/s11266-015-9651-6

Saldaña, J. (2016). *The coding manual for qualitative researchers* (3rd ed.). SAGE Publications.

Shier, M. L., & Handy, F. (2014). Research trends in nonprofit graduate studies: A growing interdisciplinary field. *Nonprofit and Voluntary Sector Quarterly*, *43*(5), 812–831. https://doi.org/10.1177/0899764014548279

Skocpol, T. (1996). Unravelling from above. *The American Prospect*, *25*, 20–24.

Skocpol, T. (1997). The Tocqueville problem: Civic engagement in American democracy. *Social Science History*, *21*(4), 455–479. https://doi.org/10.2307/1171662

Skocpol, T. (2003). *Diminished democracy: From membership to management in American civic life* (Vol. 8). University of Oklahoma Press.

Skocpol, T., & Fiorina, M. P. (2004). *Civic engagement in American democracy*. Brookings Institution Press.

Skocpol, T., Cobb, R. V., & Klofstad, C. A. (2005). Disconnection and reorganization: The transformation of civic life in late-twentieth-century America. *Studies in American Political Development*, *19*(2), 137–156. https://doi.org/10.1017/S0898588X0500009X

Skocpol, T., Ganz, M., & Munson, Z. (2000). A nation of organizers: The institutional origins of civic voluntarism in the United States. *American Political Science Review*, *94*(3), 527–546. https://doi.org/10.2307/2585829

Smith, D. H. (1994). Determinants of voluntary association participation and volunteering: A literature review. *Nonprofit and Voluntary Sector Quarterly*, *23*(3), 243–263. https://doi.org/10.1177/089976409402300305

Smith, D. H. (1997). Grassroots associations are important: Some theory and a review of the impact literature. *Nonprofit and Voluntary Sector Quarterly*, *26*(3), 269–306. https://doi.org/10.1177/08997640972630

Smith, D. H. (2000). *Grassroots associations*. SAGE Publications.

Smith, D. H. (2003). A history of ARNOVA. *Nonprofit and Voluntary Sector Quarterly*, *32*(3), 458–472. https://doi.org/10.1177/08997640972630

Smith, S. R., & Grønbjerg, K. A. (2006). Scope and theory of government-nonprofit relations. In W. W. Powell & R. Steinberg (Eds.), *The nonprofit sector: A research handbook* (2nd ed.) (pp. 221–242). Yale University Press.

Smith, S. R., & Lipsky, M. (2009). *Nonprofits for hire: The welfare state in the age of contracting*. Harvard University Press. https://doi.org/10.4159/9780674043817

Soskis, B. (2006). A history of associational life and the nonprofit sector in the United States. In W. W. Powell & P. Bromley (Eds.), *The nonprofit sector: A research handbook* (3rd ed.) (pp. 221–242). Stanford University Press.

Steinberg, R. (1997). Overall evaluation of economic theories. *Voluntas: International Journal of Voluntary and Nonprofit Organizations*, *8*(2), 179–204. https://doi.org/10.1007/BF02354194

Steinberg, R. (2003). Economic theories of nonprofit organizations. In H. K. Anheier & A. Ben-Ner (Eds.), *The study of the nonprofit enterprise: Theories and approaches* (pp. 277–309). Springer US. https://doi.org/10.1007/978-1-4615-0131-2_16

Steinberg, R. (2006). Economic theories of nonprofit organizations. In W. W. Powell & R. Steinberg (Eds.), *The nonprofit sector: A research handbook* (2nd ed.) (pp. 117–139). Yale University Press.

Stiglitz, J. E. (1989). Markets, market failures, and development. *The American Economic Review*, *79*(2), 197–203. www.jstor.org/stable/1827756
Sutton, R. I., & Staw, B. M. (1995). What theory is not. *Administrative Science Quarterly*, *40*(3), 371–384. https://doi.org/10.2307/2393788
Theiss-Morse, E., & Hibbing, J. R. (2005). Citizenship and civic engagement. *Annual Review of Political Science-Palo Alto*, *8*, 227–249. https://doi.org/10.1146/annurev.polisci.8.082103.104829
Tschirhart, M., & Gazley, B. (2014). Advancing scholarship on membership associations: New research and next steps. *Nonprofit and Voluntary Sector Quarterly*, *43*(2_suppl), 35–175. https://doi.org/10.1177/089976401351705
Van Til, J. (2008). *Growing civil society: From nonprofit sector to third space*. Indiana University Press.
Verba, S., Schlozman, K. L., & Brady, H. E. (1995). *Voice and equality: Civic voluntarism in American politics*. Harvard University Press.
Wan Utap, A. K., Zainab, A. N., & Anuar, N. B. (2009). Bibliometric studies on single journals: A review. *Malaysian Journal of Library & Information Science*, *14*(1), Article 1.
Warren, M. E. (2022). Democracy and association. In *Democracy and association*. Princeton University Press.
Weick, K. E. (1995). What theory is not, theorizing is. *Administrative Science Quarterly*, *40*(3), 385–390. https://doi.org/10.2307/2393789
Weisbrod, B. (1977). *The voluntary nonprofit sector: An economic analysis*. Lexington Books.
Weisbrod, B. (1986). Toward a theory of the voluntary nonprofit sector in a three-sector economy. In S. Rose-Ackerman (Ed.), *The economics of nonprofit institutions* (pp. 21–44). Oxford University Press.
Weisbrod, B. (2009). *The nonprofit economy*. Harvard University Press.
Winston, C. (2007). *Government failure versus market failure: Microeconomics policy research and government performance*. Brookings Institution Press.
Wolch, J. R. (1990). *The shadow state: Government and voluntary sector in transition*. Foundation Center.
Wolfram, D. (2003). *Applied informetrics for information retrieval research*. Greenwood.
Woolcock, M. (1998). Social capital and economic development: Toward a theoretical synthesis and policy framework. *Theory and Society*, *27*(2), 151–208. www.jstor.org/stable/657866
Wry, T., Cobb, J. A., & Aldrich, H. (2013). More than a metaphor: Assessing the historical legacy of resource dependence and its contemporary promise as a theory of environmental complexity. *Academy of Management Annals*, *7*(1), 441–488. https://doi.org/10.1080/19416520.2013.781862

Wuthnow, R. (1998). *Loose connections: Joining together in America's fragmented communities*. Harvard University Press.

Young, D. (1980). *Entrepreneurship and the behavior of nonprofit organizations: Elements of a theory*. Institution for Social and Policy Studies, Yale University.

Young, D. (1983). *If not for profit, for what?* Lexington Books. https://scholarworks.gsu.edu/facbooks2013/1

Young, D. (1989a). Contract failure theory. In J. Shafriz (Ed.), *International encyclopedia of public policy and administration* (Vol. 3, pp. 230–234). Routledge. https://doi.org/10.4324/9780429045097

Young, D. (1989b). Government failure theory. In J. Shafriz (Ed.), *International encyclopedia of public policy and administration* (Vol. 1, pp. 235–237). Routledge. https://doi.org/10.4324/9780429045097

Young, D. (1989c). Third party government. In J. Shafriz (Ed.), *International encyclopedia of public policy and administration* (Vol. 4). Routledge. https://doi.org/10.4324/9780429045097

Young, D. (2000). Alternative models of government–nonprofit sector relations: Theoretical and international perspectives. *Nonprofit and Voluntary Sector Quarterly*, *29*(1), 149–172. https://doi.org/10.1177/0899764000291009

Young, D. (2006). Complementary, supplementary or adversarial? Nonprofit-Government Relations. In E. T. Boris & C.E. Steuerle (Eds.), *Nonprofit and government: Collaboration and conflict* (pp. 37–80). Urban Institute Press.

Young, D. (2016a). Contract failure theory. In J. S. Ott & L. A. Dicke (Eds.), *The nature of the nonprofit sector* (3rd ed.) (pp. 230–234). Routledge.

Young, D. (2016b). Government failure theory. In J. S. Ott & L. A. Dicke (Eds.), *The nature of the nonprofit sector* (3rd ed.) (pp. 126–128). Westview Press.

Young, D. (2016c). Third party government. In J. S. Ott & L. A. Dicke (Eds.), *The nature of the nonprofit sector* (3rd ed.) (pp. 323–326). Westview Press.

4 What Makes Good Nonprofit Sector Theory?

EVA WITESMAN*

4.1 The Need for Nonprofit Sector Theory

Many have described the need for nonprofit sector theory, at least in part because of the social significance of the nonprofit sector in public life (Sager, 2010). Theory can help us to understand how and why prosocial institutions exist, how to empower and expand them, and how, when, and why they might operate in ways that do or do not effectively serve the greater good.

In addition to describing what *is*, we need theory to help us to predict what *could* be, and to intentionally create what *should* be. This prescriptive orientation may run counter to how some scholars conceptualize theory, especially for those who prefer to develop theory through the creation of formal models or propositions. Compared with these more formalized approaches, prescriptive and evaluative theory may feel overly normative and expressive rather than "scientific." Reuter et al. (2104) described this issue specifically as it applies to civil society, which, they write, is "somehow infused with all kinds of normative meanings, while at the same time being altogether rejected as irrelevant by others who are put off by that very normativity" (p. 71). However, theorizing – and more specifically, theorizing about the nonprofit sector – is not merely a dispassionate scientific endeavor; rather, it is infused with all the hope embodied in the sector itself.

Our ability to understand and communicate about the theory of the nonprofit sector requires us to first describe both what we mean by *theory* and what we mean by the *nonprofit sector*. In doing so, it seems prudent to acknowledge that the definitions that follow may not seem particularly satisfying, especially because our very intentional approach is one of inclusion rather than exclusion. That is, our

* Thanks to Curtis Child for useful comments on various drafts of this chapter.

definition for what constitutes the "nonprofit sector" is inclusive of many approaches, viewpoints, and perspectives – and our approach to "theory" is as well. This discussion, therefore, may seem so inclusive as to draw few satisfactory boundaries. However, though our views of both the nonprofit sector and of theory are fluid and broad, the intersection of these – that is, the space that constitutes nonprofit sector theory – emerges as surprisingly specific. This is because there is only a small area of overlap between the vast scholarly ocean of theory and the curiously amorphous space called the "nonprofit sector." It is in this overlap that we seek to make a contribution.

4.2 What Is "Theory"?

Theorizing about theory is a favorite pastime of scholars in many fields. Each discipline (and arguably each subfield within each discipline) has its own definitions, orientations, and arguments about what does or does not constitute theory. Abend (2008), for example, provides seven useful alternative definitions of theory that he views as covering the forms of theory as they exist in the sociological sciences.[1] Each approach to theory has its defenders and detractors, and lively debates on the subject occur in the pages of academic journals. However, given that the purpose of these debates is generally to disqualify as theory whole methods of theorizing, to favor specific methods of theorizing, or to create a hierarchy of theorizing, very little of this discussion actually expands our ability to usefully describe the world we observe. If anything, limiting what can be considered "theory" creates unnecessary overspecification that prevents robust and intellectually diverse dialogue.

Our approach in this volume is decidedly inclusive of a broad set of definitions and approaches to theory, primarily for three reasons. First, the study of the nonprofit sector is interdisciplinary and must

[1] These are, in brief, (1) a proposition or set of propositions that establish a relationship between variables; (2) an explanation of a phenomenon; (3) questioning or studying the meaning of phenomena; (4) the study of, and creating derivative works from, luminaries in the field; (5) a *Weltanschauung*, perspective or viewpoint from which phenomena can be viewed and observed; (6) accounts of phenomena that have a fundamental normative component, expressing and promoting specific values; and (7) broad philosophies about, or abstractions of, social problems or phenomena (Abend, 2008).

therefore be prepared to accommodate the views of people from a wide range of scholarly orientations and training. These disciplinary differences are likely to result in variation in the language and methodologies of theory development. Embracing this interdisciplinarity means, by necessity, being flexible regarding the form and content of theory contributions and the processes used to produce them. Second, narrowing our scope to only a subset of theoretical orientations would run counter to our purpose, which is to broaden and challenge the existing cadre of theoretical touchpoints in the field of nonprofit studies. We cannot justifiably claim to be broadening the field nonprofit sector theory and then simultaneously narrow it to approaches that favor only certain perspectives or methodologies. Finally (and related to our second point), we normatively agree with recent criticism of the academy with respect to theory-building. These critiques suggest that traditional or highly defined approaches to theory often exclude valid processes and viewpoints while privileging others, gatekeeping the term "theory" to the point of altogether preventing some perspectives and approaches from even entering the discussion (e.g., Cunliffe, 2022; Gioia & Pitre, 1990).

In order to provide new ways of thinking about the nonprofit sector, it is necessary to broaden the range of approaches to theorizing. As Gioia and Pitre (1990) observe,

> Traditional approaches to theory building in organizational study have tended to produce valuable, but nonetheless incomplete, views of organizational knowledge, mainly because they have been predicated predominantly on the tenets of one major paradigm ... theory-building discussions seem to proceed as if the principles of theory building are somehow universal and transcendent across disparate paradigms of thought and research. They are not. (p. 584)

Our intention is to take an expansive and inclusive view of what theory is, since limiting our range of appropriate theoretical approaches would also reduce the aperture of our analytic lens in ways that may exclude important perspectives and experiences about the nonprofit world.

We do not intend to be so inclusive, however, as to render *any* scholarly endeavor as theory. Rather, as Cunliffe (2022) writes, "To clarify an important distinction, theory is the end product of theorizing" (p. 3). The process of theorizing can provide the academy – and the broader world – not only with scientific utility, but also with new perspectives in the form of optimistic imagination. Speaking of political theory, Faulks et al. (2003) write, by "tackling these issues in an abstract manner, scholars are free to concentrate on 'ideals' and 'utopias,' contrasting these with the 'real world.' This has led to useful, imaginative and even inspirational interpretations.... Theory can thus be defined as the largely abstract critical study of ... motivations, values, beliefs and principles" (p. 62). This is equally the case for nonprofit sector theory.

As Turner (2010) observes, theorizing can "create a distance towards those phenomena that others routinely treat as self-evident; and it is then to encourage us to see the world a little differently" (p. 1). This scholarly imagination in the form of theory development can be conceived of as the "elaboration of a small number of interrelated concepts which dispel confusions and/or raise interesting questions on a specific problem" (Mouzelis, 1993, p. 691). This type of incremental inquiry can add clarity to the current state of affairs, raise a voice of warning about problems that may be foreseen through theorizing, and inspire the creation of ever-stronger social institutions.

While we expect theory to result from the process of theorizing, we do not dictate a specific *methodology* for theorizing, nor for *representing* theory. In our view, formal modeling is not superior to qualitatively grounded theory development; causal logic does not outweigh normative speculation; and logical legal frameworks are not more valued than observations that emerge from the in-depth study of individual cases. In the process of generating theory, then, we are agnostic regarding the form of theory or the process of theorizing.

In summary, theory is the result of theorizing – a diverse endeavor with many forms – and results in a form of useful imagination about a phenomenon – in our case, the nonprofit sector. Theorizing answers specific questions (here, the *what* and *why* of the nonprofit sector) and must abstract from observed facts to some form of broader set of claims about how the world is or how the world ought to be. Theory in this volume is centered on the nature and rationale for the nonprofit sector. In order to engage in theorizing the nonprofit sector, we must have some definitional clarity about the phenomenon or set of phenomena at question. We turn to this question in the next section.

4.3 What Is the Nonprofit Sector?

As described above, the process of defining the nonprofit sector is itself an act of theorizing. We will provide a broad definition of the nonprofit sector here, but each theorist of the nonprofit sector should also, in the process of outlining their own theories of the sector, offer their own preferred definitions. Our intent in providing a set of definitional guidelines here is simply to provide an anchor as to what may – or may not – be considered as part of the nonprofit sector for the purposes of this volume. If nonprofit sector theory is at the intersection of a broad and contested set of phenomena that comprise the "nonprofit sector" and another broad and contested set of methodologies that comprise "theory," it is necessary to provide what clarity we can about the boundaries of that intersection.

We embrace as included within the "nonprofit sector" any associational phenomena that (1) involve some form of organizing (this does not presuppose organizations), (2) are intended to improve the social welfare (as opposed to the welfare of an individual or near kin), and (3) are voluntary in nature (they do not involve coercion in the process of organizing, i.e., are not governments – see Tilly 1992 – though they may *govern* and may involve *governance*). Beyond this set of gentle constraints, we leave it to individual theorists to define the sector in ways that are analytically useful.

Concepts related to the nonprofit sector – such as social movements, social organizing, and civil society – have developed alongside nonprofit sector studies, and may overlap with the nonprofit sector definition provided here. By opening the doors of nonprofit sector theory to these broader perspectives, and to the critiques that have emerged within the study of the nonprofit sector, we prepare the way not only for a more inclusive study of the nonprofit sector but a more robust study as well.

4.4 What Is Nonprofit Sector Theory?

Nonprofit sector theory exists at the intersection of theory (broadly defined) and the nonprofit sector (also broadly defined). Though the ambiguity and inclusiveness of our definitions of both nonprofit sector and theory would suggest difficulty in determining what is nonprofit sector theory and what is not, such is actually not the case. Not all theories are nonprofit *sector* theories, even if the theory generally might apply to the nonprofit sector. For a theory to be a nonprofit sector theory, it must not only be applicable to the nonprofit sector, but the nonprofit sector itself must be the central focus of the theory and the purpose of theorizing.

Within the field of nonprofit studies, there exist studies of the nonprofit sector. And within the world of theory, there are a subset of theories that are applicable to the nonprofit sector. It is at the confluence of these two research endeavors that nonprofit sector theory exists. Figure 4.1 presents a graphic illustration of this unique intersection of research interests.

For example, we might consider theories such as symbolic interactionism (sociology; e.g., Rock, 2016), agency theory (economics; Alchian & Demsetz, 1972), or public choice theory (political science; e.g., Arrow, 2012). Each of these is broadly recognized as theory by any measure, and certainly qualifies as theory under the definition provided earlier in this chapter. Each of these theories also has relevance for the nonprofit sector: symbolic interactionism suggests that people interact at least in part based on how they assign meaning in the world. This could apply to how people assign meanings to and within the nonprofit sector. Agency theory explains how and why people hire others ("agents") to do work in their behalf and what happens if the worker's incentives are not aligned with those of the principal. This could help explain phenomena in the nonprofit sector, such as volunteering. Public choice theory explains how market tools can solve problems usually faced by governments. This approach could be used to describe the role of nonprofits in mixed market settings. Yet while symbolic interactionism, agency theory, and public choice theory can (and do) *inform* sector theory, they are not *themselves* sector theories. The purpose of these theories was not to illuminate the nature and role of the nonprofit sector, but rather to theorize sociological, economic, and political phenomena more generally. To generate a nonprofit sector theory, a scholar hoping to use insights from one of these broader theories would need to specifically define, describe, explain, prescribe, predict, or evaluate the nonprofit sector using the broader theory as a tool for generating these insights.

Not all nonprofit studies are nonprofit *sector* studies. For example, in Lohmann's (2007) paper on big questions in nonprofit management, he includes questions about the business practice of nonprofits,

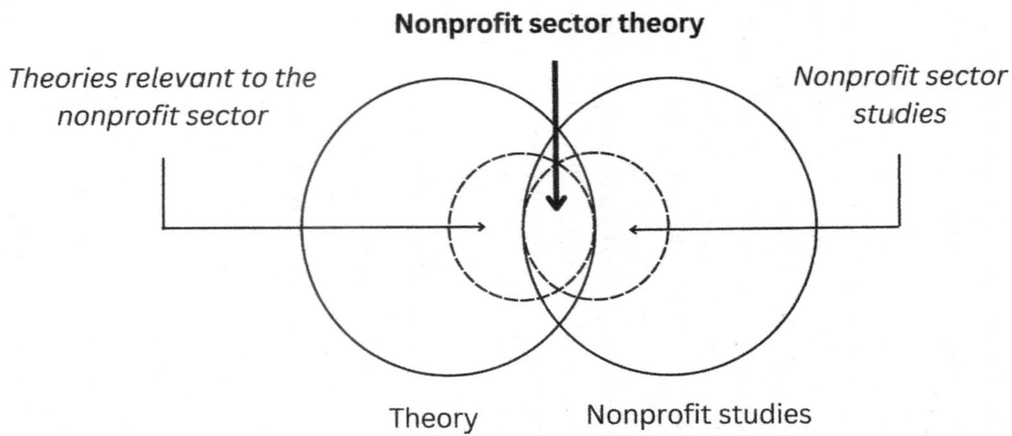

Figure 4.1 Nonprofit sector theory as an intersection of theory and nonprofit studies

accounting and accountability within nonprofit organizations, and the effectiveness of nonprofit boards. His questions invite scholars to develop theory about nonprofits, nonprofit practices, and nonprofit management – but these are not questions about the nonprofit *sector*. In contrast, Lohmann's inquiry about what the nonprofit sector *is* ("what exactly is the 'third sector' a sector of?" [p. 37]) would invite theorizing about the nonprofit sector specifically, and is the seed of nonprofit sector theory.

Not all nonprofit sector studies are nonprofit sector *theories*. Nonprofit sector studies such as those that describe the composition of the sector (e.g., Abramson, 2022), the economic impact of the sector (e.g., Flynn & Hodgkinson, 2001), or studies about how and why people opt to be employed within the sector (e.g., Mirvis & Hackett, 1983), are not *theories* about the nature and/or origin of the sector itself and would thus not qualify as nonprofit sector theory.

Though our approach is to be extremely inclusive about what qualifies as theory and what falls within our broad definitional guidelines that outline the nonprofit sector, the intersectional space of nonprofit sector theory is unique and specific.

4.5 The Role of Nonprofit Sector Theory

While we are not overly concerned about the process of generating theory or the form that theory may take, we *are* highly concerned with the function and role of nonprofit sector theory. What is the function of theory? As Lynham observes, theory serves to "describe and explain how things actually work and, in so doing, to help us improve our actions in this world" (Lynham, 2002, p. 221). Our core approach to inviting scholars to theorize the nonprofit sector in this volume has been to invite authors to consider *what* the nonprofit sector is and *why* it exists. In accordance with the work of O'Shaughnessy (1973), we expand this definition to encompass a set of specific analytic tasks, namely, definition, description, explanation, prescription, prediction, and evaluation.

A theory of the nonprofit sector could be one that examines *what* the nonprofit sector is by (a) defining the nonprofit sector or (b) describing the nonprofit sector. Nonprofit theory may also provide information about *why* the nonprofit sector exists by (c) explaining the origins of the phenomenon of the nonprofit sector or (d) providing normative prescriptions that justify its existence. The *what* and *why* of theory can be further enhanced by (e) predicting changes or evolution as yet unobserved in the nonprofit sector or (f) evaluating the nonprofit sector by examining its effect on individuals, groups, or society.

In defining, describing, explaining, prescribing, predicting, and evaluating the nonprofit sector, theory should go beyond merely observing phenomena or restating observed phenomena in a more abstract or formulaic manner. While observations (data) about the world are the core of any good theory, theory should also provide lessons and insights that push beyond what we might find in empirical research. Nonprofit sector theory simultaneously poses questions about the world and makes claims about the world. It connects observations with meaning and infuses correlations with insightful lessons about what and why the nonprofit sector exists. "The power of a theoretical explanation lies in the insight it provides in regard to how and why abstract constructs are related. Imagination disciplined by data leads to such insight but the explanation must go beyond the data and can never be fully represented in it" (Calder & Tybout, 2016, p. 119).

Nonprofit sector theory should thus seek to contribute to our understanding of the sector by engaging one or more of the following questions:

1. *What* is the nonprofit sector? (define)
2. *What* are the characteristics of the nonprofit sector? (describe)
3. *Why* does the nonprofit sector exist? (explain)
4. *Why* should the nonprofit sector exist? (prescribe)
5. *What* is the future of the nonprofit sector? (predict)
6. *What* is the value of the nonprofit sector? (evaluate)

4.5.1 The Definitional Role of Nonprofit Sector Theory

In some ways, revisiting the meaning of the term "nonprofit sector theory" feels like retreading ground we once thought solid – and finding it giving way beneath us as wade into the swamp of murkier definitions, dimmer lines, and increasing complexity. We must revisit and redefine terms we once thought common, like "nonprofit." However, "a serious impediment to better research has been a lack of clarity about the exact nature of the organisations being discussed under the non-profit banner," writes Considine (2003, p. 63), and Blakely (2002) observes, "ambiguity surrounding civil society arises not from definitional confusion, but from the conflicting norms within the concept itself" (p. 90). Thus, revisiting the boundaries for inclusion or exclusion from the nonprofit sector is itself part of the tradition of descriptive nonprofit sector theory.

4.5.2 The Descriptive Role of Nonprofit Sector Theory

A strong theory of the nonprofit sector would describe the role and operation of the sector across cultural contexts and at different points in history and identify its core relationship with the subsectors and substantive areas that are frequently served by nonprofits regardless of cultural context.

Because descriptive nonprofit sector theory has traditionally been preoccupied with distinguishing the nonprofit sector from other institutions, the sector is frequently described using theories that explain what the sector is *not*, particularly in contrast to both markets and government. Theory of the nonprofit sector is a newer area of theory and scholarship than either government or market theories (Langton, 1987), so it is reasonable and natural that the theory should use these prior theories as foils. However, we suggest that nonprofit sector theory should – even in the absence of markets and governments – effectively identify and describe characteristics unique to the nonprofit sector.

4.5.3 The Explanatory Role of Nonprofit Sector Theory

The origin story of the nonprofit sector is embedded in the explanatory role of nonprofit sector theory. Why does the nonprofit exist? How did it evolve? Why does it persist? What need does it fill? This challenging explanatory role may differ across time and across cultures and national contexts. Explanatory nonprofit sector theory is needed to understand what is happening in prosocial associational life and why it is happening – not only in the American nonprofit sector and in global nongovernmental organizations, but also in the civic, economic, and social spaces that exist throughout the world in the so-called *dark matter* of associational life (Smith, 1997). This includes the existence of organizations, institutions, and associations in autocratic regimes as well as in democratic ones, and in the unincorporated social movements of indigenous, minority, and state-oppressed peoples around the world.

While a grand explanatory theory of the nonprofit sector may prove illusive, we can expect localized theories of the sector to proliferate. The role of rich case analysis as a theorizing methodology can provide deep insight into the role and nature of the nonprofit sector where broader, more general, abstracted theories may fail to provide satisfactory answers. "[A]lthough sometimes seen as 'subjective,' well-done theory building from cases is surprisingly 'objective,' because its close adherence to the data keeps researchers 'honest.' The data provide the discipline that mathematics does in formal analytic modeling" (Eisenhardt & Graebner, 2007, p. 25). While we may be able to draw general themes across locally contextualized theories, it may be that the locally relevant theories are actually the more useful for evaluating, predicting, and prescribing the nonprofit sector within those specific contexts as well as more generally.

4.5.4 The Prescriptive Role of Nonprofit Sector Theory

Prescriptive nonprofit sector theory suggests a normative element that indicates not only the historical rationale for nonprofit institutions but also a prospective rationale. Calder and Tybout (2016) suggest that the key to making theory relevant to practice is through the application of practical imagination:

> good theories, though imagined, should to be viewed as real in that they offer a valuable viewpoint for solving practical problems. They expand the real world of the practitioner.... A different sort of imagination, however, is required to move from an abstract theory to an intervention that can be implemented in the real world. Good theory can be highly practical but it requires separating research designed to build and test theory from research designed to evaluate the efficacy of theory-inspired interventions to real world problems. (Calder & Tybout, 2016, p. 116)

4.5.5 The Evaluative Role of Nonprofit Sector Theory

Evaluative nonprofit sector theory examines whether the sector is successful in achieving the aims for which it was created. There may be a contrast in the evaluative nonprofit theory literature between cross-context views of the nonprofit sector as a global socio-institutional phenomenon and localized roles of the nonprofit sector in specific regimes and contexts. Thus evaluative nonprofit sector theory may seek to determine both (1) whether the role of the nonprofit sector in a given context is valuable to society and (2) whether the nonprofit sector is contributing value as expected. In regime settings where the nonprofit sector is used primarily to undermine social organizing and democratic voice, the institution might be viewed as questionable in its contribution to broad social aims. On the other hand, in contexts where nonprofit organizations contribute to the social welfare through meaningful creation and distribution of value, they might be evaluated according to their potential for social welfare maximization. An important role for nonprofit sector theory, therefore, is both to question the value of the nonprofit sector and to question whether that value is being maximized.

4.5.6 *The Predictive Role of Nonprofit Sector Theory*

Predictive nonprofit sector theory seeks to identify likely possible futures based on the trajectory of nonprofit sector function. These futures may include the future of the nonprofit sector itself, but more interestingly, may predict the future of human society based on the function of the nonprofit sector.

Corley and Gioia (2011) point out that the predictive role of enhances its applicability to practice: "Incorporating a future orientation can help keep our theories not only vibrant but also relevant in a constantly changing landscape of organizational realities. Additionally, we believe that over time, as prescience becomes more prominent in our theoretical formulations, the distinctions between scientifically useful and practically useful will begin to blur" (pp. 24–25).

As the world continues to rapidly evolve, the predictive role of nonprofit sector theory becomes ever-more important for identifying what the probable future states of our global society may be.

4.6 What Makes Good Nonprofit Sector Theory

Good theories of the nonprofit sector should help us to define the nonprofit sector more usefully, describe it more accurately, explain it more satisfactorily than other plausible explanations, or prescribe better practices for the sector than presently exist. Langton (1987) also suggests several criteria for its theoretical usefulness, including an analysis of the breadth, depth, and relevance of nonprofit sector theory. We further developed his work to identify specific questions that nonprofit sector theory should seek to answer (see Table 4.1). Together with the roles for nonprofit sector theory, these evaluative criteria suggest several questions that can push nonprofit sector theory in new and useful directions that will enhance our understanding of the sector in a global and historical context, as well as making theory more applicable by focusing on its prescriptive value (Calder & Tybout, 2016; Corley & Gioia, 2011).

We interpret "breadth" of theory to mean that nonprofit sector theory should effectively focus on the nonprofit sector as a major institution in society, functioning parallel to – and in concert with – markets and governments in the distribution of goods, services, and other valued assets. We interpret "depth" of theory, described by Langton (1987) as "sufficiently detailed in its level of explanation" (p. 140), as the applicability of broad nonprofit sector theory to the individual actors and organizations that comprise the sector. In other words, nonprofit sector theory should have implications at both the macro- and micro- levels. Finally, we interpret the "relevance" of nonprofit sector theory in terms of its ability to effectively contribute answers to the key questions identified above. Specifically, the theories should describe, predict, explain, prescribe, and evaluate the nonprofit sector and its actors relative to important social outcomes in the substantive areas served by nonprofits.

Table 4.1 summarizes one possible approach to evaluating the quality of sector theory. The purposes of nonprofit sector theory are identified along the horizontal axis at the top of the table, and the vertical axis identifies the substantive criteria on which the theories are to be evaluated. By combining the roles of nonprofit sector theory and the criteria for effective theory, we have identified 18 key questions on which theories of the nonprofit sector may be assessed (see Table 4.1).

The questions about breadth of theory examine the extent to which the theory is sufficiently general in scope, and include the following:

- Does it clearly define the nonprofit sector and either distinguish it from related phenomena or justify their inclusion?
- Does it describe all known nonprofit and voluntary sector activity, including activity in various cultural and temporal contexts?

Table 4.1 *The nonprofit sector theory evaluation matrix*

		Definition	Description	Explanation	Prescription	Evaluation	Prediction
		What is the nonprofit sector?	*What are the characteristics of the nonprofit sector?*	*Why does the nonprofit sector exist?*	*Why should the nonprofit sector exist?*	*What is the value of the nonprofit sector?*	*What is the future of the nonprofit sector?*
Quality of Theory Criteria	**Breadth** *Sufficiently general in scope*	Does it clearly define the nonprofit sector and either distinguish it from related phenomena or justify their inclusion?	Does it describe all known nonprofit and voluntary sector activity, including activity in various cultural and temporal contexts?	Does it explain macro-institutional structures and why they interact in specific ways?	Does it provide useful prescriptions for the role of the nonprofit sector in society?	Does it apply useful criteria when examining the success or failure of the sector as a whole in fulfilling its role in society?	Does it generate accurate predictions about the future evolution of the nonprofit sector?
	Depth *Sufficiently detailed in its level of examination*	Does it provide a definition that is relevant in describing the sector as well as the actors within it?	Does it describe the actions and decisions of individual actors in addition to broad macro-institutional phenomena?	Does it explain why individual actors in the nonprofit sector behave in specific ways?	Does it provide useful prescriptions for policymakers, individual nonprofit actors, and organizations?	Does it generate useful criteria for examining the success or failure of individual nonprofits, nonprofit actors, or nonprofit policies?	Does it make useful predictions about the actions of individual nonprofit actors?
	Relevance *Germane to recognizable need*	Is the definition applicable across cultural and national contexts, as well as the various types of actors and organizations intended for inclusion?	Does it distinguish the nonprofit sector from markets and from government?	Does it explain sector choice for individuals, organizations, and goods produced?	Do the normative prescriptions based on this theory result in substantially improved social outcomes?	Are the evaluative criteria suggested by the theory relevant to key outcomes in the substantive areas served by nonprofits?	Does it make accurate predictions about nonprofit actors and the sector in general?

Note: Criteria adapted from Langton 1987.

- Does it explain macro-institutional structures and why they interact in specific ways? Does it provide useful prescriptions for the role of the nonprofit sector in society?
- Does it apply useful criteria when examining the success or failure of the sector as a whole in fulfilling its role in society?
- Does it generate accurate predictions about the future evolution of the nonprofit sector?

The questions for assessing the depth of theory examine whether the theory includes sufficient detail, and include the following:

- Does it provide a definition that is relevant in describing the sector as well as the actors within it?
- Does it describe the actions and decisions of individual actors in addition to broad macro-institutional phenomena?
- Does it explain why individual actors in the nonprofit sector behave in specific ways?
- Does it provide useful prescriptions for policymakers, individual nonprofit actors, and organizations?
- Does it generate useful criteria for examining the success or failure of individual nonprofits, nonprofit actors, or nonprofit policies?
- Does it make useful predictions about the actions of individual nonprofit actors?

The questions that assess the relevance of nonprofit sector theory explore whether the theory meets the needs of nonprofit sector theorizing, and include the following:

- Is the definition applicable across cultural and national contexts, as well as the various types of actors and organizations intended for inclusion?
- Does it distinguish the nonprofit sector from markets and from government?
- Does it explain sector choice for individuals, organizations, and goods produced?
- Do the normative prescriptions based on this theory result in substantially improved social outcomes?
- Are the evaluative criteria suggested by the theory relevant to key outcomes in the substantive areas served by nonprofits?
- Does it make accurate predictions about nonprofit actors and the sector in general?

By considering the function of nonprofit sector theory and how we might evaluate the quality of a theory in terms of its depth, breadth, and relevance, we can examine the value, quality, and utility of a nonprofit sector theory. While these tools for evaluating nonprofit sector theory do not constitute the only possible approach, they do provide a perspective on how to evaluate nonprofit sector theory, especially in light of the breadth and ambiguity in our approach to both "theory" and the "nonprofit sector."

4.7 Conclusion

The goal of this book is to bring new and diverse perspectives to the ways we conceive of the nonprofit sector. To truly achieve the goal of moving in new directions, we must be willing to question the basic premises on which our current body of knowledge lies. We agree with Cunliffe, who writes, "There are other forms of knowing and theorizing that if accepted would mean that organization and management theory would become more pluralistic, imaginative and generative. These are forms of theorizing that embrace our humanness, are situated within experience, engaged, about living relationships with others, speculative, sensitive to people who are different to ourselves, and sensual, responsive, reflexive and impactful" (p. 12).

We have established ultimately a very inclusive definition of nonprofit sector theory. Our central intention is to open new lines of thinking and inquiry, new insights, and hopefully new perspectives that can help us to better understand the institutional, organizational, and socioeconomic landscape in which we function in our global society. Building on the world of others, we have suggested an approach for evaluating the quality of the nonprofit sector theory presented in this volume and beyond. We invite you, the reader, to apply these criteria and identify where nonprofit sector theory is strong, and where it is left wanting. From there, we hope for new ideas and theory that can move this endeavor ever forward.

References

Abend, G. (2008). The meaning of "theory." *Sociological Theory*, *26*(2), 173–199.

Abramson, A. J. (2022). Assessing the state of the US nonprofit sector: What indicators should we use? *Nonprofit and Voluntary Sector Quarterly*, 08997640221091534.

Alchian, A. A., & Demsetz, H. (1972). Production, information costs, and economic organization. *The American Economic Review*, *62*(5), 777–795.

Arrow, K. J. (2012). *Social choice and individual values* (Vol. 12). Yale University Press.

Blakeley, G. (2002). Civil society. In G. Blakeley & V. Bryson (Eds.), *Contemporary political concepts: A critical introduction* (pp. 90–107). London; Sterling, Virginia: Pluto Press. doi:10.2307/j.ctt18fs3n8.9

Calder, B. J., & Tybout, A. M. (2016). What makes a good theory practical? *AMS Review*, 6, 116–124.

Considine, M. (2003). Governance and competition: The role of nonprofit organisations in the delivery of public services. *Australian Journal of Political Science*, *38*(1), 63. https://doi-org.erl.lib.byu.edu/10.1080/1036114032000056251

Corley, K. G., & Gioia, D. A. (2011). Building theory about theory building: What constitutes a theoretical contribution? *Academy of Management Review*, *36*(1), 12–32.

Cunliffe, A. L. (2022). Must I grow a pair of balls to theorize about theory in organization and management studies? *Organization Theory*, *3*(3), 26317877221109277.

Eisenhardt, K. M., & Graebner, M. E. (2007). Theory building from cases: Opportunities and challenges. *Academy of Management Journal*, *50*(1), 25–32.

Faulks, K., Phillips, K., & Thomson, A. (2003). Political theory. In Keith Faulks, Ken Phillips, & Alex Thomson (Eds.), *Get set for politics* (pp. 61–80). Edinburgh University Press. doi:10.3366/j.ctvxcrd7k.7

Flynn, P., & Hodgkinson, V. A. (Eds.). (2001). *Measuring the impact of the nonprofit sector*. Springer Science & Business Media.

Gioia, D. A., & Pitre, E. (1990). Multiparadigm perspectives on theory building. *Academy of Management Review*, *15*(4), 584–602.

Langton, S. (1987). Envoi: Developing nonprofit sector theory. *Nonprofit and Voluntary Sector Quarterly*, *16*(1–2), 134–148.

Lohmann, R. A. (2007). Charity, philanthropy, public service, or enterprise: What are the big questions of nonprofit management today? *Public Administration Review*, 67(3), 437–444.

Lynham, S. A. (2002). The general method of theory-building research in applied disciplines. *Advances in Developing Human Resources*, *4*(3), 221–241.

Mirvis, P. H., & Hackett, E. J. (1983). Work and work force characteristics in the nonprofit sector. *Monthly Labor Review*, *106*(4), 3–12.

Mouzelis, N. (1993). The poverty of sociological theory. *Sociology*, 27(4), 675–695. Retrieved June 6, 2020, from www.jstor.org/stable/42855272

O'Shaughnessy, J. (1973). *Inquiry and decision: A methodology for management and the social sciences*. Harper and Row.

Reuter, M., Wijkström, F., & Meyer, M. (2014). Who calls the shots? The real normative power of civil society. In M. Freise & T. Hallmann (Eds.), *Modernizing democracy* (pp. 71–82). Springer, New York.

Rock, P. (2016). *Making of symbolic interactionism*. Springer.

Sager, R. (2010) Theories of nonprofit sector, sociological. In H. K. Anheier & S. Toepler (Eds.), *International encyclopedia of civil society*. Springer, New York.

Smith, D. H. (1997). The rest of the nonprofit sector: Grassroots associations as the dark matter ignored in prevailing "flat earth" maps of the sector. *Nonprofit and Voluntary Sector Quarterly*, 26(2), 114–131.

Tilly, C. (1992). *Coercion, capital, and European states, AD 990–1992*. Blackwell.

Turner, C. (2010). *Investigating sociological theory*. Sage Publications.

PART II

Reflections and Refinements

5 *Sector Theorists Should Consider How Social Values Determine Unmet Needs*

RUTH K. HANSEN AND GREGORY R. WITKOWSKI

Sociopolitical power manifests itself through for-profit, nonprofit, and public sector practices and policies. While there are differences between the sectors, socially constructed preferences and sociopolitical power supersede these differences, foregrounding the needs of people with economic, political, and social power and repeatedly leaving others' needs unmet. We argue that the dominant explanatory framework for the interaction of the market, government, and nonprofit sectors – Three Failures Theory – works only for those needs that society recognizes as important. The theory illustrates how only certain needs are met while claiming to explain provision of goods across society. In this way, it unconsciously reflects and reinforces the social constructions that deem the demands of some people as important and of others as irrelevant (e.g., Schneider & Ingram, 1990, 1993). We take special issue with the notion of "needs" that are taken for granted in Three Failures Theory. All needs are not the same, and some needs are recognized while others remain hidden. Gaps in provision are neither evenly spread nor random, but correlate with societal values. In essence, groups who are "on the margins" of society are often ignored or exploited because of culturally ascribed characteristics. For the nonprofit sector, these groups represent a challenge and opportunity to show societal leadership and to engage with these needs.

In this chapter, we draw on both critical theory and social science to propose an explanatory framework to understand which needs are likely to be met and which are likely to be excluded. We call this framework Cross-Sectoral Bias Theory, which provides one way to understand how needs are prioritized across sectors and how socially constructed biases affect which needs are met. Our theory draws on postcolonial and postmodern theory to illustrate the need for a more inclusive model that identifies populations underserved by the three sectors. We assess some of the factors that lead to the invisibility of certain populations, relying especially on warmth, competence, and behavior intentions as described in the Behaviors from Intergroup Affect & Stereotypes (BIAS) framework (Cuddy et al., 2007). We adapt this model to a societal level and apply it to understanding how the three sectors often work in concert as much as they fill gaps in service provision based on the goods delivered. We introduce this theory as a means to better understand the interaction of the three sectors after critically analyzing Three Failures Theory. While our work draws upon examples from the United States, we argue that Cross-Sectoral Bias Theory can be applied to other national contexts.

5.1 A Critique of Three Failures Theory as Sector Theory

At the heart of the discussion around Three Failures Theory is a classical liberal view that the three sectors function to meet social needs. This perspective assumes that the functions of these sectors are designed to address needs equally and to optimize social provision based on the efficiencies of different sectors. However, postmodern and postcolonial scholars challenge that view and instead argue that social institutions are a means of maintaining power and inequality more than of redressing inequality or meeting all societal needs. We first review Three Failures Theory before turning to postcolonial and postmodern criticisms of this approach.

5.1.1 A Review of Three Failures Theory

The animating notion of Three Failures Theory is that each of the three sectors, for-profit (market), government (public), and nonprofit (voluntary), is efficient at producing certain goods or meeting certain societal needs. The theory describes the nonprofit sector as meeting the diverse needs of individuals that are not met by for-profits (market failures) or public institutions (government failures) (Hansmann, 1987; Salamon, 1987; Weisbrod, 1977). Nonprofits step in to provide collective goods when the market and the government only partially meet the demands of society, particularly in the case of groups whose demands are either higher in quantity than average or more specialized (Steinberg, 2006; Weisbrod, 1977). Nonprofits are also considered more trustworthy in cases of information asymmetry, often referred to as contract failure. Because the nonprofit form does not allow for private owners who might enrich themselves by cutting quality, there is less temptation to skimp when quality cannot be directly observed (Hansmann, 1987). As such, the nonprofit sector may be viewed as functionally addressing the failures of the market and the state. Taken together, then, the three sectors are positioned as a balanced response to the gaps that would exist without the other metaphorical legs of the stool (Ghatak, 2020).

Among the criticisms of Three Failures Theory is that it focuses on demand, lacking a supply focus (Frumkin, 2002; Steinberg, 2006); however, we argue that a major weakness is that it does not adequately address the full demands of society but instead focuses on people whose needs *are* substantially met through a combination of the sectors. In so doing, we enter the discussion by highlighting the needs of people rather than focusing on the goods available. A goods-based focus admits allocative inefficiency – that is, balancing the benefits to consumers against the relative costs of production – and seeks to find Pareto efficiencies, in which people judge themselves to be happiest given the possible mix of goods. Yet in practice, critically evaluating social benefits depends on identifying which demands and preferences matter. It follows that, although perhaps unnoticed, the presence of sociopolitical power and preferences is highly relevant in determining preferred social objectives (Schneider & Ingram, 1990, 1993). And when social objectives are contested, some causes are more popular and more easily funded than others (Witesman & Heiss, 2017); yet this heterogeneity of demands is precisely the field within which the nonprofit or voluntary sector is theorized to offer the greatest strength (e.g., Lu, 2017; Weisbrod, 1989).

5.1.2 Bringing Postmodern and Postcolonial Insights to Service Provision

Postmodern theory indicates that many seemingly unrelated institutions work to advance a mainstream understanding of power and norms that can ultimately become oppressive. For instance, Foucault (1977) argued that prisons are not a means to protect society but rather maintain and enforce societal norms. In this light, institutions are neither impersonal nor benign to all but reinforce the good of some at the expense of others. Historians have often interpreted charity in a similar fashion, arguing that it serves a policing function (Andrew, 1989). For example, historically, poor houses and prisons were sometimes overseen by the same department or agency (Witkowski,

2022). Charity was also intertwined with a moral superiority based on religion, the Social Gospel, and Social Darwinism. The definitions of deserving and undeserving poor – who should be supported and who should not – related alleviating need to a moral understanding of action and belief. Charities and nonprofit institutions therefore confirmed societal expectations of how to act, focusing on the moral failings of individuals who were undeserving while ignoring more systemic problems. In blaming the people in need, charitable institutions have historically justified the system that created those needs.

Postcolonialism places these systemic failings in the context of a lopsided power dynamic. It recognizes that pervasive societal narratives reflect those of a dominant class and inherently contain judgments that diminish the contributions and personhood of people outside the dominant class. Often used to explain pervasive racial, ethnic, and nationalist discrepancies, postcolonialism addresses the legitimization of continued repression and dependency of people characterized as "Other" (Spivak, 1988).

These power dynamics are most apparent in colonial relationships, in which the colonial power (the metropole) does not view the people in the colonies (the periphery) as equals. This judgment was often justified by referencing a moral or biological difference, but, regardless, there was a split between the superior and the inferior. The notion of the "the colonized" has since expanded beyond the divide between colonies and colonized "to include women, subjugated and oppressed classes, national minorities" (Said, 1989, p. 207), and more, every group that was not valued equally, such as domestic workers in nineteenth-century England (McClintock, 1995).

We embrace the postcolonial understanding of the power dynamics embedded within society. We argue that the three sectors all represent the interests of the dominant classes more fully than the interests of those who have been marginalized. While we understand that the interests benefitted are not exclusively those of the dominant classes, we see that those mainstream interests are most often met, while others with less power are more likely to have needs that are unmet by any of the sectors.

5.1.3 Adding Insights from Social Theory

We follow Go (2016) in recognizing a connection between postcolonial theory and aspects of social theory concerned with "the other."

Empirically, we know that persistent disparities of service exist, whether in the market, the state, or the nonprofit sector (e.g., AbouAssi et al., 2019; Glied & Frank, 2009; Mosley, 2012; Rocha, 2006; Wu, 2021). These disparities are not evenly distributed; instead, those whose needs remain unmet are often members of groups that are also systematically excluded from society. Society values their demands less than those of more powerful groups. In terms of social theory, we attribute the functional mechanisms of this exclusion to persistent stereotypes and compounding inequalities that render their needs invisible, or judged as less worthy, even when the intentions of the perceivers are not malicious (West, 1993). In essence, as society weighs the many demands, the claims of these groups are repeatedly deemed less important. Our learned expectations and perceptions of what is normal, right, and fair mean that over time, just as interest compounds, so does lack of interest.

The microsociological work of Erving Goffman (1961) supports many of the insights of the humanistic postcolonial school. His observations about total institutions, such as prisons and mental hospitals, are similar to Foucault's arguments about prisons. They highlight societal norms and at the same time reify those norms by defining what is acceptable and what is punishable. Total institutions function as "the forcing houses for changing persons" (Goffman, 1961, p. 12; see also Foucault, 1977). Goffman's work addresses the theme of reducing the social status of a person – "from a whole and usual person to a tainted, discounted one" (Goffman, 1986, p. 3), to one who is "less than" others – and observes the processes that pave the way to social justification for labeling, negative stereotypes, and prejudice (Goffman, 1986). In the postcolonial view, these are the colonized, the subaltern, those whose value is diminished (Said, 1989; Spivek, 1988).

Two of the markers of a stigmatized or "other" status are the perceived possibility of threat to "normal" individuals, and lowered expectations for the life possibilities of an individual so categorized. Both lower expectations and possible threat are themes woven into narratives that correspond with and justify "othering" behaviors. Scholarly work on dehumanization has similar ideas, finding two main types: a mechanistic dehumanization that denies that others share our common human nature, and an animalistic dehumanization that denies others the presence of uniquely human attributes (Haslam, 2006).

5.1.4 Stereotypes and Behavior

Alongside these theoretical intuitions, a rich empirical scholarship helps account for which groups are more or less likely to have their needs met. Stereotypes, attributions, and in-group versus out-group status all act as heuristics that affect perceptions and, therefore, the decisions made about helping others. This dynamic is particularly important in understanding the extent of aid available through the nonprofit sector, with its reliance on voluntary action. When people perceive a shared in-group identity with others, they are more likely to help them (e.g., Ben-Ner et al., 2009; Duclos & Barasch, 2014; Turner et al., 1979). If people perceive the reason a person needs help is externally caused and beyond their control, they are more likely to help than if responsibility for the need is attributed to the recipient (Zagefka et al., 2011). Negative stereotypes can lead to impressions of unreliability, irresponsibility, and lack of credibility on the part of group members (Holstein, 1993), and describing beneficiaries in terms that activate negative stereotypes may depress giving (Hansen, 2020). Conversely, donors often choose to support groups with warm, positive stereotypes (Chapman et al., 2020).

Different stereotypes have different combinations of relative perceived warmth and competence, predicting whom we pity, admire, envy, and condemn, as well as the correlated emotional responses and behaviors (Cuddy et al., 2008). In the Behaviors from Intergroup Affect & Stereotypes (BIAS) framework, "warmth" describes groups who are perceived as friendly, honest, sincere, and kind. Groups that lack warmth are perceived as competitive or harmful. "Competence" describes groups that are considered capable and intelligent (Cuddy et al., 2007). Figure 5.1 illustrates the dimensions of warmth and competence and the emotional responses and behavioral tendencies expected for each combination.

Note that the dimension of warmth is tied to active behaviors, such as active facilitation (i.e., helping) if warmth is high or active harm (i.e., harassing) if warmth is low. The dimension of competence is tied to passive behaviors, such as associating with the target (if high) or neglecting them (if low) (Cuddy et al., 2007). It is also important to note that this map of perceptions and their attendant behavioral intentions are relative to one another, and there is no fixed map. The group identity of the perceiver and the stereotypes the perceiver holds of

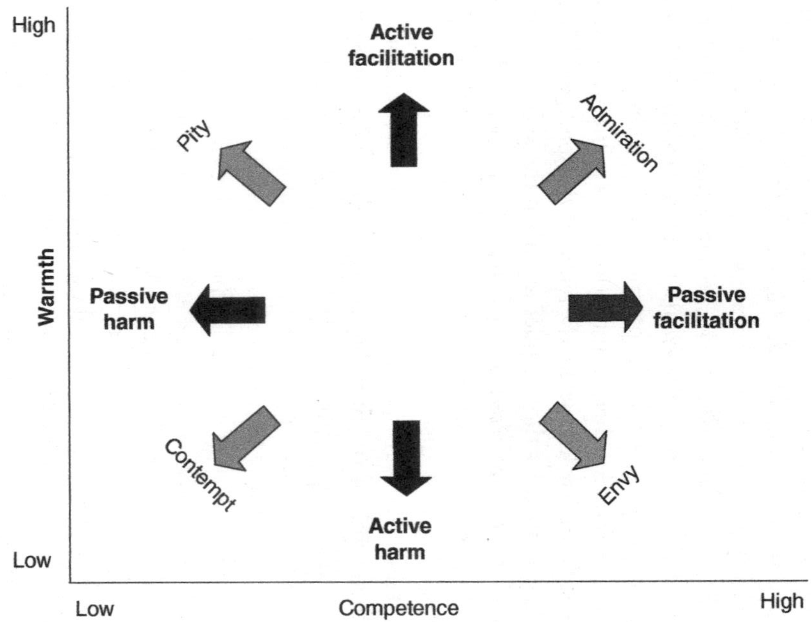

Figure 5.1 Representation of dimensions of warmth and competence
Note: Copyright © 2007 by American Psychological Association. Reproduced with permission, Cuddy et al. (2007).

the group being evaluated will affect a group's placement within this scheme. Larger societal culture will also have some influence. Thus, the positioning of the decision maker is important here. If one group has disproportionate amounts of power – whether financial or political – then the resources at their disposal will follow from that point of view, not only for themselves but for much of society through the institutions affiliated with enforcing that power.

The benefits and burdens of policy are not evenly spread but vary according to the positive or negative social constructions of different groups within society (Schneider & Ingram, 1993). The needs of those perceived positively and with power are seen as important social issues (Schneider & Ingram, 1990, 1993). People within this preferred category think of themselves as "normal" and perceive those outside this category as "other." For example, people who are white see themselves simply as people and see others as minorities (Dyer, 2005). Additionally, men's athletic teams are known by the name of the sport, while women's teams are first named by their gender and then the sport (de Beauvoir, 1953). Members of preferred groups may experience enhanced self-esteem by comparing themselves to others who are "less than" (Dovidio et al., 2000). They may also experience increased cooperation, mutual aid, commonality of interest, and social cohesion as a result of the intergroup conflict, while also diminishing competition for resources such as good jobs or other opportunities (Parker & Aggleton, 2003; Simmel, 1964). Even people in less preferred groups may agree with this social construction, since the assumption is part of the accepted societal view (Goffman, 1986). Or they may resist the characterization, insisting on their own narratives and competence and deny the moral dominance of a group whose power to shape society has increased over generations due to constant tending at the expense of others (Go, 2016). This is the very tension described in postcolonial thought.

Where the market serves those with money, and the government is theorized to reflect the interests of the median voter, Three Failures Theory views the voluntary, nonprofit sector as a stabilizing social force. Yet its very voluntariness may be, at best, insufficient to overcome these compounding inequalities; and at worst, it may compound them further. We tend to support others whom we perceive as being like us – suggesting the direction in which voluntary support is most likely to flow (Chadborn & Reysen, 2018). We tend to fear others who seem unlike us (Hatemi et al., 2013); at an extreme, we may even prefer harm to others whom we perceive as possible threats (Cikara et al., 2014). For example, after the 9/11 terrorist attacks, the United States federal government took a series of harsh actions targeted at Muslim-serving charities in what has been characterized as a "sledgehammer" approach (Chong, 2020; Sidel, 2010). Examples include closing charities and freezing assets without due process, and characterizing respected Muslim charities as terrorist groups despite lack of evidence within other governmental documents (Sidel, 2010). In this example, the rationale of keeping people safe from the threat of terrorists was used to justify actions whether or not they were effective or consistent with procedural justice.

The concerns of groups that are viewed less favorably are less likely to be considered a public responsibility. Members of these groups are more likely to be blamed for their situation, and any resources made available to them are more likely to require effort – and sometimes significant behavioral change – in exchange for the benefit. The behavior of members of these groups is more likely to be questioned, and to be treated punitively, than is the behavior of members of the dominant, more positively viewed groups (Dorfman, 2016; Schneider & Ingram, 1990, 1993).

5.2 How Cross-Sectoral Bias Theory Adjusts the Focus

In this section, we apply the BIAS framework (Cuddy et al., 2007, 2008; Fiske, 2018; Harris & Fiske, 2006) to analyze how societies meet the needs of different groups across the three sectors. Although Three Failures Theory would indicate that each sector uses a different approach, we argue that the social and political capital of those in power defines how the different groups' needs are met by all three sectors. We have named our contribution Cross-Sectoral Bias Theory because we see the same dynamics at play across all three sectors, as we explain in the following sections.

If we know who holds the reins of power in society, whether financial, political, or social, and if we know how these powerful groups perceive other groups in terms of warmth and competence, we can make some predictions about which groups' needs will likely be met and which will not. Our cross-sectoral theory thus refines our understanding of the demand side of sectoral relationships by seeking the common source of cultural power that manifests across all three sectors. In this section, we translate the implications of the BIAS framework to help us understand how decision makers in the institutions in each sector will affect that sector's likelihood of addressing the needs of different groups. We recognize that individuals have multiple identities defined by physical characteristics and environmental conditions that lead to a complicated individual identity. For many, these characteristics and identities can be reinforcing – thus the concept of intersectionality. In addition, identities may be closely tied to the frame within which one seeks help (e.g., addiction, childcare, stable housing). Our theory focuses on the positionality of different groups from the basis of those in power in a society. It is not static and can change based on who holds power and how different groups are viewed.

5.2.1 Groups High in Warmth and Competence

We argue that Three Failures Theory aptly explains the experiences of groups that are viewed as high in both warmth and competence. The general emotional reaction to these groups is admiration. From a social behavioral standpoint, we can expect others to actively want to help members of these groups, as well as to passively facilitate their best interests. Many Americans view Christians and members of the middle class as both warm and competent (Cuddy et al., 2007). Groups like these will be pursued by politicians for their votes and by companies for their consumption, and nonprofits will both seek their support and address their interests.

Since the market excels at providing private, excludable goods and services in exchange for fees, we would expect to see major companies market to and develop products for these groups. The government's focus on providing public goods to the median voter suggests that the interests of these groups will be recognized as important public issues, and their needs will generally be perceived as being those of society at large. If more money must be allocated to meet these groups' needs, then resources will likely be taken from groups whose issues are considered less aligned with society at large, potentially lessening support for other groups.

People in these groups are likely to set up private, nonprofit alternatives to public services to meet specialized demands, such as organizations to support their children's schools or organizations centered around recreational or professional interests, and it will be fairly easy to mobilize support for them. People in these groups find that citizen mobilization tends to address their needs.

5.2.2 Groups High in Warmth and Low in Competence

Three Failures Theory partly describes the experiences of groups that are perceived as high in warmth and low in competence, as there is willingness to help them, but its limits are reached sooner. From a social behavioral standpoint, we can expect others to actively want to help people who are members of these groups. Passively, people will tend to avoid spending too much time with them, and their interests are likely to be neglected (Cuddy et al., 2007). For these groups, the general emotional reaction is pity.

Many Americans view older adults as warm but lacking competence, as they do people with developmental disabilities. People with other disabilities also fall into this category but are often viewed less warmly, which likely results in more of their needs remaining unmet (Cuddy et al., 2007).

We would expect that fewer companies would market to and develop products and services for these groups. Therefore, there are likely to be fewer but more expensive choices, with less quality assurance and availability. The demands of these groups are likely to exceed the provision of government services. Although their needs will be recognized as public issues, they will be addressed at an insufficient level, with resources prioritized for those considered to reflect society at large (i.e., those perceived as warm and competent).

People in these groups are likely to seek private, nonprofit alternatives to public services for help in meeting their specialized demands, and while others will contribute to these organizations, the needs of these groups will be considered essentially a private responsibility and less important than those of others in society at large. People in these groups will also generally be perceived as unable to solve their own problems. While they may be viewed as worthy recipients of help, they will likely be required to admit that they are in a dependent role in order to have their needs met at a level and time determined by those with greater resources, assumed competence, and power (Schneider & Ingram, 1990, 1993).

We argue that people in these groups are less likely to advocate for their own needs, although others may advocate on their behalf. The market failures of overexclusion and contract failure are likely to be key factors here. Combined with the government failures of high demanders and unobservables, the voluntary sector is a presumptive source of goods and services. Within the nonprofit sector, the voluntary failures of insufficiency and paternalism are likely to be key factors for organizations serving these groups, meaning that these groups are unlikely to have their needs met satisfactorily, particularly because others with greater social and financial power will define their needs, rather than they.

5.2.3 Groups Low in Warmth and High in Competence

Three Failures Theory partially explains the experiences of groups that are viewed as low in warmth and high in competence, as willingness to help is lower for these groups. For these groups, the general emotional reaction is envy. From a social behavioral standpoint, we can expect others to be willing to harass people who are members of these groups, but passively, people will be willing to associate and cooperate with them when it is convenient or mutually advantageous (Cuddy et al., 2007). For instance, people may regularly make derogatory comments about members of these groups while still working with them in formal settings. People who are wealthy are seen as both competent and lacking warmth by many Americans. Some ethnic stereotypes also fall into this category (Cuddy et al., 2007).

Since the market excels at providing private, excludable goods and services in exchange for fees, we would expect companies to market to and develop products for these groups. However, these products are likely to be more expensive, without corresponding increases in quality. To the extent that these groups' interests differ from those recognized as belonging to society at large (i.e., those high in warmth and competence), they are unlikely to be recognized as public issues and may actually be perceived as conflicting with those of society at large. The government may want to be seen as penalizing these groups publicly, or at least as not giving them "special treatment," although these groups may have enough resources, competence, and power to push policies that actually minimize burdens.

These groups are likely to use private, nonprofit alternatives as well as informal means, such as private influence. Their needs will be considered a private responsibility and less important than those of society at large (Schneider & Ingram, 1990, 1993). Additionally, since these groups likely have the resources to address their needs, others may consider them to have an unfair advantage. The natural way for people in these groups to engage with the nonprofit sector from a demand viewpoint is through member-serving organizations, such as those centered around recreational or professional interests. The voluntary failures of free-riders and particularism are likely to be in play, as self-interest will be a key motive for engagement. From a supply standpoint, people within these groups will be sought as supporters for charitable endeavors. In addition to intrinsic interest, they may exhibit "conspicuous generosity" to burnish their own reputations (Bekkers & Wiepking, 2011; Bhati & Hansen, 2020), perhaps preferring charities that benefit warmly perceived groups in order to enhance their own reputation for warmth (Fehrler & Przepiorka, 2013).

People in these groups are likely to advocate for their own needs, whether through engaging politically, setting up their own associations, or mobilizing protests. They may engage others who are perceived more warmly to be the face of these efforts. Although the government will likely characterize these groups as "high demanders" to justify the lack of resources used to finance this groups' demands (Schneider & Ingram, 1990, 1993), the lack of warmth is a defining feature. Others are simply not inclined to help groups within this category unless it is convenient, or there is some opportunity for personal gain. More than other groups, conflict is a regular feature of how low-warmth, high-competence groups interact with society and with organizations within the three sectors. Understanding this further refines our ideas of how the sectoral dynamics interact with this subset of the population.

5.2.4 Groups Low in Warmth and Competence

We argue that Three Failures Theory is most limited in its explanation of sectoral responses to groups that are viewed as low in both warmth and competence, as they are neither liked nor respected. The general emotional reaction to these groups is contempt. From a social behavioral standpoint, we can expect others to be willing to actively harass members of these groups, as well as passively neglect their needs (Cuddy et al., 2007). Americans often consider the stereotypical "poor" to be among the better-liked groups in this category, although people on welfare are liked much less, and "the homeless" score extremely low on both competence and warmth with the general American public.

People in these groups are generally viewed as unable to solve their own problems and largely to blame for their problems, and their needs will be met at a level and time determined by others with greater resources, assumed competence, and power. People in these groups are unlikely to advocate for their own needs though conventional political engagement, although they may set up their own associations or mobilize protests. The socially perceived lack of warmth is a defining feature of these groups, meaning that others are simply not inclined to help them unless it is convenient or there is some opportunity for personal gain. Because these groups are seen as lacking competence, people may feel free to openly dismiss their needs.

We would expect to see companies largely ignore groups in this category. There is likely to be less choice in terms of products and services and less assurance of quality. The government is likely to largely dismiss issues of concern to these groups, considering their needs to be personal responsibilities and/or personal failings rather than proper public issues. The government may also deter people in these groups from seeking redress unless they change their behavior, or avoid contact with other members of the general public.

People in this category may seek help from private, nonprofit alternatives to public services for help in meeting their specialized demands, and while some nonprofits will support them, there will be insufficient resources to meet their needs. Some needs may be ignored entirely and considered a private responsibility. Organizations serving these groups may face many conflicting priorities for resources, dampening the level of advocacy for systemic change (e.g., Jones & Deitrick, 2020; Mosley, 2012). The voluntary failures of insufficiency and paternalism are likely to be heightened factors for organizations serving these groups.

5.2.5 Cross-Sectoral Bias Theory Summary

Identifying the features associated with each category is an important start, as it indicates the ways in which societal values determine whether different groups' needs are met or unmet. While Three Failures Theory describes the relationships among the three sectors, these sectors are located within broader social dynamics that affect how groups are perceived and people's willingness to help them. We recognize that different sectors have distinct priorities and tools, as stated by Three Failures Theory, but Cross-Sectoral Bias Theory indicates that groups are treated based on how society views them as well as which sector is engaging with them. While we have followed Cuddy et al. (2007, 2008) in focusing on the United States in our examples, Cross-Sectoral Bias Theory can be adapted to other cultural contexts as long as they are not homogenous. See Figure 5.2 for a summary of the analysis within this section.

High Warmth – Active Facilitation

Low Competence – Passive Harm

Emotional Reaction: Pity
Popular Opinion: Viewed as worthy recipients, but dependent
Three Failures: Partly describes
Business: Fewer choices, more expensive, lower quality
Government: Needs are recognized, insufficiently served
Nonprofits: Supports high demands, public serving organizations

Emotional Reaction: Contempt
Popular Opinion: Avoid association, likely to neglect
Three Failures: Does not describe well
Business: Largely ignore, fewer choices, lower quality
Government: Needs inadequately recognized, insufficiently served
Nonprofits: Help with basic needs, under resourced, paternalism

High Competence – Passive Facilitation

Emotional Reaction: Admiration
Popular Opinion: Easy to mobilize support, seen as important public priorities
Three Failures: Describes well
Business: Markets to, develops products for
Government: Needs are recognized, interests are prioritized
Nonprofits: Meets specialized demands, member serving organizations

Emotional Reaction: Envy
Popular Opinion: Lack of trust, self-interest needed to mobilize support
Three Failures: Partly describes
Business: Markets to, develops products for, more expensive
Government: Publicly scorns, quietly serves interests
Nonprofits: Meet specialized demands, member serving organizations

Low Warmth – Active Harm

Figure 5.2 Warmth and competency predictions

5.3 Conclusions

Cross-Sectoral Bias Theory emerged from a combination of humanistic and social science approaches that critically reevaluate the interplay of the three sectors. Drawing on postcolonial and postmodern theory, we indicate that those whose demands are undervalued are often systematically excluded from society, due to normative identities. We recognize that intersectionality points to multiple identities at play that may compound the difficulties in successfully having one's needs met. In proposing Cross-Sectoral Bias Theory, we argue that (a) not all needs are being met in society, (b) the consequential distribution of unmet needs is neither random nor benign but reflects existing social structures and assumptions, and (c) the nonprofit sector can amplify marginalized voices by being more inclusive, diverse, and representative. Our Cross-Sectoral Bias Theory follows Cuddy et al. (2007, 2008) in arguing that both warmth and competence play a role in how social groups, market forces, government, and voluntary action interact with stereotypes. We suggest three main avenues for future consideration.

The first consideration is whether movement from a less advantageous position (i.e., one low in warmth and competence) to a better position is possible. At first glance, the evolution of our social treatment of people with HIV suggests that this is possible: initial neglect (at best) and active opposition to medical responses has changed significantly over a period of decades, which has been attributed at least in part to successful social mobilization that resulted in changes in service provision in the market, government, and voluntary sectors (e.g., Gostin, 2015; Jenkins, 2006; Strub, 2014). Other identities may be more challenging. For instance, Katz (2013) has argued that we continue to view poverty as a moral failing; and Gostin (2015) noted that mental illness has been present for centuries, but as a cause, has not managed to successfully muster the will of market, state, or nonprofits to meaningfully recognize the causes or provide treatments (see also Klein, 2016).

A second consideration is what factors facilitate or hinder the development of warmth or competence. Although social movements, such as the Civil Rights Movement and the labor movement, produced important gains, it has been suggested that access to greater resources in some dimensions (such as housing, education, or financial capital) has been offset by persistent structures that retain power for a smaller, exclusive group with privilege (e.g., Dunning, 2022; Kohl-Arenas, 2015; Silver, 2005). What are the implications for a group that succeeds in improving its perceived competence at the expense of warmth? Can societal will to assist and will to harass stall progress somewhere at the center of the Cross-Sectoral Bias framework?

A third consideration is what policy and funding implications exist for a more equitable society, given the possibility of movement for some groups and the reality that other groups appear to have remained in the same social position for centuries. Can one sector lead the others, or must all work together? What dynamics exist, and how might they be navigated? As Coule et al. (2022) have observed, critical approaches to studying the nonprofit sector are not inherently negative. Instead, they assume that continuation of "divisive and destructive structures, processes, and practices is neither natural, unavoidable, nor eternal" (p. 490). Intentional change, however, relies on understanding problems and systems in order to adapt constructively. Recognizing the limitations of Three Failures Theory to explain service provision across all groups is perhaps the first step to consciously breaking down the power structures that determine whose needs are met. As the sector best able to fulfill needs for groups that are particular enough that public policy and market forces will not provide the necessary goods, nonprofit leaders have an obligation to find innovative methods to engage these groups. At a minimum, understanding how best to work within existing structures can lead to more effective service for those whose needs are often unmet. Then perhaps leaders will be able to strategically chart a course of advocacy that defies apparent constraints and moves groups sharply into the warmth and competence arena.

We present Cross-Sectoral Bias Theory as one way for scholars and practitioners to understand the interaction of the three sectors that recognizes that all three sectors fail to deliver for populations on the margins of society. While Three Failures Theory is about the relative efficiency of service provision across the three sectors, our theory focuses on why different sectors respond similarly regarding whose needs are recognized and met and whose are not. We argue that Three Failures Theory, long accepted in nonprofit studies, does not adequately reflect the full demands of society because it focuses on those whose needs are substantially met through a combination of the sectors. In doing so, it replicates embedded societal structures, foregrounding groups with economic, political, and social power without critically reflecting on social constructions that consider some demands important and others irrelevant (Schneider & Ingram, 1993). We see Cross-Sectoral Bias Theory as an important supplement to the Three Failures Theory of sectoral efficiencies by explaining why some societal needs remain unmet. Social systems and perceptions, defined by those with power, affect the behavior of decision makers in all sectors, resulting in differing access to goods and services. By bringing critical theory into dialogue with the BIAS framework and Three Failures Theory, our interdisciplinary Cross-Sectoral Bias Theory offers a refined understanding of how the three sectors define whose needs are met and how.

References

AbouAssi, K., Faulk, L., Tran, L., Shaffer, L., & Kim, M. (2019). Use and perceptions of the availability of local government and nonprofit services in diverse urban settings. *Nonprofit and Voluntary Sector Quarterly*, *48*(5), 975–997.

Andrew, D. (1989). *Philanthropy and police: London charity in the eighteenth century*. Princeton University Press.

Bekkers, R., & Wiepking, P. (2011). A literature review of empirical studies of philanthropy: Eight mechanisms that drive charitable giving. *Nonprofit and Voluntary Sector Quarterly*, *40*(5), 924–973.

Ben-Ner, A., McCall, B. P., Stephane, M., & Wang, H. (2009). Identity and in-group/out-group differentiation in work and giving behaviors: Experimental evidence. *Journal of Economic Behavior & Organization*, *72*(1), 153–170.

Bhati, A., & Hansen, R. (2020). A literature review of experimental studies in fundraising. *Journal of Behavioral Public Administration*, *3*(1), 1–19.

Chadborn, D., & Reysen, S. (2018). Moved by the masses: A social identity perspective on inspiration. *Current Psychology*, *37*(3), 625–631.

Chapman, C. M., Masser, B. M., & Louis, W. R. (2020). Identity motives in charitable giving: Explanations for charity preferences from a global donor survey. *Psychology & Marketing*, *37*(9), 1277–1291.

Chong, A. (2020). (Self-)Regulation of Muslim Charitable Sectors in the US and the UK in the Post-9/11 Era. *Journal of Muslim Philanthropy & Civil Society*, *4*(2), 180–205.

Cikara, M., Bruneau, E., Bavel, J. V., & Saxe, R. (2014). Their pain gives us pleasure: How intergroup dynamics shape empathic failures and counter-empathic responses. *Journal of Experimental Social Psychology, 55*(Nov 1), 110–125.

Coule, T. M., Dodge, J., & Eikenberry, A. M. (2022). Toward a typology of critical nonprofit studies: A literature review. *Nonprofit and Voluntary Sector Quarterly, 51*(3), 478–506.

Cuddy, A. J. C., Fiske, S. T., & Glick, P. (2007). The BIAS Map: Behaviors from intergroup affect and stereotypes. *Journal of Personality and Social Psychology, 92*(4), 631–648.

Cuddy, A. J. C., Fiske, S., & Glick, P. (2008). Warmth and competence as universal dimensions of social perception: The stereotype content model and the BIAS Map. *Advances in Experimental Social Psychology, 40*(2008), 61–149.

De Beauvoir, S. (1953). *The second sex* (H. M. Parshley, Trans.). Knopf.

Dorfman, D. (2016). Re-claiming disability: Identity, procedural justice, and the disability determination process. *Law & Social Inquiry, 42*(1), 195–231.

Dovidio, J. F., Major, B., & Crocker, J. (2000). Stigma: Introduction and overview. In T. F. Heatherton, R. E. Kleck, M. R. Hebl, & J. G. Hull (Eds.), *The social psychology of stigma* (pp. 1–28). Guilford Press.

Duclos, R., & Barasch, A. (2014). Prosocial behavior in intergroup relations: How donor self-construal and recipient group-membership shape generosity. *Journal of Consumer Research, 41*(1), 93–108.

Dunning, C. (2022). *Nonprofit neighborhoods: An urban history of inequality and the American state*. University of Chicago Press.

Dyer, R. (2005). The matter of whiteness. In P. S. Rothenberg (Ed.), *White privilege: Essential readings on the other side of racism* (2nd ed.) (pp. 9–14). Worth.

Fehrler, S., & Przepiorka, W. (2013). Charitable giving as a signal of trustworthiness: Disentangling the signaling benefits of altruistic acts. *Evolution and Human Behavior, 34*(2), 139–145.

Fiske, S. (2018). Stereotype content: Warmth and content endure. *Association for Psychological Science, 27*(2), 67–73.

Foucault, M. (1977). *Discipline and punish*. Vintage Books.

Frumkin, P. (2002). *On being nonprofit: A conceptual and policy primer*. Harvard University Press.

Ghatak, M. (2020). Economic theories of the social sector: From nonprofits to social enterprise. In W. W. Powell & P. Bromley (Eds.), *The nonprofit sector: A research handbook* (3rd ed.) (pp. 319–332). Stanford University Press.

Glied, S. A., & Frank, R. G. (2009). Better but not best: Recent trends in the well-being of the mentally ill. *Health Affairs, 28*(3), 637–648.

Go, J. (2016). *Postcolonial thought and social theory*. Oxford University Press.

Goffman, E. (1961). *Asylums: Essays on the social situation of mental patients and other inmates*. Anchor Books.

Goffman, E. (1986). *Stigma: Notes on the management of spoiled identity*. Touchstone. (Original work published 1963.)

Gostin, L. O. (2015). A tale of two diseases: Mental health and HIV/AIDS. *The Milbank Quarterly*, *93*(4), 687–690.

Hansen, R. K. (2020). Stories of strangers: Writing donor acquisition letters in the human services. *Nonprofit Management and Leadership*, *31*(1), 153–173.

Hansmann, H. (1987). Economic theories of nonprofit organizations. In W. W. Powell (Ed.), *The nonprofit handbook* (pp. 27–42). Yale University Press.

Harris, L. T., & Fiske, S. T. (2006). Dehumanizing the lowest of the low: Neuroimaging responses to extreme out-groups. *Psychological Science*, *17*(10), 847–853.

Haslam, N. (2006). Dehumanization: An integrative review. *Personality and Social Psychology Review*, *10*(3), 252–264.

Hatemi, P. K., McDermott, R., Eaves, L. J, Kendler, K. S., & Neale, M. C. (2013). Fear as a disposition and an emotional state: A genetic and environmental approach to out-group political preferences. *American Journal of Political Science*, *57*(2), 279–293.

Holstein, J. A. (1993). *Court-ordered insanity: Interpretive practice and involuntary commitment*. Aldine De Gruyter.

Jenkins, J. C. (2006). Nonprofit organizations and political advocacy. In W. W. Powell & R. Steinberg (Eds.), *The nonprofit sector: A research handbook* (2nd ed.) (pp. 307–331). Yale University Press.

Jones, J. A., & Deitrick, L. (2020). Does the theory of voluntary sector failure provide insight into food pantries? A case study of a network of food pantries in San Diego, CA. *Voluntas: International Journal of Voluntary and Nonprofit Organizations*, *31*(5), 870–880.

Katz, M. B. (2013). *The undeserving poor: America's enduring confrontation with poverty*. Oxford University Press.

Klein, J. (2016, May 4). Long ignored in global development, mental illness is declared a top priority. Voices. *Open Society Foundations*. www.opensocietyfoundations.org/voices/long-ignored-global-development-mental-illness-declared-top-priority?utm_source=news&utm_medium=email&utm_content=xrKbOkO7mGJLl7yITLBk4qmfIC8k27TmIGCDMOu2vu8&utm_campaign=news_051416

Kohl-Arenas, E. (2015). *The self-help myth: How philanthropy fails to alleviate poverty*. University of California Press.

Lu, J. (2017). Does population heterogeneity really matter to nonprofit sector size? Revisiting Weisbrod's demand heterogeneity hypothesis.

Voluntas: International Journal of Voluntary and Nonprofit Organizations, *31*(3), 1077–1092.
McClintock, A. (1995). *Imperial leather: Race, gender, and sexuality in the colonial contest.* Routledge.
Mosley, J. E. (2012). Keeping the lights on: How government funding concerns drive the advocacy agendas of nonprofit homeless service providers. *Journal of Public Administration Research and Theory*, *22*(4), 841–866.
Parker, R., & Aggleton, P. (2003). HIV and AIDS-related stigma and discrimination: A conceptual framework and implications for action. *Social Science & Medicine*, *57*, 13–24.
Rocha, M. G. D. L. (2006). Vanishing assets: Cumulative disadvantage among the urban poor. *The Annals of the American Academy of Political and Social Science*, *606*(1), 68–94.
Said, E. W. (1989). Representing the colonized: Anthropology's interlocutors. *Critical Inquiry*, *15*(2), 205–225.
Salamon, L. M. (1987). Of market failure, voluntary failure, and third-party government: Toward a theory of government-nonprofit relations in the modern welfare state. *Journal of Voluntary Action Research*, *16*(1–2), 29–49.
Schneider, A., & Ingram, H. (1990). The behavioral assumptions of policy tools. *Journal of Politics*, *52*(2), 510–529.
Schneider, A., & Ingram, H. (1993). Social construction of target populations: Implications for politics and policy. *American Political Science Review*, *87*(02), 334–347.
Sidel, M. (2010). Counter-terrorism and the Regulation of Civil Society in the USA. *Development and Change*, *41*(2), 293–312.
Silver, I. (2005). *Unequal partnerships: Beyond the rhetoric of philanthropic collaboration.* Routledge.
Simmel, G. (1964). *Conflict & the web of group affiliations* (K. H. Wolff & R. Bendix, Trans.). The Free Press.
Spivak, G. C. (1988). *In other worlds: Essays in cultural politics.* Routledge.
Steinberg, R. (2006). Economic theories of nonprofit organizations. In W. W. Powell & R. Steinberg (Eds.), *The nonprofit sector: A research handbook* (2nd ed.) (pp. 117–139). Yale University Press.
Strub, S. (2014). *Body counts: A memoir of politics, sex, AIDS, and survival.* Scribner.
Turner, J. C., Brown, R. J., & Tajfel, H. (1979). Social comparison and group interest in ingroup favouritism. *European Journal of Social Psychology*, *9*(2), 187–204.
Weisbrod, B. A. (1977). Toward a theory of the voluntary nonprofit sector in a three sector economy. In B. A. Weisbrod (Ed.), *The voluntary nonprofit sector* (pp. 51–76). Lexington Books.

Weisbrod, B. A. (1989). Rewarding performance that is hard to measure: The private nonprofit sector. *Science*, *244*(4904), 541–546.

West, C. (1993). *Race matters*. Beacon Press.

Witesman, E., & Heiss, A. (2017). Nonprofit collaboration and the resurrection of market failure: How a resource-sharing environment can suppress social objectives. *Voluntas: International Journal of Voluntary and Nonprofit Organizations*, *28*(4), 1500–1528.

Witkowski, G. R. (2022). *Hoosier philanthropy: A state history of giving*. Indiana University Press.

Wu, V. C. S. (2021). The geography and disparities of community philanthropy: A community assessment model of needs, resources, and ecological environment. *Voluntas: International Journal of Voluntary and Nonprofit Organizations*, *32*(1), 351–371.

Zagefka, H., Noor, M., Brown, R., de Moura, R., & Hopthrow, T. (2011). Donating to disaster victims: Responses to natural and humanly caused events. *European Journal of Social Psychology*, *41*, 353–363.

6 *Sector Theorists Should Embrace a Social Economy Perspective*

LAURIE MOOK AND JOHN R. WHITMAN*

Nonprofit organizations – a peculiar form of enterprise without investors or owners – are players in the capitalist economy. But how should we locate them among other types of organizations? In this chapter we examine two models[1] that classify nonprofit organizations: first, according to their *legal status*, including ownership rights, and second, according to their *purpose and function* – why and how they operate.

The first model we discuss is the three-sector model, which places organizations[2] into distinct public, private, and social sectors[3] reflecting their legal status. The public sector refers to government organizations, the private sector to private business organizations, and the social sector to organizations that serve society but are neither public nor private. The social sector has been called various terms, including the third sector, the nonprofit sector, the civic sector, the voluntary sector, and the independent sector.

The static, three-sector model of the economy provides the starting point for the emergence of the second model we discuss, the *social economy model*. As described in *Understanding the social economy of the United States*,

* We are grateful to Curtis Child, Jonathan Levy, Roger Lohmann, and Eva Witesman for their illuminating comments on this chapter.

[1] A model is a conceptual representation of reality (even though it cannot perfectly represent reality) that serves as an epistemological tool especially vital to making sense of complexity. The following definition of a model serves our purpose in this chapter: "A model is a simplified picture of a part of the real world. It has some of the characteristics of the real world, but not all of them. It is a set of interrelated guesses about the world. Like all pictures, a model is simpler than the phenomena it is supposed to represent or explain" (Lave & March, 1993, p. 3).

[2] We define organizations as "groups of individuals bound by some common purpose to achieve objectives" (North, 1990/2005, p. 5).

[3] This is not to be confused with the three-sector model of the economy – primary, secondary, and tertiary – that denotes the productive primacy, respectively, of raw materials, manufacturing, and the service industry.

the conventional sectors – private, public, and third – are useful in attempting to classify and differentiate organizations on a mutually exclusive basis. However, presenting such sectors as distinct spheres does little to convey the reality that many such organizations actually contain blended sectoral elements, and that this blending phenomenon appears to be increasing, further obscuring the clarity once presented by distinctly separate spheres. (Mook et al., 2015, p. 3)

How we transition from the three-sector model to the more dynamic social economy model is explained by examining the emergence of different types of organizations and how they evolved in the political economy.[4] In recounting this history, we begin with the origins of modern capitalism and the emergence of the three sectors in the United States and then summarize in broad terms the contest between government and business for control of the national economy.

Following the historical critique, we examine what the three-sector model gets wrong. We then envision the plausibility of shifting from a political economy that prioritizes market solutions to one that reasserts the primacy of social ends to justify economic means. Historical levels of inequality only a few generations old warn of the consequences of our currently unjust and instrumentally transactional economy. And we must draw from scientific studies of climate conditions hundreds of thousands of years prior to our civilization to anticipate the natural environmental consequences of our exploitative economy. In closing, we summon a movement to remedy the political economy balance in favor of humanity and the world.

6.1 A Critique of the Three-Sector Paradigm

The three-sector model was not designed by the hand of any architect of political economy. The sectors emerged organically through the intertwined evolution of political, legislative, and business institutions. In

[4] A final note on models: Models, sometimes referred to as conceptual frameworks, paradigms, taxonomies, and maps, can be misused, like any tool. Models have raised concerns among some scholars who take the critical view that mapping the nonprofit and voluntary sector can lead to cynical state control (Nickel & Eikenberry, 2016). Our aim is simply to increase understanding by proffering the social economy model as more accurate and testable to represent the dynamic configuration of organizations in the economy. Moreover, the organic, open-systems nature of the social economy model allows us to envision how society can move toward a more socially attuned order of organizations that reflects the social values of a liberal democracy (Hammond, 2003, pp. 103–141).

Weberian terms, the three sectors can be seen as pure, or ideal, types in the sense that they are subjectively theoretical but not necessarily objectively and empirically true (Weber, 1947, pp. 89–90). To understand the emergence of the three-sector model, we examine the divergence of for-profit and nonprofit forms of corporation since the founding of the country, the battle for control of the market, the triumph of neoliberalism, and the consequences of neoliberalism's excessive reign of control.

6.1.1 *The Early Success of Laissez-Faire and the Birth of Nonprofits*

Adam Smith is credited with formulating the modern doctrine of capitalism in *The wealth of nations* (Smith, 1776, 2003). Smith's business principles were demonstrated in the explosion of innovation and productivity in the Industrial Revolution, principally in England and then the United States. The unprecedented success and wealth associated with this new capitalism rendered an economic role for the government pointless, save for mercantilism. Laissez-faire was the default and de facto governing policy.

An interesting circumstance arose after the American Revolution. As a consequence of expelling English rule, the new nation in effect had no laws of its own. This dynamic affected commerce in that some statutory form of business organization was required to conduct legitimate private trade. Drawing on the precedent of English law, the government instituted the first corporate form in the United States, the "private corporate aggregate," which, by the law of that time, had to demonstrate a "public purpose" to be granted a charter by the legislature and was thus of a mixed "public/private character" (Levy, 2016, p. 23). According to Eric Hilt (2017), "Whether or not [this form] served the public interest was a vigorously contested issue at the time" (p. 40). Society in the post-Revolutionary era enjoyed new corporate formations, establishing a distinction between purely public-sector entities and the new, blended public/private-sector entities consisting of private corporate aggregates. Eventually, state by state, legislators began to drop the requirement for a public purpose to incorporate, requiring only that the corporation pursue a "lawful purpose" (Levy, 2016, p. 31).

The late nineteenth century was the era of the robber baron, in which some of the leading industrialists chose to allocate some of their private wealth to public purposes, in effect shifting their intent from the passive benevolence of charity to a more proactive form of social-minded engineering. During a tour of America, English biologist and polymath Herbert Spencer stated that such benevolent motivation was a form of altruism (Levy, 2016), and Andrew Carnegie (1889) codified this novel concept of altruism in a manual he wrote for his wealthy peers, encouraging them to spend their riches for social good before their death.

The courts, now facing the divergent distinction between corporations for profit and corporations for altruism, created a new corporate form predicated on its purpose to benefit society: the nonprofit corporation. The number of nonprofits, however, did not increase notably until the 16th Amendment to the Constitution was passed in 1909, establishing the first federal income tax. This development provided a fiscal as well as statutory foundation for distinguishing nonprofit organizations. The tripartite division of public, private, and nonprofit organizations formed what Jonathan Levy called "the fiscal triangle" (Levy, 2016, 2017).

Nonprofits further grew in number following the Second World War, when, among other factors, large amounts of government funds were channeled through nonprofits to provide social services as a result of the social contract embodied in the New Deal. With an appreciable number of nonprofit organizations contributing to the economy, the nonprofit sector, while nowhere near the size of the public or private sectors, nonetheless came into its own, and thus the three-sector model took shape, each sector defined by the legal status of the organizations located therein.

6.1.2 *The Contest for Market Control*

The success of the private sector at the end of the nineteenth century continued into the twentieth century but was eventually upended by the Great Depression. In 1933, unemployment reached almost 25% among the civilian labor force, and virtually all banks were closed (Collins, 1981, p. 4). Frustrated with business-friendly administrations, the country elected Franklin D. Roosevelt (FDR) as president. Addressing the distress of the nation, FDR, in his first inaugural address, stated,

> the rulers of the exchange of mankind's goods have failed, through their own stubbornness and their own incompetence, have admitted the failure,

> and abdicated .... The money changers have fled from their high seats in the temple of our civilization. We may now restore that temple to the ancient truths. The measure of the restoration lies in the extent to which we apply social values more noble than mere monetary profit. (Roosevelt, 1933, p. 1)

Having promised the electorate a "New Deal," FDR and his advisors enacted sweeping government regulations and economic control over matters formerly left to the market and undertook a significant redistribution of income through graduated income taxes with high marginal rates for the wealthy and corporations. The Second World War only deepened and extended the involvement of government in economic matters, particularly related to coordinating war production.

This gate-crashing of the market by the government, heretofore presumed to be the prerogative of business, alarmed many in the business community (Collins, 1981; Phillips-Fein, 2009). But the activist role of the government had the support of a new economic theory formulated by the British economist John Maynard Keynes. His novel theory fundamentally questioned the postulates of classical economics and advocated direct government intervention in markets to revive employment (Keynes, 1936). Skeptical of Keynes, FDR nonetheless adopted his advice. Friedrich von Hayek, an Austrian economist, espoused a wholly contrarian argument against government intervention in markets, which, as he warned in the title of his book *The road to serfdom* (1944/1994), would inevitably lead to the totalitarianism he had just fled in Europe. Hayek, himself uneasy about the denouement of laissez-faire in economic depression and world war, formulated a new conception of economic liberalism free of laissez-faire but that would nonetheless give preference to free markets (Burgin, 2012). The same year that Hayek published his warning against government intervention in markets, Austrian economist Karl Polanyi published an account of his dire prediction that unregulated markets would inevitably lead to human and natural disaster (Polanyi, 1944, 2001).

6.1.3 *The Triumph of Neoliberalism*

Milton Friedman (1962/2002), Hayek's eager disciple at the University of Chicago, perhaps best achieved Hayek's aim by shifting the policymaker's gaze away from laissez-faire per se to focus on the primacy of free markets, on which, Friedman said, freedom is predicated. The aim of business, Friedman (1970) argued, was to generate profits, and such profits should not be impeded by government regulations or by corporate social responsibility. This new economics became known as *neoliberalism*. In our view, these sources of economic authority were precisely what conservative business leaders and politicians needed to advance their ideological objective to remove the role of government in markets and the economy.

The social values of neoliberalism – free markets, individual liberty, and limited government – resonate well with the foundational values of the nation embodied in the Declaration of Independence. The triumph of neoliberalism was secured in the Reagan years (as in the United Kingdom during the Thatcher era). Declaring that "government [was] the problem," Reagan (1981, p. 1) heralded a fundamental societal shift away from the dignity of public service, exhorted by Kennedy (1961, p. 2), and toward the pursuit of what is good for the individual and private enterprise. This shift from a collectivist to an individual-centered ethos stimulated growing interest in business education and respect for business acumen. Consequently, one of the unforeseen outcomes of the resulting boom in popularity of the MBA degree was to instill a market-oriented mindset into nonprofit leaders and their boards, seen by some as a risk to civil society (Eikenberry & Kluver, 2004).

Over time, growing market power and the role of government lobbyists serving private interests would dismantle the social programs of the New Deal and shift greater wealth to the rich. Ironically, corporations, freed from government regulatory control, would lose the salutary benefit of competition and accountability and begin to fall behind in quality and performance compared to their counterparts in other countries (Philippon, 2019).

Overall, the neoliberal project has produced vast inequality and environmental fragility. The bookkeeping chart of accounts employed by private-sector corporations conveniently neglects categories for human well-being and the environment so that costs affecting these domains simply do not show up in the corporate accounting system. This practice of deliberately excluding social and environmental costs from an accounting system is called "externalizing" and has given rise to an academic cottage industry of social accounting, which critiques existing financial models and attempts to construct more encompassing frameworks to include social and environmental benefits and costs, including for nonprofit organizations (Mook, 2014).

But externalizing has also resulted in some for-profit firms utilizing their social and environmental responsibility and accountability as a way to differentiate themselves from their competition. This practice has led, for example, to a movement in which companies become certified as B Corporations or incorporate as benefit corporations expressly to use their social and environmental concerns to competitive advantage (Alexander, 2018; Marquis, 2020).

In this age of neoliberalism, then, we can see how nonprofit organizations, starved of public funding from governmental sources, have resorted to practices once unique to for-profit firms for the sake of raising needed funds from the market. Additionally, some for-profit companies once presumed to privilege their shareholders are beginning to forego profit maximization to respond to other stakeholders, including the environment. Public-private partnerships are forging operating alliances between the public, private, and social sectors. Altogether, once-established sectoral boundaries are blurring as a result of new, functional, and purposeful organizational practices.

While the three-sector model emerged organically, the quite distinct hand of neoliberalism purposely created conditions of smaller government and preferences for market solutions. These conditions led to smaller budgets for social programs and favored the adoption of business-like practices by organizations once encapsulated in separate sectors. This change upended the distinction of such spheres, which were replaced by the dynamic and overlapping sectors that are highlighted in the social economy model.

Put another way, the structural characteristics of organizations established respectively as government entities, private entities, or nonprofit entities gave rise to three sectors in the form of the three-sector model.[5] At this point, democracy held sway in the political economy, initially through government-endowed charters to enterprises, through an era of laissez-faire that in turn resulted in a more assertive role for the government to compensate for market failure. Capitalism as an economic ideology was ascending, and its proponents eventually founded

[5] Peter Dobkin Hall (2006) also made the point: "The terms *nonprofit sector* and *nonprofit organization* are neologisms. Coined by economists, lawyers, and policy scientists in the decades following World War II as part of an effort to describe and classify the organizational domain for tax, policy, and regulatory purposes, the meaning varies depending on the identity and intentions of the user" (p. 32).

an academically rigorous and persuasive neoliberal doctrine that succeeded laissez-faire but reasserted the social values of free markets, individual liberty, and limited government over collective welfare, or at least to limit the "general welfare" promoted in the Constitution. The growing signs of inequality, disparities, environmental impact, and other costs externalized by the private sector gave rise to social entrepreneurs and modified ways of functioning to address the social primacy of organizations. In effect, the former political economy of democratic capitalism, in which capitalism was regulated to serve democratic ends conveyed by the social values implicit in the general welfare, was superseded by a rebalancing of the political economy in which, through neoliberal values, private business interests gained political and market power over democratic government. Thus, it is now critical to understand the economy and its constituent players not only in terms of the principals served but also in terms of their functions and purposes, reflecting new normative, social value preferences. These new considerations provide the basis for locating organizations in the new social economy model.

Change will continue. Just as the New Deal vision for social well-being shifted to the neoliberal vision of market primacy, the economy will move in new directions in the future. Will the neoliberal logic of the market continue to prevail, perhaps even further exacerbating inequality and environmental stress? Or might we see a redux of the role of government to again rebalance the political economy in favor of well-being and environmental stewardship? As Nicholas Lemann (2019) said in recounting the message of Polanyi's *The great transformation*, "The only possible lasting solution to the problem of capitalism was for government to make itself such a forceful presence that the economy would be made the servant of society, instead of society being the servant of the economy" (p. 71).

6.2 The Social Economy Perspective as an Alternative

The three-sector model fails to describe and explain the classification of organizations in the contemporary economy.[6] Writing in the early 1970s, a time of great social upheaval in the United States, Harvard

[6] This section is based largely on *Understanding the social economy of the United States* (Mook et al., 2015).

Business School professor Theodore Levitt (1973) described how "the conventional taxonomy divides society into two sectors – private and public" but that organizations in what he called the "Third Sector, not conventionally thought of as a separate sector," met associational needs to fight back against what were seen as failures of government (pp. 48–49, 57). Levitt also noted that some organizations straddled the lines between sectors. By 1988, Jon Van Til would extend Levitt's treatment of sectors and define them as "three separate institutional worlds" in his book *Mapping the third sector: Voluntarism in a changing social economy* (p. 3). Van Til also noted the blurring of borders between the sectors. The discrete and static form of the three-sector model was proving not only unproductive but also harmful by leading us to conceive only of organizations that must conform to the model's boundaries. Moreover, the model obscured the possibility that normative changes in ideology could account for, or even inspire, highly differentiated classifications of sectors and even the possibility that all sectors could become normatively aligned, such as to serve social well-being and environmental stewardship.

To substantiate the inadequacy of the three-sector model, the following types of organizations are situated in the spaces between sectors, not within them, and these hybrid types appear to be growing in number:

6.2.1 *Public-Sector Nonprofits*

- Community health centers
- Nonprofit housing organizations
- Rape crisis centers

6.2.2 *Local Development Enterprises*

- Community development corporations
- Community development financial institutions
- Business improvement districts
- Workforce development organizations
- Workforce enterprises for marginal social groups
- Performing arts organizations
- Rural infrastructure development organizations
- Affordable home-ownership organizations

6.2.3 *Social Economy Businesses*

- Cooperatives, including consumer cooperatives, credit unions, insurance cooperatives, housing cooperatives, producer cooperatives, purchasing cooperatives, and worker cooperatives
- Benefit LLCs
- Low-profit, limited liability companies (L3Cs)
- Social purpose corporations
- Benefit corporations

While the aforementioned organizations[7] straddle sectors in the social economy, the following civil society organizations constitute the social sector in the three-sector model and do not overlap other sectors:

6.2.4 *Civil Society Organizations*

- Unions
- Professional associations
- Religious congregations and orders
- Associations of race and ethnicity
- Social clubs
- Self-help groups
- Sociopolitical organizations
- Public service organizations
- Collective campaigns and philanthropic foundations

***

In contrast to the three-sector model, the social economy framework recognizes the bridging of organizational forms and includes diverse and multifunctional organizations that transcend their incorporation.

The concept of a "social economy" is itself not new. Creating taxonomies of societies, or to use Lenski's term, "mapping the social universe," dates to ancient times, as documented by Gerhard Lenski

[7] Joyce Rothschild and J. Allen Whitt (1986) provide a major contribution to understanding how cooperatives are fundamentally different from corporate bureaucracies as classified by Weber.

(1994). The Italian Jesuit scholar Luigi Taparelli (1857/2011) critiqued the first French concepts of social economy in 1857, arguing that economic principles governing wealth must be combined with a political commitment to equitable distribution and a religious/moral commitment to ensure inclusion of the poor. The Catholic Church has long addressed the relationship between society, workers, socialism, and capitalism from a Catholic doctrinal perspective (Pope John Paul II, 1981; Pope Leo XIII, 1891; Pope Pius XI, 1931). In 2009, Pope Benedict XVI recognized the benefits of a diversity of organizational types, stating, "The very plurality of institutional forms of business gives rise to a market which is not only more civilized but also more competitive" (p. 46). As Roger Lohmann (2006) noted when pondering the "big questions" for nonprofits,[8] the social economy was described by French scholars over a century ago (p. 2). More recently, Richard McIntyre (2018) recounted the development of the social economy in France since 1945, and Gabriel Arsenault (2018) explained the emergence of the social economy in Québec beginning in the mid-1990s. Multinational organizations based in Europe are actively promoting the social economy (OECD, 2021; Social Economy Europe, 2020).

However, the social economy model described in this chapter is based on the three-sector model and is modified to better conform to contemporary empirical evidence, specifically in the Canadian and US experience (Mook et al., 2015; Quarter et al., 2009). Here, an important distinction of the social economy model is that, rather than viewing the social economy as separate from the private and public sectors, the three sectors are viewed together as a mixed economy. The Venn diagram in Figure 6.1 is useful in illustrating this idea in several ways: it is a method for classifying organizations, it emphasizes differing inter-sectoral behaviors, it emphasizes that the social economy is not an end in itself but rather exists in relation to other parts of society, and it recognizes the dynamic and changing nature of an economy.

[8] Lohmann's questions, though posed years ago, remain relevant both concerning nonprofits and also in contributing to a forward-looking conception of the social economy and the evolving relationships between nonprofit, public, and private organizational aims and norms.

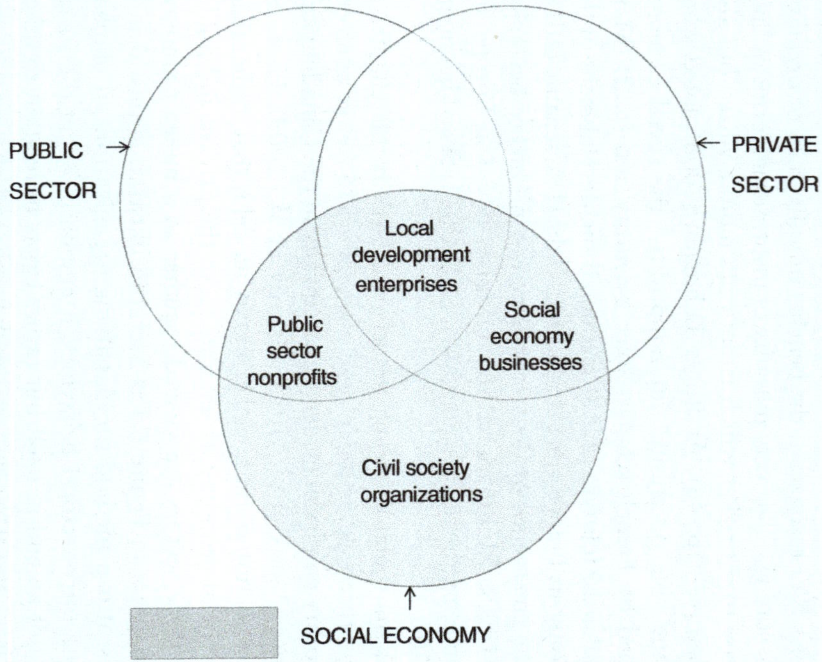

Figure 6.1 The contemporary social economy, an interactive approach

The innovation of the social economy model is that it is *organic* – in the sense that it is plastic and dynamic – and that it is open – in the sense that what characterizes the structure and functioning of organizations and locates their position in the economy is subject to both internal and environmental influences. Additionally, the leadership within an organization can control its telos (and this leadership can change), and the organization can also be controlled by external forces, whether by regulation and enforcement, competition, social regulation, or by other factors. The organic and open nature of the model evokes the dynamic systems theory introduced by Ludwig von Bertalanffy (1972) and distinguishes it from the reductionist and static nature of the three-sector model.

Social economy organizations share several features (Mook et al., 2015):

1. The primary focus of the organization's assets, income, and human resources (paid and unpaid) is to meet social objectives.
2. Social economy organizations are self-governing and relatively independent from either government or the private sector in determining their policies.
3. Distributing surplus income for individual gain is constrained, excepting a rebate to members for patronage or use of services.

It is in the overlap between the traditional sectors that organizations with multiple orientations are found. Social economy organizations interacting with the public sector ("public-sector nonprofits") receive public funding and are guided by government policies but are self-governing. The growth of government-funded nonprofits reflected a path to providing needed social services without expanding government itself to deliver such services directly. Events such as the Great Depression and World War II necessitated the initiation of social programs in response to massive unemployment and devasting social conditions. As Lester Salamon (1980) observed, the federal government began resorting to novel implementation tools, such as grant-in-aid funding to third parties, including states, during the New Deal "as a political response to the conservative argument that New Deal programs violated states' rights" (op-ed page). Government social programs continued to expand to help soldiers returning from World War II reintegrate into society. The role of government was then challenged in the 1980s, and nonprofit funding was changed from long-term to short-term contracts.

These organizations, seen as being more in touch with the needs of the communities they served, have been described as working in partnership with the government to the extent that "government has emerged as the single most important source of nonprofit sector income," constituting, in effect, a "third party government" (Salamon, 1987, pp. 30, 36–38). These organizations have also been described as serving as contractors of the government, raising questions about democratic legitimacy and the policy implications of third parties representing the government (Smith & Lipsky, 1993).

The section of the social economy that overlaps with the private sector represents organizations called "social economy businesses." These organizations earn most if not all of their revenue from market transactions. The oldest and most commonly known type of these organizations is cooperatives. Newer forms of social economy businesses include social enterprises, low-profit limited liability companies (L3Cs), and benefit corporations. Each of these types of organizations prioritizes achieving social and environmental objectives over maximizing economic profit.

Straddling both the public and private sectors are organizations called "local development enterprises," which combine public and private resources to strengthen community assets for social benefit. These organizations earn revenues from the market but also require ongoing external support from the government. They function to generate local economic and social development.

The remaining organizations in the social economy are "civil society organizations." These organizations can serve member needs, as in the case of mutual associations, or the wider public, such as the working poor or those living with disabilities, or even the environment.

Although the components in the Venn diagram appear to be the same size, in reality, economies are dynamic and continuously in flux. The size of each component varies across time in different historical, political, and economic contexts (Hall, 1987; Martin, 1985; Salamon & Sokolowski, 2004). Although the differences in scope and size of each sector can be measured, it is their relative positions that are highlighted in this model.

6.3 Conclusions

The key to understanding the future of the social economy theory is identifying the distinction between the structural and the normative functional characteristics of sectors. The public sector is grounded in the structural definition of organizations funded by the government for purposes defined by governmental codes. However, the normative character of organizations within this sector is not fixed; rather, it is determined by the ideological preferences in control of government and revealed in how the organization actually functions. Such preferences are dynamic; they may swing between more individualistic or communitarian commitments, depending on the party in power, which, in turn, is subject to change. The public sector within a liberal democracy may be even more variable in its commitments than the public sector in an authoritarian, and especially a communist, regime.

Similarly, the private sector is contingent on the structural test of private ownership of organizations. Still, depending on norms in practice, private organizations may pursue a profit-maximizing imperative characteristic of a neoliberal worldview, or, in contrast, they may function purely to donate profits to social purposes – or they may act somewhere in between profit and public purpose.

Civil society entities, in turn, are structurally defined as being neither government-controlled nor privately owned but can take various organizational forms for the sole purpose of serving a public need. This sector encompasses associations, leagues, and societies, as well as a variety of corporate forms defined by statute for public purposes. Organizations in this sector function for social purposes precisely because, unlike in the other sectors, their norms are social by definition, and, if they are 501(c)(3) tax-exempt charities, they must serve a social need by law.

As mentioned, the innovation of the social economy model is that it is open and organic, and able to explain why some organizations lie between the boundaries of the three traditionally discrete sectors because of the influence of the prevailing ideology, currently neoliberalism. While the three sectors may continue to be seen as Weberian pure types, they fail to account for observed anomalies that have led some to speak of the "blurring" of boundaries or of "hybrid" organizations that cannot neatly be assigned to one or another sector. Thus, it behooves contemporary observers to employ the social economy model in place of the three-sector model. Further, it makes sense to recognize how the social economy model easily subsumes the recently proposed "fourth sector,"[9] which in its diagrammatical representation appears strikingly similar to the social economy Venn diagram (Mook et al., 2015, p. 14).

As Salamon (1981) has noted,

> The function of theory, it is well to remember, is not simply to provide "explanations"; it is also to raise useful questions and, perhaps most important, to identify the most fruitful unit of analysis for coming to grips with the central problem of a field. (p. 256)

Reexamining societies through a social economy framework gives rise to a new set of research questions. The social economy can be considered a dependent or independent variable. Avenues of research can focus on micro, meso, and macro levels of analysis. For instance, research might explore the similarities and differences in managing such organizations; why new organizational forms arise; the efficacy of addressing different social issues through different segments of the economy; how organizations cope when their missions are constrained by environmental impediments, such as loss of financial support or the impact of economic shocks; and the effectiveness and even legitimacy of nongovernmental organizations implementing federal policies through instruments of government policy, what Salamon (1981) calls "third-party government." At the macro level, one might ask if there is a relationship between the relative size and role of each segment and inequality, health, and well-being in society. How does the relative size of each segment vary across different geographical contexts or historical periods, and with what impact? A line of research might also examine the threats to legitimacy and the public interest created by government policies that regulate organizations, for it cannot be assumed that a policy of strict government regulation necessarily precludes corruption, a danger even during the post-Revolutionary era when the government chartered public purpose corporations (Hilt, 2017).

Where does the social economy theory take us from here? The model clearly captures the dynamism of today's organizations in a way that was not accommodated in the three-sector model. But the social economy model also serves as more than a map of organizational

[9] See www.fourthsector.org/.

relationships. The dynamic nature of the model allows it to serve as a critical analytical tool not only for what is but also for what could be. One plausible scenario, by way of example, is a shift from neoliberalism, which has made society the servant of the economy, to a worldview that makes the economy the servant of society, promulgating normative values of regulated markets, collective responsibility, and good government powered by fair taxes. This shift might entail the presence of an adequately funded liberal democratic government to lead and populate its ranks with professionals who share the vision and social values of a capitalist economy that is purposefully regulated and enforced to serve social and environmental well-being. It might also entail a tax code in which all pay their fair share to ensure collective security and well-being. The social economy model would then position sectors as distinguished by structure and united by their common social purpose, thus achieving a more unified, cohesive social economy.

We argue that achieving such a coterminous social economy in which all organizations serve society requires three conditions predicated on a liberal, democratic government: (1) that public-sector organizations demonstrably serve the public interest; (2) that private sector organizations excel in producing private goods and services through competitive markets regulated by the government to eliminate social and environmental externalities; and (3) that nonprofit organizations are demonstrably trustworthy. To sustain the primacy of public benefit, these conditions must effectively eliminate government corruption, business greed, and nonprofit malfeasance.

Such a social economy might well provide a model for other capitalist economies, creating a more sustainable balance for humanity than that predicted by Polanyi (1944/2001) that would "annihilat[e] the human and natural substance of society" (p. 3). We also do not agree with Immanuel Wallerstein (2016) that "capitalism is no longer viable" (p. 202). But the needed balance in the political economy will not emerge from the boardroom, nor will it arrive spontaneously. Rather, it urgently requires a social and political movement first to ensure and protect the norms of a liberal, democratic government and then to enact and undertake the necessary legislative, regulatory, and enforcement reforms. Leadership by the United States might inspire a global trend to remedy the political economy balance to benefit humanity and the world.

References

Alexander, F. H. (2018). *Benefit corporation law and governance*. Berrett-Koehler Publishers, Inc.

Arsenault, G. (2018). Explaining Québec's social economy turn. *Canadian Journal of Nonprofit and Social Economy Research*, *9*(1), 58–75.

Burgin, A. (2012). *The great persuasion: Reinventing free markets since the Depression*. Harvard University Press.

Carnegie, A. (1889). *The gospel of wealth*. Carnegie Corporation of New York.

Collins, R. M. (1981). *The business response to Keynes, 1929–1964*. Columbia University Press.

Eikenberry, A. M., & Kluver, J. D. (2004). The marketization of the non-profit sector: Civil society at risk? *Public Administration Review*, *64*(2), 132–140.

Friedman, M. (1962/2002). *Capitalism and freedom*. University of Chicago Press.

Friedman, M. (1970, September 13). The social responsibility of business is to increase its profits. *The New York Times Magazine*.

Hall, P. D. (1987). A historical overview of the private nonprofit sector. In W. W. Powell (Ed.), *The nonprofit sector: A research handbook* (pp. 3–26). Yale University Press.

Hall, P. D. (2006). A historical overview of philanthropy, voluntary associations, and nonprofit organizations in the United States, 1600–2000. In W. W. Powell & R. Steinberg (Eds.), *The nonprofit sector: A research handbook* (2nd ed.) (pp. 32–65). Yale University Press.

Hammond, D. (2003). *The science of synthesis*. University Press of Colorado.

Hayek, F. A. (1944/1994). *The road to serfdom*. The University of Chicago Press.

Hilt, E. (2017). Early American corporations and the state. In N. R. Lamoreaux & W. J. Novak (Eds.), *Corporations and American democracy* (pp. 37–73). Harvard University Press.

Kennedy, J. F. (1961). *Inaugural address of John F. Kennedy*. Yale University: The Avalon Project. Retrieved from https://avalon.law.yale.edu/20th_century/kennedy.asp, cited March 7, 2022.

Keynes, J. M. (1936). *The general theory of employment interest and money*. Harcourt, Brace and Company.

Lave, C. A., & March, J. G. (1993). *An introduction to models in the social sciences*. University Press of America.

Lemann, N. (2019). *Transaction man: The rise of the deal and the decline of the American Dream*. Farrar, Straus and Giroux.

Lenski, G. (1994). Societal taxonomies: Mapping the social universe. *Annual Review of Sociology*, *20*, 1–26.

Levitt, T. (1973). *The third sector: New tactics for a responsive society.* AMACOM.

Levy, J. (2016). Altruism and the origins of nonprofit philanthropy. In B. Reich, C. Cordelli, & L. Bernholz (Eds.), *Philanthropy in democratic societies* (pp. 19–43). The University of Chicago Press.

Levy, J. (2017). From fiscal triangle to passing through: Rise of the nonprofit corporation. In N. R. Lamoreaux & W. J. Novak (Eds.), *Corporations and American democracy.* Harvard University Press.

Lohmann, R. (2006). Charity, philanthropy, public service or enterprise: What are the big questions of nonprofit management today? *West Virginia University Faculty Scholarship.* Retrieved from https://researchrepository.wvu.edu/faculty_publications/760/, cited March 10, 2022.

Marquis, C. (2020). *Better business: How the B Corp movement is remaking capitalism.* Yale University Press.

Martin, S. A. (1985). *An essential grace: Funding Canada's health care, education, welfare, religion and culture.* McClelland and Stewart.

McIntyre, R. (2018). The development of social economy in France since 1945. *Forum for Social Economics,* 47(2), 253–261.

Mook, L. (2014). An integrated social accounting model for nonprofit organizations. *Advances in Public Interest Accounting, 17,* 197–221.

Mook, L., Whitman, J. R., Quarter, J., & Armstrong, A. (2015). *Understanding the social economy of the United States.* University of Toronto Press.

Nickel, P. M., & Eikenberry, A. M. (2016). Knowing and governing: The mapping of the nonprofit and voluntary sector as statecraft. *Voluntas: International Journal of Voluntary and Nonprofit Organizations, 2016*(27), 392–408.

North, D. C. (1990/2005). *Institutions, institutional change and economic performance.* Cambridge University Press.

OECD. (2021). *The social and solidarity economy: From the margins to the mainstream 13–16 September 2021 Highlights.* Retrieved from https://oecd-events.org/social-and-solidarity-economy/, cited March 10, 2022.

Philippon, T. (2019). *The great reversal: How America gave up on free markets.* The Belknap Press of Harvard University Press.

Phillips-Fein, K. (2009). *Invisible hands: The businessmen's crusade against the New Deal.* W.W. Norton.

Polanyi, K. (1944/2001). *The great transformation: The political and economic origins of our time.* Beacon Press.

Pope Benedict XVI. (2009). *Caritas in veritate: On integral human development in charity and truth.* Libreria Editrice Vaticana.

Pope John Paul II. (1981). *Laborem Exercens: On human work.* Libreria Editrice Vaticana.

Pope Leo XIII. (1891). *Rerum novarum: On capital and labor*. Libreria Editrice Vaticana.
Pope Pius XI. (1931). *Quadragesimo Anno: On reconstruction of the social order*. Libreria Editrice Vaticana.
Quarter, J., Mook, L., & Armstrong, A. (2009). *Understanding the social economy: A Canadian perspective*. University of Toronto Press.
Reagan, R. (1981). *First inaugural address of Ronald Reagan*. Yale University: The Avalon Project. Retrieved from https://avalon.law.yale.edu/20th_century/reagan1.asp, cited December 8, 2019.
Roosevelt, F. D. (1933). *First inaugural address of Franklin D. Roosevelt*. Yale University: The Avalon Project. Retrieved from https://avalon.law.yale.edu/20th_century/froos1.asp, cited March 9, 2022.
Salamon, L. M. (1980, June 29). Rise of third-party government. *The Washington Post*.
Salamon, L. M. (1981). Rethinking public management: Third-party government and the changing forms of government action. *Public Policy*, *29*(3[Summer]), 255–275.
Salamon, L. M. (1987). Of market failure, voluntary failure, and third-party government: Toward a theory of government-nonprofit relations in the modern welfare state. *Journal of Voluntary Action Research*, *16*(1–2), 29–49.
Salamon, L. M., & Sokolowski, S. W. (2004). *Global civil society: Volume two, dimensions of the nonprofit sector*. Kumarian Press, Inc.
Smith, A. (1776/2003). *The wealth of nations*. Bantam Dell.
Smith, S. R., & Lipsky, M. (1993). *Nonprofits for hire: The welfare state in the age of contracting*. Harvard University Press.
Social Economy Europe. (2020). *Co-designing the action plan for the social economy*. Retrieved from www.socialeconomy.eu.org/publications/, cited March 10, 2022.
Taparelli, L. (2011/1857). Critical analysis of the first concepts of social economy (1857). *Journal of Markets & Morality*, *14*(2), 613–638.
Van Til, J. (1988). *Mapping the third sector: Voluntarism in a changing social economy*. The Foundation Center.
Von Bertalanffy, L. (1972). The history and status of general systems theory. *The Academy of Management Journal*, *15*(4), 407–426. Retrieved from www.perflensburg.se/Bertalanffy.pdf, cited July 17, 2021.
Wallerstein, I. (2016). Capitalism as an essential concept to understand modernity. In J. Kockam & M. van der Linden (Eds.), *Capitalism: The reemergence of a historical concept* (pp. 187–204). Bloomsbury Academic.
Weber, M. (1947). *The theory of social and economic organization* (A. M. Henderson & T. Parsons, Trans.). The Free Press.

7 *Sector Theorists Should Expand Three-Failures Theory to Include the Family Sector and Varied Forms of Government*

RICHARD STEINBERG, ELEANOR BROWN, AND LIZA L. TAYLOR*

Three Failures Theory (TFT), which has achieved something close to paradigmatic status (Kuhn, 1962) in the field of nonprofit studies, provides an explanation for the existence of the nonprofit sector and situates it in relationship to the government and for-profit sectors. TFT divides organizations into these three sectors, characterizing the strengths and weaknesses of each. According to TFT, each sector on its own fails to properly deliver the full range of socially needed activities, and each reacts to failures of other sectors. TFT addresses both positive questions (Why *are* activities occurring in each sector?) and normative questions (What activities *should* occur in each sector?).

Despite its significant influence on the field, TFT is not a cohesive theory; rather, it is a shorthand reference to a set of independently developed theories that, taken together, have shaped our view of the public, for-profit, and nonprofit sectors. The three-failures perspective emerged from three transformative exemplars, each focusing on specific aspects of sectoral advantage and none employing the words "three-failures theory."[1] Weisbrod (1975) focused on the choice

* We'd like to thank Bill Blomquist for his thoughts and references from political science; Pierre Englebert, Katy Herrold, and Mark Sidel for their thoughts and references on NGOs in nondemocratic societies; and Dulce Vega, Topher Anderson, and Traycee Lane for suggesting corruption as a source of government failure. We also thank Curtis Child for excellent editorial advice and Ming Hu for comments and criticisms.

[1] The first written references to these words that we could locate are in Steinberg (2006) and Smith and Grønbjerg (2006).

between government and nonprofit provision of collective goods, Hansmann (1980) on the choice between for-profit and nonprofits to remedy informational problems, and Salamon (1987) on the limits to nonprofit solutions. As a result, there is no authoritative source to resolve inconsistencies in the definitions of key terms and normative criteria across the separate originating theories. These deficits limit the influence of TFT on the development of the field.

This chapter seeks to embed TFT in a unified and comprehensive approach, which we term the Sectoral Advantage Framework (SAF), and we propose specific extensions that would make the sectoral approach more broadly applicable. Building on the insights of TFT, SAF is consciously designed with consistent definitions and criteria for evaluating sectoral performance. SAF frames a set of questions about sectoral boundaries and offers an approach to thinking about diverse puzzles in nonprofit studies that draws on the integration of the original approaches. SAF is not a theory in itself, in the sense of establishing testable predictions, but is a framework for assembling alternative theories regarding sectoral roles using common definitions and explicit criteria for judging sectoral success and failure. This flexibility enables the application of SAF to a broad range of institutions, cultures, and historical periods. In this chapter, we consider three ways in which SAF can go beyond TFT: (1) we add the family sector and consider its comparative advantages and failures, (2) we generalize government failure to make it more comprehensive and applicable outside Western democracies, and (3) we propose broadening the set of criteria used to assess sectoral advantage. In the next section, we summarize and critique TFT. We follow the summary and critique with a section illustrating how it can be improved. Our final section discusses other problems with TFT that should be addressed as we move toward an SAF.

7.1 A Critique of Three-Failures Theory

TFT draws on three exemplar studies, all of which identify the strengths and weaknesses of the various sectors, including how the failures of some organizations to provide desired goods and services help explain the presence of other types of organizations capable of providing those goods and services. The first study, Weisbrod (1975), provides an explanation of which organizations in a society provide nonexcludable collective goods ("pure public goods").[2] For-profit firms under-provide these goods because nonpayers cannot be excluded. Government monetizes through taxation and either produces the goods directly or contracts out with the other sectors. However, government is constrained by the will of the electorate. Using a simple model of democratic choice, Weisbrod assumes that governmental expenditures are set at the median-preference voter's preferred level. As a result, people who want to see higher levels of collective goods donate to nonprofits, which then supplement governmental support. This, in essence, is the reason that patrons support nonprofit organizations with their donations and purchases.

Hansmann (1980) proposed a mostly normative theory of sectoral virtues based on a kind of asymmetric information problem he called *contract failure*. Contract failure occurs when "owing either to the circumstances under which a service is purchased or consumed or to the nature of the service itself, consumers feel unable to evaluate accurately the quantity or quality of a service a firm produces for them" (Hansmann, 1987, p. 29). In such circumstances, for-profits are untrustworthy – and often untrusted by consumers – because they have the opportunity and the incentive to deliver less than the promised quality or quantity of service. Nonprofits are superior because owners cannot (legally) extract profits stemming from opportunistic behaviors, which explains why there is a demand for nonprofit organizations. Contract failure may lead managers who care about mission to preferentially work for nonprofits (Young, 1983) and, in any case, nonprofit board members presumably care about charitable outputs and therefore will check such abuses (Ben-Ner, 1986).

Salamon (1987) flipped the focus on market and government failures to examine, instead, four sources of *voluntary* failure: (1) philanthropic insufficiency contrasts the comparative difficulty of collecting donations rather than taxes; (2) amateurism stresses the difference in formal training and credentials; (3) paternalism highlights the difference between treating social problems as due to character defects of the victims or as due to social forces; and (4) particularism focuses on how nonprofits address problems for specific communities (e.g., religious denominations or ethnic groups), leading to gaps and duplications in

[2] For example, if one person helps needy people, everyone who cares about these people benefits.

services. The voluntary failure perspective suggests that nonprofits are testably distinct from governments and that governments may step in when nonprofits fail.

We have three main critiques of TFT. The first is that, notwithstanding the language of "failures" by proponents, it is unclear what failure means. The result is that sometimes a failure (as judged by one viewer) is a seen as a success (as judged by another). For example (drawing on Salamon, 1987), the same factor, particularism, creates a failure in the cases he discussed but, in other contexts, particularism *cures* failures. Case in point: particularist nonprofits serving groups that lack the power to sway majority voting can remedy government's failure to provide these groups with collective goods. Indeed, Steinberg (1995) argued that three of Salamon's (1987) four sources of voluntary failure can be seen – in certain situations – as nonprofit virtues.

More importantly, the idea of a failure presumes that *something* has not been achieved that ought to have been achieved, yet that *something* is rarely – and ought to be – identified. "Human flourishing" as envisioned in the capabilities approach pioneered by economist Amartya Sen and philosopher Martha Nussbaum provides a single criterion to assess what success or failure means. Following Nussbaum (2011), we consider human flourishing to involve 10 central capabilities, including life (normal length and functioning); bodily health; bodily integrity (freedom from violence); sensation, imagination, and reason; ability to form emotional attachments; practical reasoning (ethical reflection); affiliation (including social bases of self-respect); connection to nature; ability to engage in play; and control over one's environment (material, political). Human flourishing relies on access to an adequate minimum amount of each of these 10 capabilities; failure means that the conditions necessary to human flourishing have not been met.

Our second, and perhaps greater, critique of TFT is its lack of consideration of the productive activity that takes place within the family and the household.[3] As society has evolved, the functions traditionally assigned to the family have partly moved into the government sector (e.g., social security), the for-profit sector (e.g., assisted living facilities), and the nonprofit sector (e.g., daycare centers for children), but

[3] Acknowledging that households frequently contain persons who are not kin, and that families may be kinship groups that span many households, we refer to this sector as the family sector.

the family as an organization has remained central to modern society. The family interacts in meaningful ways with the other sectors recognized by TFT. For instance, the public, for-profit, and not-for-profit sectors provide education and socialization to children. Federal and state governments run income maintenance programs to supplement the resources available to low-income families. Public foster-care programs and nonprofit domestic violence shelters provide safety when family homes do not. Courts assign conservatorships for persons judged incompetent to care for themselves whose needs for stewardship are not met within the family.

In sum, no theory of the functions of the for-profit, not-for-profit, and public spheres is complete without an appreciation of their role in mitigating family failure. Similarly, no theory of the family is complete without an appreciation of how the family creates human flourishing in ways that the other sectors cannot. SAF is ideal for revisiting which activities are assigned to the family and which ought to be assigned to the family.

Third, we argue that governments fail in more ways than have been considered in TFT, and these failures extend beyond Western democracies. Considering democracies, Weisbrod (1975) focused on a single source of government failure predicated on the decisiveness of the median-preference voter. The median voter model is the simplest model of political equilibrium and, in many cases, predicts political outcomes accurately even though the theoretical model can be statistically rejected (Aronsson & Wikström, 1996). But the median voter model often fails empirically (for instance, in many US senatorial elections, when the same electorate picks two senators with divergent policy platforms and voting records). These and other concerns – including government's ability to restrict or eliminate the supply of nonprofits, not to mention government's relatively poor response time to social issues (Salamon, 1987) and other limitations on government action (Douglass, 1987; Wolpert, 1977) – suggest that a more nuanced treatment of the role of democratic governments is needed. Additionally, while normative discussions of government are rare within the TFT framework, they could also be integrated into the SAF framework.

TFT has little to say about the roles of government and nonprofits when governments are not, unlike Western democracies, constrained by an electorate. At best, TFT can handle cases in which the franchise is limited. But the fact that the median voter plays no role in autocracies, puppet states, or failed states is one reason that TFT has not emerged as a clear paradigm for nonprofit research in international contexts. Several studies examine state–nonprofit relationships in autocracies and failed states, which could be useful for building out a theory of nonprofits across varied contexts (see, e.g., Böhmelt, 2014; Brass, 2016; Chaudhry, 2020; Díaz-Albertini, 1993; Herrold & Atia 2016; Heurlin, 2010; Lightfoot, 2018; Najam, 2000; Ottaway & Mair, 2004; West, 2017).

7.2 What Three-Failures Theory Overlooks: An Application

In this section, we suggest how SAF can address the limitations of TFT before turning to an example. First, the family as a sector can be incorporated into SAF. Second, SAF can offer a more expansive approach to government failure. We address each of these contributions, identifying the advantages of family, as well as the ways in which family can fail. This is followed by an explanation of how notions of government failure can be expanded in the new integrated framework.

7.2.1 Advantages of the Family and Family Failure

Before there was a nonprofit sector, or formal governments and markets, there was the family. The family continues to be an important locus of economic activity, and no understanding of the nonprofit sector is complete without exploring its interaction with the family. We begin by asking what roles the modern family plays and why these economic activities are located within the family. We relate these functions to Nussbaum's (2011) 10 core capabilities and define "family failure" in terms of these multiple expectations.

Society counts on families to share resources among productive and nonproductive members; to invest in the human capital of children, including nurturance, socialization, and physical protection; and to act on behalf of family members who cannot reliably make decisions in their own self-interest. The literature on the economics of the family gives us insights into ways in which families may succeed or fail in meeting these expectations.

The first essential function of the family is resource-sharing. Young children cannot provide for themselves; neither can those adults who have functional incapacities. Families share resources across and within generations. Such resource-sharing supports Nussbaum's fundamental capabilities of living a long and healthy life.

Second, we depend on families for childrearing. Children need more than resources. They need nurturing, which is a special case of the broader category of affective labor. They need physical protection. They need education. Children also depend on their family to provide much of the socialization (e.g., whom to trust, how to behave in the presence of police, how to engage with others) needed to keep them safe, supported, and successful in the outside world. Nussbaum (2011) captured the importance of childrearing in her emphases on freedom from violence, ability to play, and capacities for reasoning, imagination, emotional attachments, and ethical reflection.

Third, sometimes adults' well-being also depends on intervention from others. Not all people are capable of effectively organizing their lives in a way that is consistent with the pursuit of their own well-being. Some people's preferences are not rational, in the sense used by economists: they cannot consistently act in accordance with their goals. Some people have preferences that are not reasonable in that their goals are evidently self-destructive. The inability of such persons to pursue their own well-being autonomously creates a dilemma for a society built on individual liberties but which additionally cares about its citizens' material well-being, since autonomy and well-being are, for these persons, at odds. Stepping into a stewardship role in caring for young children and elderly parents who have become mentally and/or physically incapable of managing their affairs is a central function of the family. Effective stewardship supports the capabilities of long life, health, and safety.

To summarize, the economic functions of the family include resource transfers to members who are not self-supporting and stewardship of those who are not reliable decision makers; nurturance and education of children; safety; and efficiency gains from comparative advantage and shared local collective goods. Most of these functions call on the altruism and love that are the comparative strength of the family as an economic unit. These functions are predicated on the presence of sufficient family resources in order to meet these goals.

Of course, families are not always successful in these functions. The literature from the economics of the family makes this clear, and we highlight only a few points here. For instance, the well-being of children may depend on the extent to which the mother controls resources: studies have found that increasing women's control over the household budget is associated with improved nutrition (Armand et al., 2020; Duflo, 2003), health outcomes (Thomas, 1990), and increased expenditures on children's clothing (Lundberg et al., 1997; Ward-Batts, 2008). Homicide data reinforce the view that families sometimes fail to behave altruistically (or even benignly) toward vulnerable members (Bennett et al., 2006). And, although people living in families are more likely to escape poverty than people living on their own, inadequate resources frequently limit the ability of families to assure the well-being of their members. In 2019, roughly 8.5% of the 262 million Americans living in families lived in a family with an income below the poverty line. Among the 60 million people in the US in 2019 who were not living in families, the poverty rate was nearly 19% (Semega et al., 2020, table B-2).

Society thus relies on the family to pool resources for the benefit of all family members, including nonproductive ones; to raise children into well-adjusted and well-functioning adulthood; and to provide stewardship services to adult members unable to manage their affairs. The successful performance of these functions relies on other-regarding behaviors motivated by the love and altruism that are the hallmark of the idealized family, as well as sufficient resources and expertise to effectively carry out these other-regarding good intentions. Nearly all the central human capabilities emphasized by Nussbaum (2011) are developed within the well-functioning family.[4] The family, however, is not always able to successfully perform these functions, which draws them into relationships with organizations in other sectors of the economy – governments, nonprofits, and businesses. Understanding any of these sectors, not to mention understanding the role of family in modern times, requires comprehending how they are all connected. A sector theory, therefore, ought to account not only for nonprofits, for-profits, and governments but for families as well.

[4] While we see these three as the core economic roles assigned to the family, we note for the record two additional roles played by the family that have consequences for the functioning of the economy. In the aggregate, fertility decisions affect the size of a country's workforce and the age distribution of its population, with implications for dependency ratios and immigration policy. Similarly, bequests to children and grandchildren are the main conduit for intergenerational transfers of wealth, with implications for social inequality and tax policy.

Family composition and kinship structures vary historically and across the globe (e.g., Henrich, 2020). Within some societies, familial expression remains distinct, whereas in others family blends with or shapes the other sectors. Examples of such sector blurring are found in government (hereditary monarchies or dictatorships), business (dynastic companies), and philanthropy (family foundations and care of children and the elderly). The strength of kinship ties, Henrich argued, affects the balance of personal (within your social network) and impersonal (to strangers and organizations) prosocial behaviors. Future research could explore how these differences affect the advantage of families, family's place within society, and the ways families interact with the other sectors.

7.2.2 Toward a Broader Analysis of Government Failures

Besides accounting for family, SAF seeks a broad view of government failure. We consider here two literatures relevant to government failure that are largely overlooked in TFT. Then we present our ideas for expanding the treatment of government in a sectoral framework. The first branch of the literature, with contributions from economics, public policy, and political science, concerns the broad category of nonmarket failures. Wolf (1979, 1993) began this stream, noting the lack of well-defined definitions and criteria for cataloguing the shortcomings of nonmarket institutions. His primary analytic goal was to see when government (or donative nonprofit) efforts to address market failure make things worse (see also Le Grande, 1991 and Luo & Kaul, 2019).

Kleiman and Teles (2006) borrowed Wolf's (1979) critical perspective on nonmarket failures.[5] After briefly discussing failures of two kinds of nonmarket institutions ("family failure" and "neighborhood failure") they enumerate and discuss government failures, including:

[5] "Unlike markets, there is not even a prima facie reason to expect them to perform optimally, because civil society lacks anything resembling the price mechanism" (Kleiman & Teles, 2006, p. 634). However, they take a less extreme position in most of their paper, suspecting that "poorly understood," "self-enforcing expectations of good behavior" may lead to better performance by nonmarket institutions.

- inadequate penetrative capacity (resistance to government information gathering)
- inadequate voluntary cooperation (requiring either costly incentive payments or costly enforcement efforts)
- institutional overhead, including corruption and principal-agent problems
- holdout problems resulting in "political transaction costs."

Some of these insights could usefully be incorporated into a paradigmatic SAF after developing the comparative aspects further.

Second, drawing from the literature on institutional failures (Derwort et al., 2019), there is room to expand our understanding of government failure by incorporating research on corruption and other self-interested behaviors of political actors. Corruption has a contested definition, but theories of corruption abound in political science, economics, management, and other disciplines. Corruption can (but need not) improve government efficiency (Holcombe, 2018). For example, bribes help citizens escape the harms created by bad laws, but the prospect of increased income from bribes incentivizes the passage of bad laws (Tullock, 1996). There is a trade-off between government interventions designed to fix market failures and governmental corruption (Acemoglu & Verdier, 2000). Corruption affects not only efficiency and the distribution of wealth but also other values such as equal power or voice and autonomy (e.g., Thompson, 2018). Moreover, corruption is not limited to governments. For-profits, nonprofits, and even families can fall prey to it. For all these reasons, it makes sense to expand our notion of government failures to include corruption, including the sectoral advantages stemming from beneficial and harmful forms of corruption.

These literatures on nonmarket and institutional failures are relevant to, and expand upon, the understanding of government failure as it is usually conceived in TFT. Incorporating them into SAF allows for a richer conceptualization of the nonprofit sector vis-à-vis other sectors in the economy. But that is not all we can do to enrich the framework. We have noted that TFT does not have obvious application to autocratic or failed states. In TFT, the role and performance of nonprofits is in part a response to the sorts of government failures endemic to Western democracies. We propose treating government failure more broadly to make TFT applicable across varying types of states, including autocracies and failed states.

A promising framework for such an expansion into an SAF is "selectorate politics," developed by Bueno de Mesquita, Morrow, Siverson, and Smith (1999) and further developed by various combinations of these authors in subsequent articles and books. Its characterization of government action is applicable to different types of regimes, so building an SAF on it, rather than on the implied Western democracy, allows for broader usage. Bueno de Mesquita and colleagues have explained how the behavior of individual political leaders depends on the size of two groups – *the selectorate* (all those who have an institutionally granted right or norm that gives them a say in choosing the government) and *the winning coalition* (members of the selectorate whose support is essential to keep the incumbent in office). For example, in the present-day US, the selectorate contains most adult citizens, and the winning coalition consists of the critical few members of the selectorate who can deliver 270 Electoral College votes to the incumbent president. According to the theory, the sole focus of leaders is on retaining power,[6] which they do by providing a combination of private benefits (special privileges, access to graft and bribes, favorable contracts, and the like) and non-excludable collective goods (national defense, political freedoms, general economic growth) to members of the winning coalition. The relative size of the selectorate and the winning coalition determines the leader's cost of securing the loyalty of members of the winning coalition, hence the mixture of private and collective goods.

Bueno de Mesquita et al.'s (1999) modeling approach strives for universality, covering autocracies as well as democracies. Endogenous threats of political revolution are introduced by Smith (2008) and Bueno de Mesquita and Smith (2009). Guriev and Treisman (2020) extend the analysis to cases of asymmetric information with their analysis of informational autocracy, and the literature provides a variety of additional applications. The approach includes the distinction between private and collective goods that is so important to TFT, making it especially promising for a general theory of government failure – that is, government failure beyond issues related to the median voter (à la Weisbrod, 1975).

[6] In this sense, the theory is Machiavellian, but this is what Machiavelli (2016) would have written had he been trained in optimization modeling and econometrics before advising the prince. Indeed, two of these authors wrote a book titled *The dictator's handbook: Why bad behavior is almost always good politics* (Bueno de Mesquita & Smith, 2011).

However, power-seekers in all four sectors seek to retain power,[7] and the selectorate approach is insufficiently comparative across the sectors. It models politics as a game between a leader, an elite, and a broader public. SAF requires, at a minimum, that the for-profit and nonprofit sectors be active players. How does nonprofit provision of collective goods affect the ability of leaders to buy the loyalty of the winning coalition? Some partial answers come from the literature on nonprofit repression, which takes the regime type as exogenous. It would be complicated to develop a fuller model with appropriate strategic relationships between the sectors, and it remains to be seen whether such generality comes at the expense of insight into the assignment of activities to sectors.

7.2.3 *Application: Elder Care in China*

Consider the vast problem of providing elder care for China's rapidly aging population. It is immediately apparent that TFT cannot fully describe sectoral roles and advantages because it omits the family sector and relies on the median voter model, which does not apply to China. Furthermore, TFT has limited value assessing the comparative successes and failures of the sectors because criteria such as efficiency and particularism do not suffice to fully evaluate elder care.

The family sector's role in elder care is important around the world, but particularly so in China. For most of China's recorded history, the tradition of filial piety ruled, and elder care was the exclusive (or almost exclusive) province of the family. As Levin (2008) noted, "For thousands of years, filial piety was China's Medicare, Social Security, and long-term care, all woven into a single-family value." Under this tradition, institutional elder care in China was limited to the "Three No's" – those with no children, no income, and no relatives and provided through stigmatizing welfare programs that placed them in lower-level government or collective facilities (Feng et al., 2012).

However, China's reliance on the family is eroding in the face of demographic change due to reductions in the number of children per family, increasing lifespans, and urbanization policies that separate working children from rural parents. Filial piety remains a powerful

[7] With some exceptions, like the private foundation seeking to spend itself out of existence.

force, but, according to three studies summarized by Feng et al. (2012, p. 2765) there are "shifting attitudes among both the old and the young toward independence and autonomy in living arrangements and the increasing tolerance of institutional care for elders."

Following the market reforms of the mid-1980s, the national Ministry of Civil Affairs adopted a policy of socializing welfare responsibilities to businesses, families, and charitable organizations (Leung 2010; Shang, 2001), changing the role of all four sectors. J. Guo and Mu summarized this new approach:

> In the field of elder care, socialization refers to the goal of a pluralistic service system that consists of residential services, community services, and home care; diversified funding sources that include government allocation, public donations, and individual payments; and the inclusion of fee-paying users. (Guo & Mu, 2015, p. 13)

Implementation of these new policies has been spotty (Feng et al., 2020) and further slowed by increases in the Communist Party's role in nonprofit registration and administration. The party balances strict control over associational activity against a desire to encourage the nonprofit sector's service to the state, and the balance has shifted toward stricter control in the Xi Jinping era, leading the National People's Congress to place revision of the Charity Law on the legislative agenda (Sidel, 2022; Snape & Weinan, 2022).

TFT speaks to some of the problems with Chinese elder care nonprofits. There is an amateurism problem due to a shortage of training opportunities for nurses and social workers that leads to maltreatment and elder abuse (Wang, 2019). Contract failure undoubtedly plays a role: like elsewhere, there are questions regarding the extent of enforcement of the non-distribution constraint and there is the likelihood that at least some organizations claiming to be nonprofit are for-profits-in-disguise (NPC, 2020).

However, a prominent feature of the provision of elder care in contemporary China is a severe shortage of nursing home facilities (Feng et al., 2020), and we need a broader framework than TFT to analyze this shortage. While TFT can describe some characteristics of the supply of nursing homes, the demand for these facilities comes from two sources addressed in SAF that lie beyond TFT. First, the increased demand stems from dynamics within the family sector. Second, the demand for elder care appeals to societal notions of value beyond consumers' willingness to pay. SAF moves beyond efficiency considerations by introducing a broader set of goals for society. For example, the capabilities approach demands that a minimum acceptable level of protection be provided. This standard of care undergirds the sense that there is a shortage of acceptable care; policies to address this shortfall will help to shape sectoral roles and advantage.

In sum, the addition of the family sector, extension of models of government failure, and inclusion of additional normative criteria foster a deeper understanding of why the sectors play the roles they do, and the role government policy can play to stimulate an efficient and humane system of elder care.

7.3 Conclusions

We identified three limitations of TFT – the absence of a family sector, the limited conception of government failure, and the narrow normative criterion – that have kept the framework from reaching its explanatory potential in nonprofit studies. In response, we developed ideas about family failure and suggested ways of combining and modifying existing approaches toward a universal, comparative, and predictive theory of government failure. To distinguish the effort toward a comprehensive sector theory framework from prior discussions of the three independent failures theories (market, contract, and voluntary) that already appear in the literature, we have suggested the term *sectoral advantage framework*. Although it is beyond the scope of this chapter to list all the fruitful possibilities for expanding on the contributions of TFT, we conclude by briefly summarizing three areas of focus that an integrative, comprehensive SAF would need to deal with moving forward: the treatment of combinations of sectors, alternative sectoral partitions, and the expansion of the theories of market and voluntary failure to accommodate normative frameworks beyond economic efficiency.

First, understanding the advantages and disadvantages of sectors operating in isolation tells us little about how each sector performs in coexistence, where the sectors may be complementary, supplementary, or adversarial (Young, 1999). For example, Hirth (1999) showed that, in certain situations, both for-profits and nonprofits will be trustworthy when they compete in the same market. In other situations, cross-sectoral competition leads to contract failure in both sectors.

Pure sectoral analysis also tells us little about performance under legal structures of interaction such as partnerships, joint ventures, contracting out, and nonprofit subsidiaries of for-profit corporations (or vice versa). TFT is also mute on the performance of cross-sectoral hybrid organizations such as low-profit limited liability companies (L3Cs), benefit corporations, or community interest companies. Do they combine the best of both sectors, the worst of both sectors, or neither? In all these cases, the whole need not be the sum of the parts. Synergies and dyssynergies exist across the sectors.

The role of the nonprofit sector may be different in societies with close collaboration between government and business than in societies where these sectors operate independently. Each possible combination of primary sectors can be regarded as a sector in and of itself, yielding its own set of relative strengths and weaknesses and changing the landscape of other sectoral advantages. Specifying that each possible combination is a distinct sector is too unwieldy to be useful in general, but when SAF is applied to cases where combinations are prevalent, some such modification is appropriate.[8]

Second, there is the question of how many sectors a sector theory should incorporate. In various contexts, informal and grassroots organizations, networks, and the press have been proposed as additional sectors. In other contexts, these entities are incorporated into the existing sectors in TFT. A related problem is whether our four sectors are too aggregated to uniformly analyze in a sectoral framework. For example, among for-profits, proprietorships are freer than traditional corporations and partnerships to sacrifice profits in the social interest (Steinberg, 2015). We might also distinguish for-profit social enterprise or worker-owned firms from other for-profits. Or we might want to subdivide nonprofits into membership organizations, foundations, and operating nonprofits, or commercial and donative nonprofits.

Third, although we have focused on government failures, market and voluntary failure theories are also incomplete. Market failure theory, for example, is elegantly complete in the treatment of market economies. However, a more universal framework such as SAF allows fuller analysis of premarket societies and centrally planned states.

[8] Marwell and Brown (2020) attempted to deal with this problem differently, developing a "governance framework" stressing the nature of interorganizational relations and coproduction to supplement sectoral analysis.

The theory of voluntary failure is less developed. Salamon (1987) listed four sources of voluntary failure and Steinberg (2006) added incompetence, inattentiveness, and indolence to the list. But there are many other ways nonprofits such as the Ku Klux Klan or QAnon fail to promote human flourishing. Nonprofits both fight and strengthen polarization, racism, distributional justice, and a host of other evils. Ben-Ner (2018) argued that the pattern of donations deepens in-group loyalty and out-group enmity, harming cooperation and trust. Lechterman and Reich (2020) noted that "some people will use their liberty to form insular associations to engage in crime, preach theocracy, or trumpet racial hatred" (p. 182). Our list of voluntary failures is incomplete without reference to these dark sides.

As our increasingly globalized society becomes more complex, there is an essential need for a more comprehensive framework that policymakers, researchers, and practitioners can use to evaluate and promote human flourishing. We take a step toward more comprehensive sector theory by proposing a Sectoral Advantage Framework (SAF) and outlining some of its characteristics. We propose that this framework incorporate elements from the disciplines of economics and political science and the fields of public affairs, nonprofit studies, and policy science, but these elements need to be modified to include a common basis for assessing sectoral successes and failures across a comprehensive set of sectors. Our specific contribution toward an SAF expands on Three Failures Theory (TFT) by adding the family sector, suggesting an analysis of government failure that can be applied to autocracies and anarchy as well as democracies, and broadening the criteria for evaluating sectors.

References

Acemoglu, D., & Verdier, T. (2000). The choice between market failures and corruption. *American Economic Review*, *90*(1), 194–211.

Armand, A., Attanasio, O., Carneiro, P., & Lechene, V. (2020). The effect of gender-targeted conditional cash transfers on household expenditures: Evidence from a randomized experiment. *Economic Journal*, *130*, 1875–1897. https://doi.org/10.1093/ej/ueaa056

Aronsson, T., & Wikström, M. (1996). Local public expenditure in Sweden: A model where the median voter is not necessarily decisive. *European Economic Review*, *40*(9), 1705–1716.

Ben-Ner, A. (1986). Non-profit organizations: Why do they exist in market economies? In S. Rose-Ackerman (Ed.), *The economics of nonprofit institutions: Studies in structure and policy*. Oxford University Press.

Ben-Ner, A. (2018). Is altruism (always) good for society? The problem of particularistic giving in a diverse society. Working paper. Carlson School of Management, University of Minnesota.

Bennett, M. D., Hall, J., Frazier, L., Patel, N., Barker, L., & Shaw, K. (2006). Homicide of children aged 0–4 years, 2003–04: Results from the National Violent Death Reporting System. *Injury Prevention*, *12*(suppl 2), ii39–ii43.

Böhmelt, T. (2014). Political opportunity structures in dictatorships? Explaining ENGO existence in autocratic regimes. *The Journal of Environment & Development*, *23*(4), 446–471. https://doi.org/10.1177/1070496514536396

Brass, J. N. (2016). *Allies or adversaries: NGOs and the state in Africa*. Cambridge University Press.

Bueno de Mesquita, B., & Smith, A. (2009). Political survival and endogenous institutional change. *Comparative Political Studies*, *42*(2): 167–197.

Bueno de Mesquita, B., & Smith, A. (2011). *The dictator's handbook: Why bad behavior is almost always good politics*. PublicAffairs.

Bueno de Mesquita, B., Morrow, J. D., Siverson, R. M., & Smith, A. (1999). Policy failure and political survival: The contribution of political institutions. *Journal of Conflict Resolution*, *43*(2), 147–161.

Chaudhry, S. (2020). The assault on civil society: Explaining state crackdown on NGOs. Draft available from the author.

Derwort, P., Jager, N., & Newig, J. (2019). Towards productive functions? A systematic review of institutional failure, its causes and consequences. *Policy Sciences*, *52*(2), 281–298.

Díaz-Albertini, J. (1993). Nonprofit advocacy in weakly institutionalized political systems: The case of NGDOs in Lima, Peru. *Nonprofit and Voluntary Sector Quarterly*, *22*(4), 317–337.

Douglas, J. (1987). Political theories of nonprofit organization. In W. W. Powell (Ed.), *The nonprofit sector: A research handbook* (pp. 43–45). Yale University Press.

Duflo, E. (2003). Grandmothers and granddaughters: Old age pensions and intra-household allocation in South Africa. *World Bank Economic Review*, *17*(1), 1–25.

Feng, Z., Glinskaya, E., Chen, H., Gong, S., Qiu, Y., Xu, J., & Yip, W. (2020). Long-term care system for older adults in China: Policy landscape, challenges, and future prospects. *The Lancet*, *396*(10259), 1362–1372.

Feng, Z., Liu, C., Guan, X., & Mor, V. (2012). China's rapidly aging population creates policy challenges in shaping a viable long-term care system. *Health Affairs*, *31*(12), 2764–2773.

Guo, J., & Mu, L. (2015). Residential care for elders in China: The private sector as a solution? *Social Development Issues*, *37*(1), 11–24.

Guriev, S., & Treisman, D. (2020). A theory of informational autocracy. *Journal of Public Economics*, *186*, 104–158.

Hansmann, H. (1980). The role of nonprofit enterprise. *Yale Law Journal*, *89*, 835–901.

Hansmann, H. (1987). Economic theories of nonprofit organization. In W. W. Powell (Ed.), *The nonprofit sector: A research handbook*. Yale University Press.

Henrich, J. (2020). *The WEIRDest people in the world: How the West became psychologically peculiar and particularly prosperous*. Penguin UK.

Herrold, C., & Atia, M. (2016). Competing rather than collaborating: Egyptian nongovernmental organizations in turbulence. *Nonprofit Policy Forum*, *7*(3), 389–407.

Heurlin, C. (2010). Governing civil society: The political logic of NGO–state relations under dictatorship. *VOLUNTAS: International Journal of Voluntary and Nonprofit Organizations*, *21*(2), 220–239.

Hirth, R. A. (1999). Consumer information and competition between non-profit and for-profit nursing homes. *Journal of Health Economics*, *18*, 219–240.

Holcombe, R. (2018). The Coase theorem, applied to markets and government. *Independent Review*, *23*(2), 249–266. www.jstor.org/stable/26591782

Kleiman, M. A., & Teles, S. M. (2006). Market and non-market failures. In M. Moran, M. Rein, & R. E. Goodin (Eds.), *The Oxford handbook of public policy* (pp. 624–650). Oxford University Press.

Kuhn, T. (1962). *The structure of scientific revolutions* (1st ed.). University of Chicago Press.

Le Grand, J. (1991). The theory of government failure. *British Journal of Political Science*, *21*(4), 423–442.

Lechterman, T., & Reich, R. (2020). Political theory and the Nonprofit sector. In W. W. Powell & P. Bromley (Eds.), *The nonprofit sector: A research handbook* (3rd ed.) (pp. 171–191). Stanford University Press.

Leung, J. C. (2010). Residential care services for older people in China: From state to market provisions? *Social Development Issues*, 32(1), 31–47.

Levin, D. (2008). Aging in China: A tradition under stress: Who will care for the nation's elders? *AARP Bulletin* [serial originally on the Internet, not currently available from 2008]. As cited in Feng et al., 2012, accessed May 11, 2012 from www.aarp.org/politics-society/around-the-globe/info-07–2008/aging_in_china_a_tradition_under_stress.html. No page for this quote was given.

Lightfoot, H. S. (2018). *Non-state actors in weak states. An exploration of NGOs and MNCs in the eastern Democratic Republic of Congo* [Master's thesis]. UiT Norges arktiske universitet.

Lundberg, S., Pollak, R., & Wales, T. (1997). Do husbands and wives pool their resources? Evidence from the United Kingdom Child Benefit. *Journal of Human Resources*, *32*(3, Summer), 463–480.

Luo, J., & Kaul, A. (2019). Private action in public interest: The comparative governance of social issues. *Strategic Management Journal*, *40*(4), 476–502.

Machiavelli, N. (2016). *The prince with related documents* (2nd ed.) (W. J. Connell, Trans.). Bedford/St. Martin's. (Original work published 1532.)

Marwell, N. P., & Brown, M. (2020). Toward a governance framework for government–nonprofit relations. In W. W. Powell & Bromley, P. (Eds.), *The nonprofit sector: A research handbook* (4th ed.). Stanford University Press.

Najam, A. (2000). The four C's of government third sector–government relations. *Nonprofit Management and Leadership*, *10*(4), 375–396.

NPC. (2020). The standing committee of the National People's Congress: Report on inspection of the implementation of the Charity Law of the People's Republic of China. www.bnu1.org/show_2066.html

Nussbaum, M. (2011). *Creating capabilities: The human development approach*. Belknap Press of Harvard University Press.

Ottaway, M., & Mair, S. (2004). States at risk and failed states. Policy Outlook: Democracy and Rule of Law Project. Carnegie Endowment for International Peace and German Institute for International and Security Affairs, 1–9.

Salamon, L. M. (1987). Of market failure, voluntary failure, and third-party government: Toward a theory of government–nonprofit relations in the modern welfare state. *Journal of Voluntary Action Research*, *16*(1–2), 29–49.

Semega, J., Kollar, M., Shrider, E. A., & Creamer, J. F. (2020). *Income and Poverty in the United States: 2019* (U.S. Census Bureau, current population reports, P60-270). U.S. Government Publishing Office, Washington, DC.

Shang, X. (2001). Moving towards a multi-level and multi-pillar system: Changes in institutional care in two Chinese cities. *Journal of Social Policy*, *30*, 259–281.

Sidel, M. (2022). Rebooting China's charity law. *U.S.-Asia Law Institute Perspectives*, 2(25). June 23, 2022, https://usali.org/usali-perspectives-blog/rebooting-chinas-charity-law

Smith, A. (2008). The perils of unearned income. *Journal of Politics*, *70*(3), 780–793.

Smith, S. R., & Grønbjerg, K. A. (2006). Scope and theory of government–nonprofit relations. In W. W. Powell & R. Steinberg (Eds.), *The nonprofit sector: A research handbook* (2nd ed.). Yale University Press.

Snape, H., & Wang, W. (2022). Towards a "command civil society"? China's Xi era rules on social organizing. Paper presented at International Society for Third Sector Research 15th International Conference, Montreal, Canada.

Steinberg, R. (1995). The clash of values in civil society. Working paper. Available from the author.

Steinberg, R. (2006). Economic theories of nonprofit organizations. In W. W. Powell & R. Steinberg (Eds.), *The nonprofit sector: A research handbook* (2nd ed.). Yale University Press.

Steinberg, R. (2015). What should social finance invest in and with whom? In A. Nicholls, R. Paton, & J. Emerson (Eds.), *Social finance* (pp. 64–95). Oxford University Press.

Thomas, D. (1990). Intra-household resource allocation: An inferential approach. *Journal of Human Resources*, *25*(4), 635–664. https://doi-org.ccl.idm.oclc.org/http://jhr.uwpress.org/ content/by/year

Thompson, D. F. (2018). Theories of institutional corruption. *Annual Review of Political Science*, *21*, 495–513.

Tullock, G. (1996). Corruption theory and practice. *Contemporary Economic Policy*, *14*(3), 6–13.

Wang, Y. (2019). The eight major changes in the Government Work Report on Social Organizations, Social Work, Charity, etc. are worthy of attention! *Philanthropy Times (China)* 3/5/2019. Accessed from https://mp.weixin.qq.com/s?__biz=MjM5NTM3MjM5Mg==&mid=2652355572&idx=1&sn=38c5ad7b2da0829a799fd57700e8445d&chksm=bd1a97f38a6d1ee5c65a8136569e61732b31dae71e44308e3e7c068e372028e572dc8fd735b7&mpshare=1&scene=1&srcid=03056h39b4Yfih8jnPWWkMbj#rd, June 7, 2021.

Ward-Batts, J. (2008). Out of the wallet and into the purse: Using micro data to test income pooling. *Journal of Human Resources*, *43*(2, Spring), 325–351.

Weisbrod, B. A. (1975). Toward a theory of the voluntary nonprofit sector in a three-sector economy. In E. S. Phelps (Ed.), *Altruism, morality, and economic theory* (pp. 171–195). Russell Sage Foundation.

West, K. (2017). *Agents of altruism: The expansion of humanitarian NGOs in Rwanda and Afghanistan*. Routledge.

Wolf Jr., C. (1979). A theory of nonmarket failure: Framework for implementation analysis. *The Journal of Law and Economics*, *22*(1), 107–139.

Wolf Jr, C. (1993). *Markets or government: Choosing between imperfect alternatives* (2nd ed.). MIT Press.

Wolpert, J. (1977). Social income and the voluntary sector. In *Papers of the Regional Science Association*, 39(1), 216–229.
Young, D. R. (1983). *If not for profit, for what?* D. C. Heath.
Young, D. R. (1999). Complementary, supplementary, or adversarial: A theoretical and historical examination of government-nonprofit relations in the U.S. In E. T. Boris & C. E. Steuerle (Eds.), *Nonprofits & government: Collaboration & conflict* (pp. 31–67). Urban Institute.

8 *Sector Theorists Should Be Wary of the Nonprofit Industrial Complex*

ANA CLARISSA ROJAS DURAZO

I write at the historical crux of a pandemic moment, an escalating climate crisis, and a post–George Floyd turn toward abolitionist thought and action. The tragedies of this moment in time have come alongside unforeseen changes to our social and daily lives, leading to a heightened time of collective and self-reflection. The unpredictability of our safety and well-being amidst tragic consequences marked by an inordinate loss of life in the material and social sense have insisted we take stock and assess what is most important – we want to keep ourselves and our loved ones safer as we move forward, building the future we want to live in.

The casualties of this historic moment have arrived differently on different bodies and peoples. Black, Brown, and Indigenous peoples – in particular, those most marginalized racially and economically – have suffered the greatest consequences. I am writing in California, where a startlingly high rate of those dying from COVID-19 are Latinx of working age. In California, 73% of people aged 35–49 who have died of COVID-19 are Latino (Romero, 2021). I am writing in the city of Oakland, where fury over centuries of police violence has led to powerful social movements that are causing people to imagine and organize societies in which Black lives matter. The unceded Ohlone lands where I write are also known as Huichin, the ancestral homeland of the Confederated Villages of Lisjan. Indigenous women here have organized a land trust called Sogorae Te' to heal and transform the genocidal and patriarchal legacies of colonization. Indigenous women are leading the work of rematriation, that is, working to restore the sacred relationship between Indigenous peoples and their ancestral lands while honoring their matrilineal ancestral languages and cultural ways.

In this chapter I invite us to consider the layout of the social landscape, its organizational forms, and institutional actors from the perspective of those most marginalized in our society. In particular,

I invite us to think about the nonprofit sector in its complex relationship to the state, to the market, and to those most disenfranchised and their relevant social movements for just and decolonial futures. This is a potent time to study, interrogate, and engage in a much-needed assessment that considers what is and is not working about this societal layout for Black, Indigenous, and people of color. I invite readers to ask what is contributing to continued disenfranchisement and death and to engage in fruitful dialogue that sparks a creative imagining of decolonial, antiracist social worlds and futures that are more just.

Many scholars have written about the historic entanglements of the state and the nonprofit sector. In its most recent history, the nonprofit sector in the United States was formalized in 1969 through the Tax Reform Act, a law that produced Section 501(c)3 in the Internal Revenue Service Code that grants tax-exempt status to charitable organizations (Internal Revenue Service, 2023). Because nonprofits are typically dependent on the state for financial and other resources, many scholars have raised concerns about the impact the state has on the nonprofit sector. Less attention has been focused on the state-driven shaping of the nonprofit sector and its effects on marginalized communities and the social movements that many of them are ostensibly designed to serve. This chapter addresses some of the understudied ways in which the deep intertwining of the state, the market, and nonprofit organizations have produced harmful consequences for Indigenous peoples, people of color, and their related social movements.

Ruth Wilson Gilmore discusses the term "shadow state" to signal the expansion of nonprofit service delivery organizations amid the neoliberal state's social abandonment in the 1970s (Gilmore, 2017). Referencing Wolch's (1990) notion of the shadow state, Gilmore (2017) speaks to the wide-scale withdrawal of government services in the 1970s and the rise of the nonprofit service-oriented industry in the 1980s. According to Gilmore, the shrinking of state social services amplified the idea and structure that uplifts the market as the most efficient to capably meet the people's needs.

Under neoliberal economic arrangements, the state's primary accountability shifts from the *people* to the *economic sector*. The nonprofit industry, which has also been labeled the third sector, stepped in to absorb what it could of the remaining unmet need, but its capacity and structural arrangements limit both its ability to do so and its work. This shift marks the third sector's turn away from political organizing toward social-service delivery. As its 501(c)(3) structure implies, the form of the nonprofit necessitates constant engagement with the state and the market; these entanglements set up the possibilities for its existence.

Amid professionalizing and fiduciary responsibilities, the nonprofit structure is principally accountable to its funders and the state, a turn that subordinates if not outrightly exterminates political organizing. As movement leader and elder Madonna Thunder Hawk (Oohenumpa Lakota from the Cheyenne River Sioux) observes, "The focus turned to raising money to keep the organization going, while the actual work of activism became secondary and watered down. And when the money disappeared, the work did too. Before we focused on how to organize to make change, but now most people will only work within funding parameters" (Thunder Hawk, 2017, p. 105).

Under tax laws and public- and foundation-grant guidelines, political nonprofit work (organizing and/or political activity) is at best belittled and underfunded; at worst it is banned. Yet, in the twenty-first century, the nonprofit model has become the dominant organizational form for social movements.

Some activists express dismay for the ways nonprofitization removes social, political, and financial power from the most marginalized communities and their efforts for social change (INCITE!, 2017). As concerns grew over the nonprofit structure's growing impact on social movements, activists in the early 2000s started using the term *nonprofit industrial complex* to describe how the structuring and expansion of the nonprofit sector reflects the interests of the state and economic sectors while also curtailing social movements concerned with social, political, and economic injustice. The INCITE! movement and affiliated scholar-activists at the University of California, Santa Barbara hosted a conference entitled, "The Revolution Will Not Be Funded: The Non-Profit Industrial Complex" in 2004. The term "nonprofit industrial complex" stems from prior activist engagement with the phrase *prison industrial complex*, which gained popularity in the late 1990s and references the ways the interests of the state and the economy converge through policing, surveillance, and imprisonment instead of addressing the social, political, and economic issues that undergird heightened police violence and the incarceration of communities of color. (This term, in turn, is a reference to Eisenhower's use of the *military industrial complex*, which he used to describe the intertwining of the state and the warfare industry that were gaining dominance in determining the country's political goals.) The term "prison industrial complex" gained popularity at the 1998 conference held at the University of California, Berkeley, "Critical Resistance: Beyond the Prison Industrial Complex." According to Critical Resistance, an organization that was created at the conference, the term "prison industrial complex" speaks to the ways the interests of the state and the economy converge through policing, surveillance, and imprisonment instead of addressing the social, political, and economic issues that undergird heightened police violence and incarceration of Black, Brown and Indigenous communities. The term "nonprofit industrial complex" builds on these prior concepts to express how state and economic sector interests converge through the structuring and expansion of the nonprofit sector and how this convergence curtails social movements concerned with social, political, and economic injustice.

Among the concerns encapsulated in the concept of the nonprofit industrial complex is a situation in which nonprofit organizations that purport to address social problems are ideologically moved to secure consistent streams of funding first instead of organizing for social change. Worse yet, in the process some nonprofits perpetuate and even exacerbate the social justice issues they claim to address. The nonprofitization of social movements strips them of efficacy, making them look like the white Western capitalist markets from whence nonprofit corporate forms emerged. This marketization, monetization, and professionalization of the nonprofit sector creates a system in which often well-meaning individuals and organizations profit from the misfortunes of others (e.g., by monetizing their pain in the form of stories sold to funders). They do so without making systematic change and often while entrenching and exacerbating the authority structures that are to blame for the problems in the first place. In other words, the nonprofit structure becomes a path to maintaining an unjust status quo and legitimating unequal social orders alongside the state and economic interests that produce such unjust arrangements and outcomes. Rather than creating a space that protects people from the overreach of both the state and the market, the nonprofit structure urges organizations toward participating in the same mechanisms that have entrenched social problems deep into the fabric of our society.

8.1 The Nonprofit Industrial Complex: Three Critiques

By partnering with the public and private sectors, the nonprofit sector extends interests that continue to subjugate Indigenous peoples, women, people of color, and other minority groups. This is particularly problematic because one rationale for the nonprofit sector is its role in remedying flaws – particularly those affecting marginalized communities – in the market and in government systems. This dissonance between the purported purpose of the sector and its actual institutional structure and sociocultural results merits deeper examination.

This section of the chapter examines three aspects of this issue in particular. The first is the state-marketization of the nonprofit sector through the corporate model, grantmaking, and state activity. These factors ensure that the interests of the state and the economy structurally reflect dominant, economic interests and ignore or exacerbate harms to marginalized communities. The second is the nonprofitization of social movements. Organizations gain dominant priority in terms of their economic survival (funding), identity, and economic structuring, while attention to social-movement work is subordinated if not left by the wayside. The third is the state's authority to use coercion and force – including policing – to address what it perceives to be social problems and issues. When the nonprofit sector is intertwined with the state in addressing social problems, it becomes complicit in the process of engaging policing and coercion to meet the state's – rather than the people's – objectives. Overall, these three points, addressed in turn below, examine the ways in which white supremacy is promoted through the state and capitalist structuring of the nonprofit sector, disadvantaging the interests and voices of communities of color and the voices of Black, Indigenous, and people of color.

8.1.1 Ideology for Sale: The State-Marketization of the Nonprofit Sector

While contemporary theories of the nonprofit sector suggest a three-sector system in which markets are distinct from the state and nonprofits are distinct from both markets and the state, a view of financial flows between these three institutions reveals that they are, in fact, part of the same industrial complex. This means that not only does money flow from the market to the state and from the state to nonprofits (as well as directly from the market to nonprofits), the interests that maintain these financial flows are linked as well.

Many scholars have documented the white colonialist interests that have undergirded American capitalism historically since the time of the founding of the US government and into the current era. Cedric Robinson coined the term *racial capitalism* to examine the ways that racialized exploitation reinforces capital accumulation and vice versa (Robinson, 2019). Put simply by Gilmore (2018), "racial capitalism is all capitalism. There was not one minute in the entire story of capitalism that it was not racial" (p. 14). What is less often acknowledged is that the nonprofit system is rooted – financially and philosophically – in the same market and state institutions, and that despite claims that nonprofits are working to address and resolve social problems, they are funded by the same market and state sources that instantiate racial capitalism, such as grantmaking and funding requirements. For example, grantmakers identify the specific interests, issues, and methodologies they will and will not fund, thus contributing to less democratic control and more centralized, self-interested control in the nonprofit system. As long as the primary funders of nonprofit efforts remain private industry heads (who benefit from the market capitalist system that subjugates women and people of color) and state actors (who are elected and maintain power by support from dominant sectors and capitalist-funded interests), the flow of funding and power to the nonprofit sector will continue to be explicitly shaped by interests that benefit from the continuation of specific power structures and social dynamics that disadvantage women and people of color.

If the sources of nonprofit funding emerge from unequal capitalist and state sources that accumulate power and wealth in the hands of the few, then funding will go toward that which continues such unequal capitalist and state social arrangements. In other words, to paraphrase the title of the book *The Revolution Will Not Be Funded*, the government and the market will not fund movements whose aim is to dismantle injustices. Doing so would cause them to fund the social transformation of racial capitalism, which instantiates the racial inequities and social violence that targets and structurally subordinates Indigenous and people of color in the first place. As I have written before, "Paolo Freire [Brazilian scholar and activist] once said that violence is an instrument of terror intended to immobilize the opponent; it stands then that the non-profit industrial complex is guilty of deploying the violence of non-profitization, an attempt to sink our movements" (Rojas Durazo, 2017, 126). This chapter builds on activist work since the early 2010s and invites us to consider some of the ways nonprofitization "immobilizes" the movements for justice wielded by marginalized communities.

8.1.2 Pathologizing Social Issues and Social Movements

One way that state and market actors target and disempower women and people of color – as well as their social movements – is by invoking a Western, scientific approach to the diagnosis of social problems. Some pathologize social ills through individualizing a problem instead of occluding the sociopolitical context that, through inequity, is responsible for producing the social problem. This practice creates significant issues that prevent us from holistically viewing and addressing the problems that continue to be pervasive in society – particularly those that affect and disenfranchise peoples of color.

When we presume that the role of the nonprofit sector is to "solve social problems," we invoke a problem-centric, medical model of diagnosis and treatment. For example, identifying the personal and social dynamics that lead to problems like domestic violence or child abuse could be considered good faith efforts to address and remedy the sources of these problems. However, identifying and classifying social ills within an already racial, capitalist order contributes to the pathologizing and targeting of Indigenous and communities of color. Building on our prior analysis that exposes the ways the state and capitalist economy are principally invested in self-perpetuation, it follows that deflecting the culpability for social ills produced by this social order leads to the pathologizing of Black, Indigenous, and women of color, and even our communities as themselves being responsible for social problems like violence. As a result, instead of rightly identifying these communities as targets of the state and market-perpetrated violence and subjugation, they become the suspect – surveilled, punished, incarcerated, separated, and disappeared – targeted doubly by the imagined ways they are viewed as principally responsible for producing social problems.

Using a scientific or medical lens, the state and market diagnose social problems like violence as originating at the level of the individual, a view that deflects attention from the ways gender and racial violence are structured by the state and the economy into the social fabric of society. Structuring society by race and gender leads to increased exposure of women to gender-based violence (Heise et al. 2002) and the disproportionate targeting, arresting, imprisoning, and killing of peoples of color (see Rucker and Richeson 2021). These phenomena are even worse for LGBTQ members of these communities (Jones 2021, Truman and Morgan 2022). While it is the state and the economy that structure the conditions that produce social problems, those conditions are rarely – if ever – addressed as a target of analysis, political interrogation, and mobilization (through grants and funding). In other words, when the state or the market invokes the authority of science to direct attention to a problem within a community of color, it misdirects attention away from the actual root cause, which is endemic in the racial capitalist system itself and within the coercive power of the state (to which point we will turn in the next section).

One way this misdirection happens systematically is through nonprofitization, a government-controlled process that regulates and prohibits a nonprofit's engagement with politics. Containing the political engagement of nonprofits limits the potential for social transformation, but it also conditions the possibility for the state-based, economic, or institutional violence against targeted groups like women and peoples of color to be relegated outside the scope of nonprofit work. Therefore, this violence is imagined to be disparate or dislodged from the interrelated, interpersonal violence within these targeted communities.

Rather than naming and considering the long history and present-day reality of state-based violence that targets these communities, the racial, capitalist state uses nonprofitization to frame *individual* and *interpersonal* issues as legitimate problems to spend time and money addressing, which leads society to ignore the *systemic* problems that the racial, capitalist state itself produces. For example, I have written in a prior essay about migrant women who are violently targeted by the border patrol or the police. Antiviolence organizations are structured toward silencing this type of violence by government agents; they are "paid" to turn their eye solely to what is deemed the legitimate and fundable social problem: women attacked by an intimate partner or domestic violence (Rojas Durazo, 2017). Nonprofits are placed in a precarious relationship to the state and other funders, whose monetary support they ultimately want to secure. This structural precarity functions as a barrier, blocking organizations from taking to task or challenging violence committed by state actors and agencies. This state of precarity is ultimately a means for co-opting or redirecting the energies of nonprofits, making them organize, behave, and operate in ways that might differ from their intent, and it merits further consideration in the literature.

As stated earlier, the Western medical model of disease deflects the political causation of social problems, instead individualizing the origin of a problem/illness. Likewise, the term *medical industrial complex*, yet another partnering of the state and capitalism by way of medical and pharmaceutical corporations, co-opts social justice issues by taking them under its jurisdiction. Just as the criminalization of violence against women emerged alongside the growth of the prison industrial complex, the medicalization of violence against women is closely linked to the growing privatization and corporatization of health care (Rojas Durazo, 2016). Through policies such as health practitioner mandatory-reporting policies, the medical industrial complex interfaces with the prison industrial complex to support state and economic interests in the criminalization of violence against women. For instance, mandatory-reporting policies require that health-care providers report suspected abuse to law enforcement. But survivor advocates argue that these policies disregard a survivor's choice in the matter of reaching out to law enforcement, especially when the survivor could be revictimized and under increased danger of being arrested or deported (Rojas Durazo, 2016). In a racial, capitalist economy, the medical industrial complex and the prison industrial complex principally promote profit, often at the expense and victimization of the most marginalized members of society, such as women of color.

The medicalization of social problems in communities of color is driven by an agenda to depoliticize our social movements. The racial, hierarchical, and organizational structures of corporations and the state are extended to nonprofit organizations, which are increasingly viewed as the "legitimate" ways to organize ourselves and pursue social change. In this way, our social movements become corporatized mini models of the market economy, driven by funding streams and concerned with survival and success of their organizations instead of social change.

Adopting a corporate structure alters the makeup of grassroots, horizontal movements and organizations into hierarchical, professionalized establishments that have limited power to enact change, and that have CEOs and CFOs to dominate them. In my work during and since the antiviolence movement of the 1990s, I have witnessed the development and growth of private and public funding that encourages, or requires, a "system-based" response. The nonprofitization of the antiviolence movement in the 1990s, for example, led to organizations being coerced to work alongside or within racial, capitalist, and white supremacist structures. Inviting – or even requiring – nonprofits to be at the table within such circumstances extended professionalization and hierarchical structuring to their organizations, redirecting their efforts toward system-supporting activities like social-service delivery. Social services – and the turn toward social servicization as a dominant, fundable aspect of the nonprofit – thus limited the amount of time, energy, and imagination nonprofits could devote to social transformation.

8.1.3 Invoking the Coercive Power of the State: Violence and Criminalization

Charles Tilly (1990) identified the coercive use of force as one of the key distinguishing features of government institutions. Whether this use of force is maintained by democracy or autocracy is almost irrelevant – the point is that one of the ways state power is mobilized is through the use of force against the citizenry in order to enforce its will. As I have discussed in this chapter, many scholars view the nonprofit sector as either deeply entwined with (in terms of interests, finances, and will) or as a direct extension of the state (Gilmore, 2017; Rodriguez, 2017; Thunder Hawk, 2017). The most obvious evidence of this interconnectedness is the granting of specific tax benefits to nonprofit organizations to enhance their ability to receive both legitimacy and funding. Nonprofit organizations enjoy significant tax benefits, and some (those designated as 501(c)(3) charities) also benefit from economic incentives such as tax-deductible donations. This entwining can be considered a symbolic, coercive force through which the state and the economy affect the life and work of a nonprofit. Through the nonprofit structure, a nonprofit's economic outlook becomes its dominant aspect, while its other work outside of its economic survival and identity becomes a byproduct of its funding. In other words, an organization's political autonomy from the state, grantmakers, and the economic sector shrinks as their accountability shifts from their prior constituents or *raison d'être* to funding-stream sources.

Not only are the financial connections between the state and the nonprofit sector formal and explicit, in many cases – particularly in situations in which communities or people of color and the state may have discord or opposing interests – the nonprofit structure also links nonprofits with military and policing interests in ways that often disadvantage peoples of color and their voices. The role of policing in peaceful protest and the role of the military and other federal bodies in immigration-related concerns are just a few of the most obvious and high-profile spaces in which nonprofit interests must institutionally align with state interests and state-sanctioned force.

As Angela Davis (2000) astutely observed, violence is not an unexpected aberration in the order of things; rather, violence is the knife that cuts and the thread that sews the racist imperial nation together: thus, violence is the order of things. The state functions not only to deploy violence but to organize it as well. As I wrote in an earlier essay, violence "creates and separates nation-states, slices us into genders and sexes, Global North and South, distances the suburbs from the inner cities, Brown and [B]lack from [w]hite" (Rojas Durazo, 2017, p. 121). The nonprofit industry, with its structural embeddedness in the state, is unavoidably summoned to be complicit with the violence the state fosters. The neoliberal state acts through incorporation, and our task is to assess the fallout.

When antiviolence movements are structured to participate directly in criminal proceedings by way of funded positions in district attorney offices or in police education and engagement opportunities, grassroots organizing and the potential for social transformation is squandered into the role of advocacy within the limits of the criminalization process and the criminal system. Creative solutions and imagination that might lead to the deep transformation of the root causes of domestic violence, for example, are siphoned into programmed responses to "call the cops," which action exposes Black, Brown, Indigenous and migrant communities to revictimization and potentially the entire criminal and detention response and process at the hands of the police. Through funding streams, the antiviolence movement is entrenched in the prison and detention industrial complex.

As Wolch (1990) described, the nonprofit industrial complex enlists a dynamic of collaboration with the state, constricting a group's or a movement's autonomy. Political imagination, one of the most vital nutrients to a social movement, is particularly affected by this arrangement. In the case of antiviolence feminist movements, such an entrenchment in practice builds an alliance between the antiviolence movement and the state. Through this alliance, the state furthers the ideological myth that it is not responsible for violence, thus evading accountability for it. The state is instead imagined and legitimated as an antiviolence partner to the antiviolence movement.

Dylan Rodriguez (2017) studied the ways such partnering or collaboration has its roots in the state's conspiratorial practices. He cited the example of COINTELPRO, which launched deliberate strikes to halt the rise of liberation struggles in the United States around the same time that the nonprofit industrial complex was forged. Rodriguez referenced Robert Allen's (1990) *Black awakening in capitalist America*, a pivotal, early, and astute assessment of the role white philanthropic organizations played in facilitating violent attempts to repress Black, Indigenous, Latinx, and other Third World liberation movements in the 1960s and 1970s. Allen argued that philanthropic efforts to absorb moderate Black capitalist or electoral-based Black organizations facilitated the targeting, criminalization, and elimination of more radical elements and leadership, which impeded, altogether eliminated, or literally killed some of the most potent leadership of contemporary social movements.

One of the ways the state moved this agenda forward in the late 1960s is through the Kerner Commission, which framed civil disobedience, riots, and similar public outcry among marginalized communities as violence. The Kerner Commission was a forerunner to the National Commission on the Causes and Prevention of Violence, a federally appointed body assigned to the task of investigating and making policy recommendations on "the problem of 'lawless acts' of violence," such as disrespecting public officials and the law or violently disrupting public order (Reiss, 1993, p. x). By calling violence "lawless," this commission was tasked to create the idea that violence is outside, and in opposition to, the jurisdiction of the state. The commission also labeled resistance strategies as criminal or behavioral issues, relegating them to the prison industrial complex or the medical industrial complex, respectively. Using these frameworks further individualized notions of violence and undergirded the turn toward the social servicization of violence against women, and the state slipped itself out of scrutiny for its role in the production, organization, and deployment of violence.

Gramsci's notion of "common sense" illustrates the ways through which consent among marginalized communities is achieved through the state's education and ideological disciplining (Gramsci, 1971). "Common sense" is a kind of ideological coercion that emerges through culture and an array of social institutions; along with the nonprofit, prison, and medical industrial complexes, "common sense" produces hegemonic rule. In the case of the antiviolence movement, as the state posits itself as an ally in ending violence against women, the antiviolence movement grows its dependence on the state's ideology of violence – in addition to its funding. Through funding and the disbursement of ideology, our society comes to expect and even need prisons, psychiatrists, and medicine as the imagined solution to the elimination of violence against women. This is executed most directly in the front lines of the nonprofit sector.

Physician, cultural, and earth worker Rupa Marya and Raj Patel's (2021) incisive *Inflamed: Deep Medicine and the Anatomy of Injustice* seeks to displace the dominance social institutions wield in their supposed ability to address violence and social problems. Marya and Patel proposed the term *deep medicine* to suggest that if the causes of violence and illness are tied to systemic oppression and target marginalized communities through colonial, racial, and sexual structural inequities, then their true remedies lie outside these institutions. "Practitioners of modern medicine," Marya posited, "are not trained to be healers." Because the causes of illness and harm lie outside the patient, doctors are at a loss: "The healing process must involve restructuring the world to make it a safe place for survivors to flourish – in other words, deep wounds require deep medicine" (p. 70). Deep medicine is a call for courageous action to dismantle/transform the structures that give rise to gross inequities as the very source of harm, violence, and illness. Marya and Patel's work invites us to deeply reckon – to account for the myriad coercive powers of the state and its state violence, and to set forth in implementing practices and structures to guide us toward another way of living.

8.2 An Application

As stated earlier, the United States uses racial capitalism to ensure the continuation of structures that support white supremacy. Although we are taught to think of racism as the expression of overt racist attitudes (e.g., when politicians express racist attitudes), white supremacy is often structured in ways that might be more subtle and difficult to discern as such, even manifesting in ways that purport to address issues faced by communities of color. White supremacist structures and attitudes are embedded in the nonprofit sector as it derives these structures and attitudes from its state and market counterparts.

While working in the "Latina program" at the Support Network for Battered Women in 1995, I learned that an immigrant Latina had been brutally beaten by "la Migra" (immigration law enforcement). In response, I wrote an op-ed on behalf of the program that opposed all forms of violence against Latinas, including both domestic violence and anti-immigrant state violence. The executive director's approval was needed prior to publishing anything, and when I approached her with the piece, she told me the organization's board would never allow such an opinion to represent it because our organization was not allowed to take political stances. Apparently, the INS-ICE beating (but not domestic violence) qualified as a political issue (Rojas Durazo, 2017).

In this example, my work with Latinas serves as an example of the many ways ethnic or race-specific programs have become a staple in nonprofits and antiviolence programs. These programs are anchored in the logic of the liberalist project of multiculturalism, but this organizational strategy employs and furthers some of the pinnacle logic of white supremacy – the assumption of universal whiteness that structurally others/marginalizes communities of color. In a similar way to how white supremacy is structured in the larger society, the use of multiculturalist ideals permit nonprofits and antiviolence organizations to continue using a hierarchically organized white supremacist structure for distributing resources (e.g., salary, benefits, and travel opportunities). However, this results in giving programs designed to serve communities of color within larger organizations the smallest share of their organization's economic resources. White supremacy is also structured in organizations through other means, such as decision-making power. Although white supremacist arrangements seem inconsistent with organizational objectives to prioritize diversity in principle and foster and promote relationships with peoples of color inside and outside of organizations, they nonetheless persevere through various aspects of hierarchical organization in nonprofits.

As I have addressed throughout this chapter, the political move to structure violence as a crime created the notion that violence is a crime.

The contemporary vernacular that normatively conflates violence with crime through such terminology as "violent crimes" or "hate crimes" reflects relatively recent iterations emerging through the prison industrial complex. Violence is imagined as a crime to serve the interests of racial capitalism and the racial state. For example, through the criminalization of domestic violence, an individual perpetrator is imagined as the sole party responsible for violence, which buttresses the state's notion that prisons are the solution to domestic violence. However, the prison industrial complex has been disastrous to the safety of women of color and our communities. The criminalization of domestic violence has, over the last 15 years of social experimentation, grown the prison industrial complex through expansionist criminalization policies for mandatory arrest, third-strike policies, new crime legislation, and steeper sentences.

Long-term antiviolence activist Suzanne Pharr (2004) poignantly addressed some of the concerns that arise with the nonprofitization of the antiviolence movement. When women doing antiviolence work sought tax-exempt status for shelters, organizers were taunted with lesbian and misogynist jokes and funders demanded of the institutions certain policies and practices, including professionalization. Soon funders were expressing their preference for degree-bearing professionals instead of community organizers, organizations were expected to have hierarchical structures, and therapeutic social services were funded over popular education work. Ideologically, violence against women became more and more a behavioral, criminal, and medical phenomenon rather than a social justice issue, and interventions and attempts at prevention became overly reliant on therapy and the courts. These individualized methods of intervention fail to address and combat the social organization of violence against women. These methods are also inextricable from institutional arrangements that carry deep histories of racism like the medical industrial complex and the prison industrial complex; as a result, the revictimization of women of color becomes more likely (Rojas Durazo, 2017).

Yet amidst recognizing, accounting, and grappling with the losses that nonprofitization delivers to social movements, all is not lost. As Rodriguez (2017, p. 31) argued,

> As the distance between state authority and civil society collapses, the civic spaces for resistance ... disperse into places unheard, unseen, by the nonprofit industry: arguably the most vibrant sites of ... organizing against

racist US state violence ... are condensing among populations that the NPIC [nonprofit industrial complex] cannot easily or fully incorporate. Organized, under-organized, and ad hoc movements of imprisoned, homeless, and undocumented peoples, as well as activists committed to working beneath and relatively autonomous of the NPIC's political apparatus, may well embody the beginnings of an alternative US-based praxis that displaces the NPIC's apparent domination of political discourse and possibility.

Such were the conditions that gave rise to the potent twenty-first-century social movements such as Black Lives Matter, the #NoDAPL movement to stop construction of the Dakota Access Pipeline, and the undocumented-student nationwide walkouts and protests against HR 4437, the Border Protection, Antiterrorism, and Illegal Immigration Control Act of 2005. Indeed, the conditions are always ripe for justice, the arc is always leaning toward decolonization, the path toward radical freedom is daily being imagined anew; and with every instance of attempts to derail it, of moves to absorb insurgencies, new and vibrant life and imagination will persist like the rose or weed growing outside my door on the broken concrete sidewalks that line the Oakland city streets.

8.3 Conclusions

The recent pandemic years, marked by heightened economic austerity and political interests that defunded many nonprofits, demonstrated the precarity the nonprofit structure straddles. They also demonstrated that the work of social justice will continue outside of fundable work and/or nonprofit structures. The work to survive and to resist unjust conditions will persist because contesting violence is human nature. The insurrections against police brutality in what some call the Black spring of 2020 taught us that some, if not most, of the effective paths toward social transformation emerge from efforts on the fringes, from movements and forms organized collectively or with horizontal (or even no) leadership structures, like the Zapatistas concept of "mandar obedeciendo [lead by obeying]." Some movements even are nonprofits on paper while they strategically navigate a focused direction toward social transformation that tactically accepts financial resources while rejecting co-opting tendencies.

Social movement leader Paula X. Rojas (2017) postulated that we may not necessarily need to get rid of nonprofits altogether. Cautioning that we must remain vigilant and critical of the risk of being co-opted through nonprofits, she shared that many revolutionary movements in Latin America and around the world use nonprofits strategically. They do not try to do movement work through the nonprofit but rather form nonprofits for strategic purposes, like technical support. They still strive to build social movements, but they do it outside their nonprofits. With these examples in mind, Rojas concluded, "the non-profit does not have the power to determine the course of the movement's direction. Rather, it is accountable to the movement" (p. 207).

Social movement work has always and will always continue to exist outside of the nonprofit sector. As social movements are successful in attaining their greater goals toward social transformation, they will find a way to keep the corporatist and state influences in check. How? For one, by ensuring that their organizations have accountability structured into their work on a daily basis, especially accountability to the people most affected by the social issues they address. Additionally, organizations should structure self-assessment and evaluation into their work; as the conditions for social change constantly shift, they will need to constantly engage the communities that are most affected to determine their needs. Organizations can also shift fundraising energies to grassroots techniques, which maintain an organization's proximity to their grassroots.

Some might choose an outright refusal to seek nonprofit status with the state, intentionally becoming part of the "dark matter" of the nonprofit institutional space (Smith, 2017). This means giving up government and corporate grants – which come with the burden of marionette strings – and seeking autonomy by relying on the visions, resourcefulness, and resources of the people in the social movement themselves. Organizations who choose to use these methods will have a better chance at inspiring social justice, though no structure is inherently exempt from co-optation.

Additionally, it is absolutely possible for social movements to challenge and end white supremacy as they organize freely from the violence and coercion of both the state and corporatized market forces. By defining a vision and identifying the ways in which the current institutional landscape fails to meet that vision, movements can create a lexicon of terms, which can become shared principles of unity. When we name the purveyors of violence, for example, we are that much closer to gathering forces to transform the conditions that give the purveyors the power to dominate. As we name violence against women and peoples of color, profit-centered interests that harm targeted communities, and the various iterations of colonialism, these names help us walk toward articulating a vision and a praxis for a free, decolonial, and just world, gathering the needed forces to help create the conditions that will usher its emergence.

"In a time of rapacious capitalism," long-term activist Suzanne Pharr asked, "what might we do to fund a radical movement?" (Rojas, 2017, 125). As the examples of Communities against Rape and Abuse, INCITE!, Sista ii Sista, and Communities United against Violence reveal, many organizations are leading the way toward disinvesting from the nonprofit industrial complex and the state. They are redirecting precious time, resources, and imagination to grassroots organizing and to mobilizing their communities. And they are emerging victorious!

Ruthie Wilson Gilmore's closing remark sums up much of the insight shared at the Revolution Will Not Be Funded Conference: "organizations will not save us, organizing will" (see Gilmore, 2004). Organizing in this case might mean letting go of organizational structure itself, intentionally trusting that a movement's work for social transformation will continue. We cannot afford to let formal structures become more important than our vision and purpose, and any structural form is at risk of corruption. We can free ourselves from organizational hierarchies (which often reproduce or mirror social hierarchies based on race, sex, class, and gender) and professionalization. We can let go of ideas from funders about doing the work in the "right" way (whether this refers to effectiveness, efficiency, using evidence-based practices, integrating community, etc.). We can instead focus on the community we want to create as we work together toward a shared vision. What would we – and what could that shared vision – create instead? The options are numerous and infinite, yet of this much I am sure, the movement toward social transformation needs us to practice vehemently being the communities we seek to create, through mutual accountability, care, and interdependent living.

That journey may itself be the destination: the creation of a community that emerges as it is practiced.

References

Allen, R. (1990). *Black awakening in capitalist America: An analytic history.* Africa World Press.

Davis, A. (2000, October 10). The color of violence against women. *Colorlines.* www.colorlines.com/articles/color-violence-against-women

Erickson-Schroth, L., Wu, S. X., & Glaeser, E. (2020). Sexual and gender-based violence in lesbian, gay, bisexual, transgender, and queer communities. Sexual and Gender-Based Violence: A Complete Clinical Guide, Springer 113–126.

Gilmore, R. W. (2004). Closing speech at Revolution Will Not Be Funded Conference, University of California, Santa Barbara.

Gilmore, R. W. (2017). In the shadow of the shadow state. In INCITE! Women of Color Against Violence (Ed.), *The revolution will not be funded: Beyond the non-profit industrial complex* (pp. 41–52). Duke University Press.

Gilmore, R. W. (2018). Making abolition geography in California's Central Valley. *The Funambulist, 21*, 14–15. https://thefunambulist.net/magazine/21-space-activism/interview-making-abolition-geography-california-central-valley-ruth-wilson-gilmore

Gramsci, A. (1971). *Selections from the prison notebooks of Antonio Gramsci.* Lawrence & Wishart.

Heise, L., Ellsberg, M., & Gottmoeller, M. (2002) A global overview of gender-based violence. International Journal of Gynecology & Obstetrics, 78, S5–S14.

INCITE! Women of Color Against Violence (Ed.). (2017). *The revolution will not be funded: Beyond the non-profit industrial complex.* Duke University Press.

Internal Revenue Service. (2023, February 6). *Exemption requirements – 501(c)(3) organizations.* www.irs.gov/charities-non-profits/charitable-organizations/exemption-requirements-501c3-organizations

Jones, A (2021, March 2). Visualizing the unequal treatment of LGBTQ people in the criminal justice system. www.prisonpolicy.org/blog/2021/03/02/lgbtq/

Marya, R., & Patel, R. (2021). *Inflamed: Deep medicine and the anatomy of injustice.* Farrar, Straus and Giroux.

Pharr, S. (2004). INCITE! The Revolution Will Not Be Funded: Beyond the Nonprofit Industrial Complex Conference, UC Santa Barbara. https://soundcloud.com/user-869100178/rwnbf-suzanne-pharr-highlander-center

Reiss, A., Jr. (1993). *Understanding and preventing violence.* National Research Council, Ed. National Academy Press.

Robinson, J. C. (2019). *Cedric J. Robinson: On racial capitalism, Black internationalism, and cultures of resistance*. H. L. T. Quan, Ed. Pluto Press.

Rodriguez, D. (2017). The political logic of the non-profit industrial complex. In INCITE! Women of Color Against Violence (Ed.), *The revolution will not be funded: Beyond the non-profit industrial complex* (pp. 21–40). Duke University Press.

Rojas, P. X. (2017). Are the cops in our heads and hearts? In INCITE! Women of Color Against Violence (Ed.), *The revolution will not be funded: Beyond the non-profit industrial complex* (pp. 197–214). Duke University Press.

Rojas Durazo, A. C. (2016). Medical violence against people of color and the medicalization of domestic violence. In INCITE! Women of Color Against Violence (Ed.), *Color of violence: The INCITE! anthology*. Duke University Press.

Rojas Durazo, A. C. (2017). We were never meant to survive: Fighting violence against women and the fourth world war. In INCITE! Women of Color Against Violence (Ed.), *The revolution will not be funded: Beyond the non-profit industrial complex* (pp. 113–128). Duke University Press.

Romero, F. J. (2021, March 30). California's working-age Latinos are disproportionately dying of COVID-19. *KQED*. www.kqed.org/news/11866749/californias-working-age-latinos-are-disproportionately-dying-of-covid-19

Rucker, J. M., & Richeson, J. A. (2021) Toward an understanding of structural racism: Implications for criminal justice. Science, 374(6565), 286–290.

Smith, A. (2017). Introduction: The revolution will not be funded. In INCITE! Women of Color Against Violence (Ed.), *The revolution will not be funded: Beyond the non-profit industrial complex* (pp. 1–18). Duke University Press.

Thunder Hawk, M. (2017). Native organizing before the non-profit industrial complex. In INCITE! Women of Color Against Violence (Ed.), *The revolution will not be funded: Beyond the non-profit industrial complex* (pp. 101–106). Duke University Press.

Tilly, C. (1990). *Coercion, capital, and European states, AD 990–1990*. Blackwell.

Truman, J. L., & Morgan, R. E. (2022). Violent Victimization by Sexual Orientation and Gender Identity, 2017–2020. US Department of Justice, Office of Justice Programs, Bureau of Justice Statistics.

Wolch, J. (1990). *The shadow state: Government and the voluntary sector in transition*. Foundation Center. https://doi.org/10.1002/nml.4130030310

9 *Sector Theorists Should Be Inclusive of Muslim and Non-Western Perspectives*

SHARIQ SIDDIQUI

Nonprofits are a highly visible instrument through which modern society organizes solutions to social problems. In the United States, nonprofit organizations have become an important part of the government's delivery of public goods. In Saudi Arabia, government institutions, such as universities, hospitals, and other public entities, are being intentionally transformed into nonprofit organizations as part of the country's Vision 2030, which seeks to intentionally reorient the country's economic and government structures in hope of a more vibrant future (Khan, 2020). Across the developing world, the nonprofit or nongovernmental organization is the partner of choice for foreign aid (Pallas & Sidel, 2020). While there is a great deal of interest in the management, leadership, capacity building, governance, and funding of nonprofit organizations, and a similar interest in the efficiencies such institutions bring to society, there is less examination of the fuel that drives this sector: the deeply personal and often heterogeneous values that individuals hold dear.

One powerful way of defining the nonprofit sector includes prosocial action by individuals, not just by formally organized corporate entities. This approach comprises prosocial behavior by every unit of society – individuals, loosely organized groups, and even formally recognized groups that have elected not to register as nonprofit organizations with the regulatory bodies of the state (Siddiqui, 2022). The advantage to nonprofit sector scholars of broadly defining the nonprofit sector in this way is that it allows them to examine the sociocultural roots of the sector, digging deeper into the question of why the nonprofit sector – including formally organized nonprofit corporate entities – actually exists. Using a sociocultural lens helps us to see the undercurrents of human behavior that shape the more rigid and institutionalized structures that might otherwise obscure the motivational roots of prosocial action.

Our modern understanding of social action is largely shaped by the actions of very wealthy or large institutions, like government and philanthropic foundations, rather than the day-to-day actions of ordinary people. Scholars have a tendency to define the nonprofit sector in terms of organizations rather than in terms of people and their actions and values. Our theories explain the rationale for legal and economic structures rather than detailing the very personal reasons that a person might, for example, donate money, provide voluntary service, or start a philanthropic organization.

The very macro-level social problems that government or nonprofit action address are actually, at their most fundamental, problems that stem from individual choices and actions. These actions are driven and justified by personal values (Schwartz & Bilsky, 1987). While scholars and practitioners look to organizations, macro-institutions, policies, and collaboratives to solve social problems, they are missing another approach that drives the prosocial engagement of nearly two billion people – about a quarter of the world's population – one informed by Muslim values and practices. The deeply held tenets of Muslim faith and tradition shape prosocial action in important ways that are rarely, if ever, accounted for in nonprofit sector theory. This gap exists because the history of nonprofit sector theory is largely driven by Western philosophies and perspectives that are – consciously or not – rooted in both Greco-Roman and Judeo-Christian perspectives (Siddiqui, 2022).

Western philosophy is so engrained in nonprofit scholarship that a ubiquitously accepted definition of nonprofit action, such as "voluntary action for the public good" (see, e.g., Payton, 1998; Payton & Moody, 2008) excludes many prosocial acts that Muslims consider to be important charitable deeds that should be included within the boundaries of the nonprofit sector. The Western framing of the nonprofit sector and prosocial behavior, with its Greco-Roman origins and transformation by the Scientific Philanthropy movement (Siddiqui, 2022), tends to prioritize the social-scientific side of prosocial action (McCully, 2012).

To achieve a more global view of prosocial action and incorporate insights from populations outside the West, the core definitions of nonprofit action need to be reframed and adapted to include Muslim perspectives. In the past, scholars who have sought to integrate Muslim philosophy and theology into studies of the nonprofit sector have used the Western definition of the sector as a lens through which to view Muslim practices, inadvertently limiting their fields of vision to the subset of Muslim practices that fit within the Western definition of nonprofit and voluntary action (Mattson 2010; Singer 2008). The dominance of Western definitions of prosocial voluntary action excludes certain Muslim charitable acts from consideration, thus limiting our view of what the global nonprofit sector includes and why it exists. The challenge to the field of study is not that there are competing "Western" and "Muslim" approaches to prosocial behavior in the nonprofit sector – rather, *all* such practices are informed by local culture and tradition. The problem is the privileging of Western scholarly framing of charitable action that has been heavily informed by scientific approaches, exclusive not only of Muslim viewpoints but of other localized and individual perspectives as well.

Unperturbed by the scholarly debate over the definition of the nonprofit sector, Muslims have engaged in charitable, humanitarian, and prosocial acts for centuries. The Quran (the holy book of Islam), the Sunnah (traditions of the Prophet Muhammad), and local customary practices influence Muslims' charitable acts. Scholars have focused on the Islamic practices of *waqf* (religious endowments), *Zakat* (obligatory giving), and *Sadaqah* (optional religious giving) as examples of Muslim prosocial activity, as these practices have natural Western correlates. However, an examination of Muslim practice suggests that while academic studies have approached understanding Muslim prosocial action through textual analysis or archival analysis, scholars have not paid enough attention to those customary practices that fall into the gap and thus are often unrecognized in scholarly discussions. Further complicating the study of Muslim prosocial behavior is the fact that many schools of thought within Islamic law permit Muslims to assimilate local social practices into Muslim religious practice, leading to regional variations in Muslim prosocial behavior.

In this chapter, I argue that a Western scholarly understanding of the nonprofit sector limits our understanding of Muslim prosocial behaviors that are less dominant in the academic literature. By examining the tenets and roots of Muslim prosocial action, we see how this specific view of social good has been limited in the broader conversation, which in turn has limited our understanding of the nonprofit sector across the world. I also explore Muslim prosocial action by examining its theological and cultural sources to create a broader conception of giving behavior within an Islamic context, and I discuss the challenges associated with strict adherence to the Western definition of the nonprofit sector for scholars who want to include Muslim perspectives and charitable acts. Ultimately, I suggest a framework that nonprofit sector scholars can use to move beyond Western-centric definitions of prosocial action to include other cultural and faith perspectives. This approach treats Muslim prosocial action as a practice-oriented religious tradition.

9.1 A Critique of Modern Conceptions of the Nonprofit Sector

The premise of this chapter is that a Muslim nonprofit sector exists and is grounded in faith, tradition, and cultural practice. I argue that faith is rooted in both theology and practice. Because faith exists within human beings, who live in disparate communities and societies at different times, the meaning of faith is constantly evolving. Finally, I argue that Muslim nonprofit action and giving behavior should not be constrained by Western-centric or modern definitions of the sector. In exploring giving behavior by Muslims in Muslim societies and communities, scholars must try and understand these behaviors in their own culturally rooted terms. To do so, they need to understand Muslim cultural practices and conceptions regarding prosocial behavior. I suggest that rather than defining the nonprofit sector in a global manner, scholars should adopt frameworks that allow them to examine localized nonprofit and voluntary action, even as it continues to change and evolve.

The concept of philanthropy is at the heart of the nonprofit sector – particularly when we consider individual giving and prosocial behavior. Philanthropy includes not only financial giving but also nonmonetary giving behavior, and is closely tied to the structure of donative nonprofits, to organizations with significant volunteer components, and to organizations associated with the organizational procurement of funds for prosocial purposes. Thus, both formal and informal philanthropy create the conceptual tie between individual giving behavior and the formal nonprofit sector.

The word "philanthropy" is derived from an ancient Greek noun translated into Latin meaning "love of humanity" (Sulek, 2005). One commonly accepted definition of philanthropy is "voluntary action for the public good," which was coined by Robert Payton of the Indiana University Center on Philanthropy in an effort to promote the establishment of an academic disciplinary subject (Hall, 1999). Another popular academic definition was developed by Salamon (1992), who defined philanthropy as "the private giving of time or valuables (money, security, property) for public purposes" (p. 10). Van Til (1990) defined philanthropy as "the voluntary giving and receiving of time and money aimed (however imperfectly) towards the needs of charity and the interests of all in a better quality of life" (p. 34).

All of these definitions tend to privilege money and wealth as a dominant aspect of philanthropy (Sulek, 2010). McCully (2008, 2012) sought to broaden this definition, describing philanthropy as "private initiatives for the public good, focusing on quality of life" (p. 1). However, his synthesis is very US-centric and focuses on formal organizations. David Billis (2010) added community and family to his definition of philanthropy in an attempt to include non-Western traditions and culture.

The search for a definition of philanthropy reaches back to the playwright Aeschylus and his ancient Greek tragedy *Prometheus Bound* (fifth-century BC). Aeschylus described the character as "humanity loving" (*philanthropos tropos*), for having given fire (symbolizing technological civilization) and "blind hope" (optimism) to the earliest proto-humans, who had no culture. This connection of philanthropy to an ancient Greek play has been altered by Western-centric scientific methods and discourse, excluding some cultures', traditions', and religions' notions of philanthropy – including Islam's.

Embracing this Greek and Roman tradition, philanthropy became part of "civil religion" discourse. Prosocial actions came to be viewed in terms of the honor and dignity of the community. Historian Paul Veyne (1990) used the Greek term *euergetism* to refer to the expectation that the rich would contribute their wealth to help members of their community and in return would receive prestige and honor. Similar to the religious practices of paying tithes, euergetism was an established custom until it was replaced by more formal taxation. Euergetism tended to perpetuate inequalities of wealth and power (Isin & Lefebvre, 2005; Nicholls, 2020).

In the late Middle Ages, during the economic transformation of Europe and the rise of cities, the Western concept of charitable work continued to evolve. The so-called Poor Laws, or the Statute of

Charitable Uses of 1601, are considered a watershed moment – the first time "poverty was addressed in an organized and official way" (Payton & Moody, 2008). Modern charitable law is considered to have been created in this era, an era that arguably signals the beginning of the formal nonprofit sector. This deeply European, highly centralized, state-connected evolution of prosocial activity has continued to evolve into the legal structures and cultural norms that we readily recognize as part of the nonprofit sector today. This perspective leaves out, however, traditions, viewpoints, and practices that do not share the same origin or history.

The formalization of the nonprofit sector – as commonly conceived – continued to evolve in the American colonies, which adopted the English model of governance and organization (Phillips & Jung, 2015). John Winthrop's 1630 sermon "A Model of Christian Charity," which analyzed concern for the community on religious grounds; Benjamin Franklin's support of community institutions through philanthropic contributions; and Tocqueville's famous description of voluntary associations as a fixture of American civic life further framed the nonprofit sector as a largely Western and uniquely American phenomenon (Hall, 2006).

As the American experiment saw economic success and the wild fortunes and philanthropic empires of the captains of industry were established at the birth of the modern era (Bremmer, 1988), the union of corporatized wealth, formal and tax-advantaged philanthropic giving, and the tax-privileged status of US charities and philanthropic organizations led to a view that the nonprofit sector was, somehow, defined by these American institutions. Missing from this historical exploration and academic development of nonprofit sector theory is the parallel development of prosocial institutions rooted in the religious and cultural traditions of other parts of the world – including Islam.

9.2 What Western Nonprofit Sector Theory Overlooks: An Application

The Western definition of the nonprofit sector excludes the perspectives of many indigenous groups, religions, and traditions from conversations about the nature, content, and boundaries of the nonprofit sector, including the perspectives of Islam and the world's over 1.8 billion Muslims. A very limited definition of the nonprofit sector prevents us from acknowledging various prosocial behaviors, such as the many Muslim practices that are foundational to understanding both prosocial behavior and prosocial organizing for many people around the world.

Prosocial behavior in Islam is understood to mean the Muslim's moral obligation to do good for God (McChesney, 1995). For Muslims, this moral obligation has been defined by Islamic law (Fauzia, 2013), of which there are two primary sources: the Quran and the Sunnah. The Quran describes various prosocial behaviors, including *Zakat*, *Sadaqah*, *birr* (righteousness), *amal al-salihat* (good deeds), *khayr* (goodness), and *ihsan* (virtue) (Fauzia, 2013). Philanthropy, as commonly understood in Western traditions and as recognized by scholarship, generally points to three examples to illustrate Islamic philanthropy: Zakat, Sadaqah, and waqf.[1]

According to both the Quran and the Sunnah, Zakat is considered one of the five pillars of Islam, requiring Muslims to give 2.5% of their surplus income and assets to eight specific causes: to help the poor (Al-Fuqara), the needy (Al-Masakin), to compensate Zakat administrators, to evangelize Islam, to free those in bondage, to free people from debt, to further the cause of God, and to help travelers. The Quran describes Zakat as a means of purification and growth (Singer, 2008): Giving a fixed proportion of one's surplus purifies the remainder of the wealth, and God promises to multiply the giver's generosity many times over.

Some scholars question whether Zakat is a philanthropic principle. For example, Ingrid Mattson has argued that Zakat is a tax, not a philanthropic obligation, because in the past, the state collected and distributed the funds. Similarly, Robert Payton has asserted that since tithing is obligatory, it does not fall within the voluntary nature of philanthropy.[2] Singer (2018) has also posited that Zakat is not philanthropy because it is not voluntary or benevolent, but she has conceded that there is little historical evidence that Zakat was paid or apportioned by any premodern polity, thus distinguishing it from a tax levied by the state for the functioning of said state (Singer, 2018).

[1] For examples of scholarship on Muslim philanthropy, see: Singer (2008), McChesney (1995), Ilchman et al. (1998), and Ismail et al. (2013).

[2] Personal communication with Payton during the Ethics, Philanthropy and Religion doctoral seminar in spring 2006.

While scholars like Singer and Mattson have disputed the notion that Zakat is charity, the consensus among Muslims is that Zakat is a form of charity that has been institutionalized in the Islamic faith (Ba-Yunus & Kone, 2006). Very few Muslim-majority nations have systems in which the state attempts to collect Zakat (Kuran, 2003). Some scholars have argued that states do not collect Zakat largely because they have failed to institutionalize the practice as well as because there is a lack of trust within the state. Kuran (2003) has argued that there has never been a consensus on how Zakat should be paid or collected. While Muslims were held accountable for not paying Zakat in the past, scholars note that today most Muslims do not pay Zakat through the government and in fact use it to further their own personal charitable interests (McChesney, 1995). According to Widaman, Zakat has long been practiced as an individual charitable act and is considered a companion to ritual prayer by Muslims (qtd. in Abraham, 2018). Rashid et al. (2017) have argued that paying Zakat is indeed an individual Muslim obligation and proposed a system to systematically distribute the funds.

Clearly, there is a disconnect between the scholarly understanding of the theology of Zakat and the practice of Zakat by Muslims. This misunderstanding, alluded to by Singer (2018), goes beyond scholarship, as Muslims across the world embrace Zakat as philanthropic behavior. Thus the operational definitions of the words "voluntary" and "involuntary," so central to many conceptions of the nonprofit sector in the Western world (McCully, 2008; Sulek, 2010; Van Till, 1990), do not help us understand charity as an ethic rooted in Islam. The idea that religious obligations are somehow involuntary discriminates against these obligations uniquely. Social obligations may be similarly involuntary but are not excluded. Religious obligations are seen within this worldview of being devoid of free will. This is the first way that Western notions of the nonprofit sector operate counter to the understanding of prosocial giving behavior – even formally institutionalized giving behavior – in Islam. If a key definitional tenet of the nonprofit sector requires that prosocial behavior be fully voluntary, then Zakat is excluded. However, for Muslims, Zakat is both individual and institutional. While paying Zakat is obligatory, the manner in which it is given and distributed varies. Most importantly, Zakat straddles the line between religious obligation and social transaction because it comprises both: it is a component of worship (*ibadat*) and it is also a benevolent action. To define the nonprofit sector in a way that excludes Zakat draws arbitrary lines through the center of Islamic faith and tradition, fracturing what is otherwise a cohesive and interlocking set of institutionalized prosocial practices.

The second form of philanthropy in Islam is Sadaqah, which, for Muslims, encompasses all forms of Muslim philanthropy. Sadaqah is voluntary charitable giving as compared to the obligatory Zakat (Singer, 2018). Both in Arabic and Hebrew, the word "Sadaqah" has a strong connection to justice, or *adl*. Sadaqah can be formal (giving to institutions) or informal (giving to individuals, including family members in need). Muslims who fail to give Sadaqah are not considered to be committing a sin. However, they are promised great religious rewards if they engage in this voluntary practice. There are no limitations on Sadaqah. It is within this realm that even a smile, intended to do good and to show devotion to God, is considered to be philanthropy. (When I was a child, family members routinely encouraged me to smile when I was upset about something, saying, "Remember, smiling is Sadaqah [charity].")

While Sadaqah may seem to more naturally fit with conceptions of the nonprofit sector as articulated in the Western world – both because of its voluntary nature and because of its correlates with volunteering and charitable donations, it is incorrect to assume that Sadaqah is included in existing nonprofit sector theory. While charitable giving and volunteering might be neatly nestled within the paradigm of the nonprofit and voluntary sector, some acts of charity and individual expressions of faith that qualify as Sadaqah would not be acceptable within the realm of Western notions of nonprofit sector activity. Smiling, for example, is not typically considered an action that is part of the nonprofit sector, nor are any number of actions carried out by Muslims in their day-to-day lives that have the dual intention of doing good and glorifying God. These actions (and even inaction to prevent harm or further good) – though deeply personal – are expressions of faith, and they are also institutions in the sense that there is a shared language and tradition for their meaning. This shared language and meaning creates an institutional presence for Sadaqah that could – and arguably should – reorient our views about the boundaries of the nonprofit sector.

The third form of philanthropy is the *waqf*, or endowment (Lev, 2005). The waqf originates from a passage in the Quran in which Umar ibn al-Khattab acquired a property and asked the Prophet whether he should donate it for charity (Garcia, 2007). The Prophet replied, "Encumber the thing itself and devote its fruits to pious purposes" (McChesney, 2004, p. 273). Thus, a waqf, or religious endowment, is a form of charity that is designed to give long after the initial act of donation. Waqfs are another example of how Muslims have transformed and institutionalized prevailing cultural traditions within Islamic law and practice (Cizakca, 2000). Muslims have borrowed from prior traditions and regifted this idea to the modern world in the form of the modern philanthropic endowment and foundation (Adam, 2020).

In Muslim spiritual practice, intention is deeply important. Focusing on intention means that charitable acts are not assessed by their efficacy alone but also by the intention of the giver. An example from the life of the Prophet illustrates this point. A man came to the Prophet asking for a pathway to heaven. The Prophet suggested that he do acts of charity. The first day, the man accidentally gave charity to a man who was a thief. When he found out that he had given charity to a thief, he decided to give charity to another person to earn the blessings of God. This time he accidentally gave charity to a rich and undeserving man. Upon learning of his mistake, he sought to correct it by giving charity to a woman. This time, he accidentally gave charity to a prostitute. When he found out that the woman he gave charity to was a prostitute, he was devastated. In despair, he went to the Prophet, who told him that his charity was still important: the money he gave to the thief may prevent him from stealing, the money he gave to the prostitute may prevent her from selling her body, and the money he gave to the rich man might teach him to give charity himself. From this story, we learn about an important element of Muslim giving: The intention to do good is more important than the eventual efficacy of the charitable act. Unlike the Western utilitarian focus on "voluntary action for the public good," the purpose of Muslim philanthropy is to demonstrate one's love of God. This shift reorients the nonprofit sector away from programs, organizations, and outcomes and refocuses it on the transformation of the human heart.

Another lesson can be learned from this story. The Prophet suggested that, regarding the final outcome of his acts of giving, the man must have faith in God. Each of the possible outcomes the Prophet mentioned could be thought of in terms of transformational development rather than the alleviation of suffering. A thief may stop stealing, a prostitute may stop selling herself, and a miser may become generous. The transformative impact, through a Muslim lens, is in God's hands, not in the hands of the giver.

This reorientation of the nonprofit sector to encompass inward devotional intentions includes concepts like charitable donation and volunteerism. However, it also expands to include other concepts from Islam that might otherwise be excluded. For example, forgiving another for their misdeeds or being kind to another are considered charitable acts in Islam: "But forgive them and overlook their misdeeds: for Allah loveth those who are kind" (Siddiqui, 2010, p. 206).

Additionally, all Muslims can engage in prosocial behavior. The Prophet stated,

> Every Muslim has to give for charity. They asked, O Prophet of Allah, how about one who has nothing to give? He said, He should work with his hands and benefit himself and also give in charity. They said: If one cannot do even that? He replied: He should help one who is eager to have help. They said: And if he couldn't do that? He answered: Then he should do good action and abstain from evil, this is a charity for him. (Siddiqui, 2010, p. 206)

Individuals who can afford to do so can give of their wealth; individuals who have nothing can give charity by refraining from doing evil deeds. Therefore, while modern Western conceptions of charitable giving emphasize time and money, Muslim notions of charitable works include voluntary *inaction* for the public good as well. This idea is particularly relevant in a modern age in which inaction by certain entities – such as companies that choose not to engage in environmentally harmful behaviors – is considered by some to "blur the boundaries" between the private and nonprofit sectors.

A recent survey of Muslims in the US showed that their definitions of charitable giving go beyond donating money and volunteering, illustrating that US Muslim definitions of philanthropy include smiling, having good intentions, helping relatives, commanding right (a principle in Islam requiring followers to demand or impose positive values), furthering good, causing no harm, and advocating for the oppressed (Siddiqui et al., 2022). It may be tempting to think that this expansive view of charity might dictate that the boundaries of the nonprofit sector be drawn in one place for people who subscribe to Western Judeo-Christian notions of charity and in another for Muslims. However, US Muslims are not alone in embracing this broader definition of philanthropy. The survey showed that the general US population, while at lower levels, also embraced a broader definition of philanthropy. This finding suggests that a nonprofit sector that encompasses a broad variety of charitable acts may capture and describe behavior by people in general, not just adherents of Islam.

If we were to reimagine the boundaries of the nonprofit sector in a manner informed by Islam, the focus would not just be on the benefits of charity to society but also on the development of a compassionate, caring, engaged human being. Just as important as the act of giving is the effect that giving has on the donor. Philanthropic acts transform an individual, drawing them closer to God, by transforming others. In this view, the nonprofit sector is filled not only with organizations but with people who are devoted to creating a more peaceful, kind, and giving society. For those formal prosocial organizations that do exist, their impact results not only from the measurable outcomes or investment in social programs but also from the deep commitment of all stakeholders to embody the values of the world they are striving to create together.

Certainly some questions about the inclusion or exclusion of certain acts or behaviors in the boundaries of the nonprofit sector might arise from a study of Muslim charitable beliefs. However, a more fundamental challenge to the field is the secular expectation that charitable acts must be independent of God. Any behavior (e.g., a smile or other kindness, an intention to do good, or the withholding of harmful action) can be secularized in a manner that satisfies the need of our scientific tradition to create boundaries and definitions around the subject about which we are trying to theorize. In this case, we could make arguments for why these acts should or should not be included in the definition of the nonprofit sector or in the rationale for the existence of the sector. However, to do so merely based on externally observable actions or expressed intentions would miss the core difference between the Muslim "nonprofit sector" and the nonprofit sector as viewed in secular Western texts – that is, for Muslims, the most fundamental boundary around charitable activity is in fact *devotion to God*. This is the line that determines whether an action or inaction belongs inside or outside the boundaries of desirable charitable activity.

9.3 Conclusions

Western scholars have sought to define the nonprofit sector in a way that makes it difficult for religious and Eastern traditions to engage in a more comprehensive self-examination of their own charitable or humanitarian acts. Focusing on the Greek and Roman origins of philanthropy creates a framework that at times excludes both religion and non-Western traditions. However, it is critical that we explore these notions to perceive their limitations in understanding the rich and valuable Muslim perspective on the role of charitable acts in society. Table 9.1 provides some examples of ways nonprofit sector theory might be shaped by a deeper consideration of the Muslim perspective.

Having a common definition of the nonprofit sector – such as those already prevalent in the extant body of nonprofit sector studies – may be a useful starting point for scholars and theorists. However, this definition should not inhibit scholars from constantly reevaluating their understanding of charitable behavior when examining norms or traditions that fall outside of the Western tradition. Developing a framework to examine the boundaries of the nonprofit sector in a more comprehensive and interdisciplinary manner will make the field more vibrant.

For centuries, Muslim patterns of giving have extended well beyond the narrow scope of the Western definition of the nonprofit sector. While some scholarly attention has recently been given to Muslim philanthropy, it has used Western definitions of philanthropy as its central frame (Siddiqui, 2022). There is a need to examine Muslim philanthropy in the context of its own cultural framing, without the preexisting definitions and boundaries imposed by Western theorists. Adopting a broader understanding of nonprofit and voluntary activity from a Muslim perspective can open new ways of understanding the nonprofit sector and the various reasons why the nonprofit sector exists at all.

Muslim scholars, practitioners, and policymakers should take the opportunity to explore their own cultural, religious, and historical traditions to develop a more resonant and inclusive definition of the nonprofit sector that can help them address some of the problems inherent in our current, limited sector theory (Smith, 1997).

Table 9.1 *Contributions of the Muslim perspective to nonprofit sector theory*

Current perspective	Muslim perspective	Implications for nonprofit sector theory
The nonprofit sector comprises only voluntary charitable activity.	Charitable activity includes Zakat.	The nonprofit sector includes charitable giving that the giver views as obligatory – including tithes and Zakat offerings.
The nonprofit sector is defined by laws and transactional rules.	The intention of an act is more important than the act itself.	Many actions currently considered to be within the nonprofit sector (such as corporate grantmaking or philanthropic giving) ought not qualify because the intentions are self-serving; conversely, many actions should be included in the nonprofit sector that are not described by the law or formal structures (such as smiling or offering kindness to others).
The nonprofit sector exists at the macro-institutional level.	Individual acts and intentions aggregate to create the charitable sector.	Legalistic and overly formal definitions of nonprofit activity that primarily describe organizations should be reframed to include individual behaviors and intentions. The nonprofit sector exists both in formal institutions and in individual expressions and beliefs.
The key inputs to the structure and function of the nonprofit sector are financial (grants, donations, tax expenditures) and human capital (volunteering, knowledge).	In addition to money and time, kindness and personal purity contribute to the charitable sector.	Morality, kindness, and intention are important inputs that help to define the boundaries of the nonprofit sector and aid in explaining its function and capacity, in addition to financial and human capital.
The nonprofit sector is primarily defined by external structures and actions.	Charity exists primarily in the personal space between a person and God.	The nonprofit sector is bounded by individual and collective devotion to God, rather than by organizations and transactions.

References

Abraham, D. W. (2018). Zakat as practical theodicy: Precarity and the critique of gender in Muslim India. *Journal on Muslim Philanthropy and Civil Society*, *2*(1), 21–41.

Adam, T. (2020). From waqf to foundation: The case for a global and integrated history of philanthropy. *Journal of Muslim Philanthropy and Civil Society*, *4*(1), 55–73.

Ba-Yunus, I., & Kone, K. (2006) *Muslims in the United States*. Greenwood Press.

Billis, D. (2010). Hybrid organisations in the overlapping territory with the personal world. In D. Billis & C. Rochester (Eds.), *Handbook on hybrid organisations*. Edward Elgar Publishing.

Bremner, R. H. (1988). *American philanthropy* (2nd ed.). The University of Chicago Press.

Bremner, R. H. (2000). *Giving: Charity and philanthropy in history*. Transaction Publishers.

Cizakca, M. (2000). *A history of philanthropic foundations: The Islamic world from the seventh century to the present*. Bogazici University Press.

Fauzia, A. (2013). *Faith, and the state: A history of Islamic philanthropy in Indonesia*. Brill.

Garcia S. A. (2007). *Till God inherits the earth: Islamic pious endowments in* al-Andalus *(9–15th centuries)*. Brill.

Hall, P. D. (1999). The work of many hands: A response to Stanley N. Katz on the origins of the "serious study" of philanthropy. *Nonprofit and Voluntary Sector Quarterly*, *28*(4), 522–534.

Hall, P. D. (2006). A historical overview of philanthropy, voluntary associations, and nonprofit organizations in the United States, 1600–2000. In W. W. Powell & R. Steinberg (Eds.), *The nonprofit sector: A research handbook* (pp. 32–65). Yale University Press.

Ilchman, W. F., Katz, S., & Queen II, E. L. (1998). *Philanthropy in the world's traditions*. Indiana University Press.

Isin, E. F., & Lefebvre, A. (2005), The gift of law: Greek euergetism and Ottoman *waqf*. *European Journal of Social Theory*, *8*(1), 5–23.

Ismail, A. G., Zaenal, M. H., & Shafiai, H. (2013) Philanthropy in Islam: A promise to welfare economics system. IRTI Working Paper Series, Islamic Research and Training Institute, WP# 1435-03.

Khan, S. (2020). Leadership, professionalisation and impact: Lessons from a national survey of non-profit leaders in the Kingdom of Saudi Arabia. *Voluntary Sector Review*, *11*(1), 79–97.

Khan, S., & Siddiqui, S. (2017). *Islamic education in the United States and the evolution of Muslim nonprofit institutions*. Edward Elgar Publishing.

Kuran, T. (2003). Islamic redistribution through zakat: Historical record and modern realities. In M. Bonner, M. Ener, & A. Singer (Eds.), *Poverty and charity in Middle Eastern contexts*. State University of New York.

Lev, Y. (2005). *Charity, endowments, and charitable institutions in medieval Islam*. University Press of Florida.

Mattson, I. (2010). *Zakat in America: The evolving role in Islamic charity in community cohesion*. Lake Institute on Faith and Giving, Indiana University.

McChesney, R. D. (1995). *Charity and philanthropy in Islam: Institutionalizing the call to do good, essay on philanthropy no 14*. Indiana University Center on Philanthropy.

McChesney, R. D. (2004). Islamic philanthropy. In D. Burlingame (Ed.), *Philanthropy in America: A comprehensive historical encyclopedia*. ABC-CLIO.

McCully, G. (2008). *Philanthropy reconsidered: Private initiatives–public good – Quality of life*. Author House, Indiana.

McCully, G. (2012). *What is-and is not-philanthropy* (Conversations on Philanthropy), retrieved from www.academia.edu/36978441/What_Is_and_Is_Not_Philanthropy_docx

Nicholls, M. (2020). Euregetism. In *Encyclopedia Britannica*. Chicago: Encyclopædia Britannica, Inc.

Pallas, C., & Sidel, M. (2020). Foreign aid reduction and local civil society: Recent research and policy guidance for donors and international NGOs. *Nonprofit Policy Forum*, *11*(1), 20190045.

Payton, R. L. (1998). *Philanthropy: Voluntary action for the public good*. American Council on Education/Macmillan.

Payton, R. L., & Moody, M. (2008). *Understanding philanthropy: Its meaning and mission*. Indiana University Press.

Phillips, S. D., & Jung, T. (2015), Introduction: A new "new" philanthropy: From impetus to impact. In T. Jung, S. D. Phillips, & J. Harrow (Eds.), *The Routledge companion to philanthropy*. Routledge.

Rashid, M., Hassan, M. K., Min, H. S., & Wali Ullah, G. M. (2017). Reporting of zakat and charitable activities in Islamic banks: Theory and practice in a multi-cultural setting. In M. K. Hassan (Ed.), *Handbook of empirical research on Islam and economic life*. Edward Elgar.

Salamon, L. M. (1992). *America's nonprofit sector: A primer*. Foundation Center.

Schwartz, S. H., & Bilsky, W. (1987). Toward a universal psychological structure of human values. *Journal of Personality and Social Psychology*, *53*(3), 550.

Siddiqui, S. (2010). Giving in the name of God. In D. H. Smith (Ed.), *Religious giving: For love of God*. Indiana University Press.

Siddiqui, S. (2022). Muslim philanthropy: Living beyond a Western definition. *Voluntary Sector Review*, *13*(3), 338–354.

Siddiqui, S., Wasif, R., Hughes, M., Paarlberg, A., & Noor, Z. (2022). Muslim American Zakat Report 2022. Muslim Philanthropy Initiative at Indiana University Lilly Family School of Philanthropy.

Singer, A. (2008). *Charity in Islamic societies*. Cambridge University Press.

Singer, A. (2018). The politics of philanthropy. *Journal of Muslim Philanthropy and Civil Society*, 2(1), 4.

Sulek, M. (2005). Recovering the original meaning in philanthropy. In G. Shaker (Ed.), *Faculty work and the public good*. Teachers College Press – Columbia University.

Sulek, M. (2010). On the modern meaning of philanthropy. *Nonprofit and Voluntary Sector Quarterly*, *39*(2), 193–212.

Van Til, J. (1990) *Critical issues in American philanthropy: Strengthening theory and practice*. AAFRC Trust for Philanthropy.

Veyne, P. (1990). *Bread and circuses: Historical sociology and political pluralism* (B. Pearce, Trans.). Penguin.

10 *Sector Theorists Should Revisit the Role of Information*

GEORGE E. MITCHELL AND JASON COUPET

According to Hansmann's (1980) theory of contract failure, a defining feature of the nonprofit organization is the so-called nondistribution constraint. The nondistribution constraint prevents the distribution of profits to those who control nonprofit organizations. This imbues nonprofits with trustworthiness because without profit distribution there is a reduced ability for the organization to maximize private benefits at the expense of the organization's social mission.[1] Trustworthiness is particularly important in situations in which purchasers – often donors who do not consume the charitable outputs produced by the organization – are unable or unwilling to evaluate the quality or quantity of the outputs, thus potentially enabling opportunistic behavior on the part of the organization. The nondistribution constraint mitigates this important probity hazard by essentially eliminating shareholding owners, circumventing what would otherwise be a contracting failure between the purchaser (donor) and the organization.

Scholars writing after Hansmann (1980) modeled the problem of so-called information asymmetry more explicitly (e.g., Andreoni, 1990; Weisbrod & Schlesinger, 1986). The term *asymmetry* implies that organizations possess information that purchasers do not, or at least that there is a meaningful difference in the respective abilities of purchasers and organizations to monitor and evaluate output production and quality. Although purchasers may be unable or unwilling to observe charitable outputs, they may still receive the "warm glow" or the "license to feel good" that comes with donating to a trustworthy nonprofit organization (Mitchell & Calabrese, 2020). A donor's perception of an organization's trustworthiness enables transactions that might not otherwise

[1] In other words, nonprofits have little residual claimancy because they are unlike firms with profit-maximizing shareholders. Thus, there is less incentive to exploit informational problems for profit. For more on residual claimancy, see Alchian and Demsetz (1972).

take place, and the nondistribution constraint reduces the extent to which informational problems might prevent these transactions.

The existence of the nondistribution constraint does not resolve so much as circumvent the informational problem at the heart of contract failure theory. The underlying lack of information about charitable outputs persists. However, this may not be due to the presence of inherently unmeasurable aspects of charitable outputs, as contract failure suggests, but rather to the cost of information itself and who is burdened with paying for it. Private purchasers may be more interested in the benefits that they personally receive from donating, such as a warm glow, than they are in purchasing credible information about whether or how their contributions ultimately affect the intended beneficiaries. Warm glow derives from the purchase of goods and services from a trustworthy organization, not necessarily from credible information about the quality of charitable outputs. Thus, private purchasers may prefer not to pay for the monitoring and evaluation costs that must be incurred to obtain information. This is especially likely if the information could potentially undermine warm glow, for example, by revealing that the charitable outputs purchased failed to have the desired effect on the intended beneficiaries.

Neither purchasers nor nonprofits are likely to have sufficient incentive to generate costly information that has significant social but not private benefits. Because of this disparity, a nonprofit may be successful at gaining donations by appearing to be trustworthy and by providing donors with warm glow while failing to produce charitable outputs that benefit the intended beneficiaries (Mitchell & Calabrese, 2020). We label this phenomenon *benefit failure*.

Thus, the market for charitable output information is largely a missing one. While the conventional argument holds that an asymmetry of information arises due to the presence of hard-to-measure outputs or output attributes, this chapter argues that a *symmetry of uninformedness* (hereafter, *ignorance*) arises due to the nature of information as a social good. Specifically, informational problems arise because private purchasers do not sufficiently value the positive externalities of information. Rather than producers having more information than purchasers (a typical information asymmetry), both nonprofit organizations and purchasers (donors in this case) are *equally uninformed* (i.e., they have a symmetry of ignorance) in a way that benefits them both but which may harm, or at least fail to optimally benefit, the intended beneficiaries of the organization. In short, weak private incentives for acquiring costly information (a social good) causes a *symmetry of ignorance*, which may in turn lead to charitable transactions that fail to benefit the intended beneficiaries (i.e., *benefit failure*). This argument has significant implications for theory as well as for public policy, suggesting that for some market segments, public subsidies for information production may increase social welfare simply by shifting the cost burden from private to public funders, without the need to increase total charitable spending.

10.1 A Critique of Contract Failure Theory

The theory of the nonprofit institutional design introduced by Hansmann (1980) has been a dominant explanatory model in the field of nonprofit studies for decades (Anheier & Ben-Ner, 1997; Hall, 1995). The "seminal influence" of this model (Steinberg & Gray, 1993, p. 297) is easily recognizable in several major efforts to advance, summarize, and reflect upon the state of nonprofit theory throughout the past several decades. Numerous edited volumes (e.g., Rose-Ackerman, 1986), special issues in major journals (e.g., Anheier & Ben-Ner, 1997; Van Til, 1995), and other overviews (e.g., Bilodeau & Steinberg, 2006; Steinberg, 2006; Steinberg & Galle, 2018) take Hansmann's contract failure theory as a primary framework. As an economic theory of the nonprofit institutional form, contract failure theory is differentiated from many other relevant nonprofit or third-sector theories that (a) depart from the neoclassical economic paradigm of methodological individualism, utilitarianism, and constrained optimization or (b) take something other than the institutional form of the nonprofit organization as the primary subject matter. Nonetheless, such theories often overlap or are presented as complementary components of a more complete theoretical repertoire, often including not only contract failure but also market, government, and voluntary failures (e.g., Steinberg, 2006).[2] Below, we critique contract failure theory specifically and proceed to argue for the importance of information structure to nonprofit sector theory.

[2] Indeed, more than two decades after the publication of *The role of nonprofit enterprise*, Hansmann (2003) reiterated the incompleteness of his theory, particularly in describing so-called commercial nonprofits.

10.1.1 Circular Logic

By focusing on institutions and contracts as the primary units of analysis, scholars have departed from neoclassical approaches to nonprofit sector theory. In the new institutional economics framework, markets are the most efficient coordination mechanisms when frictions – such as information problems and probity hazards – are negligible. But there are almost always market frictions, and when there are, institutions arise as coordinating mechanisms. This occurs when market frictions incurred by organizations are lower than those incurred in the market.[3] When individuals and institutions exchange economic goods and services, market frictions are negotiated through contracts. Contract failure occurs when transactions that would otherwise produce social value do not happen.

Probity hazards are a critical market friction. Williamson (1999, p. 322) relates probity to the "integrity of a transaction," and in a sense, public service institutions such as nonprofit organizations exist to mitigate probity hazards. Probity hazards are present when market transactions are particularly prone to unethical behavior for which there can be little market correction. For instance, a proprietary public service entity endowed with funds to distribute to the public or to a community in need would have an incentive to simply absorb the funds for itself if the principal endowing the entity could not observe any transaction after the endowment. The principal, aware of this incentive, would not endow the entity in the first place. Thus, government entities, which can be electorally penalized, and nonprofit entities, whose missing or attenuated profit motive leads to trustworthiness, can be critical institutions in markets that might otherwise be absent. Probity hazards demand trustworthiness, and nonprofit trustworthiness circumvents a critical information problem.

The information problem that makes the nondistribution constraint, and thus nonprofits, relevant, is almost universally described as an *information asymmetry*.[4] This term denotes a situation in which one

[3] Few goods are produced in a pure marketplace, and in most cases, the production of goods and services significantly involve institutions/organizations. What is most important are the transaction costs that predict the mix of market and firm mechanisms involved in certain institutional designs. See Williamson (1999) for a thorough discussion.

[4] See, for instance, Rose-Ackerman (1986).

party possesses private information that another party does not possess. Such imperfect information structures are a popular subject of inquiry in the economics of information, contract theory, and game theory.[5] Applied to nonprofit theory, information asymmetry means that nonprofit organizations possess private information that their funders lack.[6]

So, while inducing organizational trustworthiness means that the market for charitable outputs is ultimately not a missing one, it is important to emphasize that the nondistribution constraint alone does not solve the underlying information problem. Nonprofits are trustworthy *compared to proprietary institutional designs.* There is little evidence that trust-related frictions between purchasers and nonprofits are completely resolved by the nondistribution constraint (Willems & Faulk, 2019). Purchasers have choices among nonprofit sellers, but since outputs are largely unobservable to purchasers, nonprofits compete on trustworthiness (Castaneda et al., 2008). Nonprofits signal their trustworthiness through fiscal probity signaling (Mitchell & Calabrese 2019, 2020), which they often accomplish by demonstrating low overhead, little or no debt, and minimal financial reserves, among other signals. For example, many nonprofit websites and solicitations display pie charts depicting low overhead rates as a means of signaling fiscal probity and therefore trustworthiness. These and other practices signal a nonprofit's conformity with widespread sectoral financial norms.

These signaling devices impose costs on nonprofits, however. For example, trimming overhead can starve nonprofits of key resources and impede production (Lecy & Searing, 2015). Low reserves can leave nonprofits vulnerable to shocks, leading to instability in spending patterns (Calabrese, 2013). Mitchell and Calabrese (2023) found that financial norm-conforming nonprofits significantly underperform compared to so-called norm-busting nonprofits, with the latter achieving 50% more total spending over a decade. In sum, nonprofits signal trustworthiness to solve a problem of missing information, but in doing so they may incur other costs that might harm their abilities

[5] For an introduction to the economics of information, see Macho-Stadler and Pérez-Castrillo (2001), Salanié (2005), and Bolton and Dewatripont (2005).

[6] For a concise explanation of the role of information structure in nonprofit theory, see Steinberg (1993). For contract theory that involves asymmetric information structures, the goal is often to achieve incentive compatibility by inducing the informed party to reveal its information (Bolton & Dewatripont, 2005; Macho-Stadler & Pérez-Castrillo, 2001; Salanié, 2005).

to advance their social missions. We assert that this dilemma, or "double-bind" (between signaling trustworthiness and maximizing the available resources for mission impact), demands more attention in nonprofit studies (Mitchell, 2018).

Trustworthiness, like information, is costly. Moreover, trustworthiness does not induce organizations to generate the missing information. On the contrary, trustworthiness facilitates information missingness, thus exacerbating the information problem it seeks to address. The logic is circular: organizations must be trustworthy because information is absent, and information is absent because trustworthiness circumvents the need for information.

10.1.2 Failure to Account for Warm Glow

What are purchasers buying with their charitable contributions? If a nonprofit's output represents a private good with positive externalities, as Preston (1989) proposed, are those externalities *essential* or *incidental* to nonprofit production?[7] In other words, do donors care whether nonprofit organizations are actually doing good, or do they mainly care that they feel good about making their donations?

The evidence strongly suggests that giving is mostly driven by private benefits to the donor than by real or anticipated social benefits to intended beneficiaries (Bekkers & Wiepking 2011; Bhati & Hansen 2020). Private benefits such as warm glow, guilt alleviation, self-esteem, and reputation are all significant drivers of giving, while social benefits such as perceived donation efficacy are not. In one influential experiment, Crumpler and Grossman (2008) found that individuals contribute to nonprofits even when told that their contributions crowd out other donations one for one, essentially ruling out social benefit motivations.

In other experiments, information plays a central role. Karlan and Wood (2017) found that information about charity effectiveness *decreased* donations from prior donors who gave small amounts while increasing donations from prior donors who gave large amounts, interpreting the behavior as "intuitive, effortless and reactive" (p. 2) decision-making consistent with warm glow. A systematic review by Greenhalgh and Montgomery (2020) identified information costs as

[7] For example, Mitchell and Schmitz (2019) asserted that most nonprofit and governmental actors claim to produce positive externalities.

a significant impediment to more informed or evidence-based giving. Other evidence suggests that low-cost performance information can affect giving for some donors. Using a survey experiment design, Vollan et al. (2017) found that respondents were more willing to donate to a nonprofit when presented with cost-effectiveness information, but traditional charity seals had no effect. The mixed evidence suggests that while giving may be driven more by private benefits than by social benefits, some giving may be informed by an interest in results for intended beneficiaries, provided that the information is relevant and its costs are sufficiently low. Indeed, industry surveys that have employed segmentation analysis to examine philanthropic giving have identified an impact-oriented segment accounting for about 16–17% of respondents (Neighbor et al., 2015).

Informed, impact-oriented giving appears to only account for a relatively small share of all philanthropic giving. Moreover, much private giving is uninformed regardless of information availability and cost. Traditional contract failure theory – rooted in information asymmetry and the nondistribution constraint – provides no explanation for this phenomenon, nor does it explain why organizations would fail to reveal relevant private information that might otherwise inform purchasers and presumably result in more efficient giving and better outcomes for the intended beneficiaries.

10.1.3 Mis-specified Information Structure

Contract failure theory asserts that the distribution of information between purchasers and sellers is asymmetric, as is often associated with the separation between donors and nonprofits in the case of the classic donative-entrepreneurial type of nonprofit (Krashinsky, 1986). However, there are many types of nonprofit purchasers in addition to donors. Empirically, donations from individuals represent only a small share of all nonprofit income. In 2013, about 13% of all revenues to nonprofits were donative. In 2016, the figure was only 9%. By contrast, in 2013, 72% of all nonprofit revenues were from fees for services, while in 2016 the number was 81%.[8] Contracts

[8] Percentages refer to public charities, as defined by the Internal Revenue Code (2022). Fees for services include payments for medical care, school tuition, and government contracts, inter alia. See McKeever (2015) and Carter et al. (2019).

involving significant performance reporting have long been commonplace throughout the sector (Pettijohn & Boris, 2013; Salamon, 1987; Smith & Lipsky, 1993). Additionally, funding from many foundation sources often involves the regular reporting of detailed performance information. In many transactions, the purchaser is thus reasonably capable of observing performance either because they are themselves the beneficiary (as in fees for service) or because they are sophisticated enough to demand outcome information and understand how to interpret it (Coupet & Schehl, 2022).

In cases that do not involve formal contracting, the distribution of information appears to be more symmetric than asymmetric. Hansmann (1980) emphasized the difficulties of measuring hard-to-measure charitable outputs and attributes, and others introduced more precise treatments of output unobservability (e.g., Weisbrod, 1988; Weisbrod & Schlesinger, 1986). For Weisbrod, nonprofit outputs are observable in principle, but only with significant distortion effects. The efficiency benefits of measuring performance must be weighed against the distortion costs induced by imperfect measurement. So, information might be missing from the dynamics of a market exchange in part because the costs of measuring hard-to-measure outputs and output attributes outweigh the benefits. In this case, neither the purchaser nor the seller possess the desired information. The distribution of information is much closer to a symmetry of ignorance as neither party judges it to be worthwhile to acquire credible information.

While it is possible that some nonprofits are acquiring output information and are simply choosing to conceal this information, this possibility does not seem to bear out empirically. There is a large body of evidence noting the difficulty and low incentives that nonprofits have in measuring performance, especially if that measurement risks revealing failure (Altamimi & Liu, 2021; Lee, 2021; Mitchell & Berlan, 2016; Umar & Hassan, 2019). Thus, it is perhaps more likely that neither nonprofits nor purchasers have sufficiently strong incentives to incur the costs of obtaining information. This may be understandable considering the distribution of information costs and benefits. Private-purchaser utility functions will tend to not fully account for all the social benefits of information, and if purchasers do not pay for the information, then nonprofits will tend to not produce it. Nonetheless, information about nonprofit outcomes is essential if stakeholders are to understand the extent to which nonprofits serve the needs of their beneficiaries. "Indeed, information is perhaps the only pure public good in economic theory" (Kingma, 1997, p. 144), or perhaps more accurately, information may be regarded as a *social good*, defined as one that creates "positive externalities, regardless of whether external benefits accrue to all or only to some members of society" (Mitchell & Schmitz, 2019, p. 13).

Free-riding is a predictable consequence of this circumstance. Private purchasers might prefer to support program activities that produce private warm glow, such as by providing restricted contributions earmarked for program spending, leaving information costs to be borne by others, if by any party at all. Research is fairly clear on this point: purchasers prefer to support direct service activities, not indirect activities such as program evaluation, and donors reduce contributions to organizations with higher overhead (Hung et al., 2022; Mitchell & Calabrese, 2019, pp. 652–653). Moreover, many purchasers seem to be quite content to remain uninformed about output production on the part of supported nonprofits (Coupet & Broussard, 2021), particularly if this guarantees that their sense of warm glow remains intact. Evidenced-based or so-called informed giving appears to be exceedingly rare (Krasteva & Yildirim, 2013, 2016).

Nonprofits that reveal negative or unflattering information may risk dissatisfying funders. In one interpretation, donors essentially purchase so-called licenses to feel good from nonprofits (Mitchell & Calabrese, 2020). Realizing this, organizations may be reluctant to generate information that could present a risk of reducing purchaser utility (Pritchett, 2002). For example, nonprofits may selectively publicize success stories or choose to only undertake credible evaluation when doing so is most likely to reveal success.[9] Of course, such a model neglects entirely the positive externalities of information (e.g., the ability to identify, replicate, and improve successful programs, to avoid replicating failed programs, etc.). While the avoidance or suppression of credible information about performance may possibly enhance utility for some purchasers by mitigating the risk of disappointment, it reduces social welfare in terms of both allocative and productive efficiency. Not only is the performance of individual organizations not rewarded, but resources may flow to lower performance organizations at the expense of higher performance organizations,

[9] Indeed, research has found evidence of the latter. See Mitchell and Berlan (2016).

as information that could drive more effective giving remains undiscovered. If nonprofits operate exclusively for the satisfaction of risk-averse, warm glow-type purchasers and if credible information is costly to produce (and ultimately must be funded by purchasers), then the distribution of credible information will approach a symmetry of ignorance. Neither donors nor nonprofits will sufficiently incur information costs, and society will forgo significant, positive information externalities. The reason for this information structure is not necessarily due to inherently unmeasurable or hard-to-measure outputs or output attributes but to the unwillingness of private purchasers to pay for positive externalities that benefit society but do not contribute to private warm glow and may even reduce it by presenting a risk of disappointment.

10.1.4 Information Structure and Sector Theory

Contract failure theory, as applied to nonprofits, presents what is essentially a theory of information. According to Hansmann (1980), the nonprofit institutional form exists to solve an information problem and thereby coordinate markets for charitable outputs. Because there are no profit-maximizing shareholders, the nondistribution constraint attenuates, if not removes entirely, the profit motive, thus imbuing nonprofits with trustworthiness. Purchasers can then better trust nonprofits to not exploit their ignorance, avoiding what Hansmann (1980, p. 845) called contract failure. Thus, according to the theory, the nonprofit sector exists because a nondistribution constraint is needed to address an information problem. If donors give money to an organization but do not receive the organization's services for themselves, they do not have sufficient information to determine whether the outputs were produced or whether the organization took the money as profit in contravention of donor intent. However, once an organization is designated as a *nonprofit* – with little or no opportunity for profit distribution to shareholders and thus little or no incentive to sacrifice performance – donors can consider the organization "trustworthy" and essentially purchase a license to feel good with their donations. Information structure is therefore already a fundamental component of sector theory. An improved understanding of information structure and its origins – particularly the ways in which the mechanisms for improving nonprofit trustworthiness may have adverse effects on outcomes for intended beneficiaries – can improve how we understand nonprofit institutional design, public policy, performance measurement, and the production of charitable outputs.

10.1.5 Improving Contract Failure Theory, with a Focus on Information

A deeper understanding of information and its costs and benefits can advance sector theory by offering a more accurate modeling of the information structure at the heart of contract failure theory and by interrogating the causes and consequences of this information structure. We propose that a better accounting of information structure may create social value in at least three ways: it would improve (1) transactional efficiency by reducing information frictions, which would enable purchasers to reward performance and in turn motivate organizations to perform better; (2) allocative efficiency throughout the sector by channeling donor resources to the most effective organizations; and (3) the productive efficiency of society through the discovery, dissemination, and adoption of the most effective and efficient strategies for achieving social goals. Whether acquiring information is worthwhile depends on not only its *private costs* but also its *social benefits*.

10.1.5.1 Transactional Efficiency

Private information can serve as a major source of friction, introducing uncertainty into markets because of the probity hazards induced by information problems (Illing, 1992). Weisbrod (1986, 1988), Steinberg (1990), and others have considered the role of information in rewarding performance and the related perils of attempting to reward performance based on flawed performance information. For example, Steinberg (1990, p. 148) described "efficiency wages" as "an intriguing but dangerous possibility" that could introduce a reverse-screening effect, possibly attracting workers with financial rather than altruistic motivations. Similarly, "incentive contracts" risk "endangering the traditional function of nonprofit organizations as trustworthy and caring providers of service" (p. 149). Like Weisbrod, Steinberg (1990, p. 149) expressed concern about "serious perverse incentives" that may be introduced when measuring and rewarding performance. The underlying problem appears to be that measuring only the observable or verifiable dimensions of nonprofit output may lead to costly behavioral distortions, themselves market frictions (e.g., teaching-to-the-test problems, disincentivizing hard-to-measure outcome production, etc.) that overwhelm the efficiency benefits of incentivizing superior performance.

The existence of social-impact bonds, pay-for-success schemes, and similar arrangements provide a challenging case with respect to these concerns (FitzGerald et al., 2019). Parties to these arrangements, which often involve public agencies, have evidently judged the considerable information and transaction costs involved to be worthwhile. Perhaps government agencies, more so than private individuals, take into account the positive externalities or social benefits of information, altering the cost–benefit ratio such that measurement becomes worthwhile (Coupet & Schehl, 2022). When positive externalities are taken more fully into account, total benefits may increase enough to outweigh even substantial costs.

Apart from the cost–benefit ratio of information acquisition, the literature related to information in nonprofit markets has also proposed a type of distortion regarding the potential underproduction of outputs with attributes that are hard-to-measure. However, the actual extent of any such problem empirically is unclear. In the United States, the service sector of the economy, much of which produces hard-to-measure outputs, accounts for more than two-thirds of all economic production, mostly performed by proprietary firms not subject to the nondistribution constraint (Bureau of Economic Analysis, 2022). It may be that the approximately 5–6% of GDP credited to nonprofit production roughly corresponds to those outputs for which acquiring information is unworthwhile, but this proposition appears to have not yet been formally evaluated (Independent Sector, 2023). Nonprofit output purchasers may insufficiently value the positive externalities of information and thus may be unwilling to pay for it. In the proprietary sector, by contrast, purchasers may have much stronger private incentives to acquire information, particularly information that yields mostly private benefits. A given purchaser might willingly incur significant private costs to acquire information about the quality of a private good, yet still be unwilling to pay even a modest sum for information about the quality of a social good. This would seem to be a fruitful area for future research.

10.1.5.2 Allocative Efficiency

The prospect of an allocatively efficient nonprofit sector in which resources flow to the most impactful organizations based on credible performance information is intuitively appealing, but it faces many practical difficulties. The effective altruism movement (MacAskill, 2016, 2017; Singer, 2017) and many other allied initiatives that take this possibility as their object have encountered considerable skepticism and even fervent opposition. The numerous criticisms may reduce to irreconcilable ideological and philosophical commitments. However, criticisms should acknowledge not only the obvious costs but also the potential benefits of allocative efficiency (Lall, 2017).

Allocative efficiency failures endemic to the nonprofit sector have motivated pronounced criticisms. In one popular critique, Giridharadas (2019) noted that allocative and distributional failures attending popular vehicles like donor-advised funds are so pronounced that they do more to exacerbate existing inequalities than to produce social goods. Reich (2018) argued that these allocative inefficiencies have *always* been a problem, highlighting among other examples John D. Rockefeller's exchanges with Congress regarding the distributional benefits of his foundation (p. 64). The underlying problem is that resources disproportionately flow to relatively low marginal-impact organizations, which are already comparatively well funded, to the exclusion of many other organizations for which additional contributions would have much higher marginal impact. In such cases, the lack of a marketplace for performance information contributes to the invisibility and underfunding of more deserving, higher-impact organizations.

While the historical intractability of problems related to allocative efficiency suggests that eliminating allocative frictions would be impractical, the volume and popularity of critiques of the sector's role and the allocative equilibrium of goods and services makes movement toward higher allocative efficiency important. A more allocatively efficient nonprofit marketplace would mean that the most productive nonprofits would be more likely to receive resources at the margin when information problems are mitigated. *Ceteris paribus*, this increases the marginal productivity of donations and should improve aggregate social welfare. While accurately estimating the aggregate benefit of potentially realized gains in allocative efficiency for the nonprofit sector would be extremely difficult, the magnitude of such potential gains would seem to be substantial.

10.1.5.3 Productive Efficiency

Productive efficiency refers to a state in which organizations are employing the best available techniques and strategies for meeting societal needs. Over time, organizations gradually replace less effective strategies with more effective strategies as new evidence becomes available. For example, J-PAL, Innovations for Poverty Action (IPA), the International Initiative for Impact Evaluation (3ie), and others offer searchable, online repositories containing credible impact evaluations about intervention effectiveness. Rather than risk unknowingly duplicating or scaling up programs known to be ineffective, organizations can learn from one another's experiences to design better-quality programs with higher chances of success (Coupet et al., 2021). Information stands to improve the effectiveness not only of individual programs and organizations but of the entire sector by raising the overall extent of knowledge at the level of fundamental social science.

The potential value of such information to society is significant, although obviously difficult to quantify. The equally important point is that private purchasers are unlikely to consider the value of such information externalities when transacting with nonprofits. Thus, nonprofits are unlikely to be provided with the necessary resources to produce this information. Indeed, research has found that insufficient resources is a top obstacle to evaluation for nonprofits (Mitchell & Berlan, 2016). Government and foundation funders may be more willing to provide resources to help incentivize nonprofits to evaluate supported programs, but even they are often unwilling to pay for "overhead" costs associated with evaluation itself, forcing nonprofits to use scarce unrestricted funds from private individuals to cover these costs.

Research does suggest that private purchasers may not be willing to incur significant information costs. In one experiment, Null (2011, p. 455) found that "few subjects were willing to pay for information that could have enabled them to increase the social benefit of their gifts." The author concluded that this aversion may explain the rarity of credible impact evaluations throughout the nonprofit sector: "Evaluations might be rare in part because they are costly to charities and largely ignored by donors. Moreover … subjects focused on the fixed cost of acquiring information rather than the benefits of knowing which programs are most effective" (p. 464).

The limited willingness of purchasers to pay for information that would improve the efficiency and impact of giving suggests that private-purchaser utility functions do not sufficiently value the positive externalities associated with information production more generally. Specifically, individual transactions between donors and nonprofits may neglect the social value of having a superior body of scientific evidence that could lead to improved programs and policies for society as a whole.

10.2 What Contract Failure Theory Gets Wrong: An Illustration

It is hard to quantify the forgone social impact associated with the inefficiencies in the nonprofit sector that are caused by information problems, but a hypothetical example can illustrate the logic of the issue.[10] Imagine a hypothetical nonprofit sector consisting of 100 nonprofits. Each organization can be assigned a value, E, ranging from 0 to 1, that quantifies its output per dollar. A value of 0 indicates no output per dollar, while a value of 1 indicates one unit of output per dollar. Assume further that this sector exhibits an unusual mirror symmetry: for every effective nonprofit organization, i, with efficiency $E = 1$, there is an identical but ineffective counterpart organization, i', with efficiency $E = 0$. Thus, half of the organizations are effective, half are not. Assume further that these two types of organizations are indistinguishable from one another, so that each contribution made by a donor has an equal probability of supporting an effective or an ineffective organization.

For simplicity, suppose that this sector is supported by 50 donors, each contributing $1, for a total of $50. Without knowing E, donors spread their contributions randomly. Each nonprofit, on average, receives about $0.50 and the sector's total output is about 25, implying a unit output price of about $2 ($50 for 25 units of output).

Now imagine that society could reallocate some of its $50 to discover E so that donors could favor more effective nonprofits. What is

[10] Many authors, including Hansmann (1981, p. 507) and Weisbrod (1988, pp. 43–58), have acknowledged the inherent inefficiency of the nonprofit form due to profit-motive attenuation or elimination, as well as shirking incentives caused by the inability to monitor outputs.

this information worth to society? After discovering *E*, donors only need to spend $25 instead of $50 to obtain the same 25 units of output: they simply could reallocate their contributions from ineffective to effective nonprofits. Essentially, one informed dollar is worth two uninformed dollars. Society saves $25 and should therefore be willing to spend up to that amount to acquire the information about *E*. Total charitable output could be as much as doubled (less the cost of discovering *E*) by applying the information about *E* to support more effective nonprofits.

This example is obviously simplistic, but the logic demonstrates the high potential value of information. Even extremely coarse information that designates nonprofits as belonging to a higher efficiency category could potentially drive dramatic improvements in total benefit. Indeed, several information intermediaries are already attempting this (e.g., GiveWell, TheLifeYouCanSave, and Charity Navigator). Based on prior research, the example provided above, in which the value of information is equal to the combined social benefit of the entire sector without the information, may actually be conservative. In one set of studies, researchers found that lay people severely underestimate the difference in cost-effectiveness between the average charity and the most effective charities: they estimate a median multiple of only 1.5, whereas highly informed experts estimate a multiple of 100 (Caviola et al., 2020). In theory, society should be willing to incur significant costs to acquire information that could so dramatically increase the aggregate social impact of giving.

Contract failure theory incorrectly implies – and without empirical evidence – that no amount of social benefit is worth incurring the cost of discovering *E*. While contract failure theory may be correct in assuming that significant costs make information difficult to obtain, it neglects the countervailing benefits of information for improving society at large.[11]

10.3 Conclusions

Classical contract failure theory provides an incomplete and inaccurate theory of information, which has contributed to a radical discounting of information's social value. Future research should seek to

[11] For a discussion of information costs, see Mitchell and Calabrese (2020).

(a) ascertain the nature, extent, and distribution of information costs and benefits, especially positive information externalities; (b) develop more accurate and complete models of information structure, particularly ones that account for the prevalence of nonprofits in markets for contractable outputs (e.g., government contracting, institutional grants requiring output reporting, social impact bonds, etc.) and the dearth of nonprofits in markets characterized by classic information asymmetries (e.g., used cars, consulting services, prisons, etc.); and (c) study the relationships among information, organizational performance, and sectoral efficiency. Additionally, future theoretical development should (d) explicitly account for warm-glow transactions and (e) avoid circularities that induce the very circumstances (i.e., missing information) that theory seeks to describe. The cost of missing information in social welfare terms is not well understood and deserves significant attention.

Other fruitful areas of inquiry concern the practical policy implications of theory. For example, future research could study the possibility of public policies that subsidize the production of output information, given that many private purchasers may be insufficiently motivated to pay for this information. This research could also examine information utilization and whether and under what circumstances government should play a more substantial role in supporting information production to improve social welfare.

Another promising area for future policy research concerns the use of performance signaling as a substitute or complement to fiscal probity signaling. A primary rationale for ignorance under contract failure theory is that nonprofit output is usually not third-party verifiable. That is, no court or arbitrator would be willing or able to adjudicate a dispute over whether a nonprofit satisfactorily produced a specified output. Contracts would therefore be unenforceable, and there would be no way to resolve a disagreement over performance. Indeed, unlike the business sector, the nonprofit sector still lacks a mature institutional infrastructure for auditing and arbitration that could, in principle, enable third-party verification. Whether this might be worthwhile would depend on the ratio of costs to benefits. Some nonprofit outputs may not be worth verifying, others may be. In cases in which donors are indifferent to verification, unwilling to pay for it, or averse to disappointment, verification may remain unlikely in the absence of government intervention.

However, third-party verification may not be necessary. Scharf (2013, p. 57) presented an instructive model showing how "donor discretion can promote efficient charity selection." In this model, nonprofits themselves receive warm glow from their own provision of output, potentially diverting resources away from higher-performing peers. Purchasers condition funding on signals correlated with performance. What is notable is that even unverifiable signals of performance can improve efficiency, provided of course that they are correlated with actual output and that the signals themselves do not induce more friction than they solve. Although many information intermediaries have traditionally relied upon signals of trustworthiness (based largely on financial data) rather than signals of efficiency (based on cost-effectiveness data), this landscape is changing (Coupet & Haynie, 2019; Mitchell & Calabrese, 2019, 2020). Private information intermediaries have an important role to play in facilitating this signaling behavior through online information platforms (Ruff, 2013; Ruff & Olsen, 2016).

If purchasers have no means of verification, nonprofits have an incentive to report the best picture possible regardless of outcomes, and the resulting warm glow may be precisely what purchasers are buying. False signaling can already be seen in pervasive practices such as so-called zero-cost fundraising, in which nonprofits underreport or fail to report fundraising costs, presumably as a fiscal probity signal meant to assure purchasers that their donations will support programs and not further fundraising. The suspiciously high ratio of success stories to failure stories in nonprofit storytelling may also represent false signaling. Future research might examine whether credible information is simply costly or whether purchaser ignorance is strategic. On one hand, organizations may have information about poor performance and withhold that information from donors and the public (information asymmetry); on the other hand, it is possible that organizations simply do not invest in the kind of data collection and analysis that would discover underperformance and risk undermining their appeal to donors (symmetry of ignorance).

Contract failure theory has been a cornerstone of nonprofit theory for decades. It defines the nonprofit institutional form in terms of the nondistribution constraint. This essential feature gives nonprofits a comparative advantage in trustworthiness when informational problems might otherwise lead to contract failure and thus the underprovision of charitable outputs. We argue that informational problems arise because private purchasers fail to sufficiently value the positive externalities of information, not because nonprofit outputs are inherently unobservable or not worth observing. The undervaluing of information as a social good by private parties results in a symmetry of ignorance that leads to benefit failure in the form of foregone social impact. Information is a social good, and its increased production has the potential to substantially improve aggregate social welfare even while holding total charitable spending constant. Future research should reexamine the role of information in sector theory.

References

Alchian, A. A., & Demsetz, H. (1972). Production, information costs, and economic organization. *American Economic Review*, *62*(5), 777–795.

Altamimi, H., & Liu, Q. (2021). The nonprofit starvation cycle: Does overhead spending really impact program outcomes? *Nonprofit and Voluntary Sector Quarterly*, *51*(6), 1324–1348. https://doi.org/10.1177/08997640211057404

Andreoni, J. (1990). Impure altruism and donations to public goods: A theory of warm-glow giving. *Economic Journal*, *100*(401), 464–477.

Anheier, H. K., & Ben-Ner, A. (1997). Economic theories of non-profit organisations: A Voluntas Symposium. *Voluntas: International Journal of Voluntary and Nonprofit Organizations*, *8*(2), 93–96.

Bekkers, R., & Wiepking, P. (2011). A literature review of empirical studies of philanthropy: Eight mechanisms that drive charitable giving. *Nonprofit and Voluntary Sector Quarterly*, *40*(5), 924–973.

Bhati, A., & Hansen, R. K. (2020). A literature review of experimental studies in fundraising. *Journal of Behavioral Public Administration*, *3*(1), 1–19.

Bilodeau, M., & Steinberg, R. (2006). Donative nonprofit organizations. In S.-C. Kolm and J. M. Ythier (Eds.), *Handbook on the economics of giving, altruism and reciprocity* (pp. 1271–1333). Elsevier.

Bolton, P., & Dewatripont, M. (2005). *Contract theory*. MIT Press.

Bureau of Economic Analysis. (2022, December 22). *Value added by industry as a percentage of gross domestic product*, https://apps.bea.gov/iTable/?reqid=150&step=2&isuri=1&categories=gdpxind#eyJhcHBpZCI6MTUwLCJzdGVwcyI6WzEsMiwzXSwiZGF0YSI6W1siY2F0ZWdvcmllcyIsIkdkcHhJbmQiXSxbIlRhYmxlX0xpc3QiLCI1Il1dfQ==

Calabrese, T. (2013). Running on empty: The operating reserves of US nonprofit organizations. *Nonprofit Management and Leadership*, *23*(3), 281–302.

Carter, T. G., Chandler, J., Cohen, R., Delaney, T., Higgins, A., O'Leary, A. S., & Thompson, D. L. (2019). *Nonprofit impact matters*. National Council of Nonprofits.

Castaneda, M. A, Garen, J., & Thornton, J. (2008). Competition, contractibility, and the market for donors to nonprofits. *Journal of Law, Economics, & Organization*, *24*(1), 215–246.

Caviola, L., Schubert, S., Teperman, E., Moss, D., Greenberg, S., & Faber, N. S. (2020). Donors vastly underestimate differences in charities' effectiveness. *Judgement and Decision Making*, *15*(4), 509–516.

Coupet, J., & Broussard, P. (2021). Do donors respond to nonprofit performance? Evidence from housing. *Public Performance & Management Review*, *44*(1), 108–135.

Coupet, J., & Haynie, J. L. (2019). Toward a valid approach to nonprofit efficiency measurement. *Nonprofit Management & Leadership*, *29*(2), 299–320. https://doi.org/10.1002/nml.21336

Coupet, J., & Schehl, M. (2022). Government grants, donors, and nonprofit performance. *Journal of Public Administration Research and Theory*, *32*(1), 97–110.

Coupet, J., Berrett, J., Broussard, P., & Johnson, B. (2021). Nonprofit benchmarking with data envelopment analysis. *Nonprofit and Voluntary Sector Quarterly*, *50*(3), 647–661.

Crumpler, H., & Grossman, P. J. (2008). An experimental test of warm glow giving. *Journal of Public Economics*, *92*, 1011–1021.

FitzGerald, C., Carter, E., Dixon, R., & Airoldi, M. (2019). Walking the contractual tightrope: A transaction cost economics perspective on social impact bonds. *Public Money & Management*, *39*(7), 458–467.

Giridharadas, A. (2019). *Winners take all: The elite charade of changing the world*. Vintage.

Greenhalgh, C., & Montgomery, P. (2020). A systematic review of the barriers to and facilitators of the use of evidence by philanthropists when determining which charities (including health charities or programmes) to fund. *Systematic Reviews*, *9*(199), 1–13.

Hall, P. D. (1995). Theories and institutions. *Nonprofit and Voluntary Sector Quarterly*, *21*(1), 5–13.

Hansmann, H. (1980). The role of nonprofit enterprise. *Yale Law Journal*, *89*(5), 835–902.

Hansmann, H. (1981). Reforming nonprofit corporation law. *University of Pennsylvania Law Review*, *129*(3), 497–623.

Hansmann, H. (2003). The role of trust in nonprofit enterprise. In H. K. Anheier & A. Ben-Ner (Eds.), *The study of the nonprofit enterprise* (pp. 115–122). Springer.

Hung, C., Hager, M. A., & Tian, Y. (2022). Do donors penalize nonprofits with higher non-program costs? A meta-analysis of donor overhead aversion. *Nonprofit and Voluntary Sector Quarterly*. 10.1177/08997640221138260

Illing, G. (1992). Private information as transaction costs: The Coase theorem revisited. *Journal of Institutional and Theoretical Economics (JITE)/Zeitschrift für die gesamte Staatswissenschaft*, *148*(4), 558–576.

Independent Sector. (2023). Health of the U.S. Nonprofit Sector Quarterly Review. Accessed online on February 21, 2023 from https://independentsector.org/resource/health-of-the-u-s-nonprofit-sector

Internal Revenue Code, 26 U.S.C. § 501(3)(c) (2022).

Karlan, D., & Wood, D. H. (2017). The effect of aid effectiveness: Donor response to aid effectiveness in a direct mail fundraising experiment. *Journal of Behavioral and Experimental Economics*, *66*(1), 1–8.

Kingma, B. R. (1997). Public good theories of the non-profit sector: Weisbrod revisited. *Voluntas: International Journal of Voluntary and Nonprofit Organizations*, *8*(2), 135–148.

Krashinsky, M. (1986). Transaction costs and a theory of the nonprofit organization. In S. Rose-Ackerman (Ed.), *The economics of nonprofit institutions* (pp. 114–132). Oxford University Press.

Krasteva, S., & Yildirim, H. (2013). (Un)informed charitable giving. *Journal of Public Economics*, *106*, 14–26.

Krasteva, S., & Yildirim, H. (2016). Information, competition, and the quality of charities. *Journal of Public Economics*, *144*, 64–77.

Lall, S. (2017). Measuring to improve versus measuring to prove: Understanding the adoption of social performance measurement practices in nascent social enterprises. *Voluntas: International Journal of Voluntary and Nonprofit Organizations*, *28*(6), 2633–2657. www.jstor.org/stable/44668907

Lecy, J. D., & Searing, E. A. (2015). Anatomy of the nonprofit starvation cycle: An analysis of falling overhead ratios in the nonprofit sector. *Nonprofit and Voluntary Sector Quarterly*, *44*(3), 539–563.

Lee, C. (2021). Factors influencing the credibility of performance measurement in nonprofits. *International Review of Public Administration*, *26*(2), 156–174.

MacAskill, W. (2016). *Doing good better: How effective altruism can help you help others, do work that matters, and make smarter choices about giving back*. Avery.

MacAskill, W. (2017). Effective altruism: An introduction. *Essays in Philosophy*, *18*(1), 1–5.

Macho-Stadler, I., & Pérez-Castrillo, D. (2001). *An introduction to the economics of information: Incentives and contracts* (2nd ed.) (R. Watt, Trans.). Oxford University Press.

McKeever, B. S. (2015). *The nonprofit sector in brief 2015: Public charities, giving, and volunteering*. Urban Institute Center on Nonprofits and Philanthropy.

Mitchell, G. E. (2018). Modalities of managerialism: The "double bind" of normative and instrumental nonprofit managerial imperatives. *Administration & Society*, *50*(7), 1037–1068. https://doi.org/10.1177/0095399716664832

Mitchell, G. E., & Berlan, D. (2016). Evaluation and evaluative rigor in the nonprofit sector. *Nonprofit Management & Leadership*, 27(2), 237–250. https://doi.org/10.1002/nml.21236

Mitchell, G. E., & Calabrese, T. D. (2019). Proverbs of nonprofit financial management. *American Review of Public Administration*, *49*(6), 649–661. https://doi.org/10.1177/0275074018770458

Mitchell, G. E., & Calabrese, T. D. (2020). Instrumental philanthropy, nonprofit theory, and information costs. *Nonprofit Policy Forum*, *11*(2), 1–15. https://doi.org/10.1515/npf-2019-0050

Mitchell, G. E., & Calabrese, T. D. (2023). The hidden cost of trustworthiness. *Nonprofit and Voluntary Sector Quarterly*, *52*(2), 304–326. https://doi.org/10.1177/08997640221092794

Mitchell, G. E., & Schmitz, H. P. (2019). The nexus of public and nonprofit management. *Public Performance & Management Review*, *42*(1), 11–33. https://doi.org/10.1080/15309576.2018.1489293

Neighbor, H., Drake, J., Eagle, T., Vandermark, J., Wilkie, B., Willer, R., Durbin, T., Haji, S., & Horberg, L. (2015). *Money for good 2015: Revealing the voice of the donor in philanthropic giving*. Camber Collective. www.cambercollective.com/moneyforgood

Null, C. (2011). Warm glow, information, and inefficient charitable giving. *Journal of Public Economics*, *95*, 455–456.

Pettijohn, S. L., & Boris, E. T. (2013). *Nonprofit-government contracts and grants: Findings from the 2013 national survey*. Urban Institute.

Preston, A. E. (1989). The nonprofit worker in a for-profit world. *Journal of labor economics*, 7(4), 438–463.

Pritchett, L. (2002). It pays to be ignorant: A simple political economy of rigorous program evaluation. *Policy Reform*, *5*(4), 251–269.

Reich, R. (2018). *Just giving*. Princeton University Press.

Rose-Ackerman, S. (Ed.). (1986). *The economics of nonprofit institutions: Studies in structure and policy*. Oxford University Press.

Ruff, K. (2013). The role of intermediaries in social accounting. In L. Mook (Ed.), *Accounting for social value* (pp. 320–248). University of Toronto Press.

Ruff, K., & Olsen, S. (2016, May 10). The next frontier in social impact measurement isn't measurement at all. *Stanford Social Innovation Review*. https://ssir.org/articles/entry/next_frontier_in_social_impact_measurement

Salamon, L. M. (1987). Of market failure, voluntary failure, and third-party government: Toward a theory of government-nonprofit relations in the modern welfare state. *Journal of Voluntary Action Research*, *16*, 29–49.

Salanié, B. (2005). *The economics of contracts* (2nd ed.). MIT Press.

Scharf, K. (2013). Impure prosocial motivation in charity provision: Warm-glow charities and implications for public funding. *Journal of Public Economics*, *114*, 50–57.

Singer, P. (2017). *The most good you can do: How effective altruism is changing ideas about living ethically*. Yale University Press.

Smith, S. R., & Lipsky, M. (1993). *Nonprofits for hire: The welfare state in the age of contracting*. Harvard University Press.

Steinberg, R. (1990). Profits and incentive compensation in nonprofit firms. *Nonprofit Management & Leadership*, *1*(2), 137–151.

Steinberg, R. (1993). Public policy and the performance of nonprofit organizations: A general framework. *Nonprofit and Voluntary Sector Quarterly*, *22*(1), 13–31.

Steinberg, R. (2006). Economic theories of nonprofit organizations. In W. W. Powell & R. Steinberg (Eds.), *The nonprofit sector: A research handbook* (pp. 117–139). Yale University Press.

Steinberg, R., & Galle, B. (2018). A law and economics perspective on nonprofit organizations. In M. Harding (Ed.), *Research handbook on not-for-profit law*. Edward Elgar.

Steinberg, R., & Gray, B. H. (1993). "The role of nonprofit enterprise" in 1993: Hansmann revisited. *Nonprofit and Voluntary Sector Quarterly*, *22*(4), 297–316.

Umar, S., & Hassan, S. (2019). Encouraging the collection of performance data in nonprofit organizations: The importance of organizational support for learning. *Public Performance & Management Review*, *42*(5), 1062–1084.

Van Til, J. (1995). Theory of the third sector. *Nonprofit & Voluntary Sector Quarterly*, *24*(1), 3–4. https://doi.org/10.1177/089976409502400102

Vollan, B., Henning, K., & Staewa, D. (2017). Do campaigns featuring impact evaluations increase donations? Evidence from a survey experiment. *Journal of Development Effectiveness*, *9*(4), 500–518.

Weisbrod, B. A. (1986). Toward a theory of the voluntary nonprofit sector in a three-sector economy. In S. Rose-Ackerman (Ed.), *The economics of nonprofit institutions: Studies in structure and policy* (pp. 21–44). Oxford University Press.

Weisbrod, B. A. (1988). *The nonprofit economy*. Harvard University Press.

Weisbrod, B. A., & Schlesinger, M. (1986). Public, private, nonprofit ownership and the response to asymmetric information: The case of nursing homes. In S. Rose-Ackerman (Ed.), *The economics of nonprofit institutions: Studies in structure and policy* (pp. 133–151). Oxford University Press.

Willems, J., & Faulk, L. (2019). Does voluntary disclosure matter when organizations violate stakeholder trust? *Journal of Behavioral Public Administration*, 2(1). https://doi.org/10.30636/jbpa.21.45

Williamson, O. E. (1999). Public and private bureaucracies: A transaction cost economics perspective. *Journal of Law, Economics, & Organization, 15*(1), 306–342. www.jstor.org/stable/3554953.

11 *Sector Theorists Should Borrow Epistemologies*

ELIZABETH A. CASTILLO

Even though the field of nonprofit research is now over 50 years old, the nonprofit sector remains undertheorized (Chapter 1 of this volume; Flynn & Hodgkinson, 2001) despite an interdisciplinary approach. Conventional theories of the nonprofit sector (e.g., market failure, government failure, contract failure, and supply-side) have difficulty predicting and explaining trends such as hybrid organizing, sector blurring, global variation, and the emergence of social enterprises. The lack of nonprofit sector theories that can explain these phenomena may stem from an overreliance on human-centric theories and processes rooted in the soft sciences (e.g., economic, political, organizational, and sociological). A promising alternative is to consider the nonprofit sector through a deeper interdisciplinary lens, drawing on principles from distant disciplines in the hard sciences (e.g., physics, ecology, and evolutionary science) to explore the boundaries, nature, and *raison d'être* for the sector.

Looking at phenomena through multiple knowledge domains generates fresh insights through synthesis (Klein, 2008). Importantly, the hard sciences acknowledge that humans are embedded in larger biological, geological, physical, and technical systems that shape our interactions with the world. Frameworks for the nonprofit sector that use principles and knowledge from the hard sciences may contribute to a more robust understanding of what the nonprofit sector is, why it exists, and how it operates.

Market, government, and voluntary failure theories represent some of the earliest attempts by scholars to explain the nonprofit sector through economic, legal, and sociological perspectives (Steinberg, 2003). Through these structural-operational lenses, the nonprofit sector is often characterized by its constraints (e.g., what it is not; see Chapter 2 of this volume). For instance, nonprofits are often distinguished from for-profit organizations by what limitations they have (e.g., prohibitions against shareholders, excessive executive compensation, and self-dealing) rather than by what functions they enable (Ben-Ner & Gui, 2003). Such "failure" theories have been criticized for their Western bias and their failure to explain nongovernmental organizations (NGOs) in global and transnational contexts (Corry, 2010).

Other theoretical conceptualizations of the nonprofit sector draw upon institutional logics, discourse, and identity theories. The institutional logics perspective sees the nonprofit sector as a product of ever-changing environmental conditions and rationalities. Identity and discourse-based theories consider the nonprofit sector through the lens of people's lived experiences and communicative rationality. They posit that the nonprofit sector orders ideas and relationships to achieve individual and collective aspirations and to resolve tensions between competing values, actors, and power structures (Koschmann, 2012). Ideally, this ordering uses deliberative democratic principles (Eikenberry, 2009) and integrates cognitive-instrumental, moral-practical, and aesthetic-expressive reasoning in ways that create mutual understanding and effective action (Habermas, 1989). Because the nonprofit sector is primarily composed of people who organize voluntarily around prosocial principles such as care, dignity, and belonging, the sector offers expressive alternatives to state bureaucracy, rationalization, compulsion (e.g., imposed order through command and control), and market economism (e.g., dehumanization, commodification, and opportunism; Kaldor, 2003).

While each of these theoretical approaches has produced valuable insights, they also leave gaps. Questions still arise regarding the sector's efficiency, beneficiaries, and special tax treatment (Ben-Ner & Gui, 2003). To address such knowledge gaps, this chapter draws from principles found in the hard sciences (e.g., thermodynamics, computer science, ecology, and evolution) to make sense of nonprofit sector dynamics, prosocial organizing, and nonprofit organizational forms.

11.1 Toward Theory Inspired by Distant Disciplines

Privileging psycho-social, political, and economic processes without considering how they are embedded in physical, geologic, ecologic, and technical systems isolates parts of the system from the whole (e.g., analyzing organizations as if they existed as standalone entities), making it harder to see system dynamics such as bidirectional causation, feedback loops, and interaction effects across micro, meso, and macro levels. Without expanding the theoretical approach we apply to the nonprofit sector, the interdependencies and tradeoffs between natural, symbolic, human, economic, social, political, and technological dimensions might be overlooked. While there may be limits to the extent that human processes mirror those of other parts of the natural world, embracing a broader set of theories and perspectives can guide theoretical development and stimulate novel insights into phenomena that may be missed using the social sciences alone.

Biglan (1973, p. 207) was one of the first to classify scholarly inquiry into "hard" and "soft" sciences, distinguishing between "pure" (e.g., math, anthropology) and "applied" (e.g., civil engineering, educational administration) disciplines and between those related to "life systems" (e.g., botany, psychology) and "nonlife systems" (e.g., geology, accounting). Remarkably, this classification scheme has persisted empirically even in light of newer disciplines, such as nonprofit studies (Stoecker, 1993). Of note for this study is the metaphorical distance in Biglan's classification between the soft sciences typically used in nonprofit sector theory and the hard sciences, like physics, computer science, and biology. The distance between these groupings makes it less likely that soft science-trained scholars will employ hard-science perspectives.

Some hard-science fields are more closely related to the nonprofit sector than others. Disciplines labeled in Biglan's (1973) classification as *life-system hard sciences* (e.g., biology) might be seen as nearer kin to the typical ones used in the nonprofit space (many of which are *life-system soft sciences*) than those labeled as *nonlife-system hard sciences* (e.g., physics). Relative to the life-system soft sciences often employed to study and develop theories of the nonprofit sector, I consider *nonlife-system soft sciences* and all of the hard sciences (*life-system* and *nonlife-system hard sciences*) as "distant disciplines."

In spite of this distance, some scholars already apply hard-science perspectives to the study of organizations and other human phenomena. For example, the application of population ecology principles by Hannan and Freeman (1977) has been tremendously influential in the field of management science. Around the same time, Hoffman (1978) collated psychological and biological imperatives for altruism, research that has shaped a relatively small but continuous stream of related studies into contemporary times. While studies that incorporate distant disciplines (such as those from the hard sciences) do exist, they are by far the minority in the corpus of general nonprofit studies literature. Further, most do not specifically broach the subject of nonprofit sector theory. Viewpoints that come close to a distant-discipline approach to nonprofit sector theory-building are Smith's (2014) assertion that "a person's tendency to feel and practice altruism is based on our genes and DNA ... [T]here is a Global Spirit of Altruism, hardwired into the human species" (177); Ben-Ner's (2022) description of the biological imperative for in-group and out-group behavior that is manifested in nonprofit organizing; and Moeller and Valentinov's (2012) application of "von Bertalanffy's general systems theory to argue that nonprofit organizations are open systems maintaining themselves in an environment in which the supply of critical resources is insecure" (p. 365). Few nonprofit scholars use hard-science perspectives to explain the functional and causal mechanisms of what the nonprofit sector is, how it has evolved, and why it exists.

While the application of both distant and less-distant hard-science disciplines has value to nonprofit sector theory, I will focus in this chapter first on *life-system hard sciences* because the insights from this group are likely to be more naturally connected to the social science perspectives that most nonprofit scholars are accustomed to. Thus, the barrier to gaining tools and knowledge from these disciplines is likely to be lower than for some of the nonlife-system hard sciences. After life-system hard sciences, however, I will also discuss nonlife-system hard sciences. The value of applying these distant disciplines (e.g., physics and engineering) to nonprofit sector theory is that they can potentially yield more novel insights than those of other disciplines – their way of viewing, testing, and theorizing about the world is usually very different from approaches in the life-system sciences. But while the potential for novel insights may be greater, so, too, is the cost of acquiring the necessary interdisciplinary knowledge to identify and apply those insights.

11.1.1 Life-System Hard Sciences: Less Distant Disciplines

Biglan's (1973) category of life-system hard sciences includes fields such as biology and ecology, in which scholars view humans as part of nature rather than entities operating outside of nature. While distinct enough from the social sciences to offer novel insights, life-system hard sciences are also close enough to make conceptual understanding reasonably intuitive. Nonprofit sector dynamics such as resource flows, competition versus cooperation, and the emergence of new organizational forms have recognizable parallels with ecological dynamics like food webs, symbiosis (how different species interact with each other), and speciation (how biological species become distinct from one another). Life-system hard sciences also tend to describe and explain phenomena in terms of relationships, interdependencies, and change over time. Finally, theories from life-system hard sciences typically examine dynamics as processes across multiple units of analysis (e.g., organisms, species, and population), akin to multilevel interactions between individuals, organizations, networks, sectors, and communities in the nonprofit sector. This type of analysis makes life-system hard sciences a good locus for discovering insights relevant to nonprofit sector theory.

11.1.2 Insights from Life-System Hard Sciences

Principles of evolutionary science such as niche construction, mutualism, and recombination offer new ways of looking at the nonprofit sector. *Niche construction* is a process whereby agents (e.g., organisms) make changes to their habitat to increase functional benefits to them (Laland et al., 2016). In the human domain, niche construction includes the social transmission of cultural values and knowledge (Kendal et al., 2011). In this light, the emergence of the nonprofit sector can be seen as a process of reshaping a context to better support collective aspirations and expressive values. From a structural perspective, actions such as advocacy provide the functional benefit of promoting permanence and stability to nascent, emergent collective action.

Mutualism is the interaction between two or more species that benefits both, sometimes producing systemic benefits as well (Leigh, 2010). An example is cross-pollination, a process in which interactions between bees and flowers benefit both species while increasing the biodiversity and the resilience of ecosystems by changing the structure and diversity of plant communities (Steffan-Dewenter et al., 2006). Mutualism often arises as species experience a decreased capacity to flourish individually (Chomicki et al., 2020). In the nonprofit sector, mutualism can occur as the interaction and collaboration between organizations from different sectors create cooperative partnerships that create interdependent hybrid forms, such as corporate–nonprofit funding relationships, government-nonprofit contracting, or collective action networks that span multiple sectors.

Recombination is the exchange of genetic information between different organisms that results in offspring with novel traits. Socially learned information (e.g., culture) can also be recombined to create new traits and environments (Richerson et al., 2010). However, if this information is not valued through a market lens, it risks being discarded. This loss of information depletes the evolutionary potential of a system by reducing recombination possibilities and eroding a network's distributed knowledge transmission infrastructure (Hidalgo, 2015). If we think of the nonprofit sector as an evolutionary process where people and organizations combine their values and resources in novel ways (like genetic recombination), trying to survive the selective evolutionary force of the market, we may gain novel insights into the "survival of the fittest" in the nonprofit sector.

Another example of a life-system hard science that seems applicable to nonprofit sector theory is ethology. *Ethology* is the study of animal behavior, including human behavior and social organization, from a biological perspective (Tinbergen, 1963). The discipline focuses on four main ideas: (a) *function* (the survival value of an animal's behavior), (b) *causal mechanisms* (how and why the behavior works), (c) *development* (the behavior's development over the animal's lifetime), and (d) *evolutionary history* (the behavior's evolution over the history of the species). Interestingly, these concepts mirror some of the knowledge gaps in nonprofit sector theories. For example, applying ethology's focus on an entity's function and mechanisms to the nonprofit sector can help us identify traits that are unique to the nonprofit sector (e.g., nondistribution of profits to shareholders, board governance, or donative redistribution) and study how these traits (which we might otherwise consider as merely definitional or legalistic) have evolved over time, why they came into existence, and what pressures keep them in place. Examining the boundaries of the nonprofit sector as a set of evolving traits can improve our efforts to determine how and when one species (nonprofits) might have descendants that evolve into something else entirely, such as a fourth sector comprised of social enterprises (Sabeti, 2011).

11.1.3 Nonlife-System Hard Sciences: More Distant Disciplines

Adding biological and evolutionary perspectives to the nature and origin of the nonprofit sector is not a significant stretch once we acknowledge that humans and their institutions are, in fact, part of nature. But what of the nonlife-system hard sciences? To what extent can these disciplines provide useful perspectives on the theory of the nonprofit sector?

The nonlife-system hard sciences are rich with opportunity to inform nonprofit sector theory. One illuminating perspective comes from thinking about the sector in terms of *energy* (i.e., the ability to do work) and *entropy* (i.e., the tendency of a system to become less ordered over time). For example, collective action in the nonprofit sector might be seen as a process of transforming potential energy (e.g., shared goals and aspirations) into kinetic energy (e.g., establishing a social movement). This kinetic energy can be stabilized by creating supportive regulations that incentivize the infusion of new energy sources, such as authorizing tax deductions for philanthropic and financial support of 501(c)(3) organizations. In this light, prosocial organizing could be seen as a process that structures and facilitates sustained cooperation by creating architectures that channel energy exchange across multiple levels (individual, organization, network, community) in ways that expand novelty and complexity over time. Principles of entropy might suggest the opposite force to that of formal organizing – suggesting that in the absence of intervention, resources once mobilized in social movements and nonprofit organizations will eventually return to a chaotic state.

The nonlife hard sciences that are most relevant to the nonprofit sector entail nonlinear complex adaptive system dynamics. Understanding these complex systems invites learning about concepts such as self-organization and emergence. *Self-organization* is a relational process that describes the spontaneous formation of structures in a system through interactions of component parts. *Emergence* is a qualitative state change (i.e., the spontaneous generation of higher-level order through lower-level local interactions; Haken, 1987). Learning about and applying these concepts about complex systems provides a lens to see and explain heretofore poorly understood patterns, structures, processes, and phenomena in the nonprofit sector. For example, the Schelling segregation model uses self-organization and emergence to demonstrate how seemingly innocuous choices by individual agents can create the unintended macro effect of social segregation (Schelling, 1971). Applied to the nonprofit sector, nonlife-system models can provide language and models that can deepen insights and accelerate learning and theorizing about the sector.

11.1.4 Insights from Nonlife-System Hard Sciences

By considering some other principles found in nonlife-system hard-science disciplines, we can develop explanations for how and why the nonprofit sector spurs individuals into action. For example, thermodynamics offers a model for how order can emerge spontaneously rather than having to be imposed through force, and physics describes systems as becoming organized by the process of energy moving through them (Morowitz, 1979). While for elements *self-organization* occurs through the interactions between environmental conditions (e.g., temperature and pressure) and the system's own compositional elements and structure, similar patterns might be observed in the nonprofit sector by considering the social pressures and fiery energy that cause people to self-organize. As a system experiences a positive *feedback loop* (energetic recursion, e.g., when an output returns to become a new input), it can reach a critical point of energy buildup that produces a qualitative state change. An example in the natural world is boiling water. As water molecules reach a critical temperature threshold, a phase transition occurs to redistribute the energy flow more efficiently, creating a new conduit between the system and the environment (Morowitz, 1979). Thinking about voluntary action and social-capital mobilization as the reconfiguration of energy that creates new outlets for the buildup of energy may spur new insights for the nonprofit sector. Grassroots organizing, for example, can be seen as the process in which the activation of independent autonomous agents, such as the pressure and "heat" of a new policy environment or social need, can create something like an energetic buildup that produces a qualitative state change, morphing individuals into a collective, social movement or organization.

11.1.5 Blended Applications: Combining Insights from Life-System and Nonlife-System Hard Sciences

While thermodynamics offers insights into how systems self-organize and how they secure and convert energy across multiple levels, this field's perspective does not explain increasing complexity, such as innovation or sociotechnical progress in the nonprofit sector. To understand such phenomena, blending ideas from both life-system and nonlife-system hard sciences is required.

Borrowing from ecology (a life-system hard science), the functional value of the nonprofit sector can be seen as creating cooperative surplus and distributing those returns across multiple levels in ways that expand the capabilities of stakeholders, organizations, communities, and society. This continuous expansion of capabilities generates *open-endedness*, a concept from computer science (a nonlife-system hard science). Banzhaf et al. (2016) defined open-endedness as the ability to continuously produce complexity and novelty (e.g., variation, innovation, and emergence over multiple levels). Rather than seeking predetermined goals and outcomes, open-ended systems seek to generate new options by continuously increasing degrees of freedom and processing energy and information across different scales, which promotes evolvability and antifragility. *Evolvability* is the propensity for a system to discover adaptations in a particular environment that promote the ability to survive and reproduce (Whitacre & Bender, 2010; Whitacre et al., 2010). *Antifragility* is a related macro-level property that increases a system's capacity to thrive under unstable conditions, transforming disturbances, surprises, pressures, noise, and ambiguity into beneficial resources (Taleb & Douady, 2013). Thus, the expansion of the nonprofit sector naturally fosters open-endedness, which in turn sustains the sector's evolvability and antifragility.

Evolvability and antifragility are useful for understanding innovation in the nonprofit sector. Jones (2014) suggested using open-endedness, evolvability, and antifragility as qualitative design principles for sociotechnical systems because they enhance fitness and innovation under adverse conditions. Evolvability and antifragility emerge through adaptive approaches that recombine elements and leverage mutation, selection, and the development and identification of high-quality areas in a search space (Back, 1996; Blum & Roli, 2003). Through these principles, the nonprofit sector can be seen as a container for process mechanisms that foster generativity, evolvability, and antifragility. These in turn facilitate the production of cooperative surplus while helping socioeconomic systems prevent ossification and/or environmental decoupling. In this way, the nonprofit sector remains dynamically stable and innovative.

11.2 Implications of Applying Distant Disciplines to Nonprofit Sector Practice and Policy

While conventional resource theories focus on human-centered explanations like economics, governance, and decision-making (e.g., bounded rationality), concepts from the hard sciences (e.g., thermodynamics, ecology, and computer science) offer a novel investigatory pathway to nonprofit theory-building. In this section, I will consider resourcing challenges in the nonprofit sector as a case study to show how applying hard-science principles to the sector can stimulate new insights into the field.

Resourcing challenges in the nonprofit sector have conventionally been theorized through the lens of market failure, which results when individuals' pursuit of self-interest prevents the efficient or sufficient production of public goods. The nonrivalrous and nonexcludable qualities of public goods makes it difficult for them to be offered in a market context since all participants automatically benefit whether or not they contribute resources toward the costs of production. And because positive externalities of public goods (e.g., national defense, safe neighborhoods) are not remunerated, private organizations have no incentive to produce these goods voluntarily (Samuelson, 1954). Additionally, collectively acting to create public value is costly (Heckathorn, 1996). How may nonprofit organizations solve these resource problems while operating efficiently? Principles from the hard sciences offer some clues.

To understand a resource-based view of the nonprofit sector, it may be useful to look at Odum's (1988) ecological principle of *maximum empower*. Odum investigated how energy moves through different levels within food webs, trying to explain what he initially saw as an inefficient process (since only a small amount of energy is typically transferred from one level to the next). Through his research, Odum came to see that energy was not necessarily being lost from organisms (i.e., entropy). Rather, it was sometimes stored for future use, with the environment functioning as a storage mechanism from which energy could be reclaimed later. For example, as a deciduous tree drops its leaves each autumn, the decaying leaves provide energy to microorganisms in the soil. When those organisms process the leaves, they enrich both themselves and the soil, creating conditions that enhance the tree's potential for future growth. If we view different economic systems as links in a food web or food chain, we start to not only see the ways in which the nonprofit sector may be distinct from other sectors in a sort of "trophic level" sense, but we can also discover new ways of thinking about resource transfers between the sectors as a sector theory. We could explore, for example, the possibility that the nonprofit sector is a resource-storage mechanism within the economic value chain. Excess "energy" in the form of resources might be transferred to the nonprofit sector in a manner that appears inefficient at the outset but in reality serves to maintain the value of those excess resources so they are not lost. The principle of maximum empower balances tradeoffs between maximizing energy output/transfer across levels with reducing the amount of time required for that energy conversion.

Viewing the nonprofit sector through a maximum empower perspective can also help prevent policy failure. Many public policy failures arise in part because people do not understand dynamics within complex systems and the interdependencies of a system's component parts (Mueller, 2020; Vester, 1988). Without a systemic understanding of resources (e.g., natural, human, social, or economic) across multiple scales (individual, organizational, regional, national, and global), it is difficult to recognize interdependencies, avoid false tradeoffs, develop policies, and make wise decisions that facilitate the production of cobenefits (Roseland, 2012). Careful application of hard-science principles can facilitate a richer understanding of the nonprofit sector, leading to better theory development and explanations.

11.3 Conclusions

This chapter suggests that distant-discipline perspectives and epistemologies can provide a conceptual foundation for theorizing the emergence and evolution of the nonprofit sector. It outlines potential starting points by sharing examples of concepts and principles from life-system and nonlife-system hard sciences that can expand nonprofit sector theory. Conceptual approaches like ethology, evolutionary science, thermodynamics, computer science, and ecology point the way to functional explanations of previously unexplained phenomena in the nonprofit sector and nonlinear causal mechanisms grounded in complex system dynamics.

Scholarly contributions of this chapter include: (a) moving the field of nonprofit sector studies beyond failure theories and human-centric schemas; (b) outlining how structural and symbolic theories (e.g., values expression) gain explanatory power when considered through the lens of evolutionary science; and (c) opening new pathways for inquiry by drawing from complex adaptive systems and process dynamics described in the hard sciences (Louie, 2010; Rosen, 1991).

A variety of research methodologies have been developed over the past three decades to study, analyze, and model nonlinear dynamic systems. However, these methods are not often taught to students or incorporated into social science education generally. Castellani (2014, par. 5) observed that "the pathway to scientific literacy in the social sciences remains pretty much the same: conventional quantitative methods and statistics, grounded in mechanistic and reductionist experimental or quasi-experimental design." The ontological and epistemological assumptions that underpin much nonprofit sector research, analysis, and theory-building (e.g., notions of separation, subject/object, humans/nature, linear causality, and how to analyze variability) often remain unquestioned. But there is a whole world of alternative methods, approaches, and ideas that remains unexplored if we avoid the distant disciplines.

There is little risk and much to gain in exploring new epistemologies and approaches inspired by the hard sciences. Our soft-science methodologies limit us by thinking too atomistically and not enough in terms of larger integrated systems. As Ragin (1987) noted, the conventional view of causation isolates individual variables to explain variance and impact. However, when causation is investigated from a complexity-oriented view, a multiplicity of factors combine in different ways and at different levels to produce an outcome. To address such issues, Wallerstein (1996) urged social scientists to conduct research through the lens of complexity science using methods such as computational science and dynamic modeling. Because complex systems have unique properties that conventional statistical analysis cannot accommodate (e.g., nonlinearity, dynamism, emergence, self-organization), they require specialized conceptual, mathematical, and computational tools to investigate structural, relational, and motional properties over time (Sayama, 2015). Examples include spectral analysis that decomposes time series data to understand underlying structural and periodic behavior at different time scales (Iacobucci, 2005) and agent-based modeling that uses abductive logic and experiments *in silico* to test potential explanations (Castillo & Trinh, 2018). Such methods can accommodate change and development over time, bidirectional causation, and mutual interaction effects. Adopting these methods, along with larger theories and approaches to thinking about the interactions between individuals and systems, are among the promising paths offered by engaging hard-science principles in the process of developing new nonprofit sector theories.

References

Back, T. (1996). *Evolutionary algorithms in theory and practice: Evolution strategies, evolutionary programming, genetic algorithms*. Oxford University Press.

Banzhaf, W., Baumgaertner, B., Beslon, G., Doursat, R., Foster, J. A., McMullin, B., de Melo, V. V., Miconi, T., Spector, L., Stepney, S., & White, R. (2016). Defining and simulating open-ended novelty: Requirements, guidelines, and challenges. *Theory in Biosciences*, *135*(3), 131–161.

Ben-Ner, A. (2022). The dark side of the nonprofit sector: Polarization in contemporary society. In M. Hoelscher, R. A. List, A. Ruser, & S. Toepler (Eds.), *Civil society: Concepts, challenges, contexts* (pp. 285–306). Springer.

Ben-Ner, A., & Gui, B. (2003). The theory of nonprofit organizations revisited. In H. K. Anheier & A. Ben-Ner (Eds.), *The study of the nonprofit enterprise: Theories and approaches* (pp. 3–26). Kluwer Academic.

Biglan, A. (1973). Relationships between subject matter characteristics and the structure and output of university departments. *Journal of Applied Psychology*, *57*(3), 204–213.

Blum, C., & Roli, A. (2003). Metaheuristics in combinatorial optimization: Overview and conceptual comparison. *ACM Computing Surveys (CSUR)*, *35*(3), 268–308.

Castellani, B. (2014, November 4). Focus: Complexity and the failure of quantitative social science. *Discover Society*. https://archive.discoversociety.org/2014/11/04/focus-complexity-and-the-failure-of-quantitative-social-science/

Castillo, E. A., & Trinh, M. P. (2018). In search of missing time: A review of the study of time in leadership research. *The Leadership Quarterly*, *29*(1), 165–178.

Chomicki, G., Kiers, E. T., & Renner, S. S. (2020). The evolution of mutualistic dependence. *Annual Review of Ecology, Evolution, and Systematics, 51*(1), 409–432.

Corry, O. (2010). Defining and theorizing the third sector. In R. Taylor (Ed.), *Third sector research* (pp. 11–20). Springer.

Eikenberry, A. M. (2009). Refusing the market: A democratic discourse for voluntary and nonprofit organizations. *Nonprofit and Voluntary Sector Quarterly, 38*(4), 582–596.

Flynn, P., & Hodgkinson, V. A. (2001). *Measuring the impact of the nonprofit sector*. Kluwer Academic/Plenum Publishers.

Habermas, J. (1989). *The structural transformation of the public sphere: An inquiry into a category of bourgeois society*. MIT Press.

Haken, H. (1987). Synergetics: An approach to self-organization. In F. E. Yates (Ed.), *Self-organizing systems: The emergence of order* (pp. 417–434). Springer.

Hannan, M. T., & Freeman, J. (1977). The population ecology of organizations. *American Journal of Sociology, 82*(5), 929–964.

Heckathorn, D. D. (1996). The dynamics and dilemmas of collective action. *American Sociological Review, 61*(2), 250–277.

Hidalgo, C. (2015). *Why information grows: The evolution of order, from atoms to economies*. Basic Books.

Hoffman, M. L. (1978). Psychological and biological perspectives on altruism. *International Journal of Behavioral Development, 1*(4), 323–339.

Iacobucci, A. (2005). Spectral analysis for economic time series. In J. Leskow, M. Puchet, & L. F. Punzo (Eds.), *New tools of economic dynamics* (pp. 203–219). Springer.

Jones, P. H. (2014). Systemic design principles for complex social systems. In G. S. Metcalf (Ed.), *Social systems and design* (pp. 91–128). Springer.

Kaldor, M. (2003). *Global civil society: An answer to war?* Polity Press.

Kendal, J., Tehrani, J. J., & Odling-Smee, J. (2011). Human niche construction in interdisciplinary focus. *Philosophical Transactions of the Royal Society B: Biological Sciences, 366*(1566), 785–792.

Klein, J. T. (2008). The rhetoric of interdisciplinarity. In A. A. Lunsford, K. H. Wilson, & R. A. Eberly (Eds.), *The Sage handbook of rhetorical studies* (pp. 265–284). SAGE.

Koschmann, M. A. (2012). Developing a communicative theory of the nonprofit. *Management Communication Quarterly, 26*(1), 139–146.

Laland, K., Matthews, B., & Feldman, M. W. (2016). An introduction to niche construction theory. *Evolutionary Ecology, 30*(2), 191–202.

Leigh, E. G. (2010). The evolution of mutualism. *Journal of Evolutionary Biology, 23*(12), 2507–2528.

Louie, A. H. (2010). Robert Rosen's anticipatory systems. *Foresight, 12*(3), 18–29.

Moeller, L., & Valentinov, V. (2012). The commercialization of the nonprofit sector: A general systems theory perspective. *Systemic Practice and Action Research*, *25*(4), 365–370.
Morowitz, H. J. (1979). *Energy flow in biology*. Oxbow Press.
Mueller, B. (2020). Why public policies fail: Policymaking under complexity. *EconomiA*, *21*(2), 311–323.
Odum, H. T. (1988). Self-organization, transformity, and information. *Science*, *242*(4882), 1132–1139.
Ragin, C. C. (1987). *The comparative method: Moving beyond qualitative and quantitative strategies*. University of California Press.
Richerson, P. J., Boyd, R., & Henrich, J. (2010). Gene-culture coevolution in the age of genomics. *Proceedings of the National Academy of Sciences*, *107*(supplement 2), 8985–8992. https://doi.org/10.1073/pnas.0914631107
Roseland, M. (2012). *Toward sustainable communities: Solutions for citizens and their governments*. New Society Publishers.
Rosen, R. (1991). *Life itself: A comprehensive inquiry into the nature, origin, and fabrication of life*. Columbia University Press.
Sabeti, H. (2011). The for-benefit enterprise. *Harvard Business Review*, *89*(11), 98–104.
Samuelson, P. A. (1954). The pure theory of public expenditure. *Review of Economics and Statistics*, *36*(4), 387–389.
Sayama, H. (2015). *Introduction to the modeling and analysis of complex systems*. Open SUNY Textbooks.
Schelling, T. C. (1971). Dynamic models of segregation. *Journal of Mathematical Sociology*, 1(2), 143–186.
Smith, D. H. (2014). The global spirit of philanthropy and altruism: Meanings, experiences, and some biological roots. *China Nonprofit Review*, *6*(2), 177–196.
Steffan-Dewenter, I., Klein, A. M., Gaebele, V., Alfert, T., & Tscharntke, T. (2006). Bee diversity and plant-pollinator interactions in fragmented landscapes. In N. M. Waser & J. Ollerton (Eds.), *Specialization and generalization in plant-pollinator interactions* (pp. 387–410). University of Chicago Press.
Steinberg, R. (2003). Economic theories of nonprofit organizations. In H. K. Anheier & A. Ben-Ner (Eds.), *The study of the nonprofit enterprise: Theories and approaches* (pp. 277–309). Kluwer Academic.
Stoecker, J. L. (1993). The Biglan classification revisited. *Research in Higher Education*, *34*(4), 451–464.
Taleb, N. N., & Douady, R. (2013). Mathematical definition, mapping, and detection of (anti)fragility. *Quantitative Finance*, *13*(11), 1677–1689.
Tinbergen, N. (1963). On aims and methods of ethology. *Zeitschrift fur Tierpsychologie*, *20*(4), 410–433.

Vester, F. (1988). The biocybernetics approach as a basis for planning our environment. *Systems Practice*, *1*(4), 399–413.

Wallerstein, I. (1996). *Open the social sciences: Report of the Gulbenkian Commission on the restructuring of the social sciences*. Stanford University Press.

Whitacre, J. M., & Bender, A. (2010). Degeneracy: A design principle for achieving robustness and evolvability. *Journal of Theoretical Biology*, *263*(1), 143–153.

Whitacre, J. M., Rohlfshagen, P., Bender, A., & Yao, X. (2010). The role of degenerate robustness in the evolvability of multi-agent systems in dynamic environments. In R. Schaefer, C. Cotta, J. Kolodziej, & G. Rudolph (Eds.), *International conference on parallel problem solving from nature, PPSN XI* (pp. 284–293). Springer.

PART III

New Directions

12 Nonprofits as Organizational Actors

PATRICIA BROMLEY AND HEITOR SANTOS

The nonprofit sector is a recent invention, arising mainly in the latter half of the twentieth century. There are some historical precursors, such as religious groups and civil society, but these forms of association fail to directly capture contemporary meanings of the term "nonprofit sector." The editors of this volume define the nonprofit sector as "voluntary (and organized) action that is not aimed at generating profit" (Child & Witesman, this volume, p. 7). Appropriately, the organized nature of the sector is explicitly called out. In this chapter we argue that "organization" is an elemental feature of the nonprofit sector. What makes the nonprofit sector distinct from earlier manifestations of prosocial activity is its dependence on formal organization[1] and organizing. By embedding the emergence of the nonprofit sector within the evolution and institutionalization of organization as a central feature of modern society, our chapter provides new insight into core questions about the sector, such as how to explain blurring between boundaries of business, government, and nonprofit domains and how to explain variation in the size of the nonprofit sector over time and around the world.

One purpose of this volume is to understand why nonprofit organizations and sectors exist. The answer we offer here is that they are part of a dramatic historical phenomenon: the rise and globalization of modern organization and organizing. The contemporary social

[1] In this account, "organization" is a socially constructed category or model composed of entities that are defined, by law and cultural tradition, as autonomous social actors with rationalized identities, purposes, and responsibilities. "Organizing" is the body of activity intended to rationalize, systematize, or standardize arenas of the human and natural world, such as formal planning around setting goals and how to achieve them, spelling out roles and responsibilities, linking resources to plans, tracking and measuring activities, or conforming to various standards and certifications. Organizing can take place outside the boundaries of formal organization.

structure we now call "organization" evolved out of the massive social transformations wrought by the Enlightenment and the related principles of Western liberal culture. Functionalist accounts of the emergence of a nonprofit sector, rooted in ideas of preexisting needs or government and market failures, overlook the role of this broader cultural context in shaping the nature of prosocial activity into its distinctly organizational character. We propose that the form and size of the nonprofit sector in part reflects the dominance of formal organization as the preferred way of structuring activity.

We start with a brief explanation of the neo-institutional view of organization that guides our arguments. Next, keeping in mind our definition of an organization as a model born from social construct and tradition, we provide a brief sketch of the historical evolution of organization, including nonprofits. The concept of formal organization, and the accompanying idea of a three-sector society with a distinct nonprofit sphere, has roots in liberal philosophy and the history of the Western world. But after the fall of the Soviet Union, the tripartite model of society with a private sphere populated largely by for-profit and nonprofit organizations diffused widely around the world. Last, we discuss how our view contributes to core questions about the sector and conclude with reflections on how the recent fragmentation of the liberal and neoliberal world order could portend critical changes for nonprofits.

Before proceeding, three clarifications are important. First, new social developments, like the "nonprofit sector," emerge from existing phenomena. Thus, although the term "nonprofit sector" is relatively new, we can retrospectively observe nonprofit-like examples that existed before society coined the term. For instance, Aristotle spoke of the "civil society," which was envisioned as a political community of citizens in the ancient Greek polis (DeWiel, 1997). In this early manifestation of prosocial activity, there was no vision of an independent sector as we understand it today. Much later, during the Enlightenment, civil society became redefined as distinct from the state. Societies were thought to be best governed by the free self-organization of individuals and groups, including the market and economic entities (Kocka, 2004). At the time, businesses were more integral to civil society than we expect in contemporary definitions of the nonprofit sector. As another example, religious institutions have long carried out many activities that are now recast as part of the nonprofit sector. However, as we will discuss later, when religious activity and older forms of civil society are recast as part of the nonprofit sector, they are also transformed. These precursors do not quite capture contemporary meanings of "nonprofit sector," and they are changed by becoming more nonprofit-like.

The second clarification that is vital to this analysis is the argument that the pervasiveness of formal organization and organizing is what differentiates a nonprofit sector from precursors. This does not mean that all activity in the sector is legally incorporated. Instead, formal organization is a dominant cultural model that provides legitimacy and visibility, but it is often more aspirational than achievable. Under conditions in which formal organization is a celebrated model, even informal clubs and grassroots associations are more likely to adopt some of its trappings, such as meeting minutes and rules of order or strategic plans.[2]

Third, our observation that formal organization is a defining feature of the nonprofit sector is analytic rather than normative. Later, we discuss what may be gained and lost as a result of structuring prosocial activity this way, but our primary goal is to explain rather than prescribe.

12.1 A Theory of Organizational Actorhood

12.1.1 The Rise of Organizations

The Introduction to this volume began with a valuable thought experiment. Editors Curtis Child and Eva Witesman asked us to imagine a group of people appearing on an uninhabited and ungoverned land, tasked with determining "how they might organize their world." They

[2] We do not conflate "organization" with the legal incorporation of a bounded entity but rather see it as an aspirational cultural model. As a result, we use the term in two distinct but connected ways. On the one hand, "organization" refers to the social construction of imagined bounded actors, including the rise of "corporate personhood" laws to institutionalize this status, as well as to the general social tendency to anthropomorphize organizations and treat them as bounded entities in management theory and practice (Ashforth et al., 2020; Bromley & Sharkey, 2017). On the other hand, we also refer to "organize" as a verb, a set of practices that, while not referring to the bounded entity, is ultimately situated in the same semantic field. For instance, when we talk about social movements getting organized, we mean the adoption of practices such as professionalization, monitoring and evaluation, and accountability, which are connected to the domain of formal organization, despite being adopted and enacted outside of this legal form.

asked, "What will be the nature of the organizations that they create to carry out the work of building and maintaining a society?" (p. 3). From our view, there is a critical distinction between how a society is organized and the nature of its organizations. "Organizations" are not the only option available for structuring human activity. Looking historically and cross-nationally, there are multiple alternatives, such as kinship or tribal networks, caste systems, autocratic forms of government, or empires. None of these alternatives fits the model of a society that is thickly populated with formal organizing and organizations that are considered to be a private sphere separate from government. A key facet of our argument is that the concept of a nonprofit sector takes for granted (often implicitly) the existence of a private, nongovernmental arena that has become largely filled by "organizations." But organizations are a distinct form of social structure that emerged in modern times out of specific historical and cultural conditions, and they remain institutionalized to varying degrees around the world.

Many organization scholars have documented that the modern concept of organization as an autonomous cultural and legal entity was uncommon until the 1950s (Coleman, 1982; Drucker, 1992; Perrow, 1991). Prior to this period, the word "organization" was mainly used to refer to a pattern or particular way of structuring or arranging items, ideas, or groups. In contrast, the contemporary use of the word "organization" refers to a bounded social actor that is distinct from its predecessors, such as states, churches, universities, or hospitals (King et al., 2010; Krücken & Meier, 2006; Krücken et al., 2013). For example, whereas bureaucracies were envisioned as a tool of a sovereign, organizations are themselves constructed as sovereign social actors.

By our definition, organization is an idealized model with three main characteristics: it is bounded, rationalized, and responsible (Bromley & Sharkey, 2017; Hwang et al., 2019).[3] The modern organization is

[3] To say "organization" is a model does not suggest it is pure ceremony. As the model of organization becomes institutionalized through normative, regulative, and cultural-cognitive mechanisms (Scott, 2013), it exerts both coercive and symbolic control over local contexts, thereby taking on material consequences. Real-world efforts to conform to the model of proper organizations are coercively imposed (e.g., by law) or aspirationally embraced (e.g., by management recommendations) to varied degrees, and this "decoupling" or variation around the enactment of the ideal model represents an important area of inquiry for scholars and managers alike (Meyer & Rowan, 1977).

conceived of as *bounded*, meaning it is intended to be autonomous, with an identity and purposes of its own that are separate from the identities and purposes of its individual members or creators. In some legal systems, organizations even come to have certain rights of their own. Proper modern organizations are also expected to be *rationalized*, which is to say that the way they go about enacting their mission involves adopting scientized practices. A modern organization concerned with eradicating hunger does not achieve its mission by simply buying food and distributing it to the poor; instead, it does so in a measurable, trackable, and optimizable way. Finally, as organizations assert their place as autonomous entities and adopt rationalized practices to enact their goals, they are expected to be *responsible*. Just as individual human actors are accountable to the wider society, the modern organization, as an actor, also ought to abide by prescribed legal and moral standards in order to maintain its legitimacy in the organizational society.

Two long-term historical trends are most salient to the rise of formal organization, including nonprofits (Bromley & Meyer, 2015; Meyer & Bromley, 2013). Starting especially in the eighteenth century, Enlightenment-era individuals were redefined as, first, having the capability to reason about science and nature, and second, as having the right and responsibility to do so (Baker, 2001). These shifts provided the basis for establishing a sphere of life meant to be independent of government, a phenomenon that has been described as "the invention of society" (e.g., Kaviraj & Khilnani, 2001; Rudan, 2016; for a critical take, see Foucault et al., 2008, pp. 4–5). One central outcome of the emergence of an independent sphere of life was the establishment of a social structure intended to enable and protect collective action separate from the state – the *corporate form* (Bromley & Meyer, 2015; Drori et al., 2006). Although contested in their early phases, corporations and their modern counterparts, organizations, have become the dominant social structure of our time. Broadly speaking, this view of organizations as dependent on, and constructed by, the external cultural environment is called *neo-institutional theory* (DiMaggio & Powell, 1983; Meyer, 2010; Meyer & Rowan, 1977; Scott, 2013). These foundational arguments are especially spelled out in a seminal work by Gili Drori, John Meyer, Hokyu Hwang, and collaborators (2006) called *Globalization and organization: World society and organizational change.*

12.1.2 Nonprofit Forms of Organization

Early on in the history of the corporate form, there was little distinction between nonprofits and for-profits (Kaufman, 2008). However, as the corporate form took hold and expanded, it became increasingly differentiated and elaborate: Rules and regulations emerged to define and govern organizations of different sizes, industries, and goals (e.g., for the public good or profit). Only after society became populated by a dense ecology of organizations did it become possible to theorize about differences between types, such as nonprofit and for-profit.

Efforts to demarcate a sharp line between nonprofit and for-profit organizations developed most forcefully starting in the mid- to late twentieth century. Especially during the 1980s, several related strands of economic thinking sharpened the focus on nonprofits and a distinct nonprofit sector. One key set of arguments speculated that nonprofits would arise when consumers did not have enough information to evaluate a product or service, and therefore must place trust in an organization (Hansmann, 1980). A second, more macro, set of arguments (often captured in the term "neoliberalism") speculated that private service provision would provide the most effective and efficient means of meeting public needs. These trends contributed to the celebration of the three-sector model of society, which was pushed widely across the world, especially following the fall of the Soviet Union, and together created today's "society of organizations" (Perrow, 1991). For better or worse, organizations have become the dominant social structure of late modern societies, often touching people's lives more deeply and routinely than the distant structures of government and sometimes having great influence over public life.

As the organizational form gained legitimacy, earlier entities started taking on some of the features of what is now called "organization." Establishing mission and vision became elaborate processes, as did developing plans for achieving goals through logic models, theories of change, and detailed evaluation and reporting metrics. For example, in *American grace*, Putnam and Campbell (2012) described one minister's internal struggle over his growing role as an events coordinator. His time was increasingly spent providing entertainment-focused social gatherings as a rationalized organizational tactic to build market share and improve customer satisfaction. In an earlier era, religious leaders would attend to otherworldly matters. As churches start to adopt the features of a modern organization, they begin to follow the latest management practices and aim to measure their impact.

As one signal of these transformations of older structures, new language evolved. When firms became contemporary organizations, they started to be described as "postmodern" (Caporaso, 1996; Hirschhorn, 1997; Kumar, 2009; Parker, 1992) or "postindustrial" (Bell, 1976; Huber, 1984; Masuda, 1980; Touraine, 1971). Similarly, government agencies and other large bureaucracies shifted to become "postbureaucratic" (Brunsson & Sahlin-Andersson, 2000; Kernaghan, 2000). And previous forms of associational and prosocial activity become "nonprofit organizations" constituting a "nonprofit sector" as they are transformed into modern organizational actors (Hwang & Suárez, 2019). As an illustration, Figure 12.1 shows the relative frequency of the phrase "nonprofit sector" in the Google Ngram corpus of digitized books (Google Inc., 2021), that is, how often the phrase appears in a sample of more than one million books published in American English. This phrase hardly appears until the 1970s and then increases dramatically. An examination of a different database, the Corpus of Historical American English (Davies, 2010–), revealed a similar pattern: the phrase "nonprofit sector" does not appear from 1800 until the 1970s, at which point 0.07 words per million include the phrase; this doubles by the 2010s when 0.14 words per million are "nonprofit sector." Related, the top co-locate of the word "nonprofit" is "organization" (a co-locate is the word appearing most commonly just before or after in the text corpus). In sum, the nonprofit sector is co-constructed with the expansion of the model of organization, and it reflects the culmination of a much longer process of societal and organizational transformation.

12.2 Implications for Understanding the Nonprofit Sector

What does a neo-institutional theory of organization suggest for the nonprofit sector? Applying our arguments to foundational questions and trends in the sector yields novel insights. As a start, observations of "blurring boundaries" are now commonplace and are typically attributed to pressures of marketization (e.g., Eikenberry & Kluver, 2004). But economic explanations only go so far; they fail to account

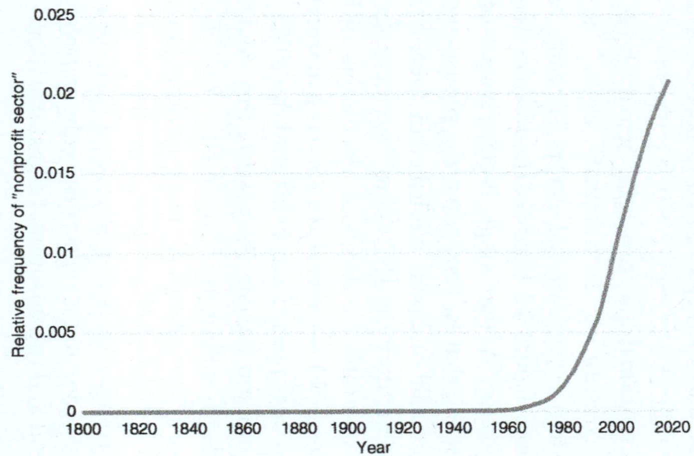

Figure 12.1 Relative frequency of the bigram "nonprofit sector" in Google's English-language book corpus

Note: Y-axis scaled at 1×10^5. Smoothing of 20. Source: Google Inc., 2021.

for why firms are transformed as well as nonprofits, and why many of the changes go far beyond direct marketization (Bromley & Meyer, 2017). We argue that as pre-organizational structures – such as family firms, guilds, townships, universities, and churches – become instances of "organization," they become more alike. By definition, all organizations possess similarities that make them recognizable members of that category. And what it means to be a proper organization continues to evolve and shift; for example, increasingly including broad emphases on social responsibility in both firms and nonprofits (Lim, 2021; Pope et al., 2018). Our view offers a cultural account for why we see similarities between for-profit and nonprofit entities.

Importantly, our account of the rise of organizational actors as a socially constructed metacategory does not predict an unending and inevitable march toward similarity between firms and nonprofits. Following classical social theory arguments, we posit that social structures are constituted by, and therefore reflect, underlying culture and society (as in, e.g., Weber's canonical discussion of how the Protestant ethic underpinned the evolution of capitalist structures). As social norms and culture shifts over time, the form and content of social structures also change. It is an open question what the future will hold as society and culture change.

The neo-institutional theory we advance can also be applied to form a better understanding of variation in the size of the nonprofit sector over time and between countries. Canonical explanations predict larger nonprofit sectors in countries with greater diversity in the population (as there is more divergence from a "typical" citizen and therefore more needs to be filled) or in which government service provision is limited (James, 1989). Our view, which is complementary to traditional arguments rather than logically competing, asserts that societies that are more linked to the liberal cultural principles underpinning the model we call "organization" will have more of these entities. In a sophisticated empirical test of this argument, Schofer and Longhofer (2011) and Longhofer and Schofer (2010) showed that countries have larger domestic nonprofit sectors if they are more connected to liberal culture through their associations with international organizations and have policies and laws that reflect liberal ideals.

The expansion of nonprofit sectors worldwide occurs in part due to the (sometimes coercive) globalization of liberal cultural principles, beyond the instrumental needs imposed by population and economic growth in each country. As a result, over time, a highly diverse group of countries have experienced growth in the nonprofit sector. At the same time, persistent and meaningful differences between countries continue to exist. In fact, major differences should be expected given the immense diversity in historical legacies, resources, political structures, and demographics. Excellent research has focused on highlighting the differences between countries or country types, especially as rooted in their social origins (for a classical perspective, see Salamon & Anheier, 1998; for a recent revision and review, see Anheier et al., 2020). Despite important and expected cross-national differences, there are unexpected similarities in the growth and form of nonprofit sectors around the world. Neo-institutional theory provides an account of similar changes to many national nonprofit sectors, as emerging from liberal cultural influences in the external environment.

Our theoretical view also has applications for the direction of future research. The term "nonprofit sector" has evolved into a significant concept, but the various meanings and changing nature of this category ought to be an object of study rather than treated as a social fact that is taken for granted. A reification of the category of "nonprofit" can lead us to overlook important trends and to inaccurately specify the causes and consequences of key features of the sector. Nonprofits are often defined as voluntary, independent from government, and subject to the nondistribution constraint (Frumkin, 2009). But, as is well known, these features prove to be problematic when we start digging into individual cases. Moreover, such definitions say nothing about contributions to the public good, a dimension of great interest to many nonprofit scholars. Harmful associations such as the Ku Klux Klan can fit the traditional definition of nonprofits but are likely not what most scholars have in mind. To be sure, in the United States, such groups are unable to obtain the "public good" certification from the Internal Revenue Service (IRS); but tax-exempt status alone does not identify the "goodness" of a group. For example, as discussed in Chapter 8 of this volume, many indigenous organizations purposefully do not formally incorporate because the government has long been complicit in egregious forms of exploitation. Similarly, support associations for some of the most vulnerable groups in society, such as illegal immigrants, may be wary of drawing government attention and thus face a form of "civic invisibility" (De Graauw et al., 2013). The public good is somewhat arbitrarily defined in the US tax code and is always contested (perhaps notably so in the current era of extreme polarization). Overall, the meanings of "nonprofit organization" and "nonprofit sector" remain in flux, and there is often a disconnect between formal definitions and on-the-ground realities. We call attention to these features as central areas in which research is needed.

Alongside the need for greater study of the creation, evolution, and meaning of "nonprofit" and its features, our theory calls for careful attention to the conceptual goal of research when developing empirical measures (see Eliasoph, 2020 for an analysis of the meaning of voluntary action). For example, if our interest is in prosocial action, by focusing solely on nonprofits, we fail to recognize a large amount of relevant work and innovation that happens outside of this sphere. One example from the past year is the groundbreaking efforts of Engine No. 1, a "green" activist investment firm, to take over two board seats at Exxon. Engine No. 1 pressures firms in which it holds investments to change their practices, unlike many prosocial investors that focus on investing in "green" firms. This innovative shift changes the meaning and scope of traditional environmental activism. Related to this example, there is a striking rise of new organizational forms around the world, such as B-Corps, social enterprises, and the use of limited liability companies for philanthropy, which could affect how organizations are defined in the future (Lee et al., 2014; Mair & Noboa, 2003).

We are not suggesting that one should abandon existing classifications, such as the distinction between nonprofit and for-profit. Rather, we advocate investigating the conditions under which these classifications carry more or less importance (e.g., in terms of material consequences, legitimacy, or conformity) and their evolving meanings. And we urge moving toward more precise measurement motivated by clearly specified conceptual purposes. There are many ways to differentiate between organizations – degree of voluntariness, size, industry, internationalization, formalization, profitability, prosocialness, legal status, and so on. We assert that the goal is to identify which dimension(s) is of interest, specify why, and seek to measure it more directly in the empirical world. For example, Langer (2021) developed a measure of both the individualistic and collectivistic orientation of organization. As another example, Bloom and colleagues developed the World Management Survey, a tool to compare management practices across multiple countries and industries (Bloom & Van Reenen, 2007; see Bloom et al., 2020 for a recent example of hospital practices). To be sure, legal nonprofit status is a convenient and oftentimes useful indicator: it may be highly correlated with (and thus a proxy for) some other factor of interest, such as profit motivations. Furthermore, legal status itself, or the choice of legal form, may have important causes and consequences worth studying (Child et al., 2015). Seeking greater conceptual and empirical precision regarding these issues is a big task. But the potential gains for understanding what we call the nonprofit sector are great.

12.3 Conclusions

Looking to the future, recent research has suggested that the hegemony of Western liberal culture may have peaked in the 1990s and eroded in the past 20 years (e.g., Guillén, 2018; Norris & Inglehart, 2019). Some scholars have even claimed we have reached the end of the society of organizations (Davis, 2009). According to our arguments, if there is an erosion of the cultural foundations that generated organizational expansion, then the nonprofit sector will be dramatically altered. Speculatively, in the US, we expect that increasing polarization and populism would undercut the myth of a shared vision of the public good that is required to support the tax-exemption system for nonprofits. If such trends continue, we might see new challenges to the IRS classifications, or legal redefinitions of the public good. Given the universalism of liberal principles, international organizations might be particularly negatively affected if illiberal culture takes center stage; indeed, recent research shows a decline in founding rates of international nonprofits in the US (Bush & Hadden, 2019). Cross-nationally, a liberal backlash may threaten nonprofit sectors; already, countries around the world are placing more restrictions on establishing and financing formal nonprofit organizations, especially regarding the receipt of foreign funding (Bromley et al., 2020; Dupuy et al., 2016).

Our arguments reinforce the importance of efforts like this volume, which addresses the fundamental questions of what we mean by "nonprofit" and why it matters. Our phenomenological approach views nonprofits and the nonprofit sector as socially constructed categories that evolve and change over time in ways that extend beyond functional exigencies. A dominant feature of the nonprofit category, in contrast to alternatives like "civil society," is its interdependence with formal organization (sometimes, but not always or solely, indicated by legal status). The rise and evolution of a metacategory of "organization" accounts for many of the similarities between firms and nonprofits but also provides a framework in which the differentiation and elaboration of subspecies within organizations can occur, such as the invention of nonprofits and B-Corps. Because of the evolving nature of these organizations, it remains an important task to track and explain the transformation of these constructed categories. Although categories are social constructions, they carry important material implications (such as tax-exempt status) and have symbolic value (such as perceptions of legitimacy or worth, which can bring additional material consequences). Recognizing the contingent nature of contemporary social structures opens the door to asking the key ethical and philosophical questions of our time: Given that the structure of society is mutable, what should it look like? Should there be a sharper distinction between for-profit and nonprofit activity, or more independence from government? Should we hold nonprofit and for-profit organizations to different moral or ethical standards?

Globally, our current era is marked by growing challenges to the liberal and neoliberal framework that provided the cultural foundation for the rise of nonprofit organizations. Populism and authoritarianism are on the rise, polarization and income inequality has increased, and a sense of optimism has eroded. For some, the recent challenges to democracy, nonprofits, and capitalism are an existential threat. For others, the upheaval indicates a respite from Western, liberal hegemony. As for our part, we do not believe that a shift away from liberal or neoliberal principles portends a decline in the amount of prosocial activity in the world – just that its nature will change to become less organizational. A move away from the dominance of formal organization as a key feature of prosocial activity may pose challenges such as decreased emphasis on professionalism and effectiveness if rationalizing tendencies are lessened, or reduced independence from the state if the autonomy dimension of organization is undermined. But a less formally organized sphere could also reduce barriers to inclusion for highly marginalized groups and could generate innovative forms of informal network activity that may be temporary and highly responsive or flexible (e.g., Højgaard, 2020; Sydow & Windeler, 2020). Although these factors may not be fully determined, what is certain is that now is the time for seeking out and evaluating alternative futures for society.

References

Anheier, H.K., Lang, M., & Toepler, S. (2020).Comparative nonprofit sector research. In W. W. Powell & P. Bromley (Eds.), *The nonprofit sector: A research handbook* (3rd ed., pp. 648–676). Stanford University Press. https://doi.org/10.1515/9781503611085-040

Ashforth, B. E., Schinoff, B. S., & Brickson, S. L. (2020). "My company is friendly," "Mine's a rebel": Anthropomorphism and shifting organizational identity from "what" to "who". *Academy of Management Review*, *45*(1), 29–57. https://doi.org/10.5465/amr.2016.0496

Baker, K. M. (2001). Enlightenment and the institution of society: Notes for a conceptual history. In S. Kaviraj & S. Khilnani (Eds.), *Civil society: History and possibilities* (pp. 84–104). Cambridge University Press.

Bell, D. (1976). *The coming of the post-industrial society*. Basic Books.

Bloom, N., Lemos, R., Sadun, R., & Van Reenen, J. (2020). Healthy business? Managerial education and management in health care. *Review of Economics and Statistics*, *102*(3), 506–517. https://doi.org/10.1162/rest_a_00847

Bloom, N., & Van Reenen, J. (2007). Measuring and explaining management practices across firms and countries. *The Quarterly Journal of Economics*, *122*(4), 1351–1408.

Bromley, P., & Meyer, J. W. (2015). *Hyper-organization: Global organizational expansion*. Oxford University Press.

Bromley, P., & Meyer, J. W. (2017). "They are all organizations": The cultural roots of blurring between the nonprofit, business, and government sectors. *Administration & Society*, *49*(7), 939–966. https://doi.org/10.1177/0095399714548268

Bromley, P., Schofer, E., & Longhofer, W. (2020). Contentions over world culture: The rise of legal restrictions on foreign funding to NGOs, 1994–2015. *Social Forces*, *99*(1), 281–304. https://doi.org/10.1093/sf/soz138

Bromley, P., & Sharkey, A. (2017). Casting call: The expanding nature of actorhood in U.S. firms, 1960–2010. *Accounting, Organizations and Society*, *59*, 3–20. https://doi.org/10.1016/j.aos.2017.06.001

Brunsson, N., & Sahlin-Andersson, K. (2000). Constructing organizations: The example of public sector reform. *Organization Studies*, *21*, 721–746. https://doi.org/10.1177/0170840600214003

Bush, S. S., & Hadden, J. (2019). Density and decline in the founding of international NGOs in the United States. *International Studies Quarterly*, *63*(4), 1133–1146. https://doi.org/10.1093/isq/sqz061

Caporaso, J. A. (1996). The European Union and forms of state: Westphalian, regulatory or post-modern? *JCMS: Journal of Common Market Studies*, *34*(1), 29–52. https://doi.org/10.1111/j.1468-5965.1996.tb00559.x

Child, C., Witesman, E. M., & Braudt, D. B. (2015). Sector choice: How fair trade entrepreneurs choose between nonprofit and for-profit forms. *Nonprofit and Voluntary Sector Quarterly*, *44*(4), 832–851. https://doi.org/10.1177%2F0899764014542688

Coleman, J. S. (1982). *The asymmetric society*. Syracuse University Press.

Davies, M. (2010–). *The Corpus of Historical American English: 400 million words, 1810–2009*. www.english-corpora.org/coha/

Davis, G. F. (2009). The rise and fall of finance and the end of the society of organizations. *Academy of Management Perspectives*, *23*(3), 27–44. https://doi.org/10.5465/amp.2009.43479262

De Graauw, E., Gleeson, S., & Bloemraad, I. (2013). Funding immigrant organizations: Suburban free riding and local civic presence. *American Journal of Sociology*, *119*(1), 75–130. https://doi.org/10.1086/671168

DeWiel, B. (1997). A conceptual history of civil society: From Greek beginnings to the end of Marx. *Past Imperfect*, 6. https://doi.org/10.21971/P7MK5N

DiMaggio, P. J., & Powell, W. W. (1983). The iron cage revisited: Institutional isomorphism and collective rationality in organizational fields. *American Sociological Review*, *48*, 147–160. https://doi.org/10.2307/2095101

Drori, G., Meyer, J. W., & Hwang, H. (Eds.) (2006). *Globalization and organization: World society and organizational change*. Oxford University Press.

Drucker, P. F. (1992). The new society of organizations. *Harvard Business Review*, *70*(5), 95–104.

Dupuy, K., Ron, J., & Prakash, A. (2016). Hands off my regime! Governments' restrictions on foreign aid to non-governmental organizations in poor and middle-income countries. *World Development*, *84*, 299–311. https://doi.org/10.1016/j.worlddev.2016.02.001

Eikenberry, A. M., & Kluver, J. D. (2004). The marketization of the nonprofit sector: Civil society at risk? *Public Administration Review*, *64*(2), 132–140. https://doi.org/10.1111/j.1540-6210.2004.00355.x

Eliasoph, N. (2020). What do volunteers do? In W. W. Powell & P. Bromley (Eds.), *The nonprofit sector: A research handbook* (3rd ed.) (pp. 566–578). Stanford University Press. (Originally published 1987)

Foucault, M., Davidson, A. I., & Burchell, G. (2008). *The birth of biopolitics: Lectures at the Collège de France, 1978–79*. Palgrave Macmillan.

Frumkin, P. (2009). *On being nonprofit*. Harvard University Press.

Google Inc. (2021). Google Books Ngram Viewer. https://books.google.com/ngrams/

Guillén, M. F. (2018). *Rude awakening: Threats to the global liberal order*. University of Pennsylvania Press.

Hansmann, H. B. (1980). The role of nonprofit enterprise. *Yale Law Journal*, *89*, 835–898. https://doi.org/10.2307/796089

Hirschhorn, L. (1997). *Reworking authority: Leading and following in the post-modern organization*. MIT Press.

Højgaard, C. D. (2020). *Elastic integration in civic do-ocracies: How organizing shapes collective civic engagement in informal, non-membership based networks*. [Paper presentation]. 36th EGOS Colloquium 2020, Hamburg, Germany.

Huber, G. P. (1984). The nature and design of post-industrial organizations. *Management Science*, *30*(8), 928–951. https://doi.org/10.1287/mnsc.30.8.928

Hwang, H., Colyvas, J. A., & Drori, G. S. (2019). The proliferation and profusion of actors in institutional theory. In *Research in the sociology of organizations* (pp. 3–20). Emerald. https://doi.org/10.1108/S0733-558X20190000058002

Hwang, H., & Suarez, D. (2019). Beyond service provision: Advocacy and the construction of nonprofits as organizational actors. In H. Hwang, J. A. Colyvas, & G. S. Drori (Eds.), *Agents, actors, actorhood: Institutional perspectives on the nature of agency, action, and authority* (vol. 58, pp. 87–109). Emerald. https://doi.org/10.1108/S0733-558X20190000058007

James, E. (Ed.) (1989). *The nonprofit sector in international perspective: Studies in comparative culture and policy*. Oxford University Press.

Kaufman, J. (2008). Corporate law and the sovereignty of states. *American Sociological Review*, *73*, 402–425. https://doi.org/10.1177/000312240807300303

Kaviraj, S., & Khilnani, S. (Eds.) (2001). *Civil society: History and possibilities*. Cambridge University Press.

Kernaghan, K. (2000). The post-bureaucratic organization and public service values. *International Review of Administrative Sciences*, *66*(1), 91–104. https://doi.org/10.1177/0020852300661008

King, B. G., Felin, T., & Whetten, D. A. (2010). Finding the organization in organizational theory: A meta-theory of the organization as a social actor. *Organization Science*, *21*(1), 290–305. https://doi.org/10.1287/orsc.1090.0443

Kocka, J. (2004). Civil society from a historical perspective. *European Review*, *12*(1), 65–79. https://doi.org/10.1017/S1062798704000067

Krücken, G., Blümel, A., & Kloke, K. (2013). The managerial turn in higher education? On the interplay of organizational and occupational change in German academia. *Minerva*, *51*(4), 417–442. https://doi.org/10.1007/s11024-013-9240-z

Krücken, G., & Meier, F. (2006). Turning the university into an organizational actor. In G. Drori, J. W. Meyer, & H. Hwang (Eds.), *Globalization and organization: World society and organizational change* (pp. 241–257). Oxford University Press.

Kumar, K. (2009). *From post-industrial to post-modern society: New theories of the contemporary world*. John Wiley & Sons.
Langer, J. (2021). Understanding the spirit of the sectors: Exploring identity in a new era of organizing. *Administration & Society*. https://doi.org/10.1177/00953997211041131.
Lee, M., Battilana, J., & Wang, T. (2014). Building an infrastructure for empirical research on social enterprise: Challenges and opportunities. In *Social entrepreneurship and research methods* (Vol. 9, pp. 241–264). Emerald. https://doi.org/10.1108/S1479-838720140000009017
Lim, A. (2021). Nonprofits as socially responsible actors: Neoliberalism, institutional structures, and empowerment in the United Nations global compact. *Current Sociology*, https://doi.org/10.1177/0011392120986216.
Longhofer, W., & Schofer, E. (2010). National and global origins of environmental association. *American Sociological Review*, *75*(4), 505–533.
Mair, J., & Noboa, E. (2003). *Social entrepreneurship: How intentions to create a social enterprise get formed* [SSRN Scholarly Paper ID 462283]. Social Science Research Network. https://doi.org/10.2139/ssrn.462283
Masuda, Y. (1980). *The information society as post-industrial society*. Transaction.
Meyer, J. W. (2010). World society, institutional theories, and the actor. *Annual Review of Sociology*, *36*(1), 1–20. https://doi.org/10.1146/annurev.soc.012809.102506
Meyer, J. W., & Bromley, P. (2013). The worldwide expansion of "organization". *Sociological Theory*, *31*(4), 366–389. https://doi.org/10.1177/0735275113513264
Meyer, J. W., & Rowan, B. (1977). Institutionalized organizations: Formal structure as myth and ceremony. *American Journal of Sociology*, *83*, 340–363. https://doi.org/10.1086/226550
Norris, P., & Inglehart, R. (2019). *Cultural backlash: Trump, Brexit, and authoritarian populism*. Cambridge University Press.
Parker, M. (1992). Post-modern organizations or postmodern organization theory? *Organization Studies*, *13*(1), 1–17. https://doi.org/10.1177/017084069201300103
Perrow, C. (1991). A society of organizations. *Theory and Society*, *20*(6), 725–762.
Pope, S., Bromley, P., Lim, A., & Meyer, J. W. (2018). The pyramid of nonprofit responsibility: The institutionalization of organizational responsibility across sectors. *VOLUNTAS: International Journal of Voluntary and Nonprofit Organizations*, *29*(6), 1300–1314. https://doi.org/10.1007/s11266-018-0038-3
Putnam, R. D., & Campbell, D. E. (2012). *American grace: How religion divides and unites us*. Simon & Schuster.

Rudan, P. (2016). Society as a code: Bentham and the fabric of order. *History of European Ideas*, *42*(1), 39–54. https://doi.org/10.1080/01916599.2015.1077147

Salamon, L. M., & Anheier, H. K. (1998). Social origins of civil society: Explaining the nonprofit sector cross-nationally. *VOLUNAS: International Journal of Voluntary and Nonprofit Organizations*, *9*(3), 213–248. https://doi.org/10.1023/A:1022058200985

Schofer, E., & Longhofer, W. (2011). The structural sources of association. *American Journal of Sociology*, *117*(2), 539–585. https://doi.org/10.1086/661593

Scott, W. R. (2013). *Institutions and organizations: Ideas, interests, and identities*. SAGE Publications.

Sydow, J., & Windeler, A. (2020). Temporary organizing and permanent contexts. *Current Sociology*, *68*(4), 480–498. https://doi.org/10.1177/0011392120907629

Touraine, A. (1971). *The post-industrial society: Tomorrow's social history: Classes, conflicts and culture in the programmed society* (1st American ed.). Random House.

13 *Nonprofits as Enablers of Multilayered Representation*

CATHERINE E. WILSON*

In the United States, the role of representation is often understood in political and partisan terms. A common response to the question "Who represents me and/or us?" is that one's elected officials – especially those at the national level – are those who have the primary responsibility for representation. However, such a response does two things: it locates the domain of representation mainly within government, and it recognizes representation as a partisan phenomenon by associating representation with individuals in elected office. But what if representation also includes institutions that transcend partisan politics? If that is the case, then for-profit businesses, government agencies, and nonprofit organizations may all take part in representation to some degree. Nonprofit organizations play a significant role in representing individuals and communities in the United States. Not only do nonprofits advance a diverse range of viewpoints, but they also allow individuals and communities to find meaning, purpose, and belonging through their interactions and involvement with them.

In this chapter, I present the theory of *multilayered representation*,[1] which maintains that public, private, and nonprofit organizations are important institutional outlets that reflect the multifaceted nature of

* This chapter is an expansion of a short presentation I delivered at the 2019 Association for Research on Nonprofit Organizations and Voluntary Action (ARNOVA) conference in San Diego, CA on the same topic. I am deeply grateful to Drs. Curtis Child and Greg Witkowski for the valuable insights and feedback they provided in their review of this chapter. In addition, I am deeply grateful to Drs. John DiIulio, Chao Guo, and Lia Howard who offered helpful feedback after reading this chapter.

1 The concept of multilayered representation was examined in the edited book, *Multilayered representation in the European Union* (2012). The editors claim that the book explores national and supranational forms of representation through parliaments and elections, the courts, and civil society (Evas et al., 2012). To my knowledge, no such theory of multilayered representation has been developed with respect to the nonprofit sector in the United States.

individuals and their unique needs and aspirations. This chapter will discuss how US nonprofit organizations enable multilayered representation. The chapter will focus its attention on social movements and all kinds of nonprofit organizations in the United States, with the exception of political organizations whose purpose is to "engage in political campaign activity" (IRS, 2022). Building on Tocqueville (see Chapter 2), I argue that nonprofit organizations produce social value (Renz, 2016) while simultaneously creating opportunities for identity development at both the individual and community levels. Identity development in this context is an important consideration because nonprofits are organizations that foster social connectedness, rootedness, and attachment to values, causes, and beliefs. Moreover, nonprofits provide additional layers of representation outside of established party platforms. Multilayered representation is an original application of James Madison's *Federalist no. 10* to the US nonprofit sector. While scholars have tended to focus on the issue of political representation in Madison's *Federalist no. 10*, this chapter will demonstrate that, through the theory of multilayered representation, Madison's essay can be applied to nonprofit organizations.

13.1 A Theory of Multilayered Representation

13.1.1 Nonprofits as Part of a Representative System

While there was debate among the delegates at the Constitutional Convention of 1787 regarding the issue of political representation (Madison, 1840/1985), debate between Federalists and Anti-Federalists continued throughout the constitutional ratification process of 1787–1788. Whereas Federalists supported the ratification of the Constitution and a stronger national government, Anti-Federalists opposed ratification and favored safeguarding states' rights (Carey & McClellan, 2001). In response to Anti-Federalist essays critiquing the Constitution, printed in New York newspapers, Alexander Hamilton, John Jay, and James Madison published 85 essays in support of constitutional ratification, also in New York newspapers, which resulted in the *Federalist papers* or *The federalist* (Carey & McClellan, 2001). In *Federalist no. 10*, Madison (1787/2001) argued that political representation was one way to limit the influence of faction. Madison (1787/2001) defined faction as a number of citizens, whether amounting to a majority or minority of the whole, who are united and actuated by some common impulse of passion, or of interest, adverse to the rights of other citizens, or to the permanent and aggregate interests of the community. (p. 43)

Instead of "removing its causes," which would amount to eliminating liberty and the freedom of expression (Madison, 1787/2001, p. 43), Madison responded to the natural occurrence of faction by "controlling its effects" (Madison, 1787/2001, p. 45) and proposed two solutions. The first solution was the establishment of a representative government which would "refine and enlarge the public views" as opposed to a direct democracy in which passions and interests could reign in an unchecked manner (Madison, 1787/2001, p. 46). The second solution was to "extend the sphere" with a large republic that, by its sheer size, would allow for "a greater variety of parties and interests," resulting in less likelihood that a majority faction would arise (Madison, 1787/2001, p. 48). Ultimately, Madison (1787/2001) argued that the Constitution, with its federalist structure, enabled the representation of aggregate interests at the national level and local interests at the state level. Tragically, however, under the newly ratified US Constitution, the cruel and unjust system of slavery persisted and those who were enslaved were wrongly denied their human and political rights.

The theory of multilayered representation, as applied here, suggests that nonprofit organizations "refine and enlarge the public views" by representing, or "acting for the sake of" (Pitkin, 1967, p. 126), individual and community interests. In addition, given the size of the US nonprofit sector – roughly 1.8 million registered nonprofits as of 2020 (Candid, 2021)[2] – these organizations "extend the sphere" by the variety of viewpoints they represent, providing a number of ways for individuals and communities to participate in activities and initiatives outside of the election cycle and two-party system. Multilayered representation thrives in pluralist political systems in that pluralist politics "respects the diverse spheres of human activity" and does not expect every sphere to "mirror the structure and principles of basic political institutions" (Galston, 2005, p. 41). Political theorist William Galston (2005) has admitted that political pluralism is a "messy and

[2] These nonprofits refer to those registered under section 501(c) of the Internal Revenue Code (Candid, 2021).

conflictual" enterprise due to co-existing claims made by political institutions, civil associations, and individuals in the name of the common good or the good for oneself (p. 65). Moreover, political scientist Robert Dahl (1982) acknowledged the "sheer complexity of organized pluralism" (p. 51) and claimed that "complexity increases with an increase in the variety and number of relatively independent subsystems and with an increase in the extent of variation in possible relations between the subsystems" (p. 52).

According to historian Olivier Zunz (2012), Madison's *Federalist no. 10* served as a foundation for a theory of interest group politics elaborated by Progressives at the start of the twentieth century. Zunz (2012) claimed that political scientists familiarized themselves with this Progressive Era research in the 1970s and developed a pluralist theory of American politics, which Senator Daniel Patrick Moynihan (D-NY) applied to nonprofit organizations. A political scientist himself, Moynihan stated in 1978 that pluralists had maintained that "in the strength of ... voluntary, private associations – church, family, club, trade union, commercial association – lay the chief strength of democratic society" (Moynihan, as cited in Zunz, 2012, p. 244; n. 41, p. 339). More recently, scholars have referred to Madison's *Federalist no. 10* in research on civil society, community-building, civic and political engagement, and philanthropy (Bresler et al., 2016; Chaskin, 2003; Frumkin, 2002; Hall, 2013; Mandeville, 2007; Weber, 2015), or to one of Madison's other *Federalist* essays in research on representation in networked governance (Guo & Marietta, 2015), as well as have included *Federalist no. 10* in a reader on the US nonprofit sector (Hammack, 1998). Scholars also have examined Madison's *Federalist no. 10* in research on interest groups, lobbying, and advocacy (Berry & Arons, 2003; Berry & Wilcox, 2018; Jenkins, 2006; La Pira, 2016; Loomis & Cigler, 2016; Schuck, 1997). While scholars have discussed the relevance of solutions that Madison provides regarding the issue of faction in research on interest groups, lobbying, and advocacy (Berry & Wilcox, 2018; Jenkins, 2006; La Pira, 2016; Loomis & Cigler, 2016), there has not been a comprehensive treatment of the relevance of these solutions to the nonprofit sector as a whole. Missing from scholarship is the applicability of Madison's understanding of representation, as elaborated in *Federalist no. 10*, to nonprofit organizations.

Politics is not the only institution that expresses meaning, purpose, and belonging in life. While political representation involves responsiveness to the public's aspirations (Pitkin, 1967), the realm of politics simply does not offer the variety of outlets that nonprofit organizations provide. These outlets decrease the possibility of faction through the social value that the nonprofit sector produces (Renz, 2016). Nonprofits represent a diversity of values and interests and create opportunities for identity development. As scholar David Mason (1996) argued, the nonprofit sector "meets a wider range of needs than the more specialized sectors of government and business" (p. 3). For this reason, Mason (1996) claimed that the sector possessed an "expressive dimension" (p. 3). The activity generated by nonprofits invites voluntary participation by individuals (Mason, 1996) who share both similar and distinct values, pursuits, and aspirations. Some examples of the range of nonprofit experiences in which individuals can participate (Mason, 1996) include mentoring, social outings, and rallies. According to Mason (1996), "the opportunity for expressive activity" in nonprofit organizations also serves "instrumental purposes" as this activity can be goal-directed (p. 14). Nonprofits act as representatives of meaningful interests and causes as well as sought-after goals. In doing so, they provide an organizational point of reference for the fashioning of identity at the individual and community levels.

13.1.2 Nonprofits and Identity Development

In *Federalist no. 10*, Madison (1787/2001) argued that factions arose most frequently from an unequal distribution of property. However, Madison (1787/2001) also maintained that factions resulted from differing opinions formed along religious and political lines as well as from affiliations with distinct leaders vying for power. Given this argument, one way to diminish the power of faction is by developing identities that cross simple divisions, which are rich and complex. The theory of multilayered representation extends Madison's *Federalist no. 10* to the nonprofit sector by acknowledging the development of identities that occurs within nonprofit organizations. Identities are not merely cultivated by the individual alone but through a variety of experiences with nonprofit organizations throughout one's lifetime. This identity development helps to restrain the effects of faction since it allows individuals and community members to align themselves with a wide array of nonprofit organizations, and thereby causes, issues, and pastimes.

Nonprofit organizations assist in the development of familial, social, cultural, professional, and associational identities, and, therefore, broaden the scope of representation beyond partisan politics (see Figure 13.1). Nonprofits offer outlets for the cultivation of familial and social identity through, among other things, the family legacies carried out by private foundations, membership in social and recreational clubs as well as in homeowners' associations (HOAs), and commitment to alma maters. Cultural identity is shaped, for instance, by participation in nonprofit organizations dedicated to the representation and celebration of diverse racial and ethnic identities as well as traditions. Cultural identity is also formed by involvement in nonprofits with an artistic or religious mission. Nonprofit organizations also offer ways for individuals to develop their professional identity through engaging in professional and scholarly associations, chambers of commerce, labor unions, and even as an employee in one's own nonprofit workplace. Finally, associational identity is fostered through support for charitable causes and policy issues promoted by nonprofit organizations.

Through the variety of identities being developed, multilayered representation by nonprofit organizations provides a broader response to the question posed in the Introduction, "Who represents me and/or us?" Such representation enables individuals and communities to "pick and choose" which aspects of the identities being formed through interactions with nonprofits matter most and allows them to focus on specific values and interests, shift loyalties, and/or synthesize elements that may otherwise appear to be contradictory. In addition, multilayered representation advances a concern for meaning, purpose, and belonging. Acknowledging the significant role that identities play in the decision-making process, multilayered representation gives individuals the opportunity to weigh and prioritize different aspects of their identities at select and important times.

Figure 13.2 provides an example of how familial, social, cultural, professional, and associational identities – developed by exposure to and alignment with nonprofit organizations – can inform an important decision-making process. In this hypothetical but realistic scenario, parents are deliberating about what kind of education (e.g., public school, private school, or homeschooling) would be best for their elementary school-aged child. If they approached the question by reflecting solely on their partisan identity, these parents might be influenced

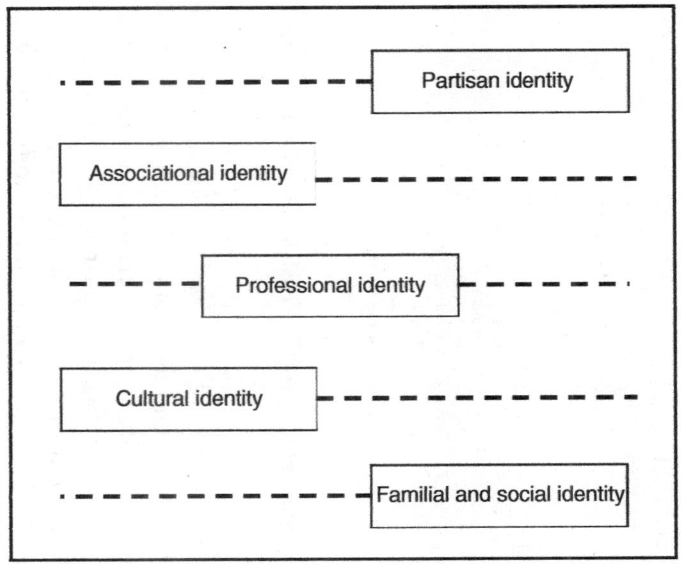

Figure 13.1 Development of identities through multilayered representation

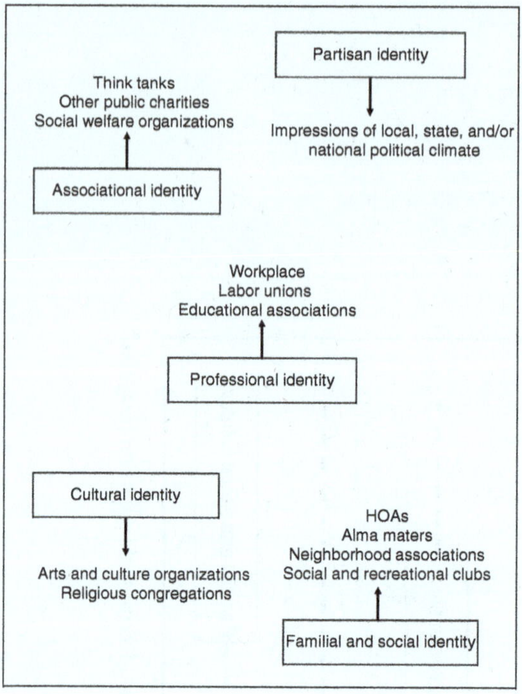

Figure 13.2 Decision-making process – elementary school education

by their impressions of the local, state, and/or national political climate. However, relying on this identity alone overlooks other potential factors guiding the decision-making process. First, parents might be motivated in their decision by their familial and social identity. They might reflect on their own experience, or family members' experiences, of attending or not attending a private (nonprofit) school as well as the influence of their social circles, such as HOAs, social and recreational clubs, and neighborhood associations. Second, parents might turn to the cultural identity they have developed as a family, for instance, as members of religious congregations and their involvement in arts and culture organizations as well as in other groups that have shaped their cultural commitments. Third, if they are a member of an educational association or labor union or an employee of the nonprofit workforce, they might consider how that would impact their decision. Finally, parents might be persuaded in their decision by their connection to think tanks, other public charities, or social welfare organizations. Through this decision-making process, parents must consider which aspects of their identities most influence the kind of education that would be desirable for their elementary school-aged child. At the same time, parents must recognize which nonprofit organizations best represent their and their child's values and interests.

By offering points of interaction outside of partisan politics, and, consequently, additional layers of representation, nonprofit organizations aid in "controlling the effects of faction" (Madison, 1787/2001, p. 48) in two ways. First, interaction with nonprofits allows individuals and communities to both develop their identities and select which identities are most relevant during specific times, as the scenario above demonstrated. Second, exposure to social movements provides additional opportunities for identity development as nonprofit organizations may form part of a movement's leadership or coalition of supporters. Social movements include ones that can create "new possibilities for being," such as the Feminist movement which exposed the existing system of gender hierarchy (Connolly, 1995, p. 182), as well as ones that triumph over social injustice, resulting in greater social, cultural, economic, and/or political inclusion. Some examples of social movements that triumphed over social injustice were the Abolitionist, Women's Suffrage, and Civil Rights movements.

In social movements such as these, identity development can occur, which may result in cohesion among those with distinct life experiences. Political scientist Robert Putnam (2000) referred to this cohesion as "bridging capital," which is characterized by "networks [that] are outward looking and encompass people across diverse social cleavages" (p. 22). Putnam (2000) considered the Civil Rights Movement as one example of bridging capital. Sociologist Aldon Morris (1984) pointed out several factors influencing the Civil Rights Movement, such as the significant role played by the Black church and the Southern Christian Leadership Conference (SCLC), as well as other organizations with strong connections to the Black community, such as the National Association for the Advancement of Colored People (NAACP), and involvement by predominantly white organizations, like the Fellowship of Reconciliation (FOR). Morris (1984) also underlined strong cultural influences in the movement, "music, trenchant sermons, and challenging oratory" (p. xiii). Co-authors Robert Putnam and Shaylyn Romney Garrett (2020) mentioned additional factors that contributed to the path of racial inclusion in the United

States, namely, increasing support for racial equality by white people on issues like interracial schools, equal job access, and integrated transportation, and the return of Black servicemen from World War II who had chosen to "join the political effort for change" in the United States (p. 229).

As an example of bridging capital, the Civil Rights Movement demonstrates how individuals, communities, and organizations came together in support of overturning social injustice. A faction that blatantly disregarded the "rights of other citizens" and the "permanent and aggregate interests of the community" (Madison, 1787/2001, p. 43) – those who opposed civil rights – was overcome by tapping into various dimensions of identity, developed both within and outside of nonprofit organizations, which shaped and influenced viewpoints on the issue. The political actions of elected officials and the US Supreme Court also helped to defeat this faction. For Civil Rights and other social movements, multilayered representation has been instrumental in fighting social injustice, thereby influencing historic and impactful policy changes.

13.1.3 The Distinctive Role of Nonprofits

For-profit businesses, government agencies, and nonprofit organizations all play a part in multilayered representation. However, what makes nonprofits distinct from their private and public sector counterparts is the variety of activities and experiences available in the nonprofit sector, from appreciating music and art, to serving the homeless, to environmental lobbying. Nonprofit organizations inspire support for their work through attachment to their missions, participation in their services and programs, and the issues about which they care. These organizations can provide an antidote to the social polarization of political parties, as noted by political scientist Lilliana Mason (2018), whereby "a single vote can now indicate a person's partisan preference as well as his or her religion, race, ethnicity, gender, neighborhood, and favorite grocery store" (p. 14), by allowing for the flourishing of cross-cutting cleavages. And yet, nonprofit organizations can also assist in fostering an "us versus them" mentality, mirroring the tactics of the two-party system. Some nonprofits may tend to align themselves with either political party by the policies they support. Consequently, nonprofit stances on policy issues can divide not only the nonprofit organizations that hold different positions on the issue, but also the individuals for whom the organizations hold some importance.

Even so, as members of the third sector, nonprofit organizations, can deftly navigate the political landscape and marketplace while maintaining their distinctive, mission-driven focus on behalf of the communities they serve. In volume II of *Democracy in America*, French historian and political philosopher Alexis de Tocqueville (1840/2000) proposed the possibility of government replacing some of the work conducted by "the greatest American associations" but asked the rhetorical question, "What political power would ever be in a state to suffice for the innumerable multitude of small undertakings that American citizens execute every day with the aid of an association?" (p. 491). Moreover, unlike their private sector counterparts, nonprofit organizations are not driven solely by a profit motive. A central focus for nonprofits is how well they deliver on their missions. Scholar J. Gregory Dees (2003/2016) wrote that social entrepreneurs "have only one ultimate bottom line by which to measure their success," that is, "their intended social impact" (p. 302).

In *Federalist no. 10*, Madison (1787/2001) introduced two solutions for the problem of faction: representative government and a large republic. Elected officials, however, are not the only actors involved in the important work of representation. Nonprofit organizations accompany their political counterparts in the effort to limit the effects of faction, creating additional layers of representation – a multilayered representation – for the American public at large. Tocqueville (1840/2000) reminded us that even in the mid-nineteenth century, "the political associations that exist in the United States form only a detail in the midst of the immense picture that the sum of associations presents there" (p. 489). This makes good sense given the multidimensional nature of individuals.

13.2 How Nonprofits Refine, Enlarge, and Extend Representation in a Federalist System

Let us return to the question raised in the Introduction, "Who represents me and/or us?" A common response would be one's elected officials. But what happens if individuals do not agree with the elected officials in office? Does that mean that those individuals would not be represented during the period in which their party was out of power?

When considering a multilayered landscape, the answer to this query would certainly beget additional questions, such as, "Where do my interests lie?," "What do I value?," and "Where do I find meaning, purpose, and belonging?" The reply to these questions may indicate three different responses: (1) one regards representation by elected officials as the most significant kind of representation; (2) one recognizes the importance of elected officials and understands that representation can take place both within and outside of partisan politics; or (3) one dismisses the idea that elected officials truly represent and seeks representation beyond the partisan realm. However, even those responses themselves are subject to change given that values and interests are not fixed. The process of identity development in a multilayered landscape involves a receptivity to, reflection on, and active selection of a range of viewpoints in American public life that are relevant to individuals and communities at particular times and in particular ways. The sections below will discuss how the theory of multilayered representation is applied by nonprofit organizations in the United States by discussing examples of how nonprofits – at both the local and national levels – "refine and enlarge the public views" and "extend the sphere."

13.2.1 Refine and Enlarge the Public Views

Nonprofits are unique organizations to the degree that they enable a multilayered representation of individuals and communities. These organizations "refine and enlarge the public views" through their roles as *memory-makers, community-builders, and isolation buffers*. At any given time, nonprofit organizations provide opportunities through which individuals and communities can explore, confirm, or reevaluate what is meaningful or important to them. Albeit not exhaustive, Table 13.1 provides some ways that nonprofits act as memory-makers, community-builders, and isolation buffers. There is some overlap in nonprofits serving in these roles, in that, taken together, each one of these roles aims to unite the individual with the larger community. This section, however, will treat each role separately and give examples of how nonprofit organizations "refine and enlarge the public views."

Nonprofits are memory-makers. Involvement with nonprofit organizations fosters the active cultivation of memories that individuals take with them throughout the course of their lives. Emotional and sensory engagement play a prominent role in this cultivation. Through

Table 13.1 ***How nonprofit organizations refine and enlarge the public views***

Role	Description	Examples
Memory-makers	• Cultivation of memories • Emotional and sensory engagement	• Theatrical performances • Sports league games • Alma maters
Community-builders	• Points of community contact • Cultivation of relationships	• Chambers of commerce • Park clean-ups • Walks/runs • Religious congregations
Isolation buffers	• Prevention from turning inward and feeling alone	• Days of Service • Volunteering • Local humane societies/SPCAs

attending theatrical performances and participating in school and extracurricular activities, identity development takes shape. Life celebrations, sports league games, and social club events instantly conjure up a range of feelings from days past. Meanwhile, attachment to one's alma mater can be strengthened through reunions, sporting events, and alma mater songs. And the sales of cookies by the Girl Scouts (2022) or the red kettle rung by employees and volunteers of The Salvation Army (2022) outside of stores, for instance, provide ways to both remember and reinforce one's relationship with organizations that held a particular meaning at a certain point in one's life.

Nonprofits are also community-builders. The presence of nonprofit organizations allows individuals to develop points of community contact and cultivate relationships, whether through involvement with chambers of commerce or participation in park clean-ups, blood drives, or walks/runs for specific causes. For years, individuals have taken part in local blood drives sponsored by the American Red Cross (2022) or walked or run in the Susan G. Komen Race for the Cure (2022) in their own cities, wearing pink clothing. Participation in these events fosters strong community ties by supporting important issues such as a reliable supply of blood reserves and cancer research. The relationships that are developed and nurtured in religious congregations also help to build community at the local level. In addition to providing opportunities for worship, congregations may hold social events, participate in interfaith gatherings, and serve as trusted resources for information on relevant issues impacting the community. One example of the community-building nature of congregations was the significant role that Black churches played as vaccination centers during the COVID-19 pandemic (Bunn, 2021).

Finally, nonprofits are isolation buffers. Some nonprofit organizations exist to prevent individuals from turning inward and feeling alone. One need only consider the important work of Alcoholics Anonymous (AA) chapters as well as local suicide prevention groups and hotlines in providing outlets for individuals who feel isolated. In addition to the "Big Book" (Alcoholics Anonymous, 2022), AA makes regular use of sayings to help people cope with their challenges and struggles. One such saying is "One day at a time" (Alcoholics Resource Center, 2022). Nonprofits also provide individuals who might otherwise feel lonely with ways to serve the larger community, through support for meaningful causes as well as participation in Days of Service and a range of other volunteering opportunities. Local humane societies and societies for the prevention of cruelty to animals (SPCAs) offer individuals the option of adopting or fostering a pet. The American Society for the Prevention of Cruelty to Animals (ASPCA), whose motto is "We are their voice," presents opportunities to get involved in advocacy against animal cruelty and abuse (ASPCA, 2022a, 2022b).

13.2.2 Extend the Sphere

While refining and enlarging the public views, nonprofit organizations also "extend the sphere" by cultivating a range of diverse voices that oftentimes do not mirror the nation's two-party system. Furthermore, nonprofit organizations allow individuals who otherwise identify with a political party to align themselves with something that might be considered on the "opposite side of the aisle." Once individuals select a political party, they may feel unsatisfied when the party platform does not reflect or represent their views on a particular issue. As a result, where do these individuals go if their political party does not fully represent them? One way is to support or get involved in a nonprofit organization that holds the very views that their party's platform, candidates, or elected officials lack.

Nonprofits interested in finding bipartisan solutions to policy issues help to "extend the sphere" through *issue framing*. In this context, issue framing refers to how nonprofits may lead with a discussion of "valence issues," issues for which there is consensus, before emphasizing "positional issues," issues that highlight opposing points of view in political candidates and sources of division in voters (Wilson et al., 2022, p. 224). For instance, advocacy organizations like Unidos US (2022) and the American Immigration Council (2022) have presented data on the economic contributions of immigrants and immigrant entrepreneurs in the United States, and, in doing so, assist in building support for immigration and immigrant rights. Meanwhile, Feeding America (2022a) inspires supporters by advancing its mission of "ensuring equitable access to nutritious food" through its national network of food banks and food programs. To fulfill this mission, Feeding America (2022b) also recognizes the necessity of bipartisan efforts to enhance federal programs to combat food insecurity. Nonprofit organizations can provide ways for individuals and communities to identify with public issues and concerns beyond the scope of American politics. As a result, nonprofits help to reduce the power of faction by championing ideas and causes outside of the partisan landscape to which individuals and communities may be dedicated.

Messaging is an influential tactic in extending the sphere. Think about the messages employed in recent social movements: "We are the 99%" in the Occupy Wall Street Movement (Reed, 2011), "Never again" (Kramer & Harlan, 2019) in the March for Our Lives Movement, and "Black Lives Matter" (2022a), which is the message, the movement, and a shortened version of the organization, the Black Lives Matter Global Network Foundation. All three movements set forth ways for individuals to situate themselves within a larger organizational, societal, and political context. Occupy Wall Street not only inspired the reemergence of the Democratic Socialists of America (DSA) and core tenets of the Democratic party platform, such as tuition-free college and an increase in the minimum wage (Stewart, 2019), but also the acceptance of "the topic of wealth and income inequality into the mainstream" (Olen, 2021, para. 9). Meanwhile, in addition to "Never again," March for Our Lives has made use of messages like "Not one more" (March for Our Lives, 2022) and "Enough is enough" (Kennedy, 2022) to convey its dedication to ending gun violence. As a movement, March for Our Lives (2022) has expanded the base of advocates who are resolved to eradicate gun violence by mobilizing youth and students across the country to participate in direct action, lobbying efforts, and walkouts at high schools, as well as encouraging voter registration. Lastly, the Black Lives Matter Global Network Foundation extends the sphere through its commitment to eliminating racism, "interven[ing] in violence inflicted on Black communities by the state and vigilantes," and building a diverse and inclusive Black liberation movement (Black Lives Matter, 2022a). The Black Lives Matter (2022b) Movement works alongside nonprofit partners like the Black Alliance for Just Immigration, Color of Change, and the NAACP Legal Defense and Educational Fund, Inc. to advance the cause of racial justice.

13.3 Conclusions

The kind of identity development that takes place in a multilayered landscape may provide some relief to those who are not satisfied with the political party in power at the local, state, or national level and those who are politically independent. Acknowledging the multifaceted nature of individuals and their desire for meaning, purpose, and belonging in life allows individuals to realize that this desire cannot be entirely fulfilled in the realm of politics alone. This is precisely why nonprofit organizations are so important. While Madison (1787/2001) understood that it would be unrealistic to assume that individuals would hold the "same opinions, the same passions, and the same interests" (p. 43), the scope of representative government is not comprehensive enough to speak on behalf of the variety and range of individual differences. Individuals are multidimensional and seek multilayered representation. This section addresses the future of multilayered representation through a discussion of: (1) structural inequality and inequity, (2) community and grassroots organizations, and (3) the extension of this theory to the private sector and the global context.

A majority faction may have more difficulty gaining traction in a multilayered landscape given the variety of concerns, issues, and needs that pull individuals and communities in different directions. It would be erroneous, however, to claim that a majority faction cannot arise in a flourishing civil society. Structural inequality and inequity are present in American public life, as demonstrated by unequal access to resources and a lack of power in certain neighborhoods and communities. As a result, the range of opportunities available for identity development may differ based on one's socioeconomic and demographic status. It is important to note that not all communities have similar access to nonprofit organizations. This should be examined in more detail from the standpoint of multilayered representation. There is a need to study how diverse nonprofit organizations can be strengthened and supported, especially in underserved urban and rural neighborhoods, so that individuals may find ways to equitably access services, advocate for relevant issues and causes, and participate in expressive outlets (Mason, 1996).

Community and grassroots organizations play a valuable role in the United States for their understanding of and response to local needs and concerns. These organizations also represent community interests by providing a range of services and expertise on neighborhood issues. Some community and grassroots organizations, though, may face challenges in their delivery of services and advocacy efforts due to issues with raising funds and implementing best practices because of their smaller size. Therefore, what is needed – at both the scholarly and practitioner levels – is a focus on how best practices in nonprofit management (including fundraising) can be adapted for smaller-sized organizations, such as public charities with under $500,000 in annual expenses, which accounted for roughly 88% of public charities in the United States in 2016 (National Council of Nonprofits, 2019). In light of this statistic, the National Council of Nonprofits (2019) maintains that "the 'typical' nonprofit is community-based, serving local needs" (p. 17). Thus, any discussion of multilayered representation should include a recognition of the vital work of community and grassroots organizations as well as recommendations to assist these organizations with effectively carrying out their missions.

Finally, given the involvement of businesses in corporate social responsibility, the theory of multilayered representation could be extended to the private sector. Consumers (especially those who are members of the Millennial and Generation Z groups) have become more discerning about how they intend to spend their money by investigating the kinds of social and environmental causes that businesses are supporting (Deloitte, 2021). The notion of businesses having a "double bottom line" (i.e., assessment of financial and social impact; Clark et al., 2004) or a "triple bottom line" (i.e., assessment of financial, social, and environmental impact; Elkington, 1998/2008) would serve as key reasons to extend the theory of multilayered representation beyond government agencies and nonprofit organizations to the private sector. Additionally, this theory should also be examined in a global context. A comparative study on the topic would highlight the uniqueness not only of the US nonprofit sector but also of nonprofit sectors in different parts of the world, such as in the Global South.

This chapter introduced the theory of multilayered representation as an application of James Madison's *Federalist no. 10* to the US nonprofit sector. Even though political representation plays a critical role in addressing the needs and aspirations of constituents, this kind of representation can never fully account for the multifaceted nature of individuals and the communities to which they belong. Nonprofit organizations enable multilayered representation. Nonprofits are institutional outlets through which individuals can find meaning, purpose, and belonging. These organizations also offer a diverse range of interactions and experiences, which present opportunities for identity development at the individual and community levels. While nonprofits "refine and enlarge the public views" in their roles as memory-makers, community-builders, and isolation buffers, they also "extend the sphere" by providing an organizational point of reference outside of partisan politics. In doing so, nonprofit organizations assist in limiting the effects of faction in American public life.

References

Alcoholics Anonymous. (2022). *The big book*. www.aa.org/the-big-book

Alcoholics Resource Center. (2022). *What does it mean to live one day at a time?* https://alcoholicsanonymous.com/one-day-at-a-time-aa/

American Immigration Council. (2022, June 9). *New American Fortune 500 in 2022: The largest American companies and their immigrant roots* [Data interactive]. https://data.americanimmigrationcouncil.org/en/fortune500-2022/?_gl=1*1g17fqa*_ga*NDQzMDQ1MTQuMTY4ODIyNzIxOQ.*_ga_W0MSMD2GPV*MTY4ODIyNzIxOS4xLjEuMTY4ODIyNzIzMC4wLjAuMA

American Red Cross. (2022). *Give blood*. www.redcross.org/give-blood.html

ASPCA. (2022a). *About us*. www.aspca.org/about-us

ASPCA. (2022b). *Get involved – Advocacy center*. www.aspca.org/get-involved/advocacy-center

Berry, J. M., & Arons, D. F. (2003). *A voice for nonprofits*. Brookings Institution Press.

Berry, J. M., & Wilcox, C. (2018). *The interest group society* (6th ed.). Routledge.

Black Lives Matter. (2022a). *About*. https://blacklivesmatter.com/about/

Black Lives Matter. (2022b). *Partners*. https://blacklivesmatter.com/partners/

Bresler, R. J., Krasynska, S., Arugay, A. A., Pikulik, A., & Smith, D. H. (2016). Civil liberties and freedoms as association contexts. In D. H. Smith, R. A. Stebbins, & J. Grotz (Eds.), *The Palgrave handbook of volunteering, civic participation, and nonprofit associations* (pp. 1093–1115). Palgrave Macmillan.

Bunn, C. (2021, March 8). Black churches have become indispensable in Covid-19 vaccination effort. *NBC News*. www.nbcnews.com/news/nbcblk/black-churches-become-indispensable-covid-19-vaccination-effort-rcna364

Candid. (2021, June). *Key facts on U.S. nonprofits and foundations*. www.issuelab.org/resources/38265/38265.pdf

Carey, G. W., & McClellan, J. (2001). Editors' introduction. In A. Hamilton, J. Jay, & J. Madison (Eds.), *The federalist* (pp. xvii–lv). Liberty Fund.

Chaskin, R. J. (2003). Fostering neighborhood democracy: Legitimacy and accountability within loosely coupled systems. *Nonprofit and Voluntary Sector Quarterly*, *32*(2), 161–189. https://doi.org/10.1177/0899764003032002001

Clark, C., Rosenzweig, W., Long, D., & Olsen, S. (2004). *Double bottom line project report: Assessing social impact in double bottom line ventures. Methods catalog* (Working paper no. 13). Center for Responsible Business, University of California, Berkeley. http://staging.community-wealth.org/sites/clone.community-wealth.org/files/downloads/paper-rosenzweig.pdf

Connolly, W. E. (1995). *The ethos of pluralization* (Borderlines, vol. 1). University of Minnesota Press.

Dahl, R. A. (1982). *Dilemmas of pluralist democracy: Autonomy vs. control*. Yale University Press.

Dees, J. G. (2016). Social entrepreneurship is about innovation and impact, not income. Nash, M. T. A. (2016). Social entrepreneurship and social innovation. In D. O. Renz & Associates (Eds.), *The Jossey-Bass handbook of nonprofit leadership and management* (4th ed., pp. 295–333). John Wiley & Sons. https://doi.org/10.1002/9781119176558. (Reprinted from "Social entrepreneurship is about innovation and impact, not income," September 2003, *Social Edge*.)

Deloitte. (2021). *A call for accountability and action: The Deloitte Global 2021 Millennial and Gen Z survey*. www2.deloitte.com/content/dam/Deloitte/global/Documents/2021-deloitte-global-millennial-survey-report.pdf

Elkington, J. (2008). The triple bottom line: Sustainability's accountants. In M. V. Russo (Ed.), *Environmental management: Readings and cases* (2nd ed., pp. 49–66). Sage Publications. (Reprinted from *Cannibals with forks: The triple bottom line of 21st century business*, 1998, New Society Publishers.)

Evas, T., Liebert, U., & Lord, C. (2012). Multilayered representation across the European Union in dialogue: Introduction. In T. Evas, U. Liebert, & C. Lord (Eds.), *Multilayered representation in the European Union: Parliaments, courts, and the public square* (pp. 11–24). Nomos Verlagsgesellschaft.

Feeding America. (2022a). *Our work*. www.feedingamerica.org/our-work

Feeding America. (2022b). *Your investments in action. Fall 2022 impact report*. www.feedingamerica.org/sites/default/files/2022–10/Fall%202022%20Impact%20Report_Individual_Digital_FINAL.pdf

Frumkin, P. (2002). *On being nonprofit: A conceptual and policy primer*. Harvard University Press.

Galston, W. A. (2005). *The practice of liberal pluralism*. Cambridge University Press.

Girl Scouts. (2022). *About Girl Scout cookies*. www.girlscouts.org/en/cookies/about-girl-scout-cookies.html

Guo, C., & Marietta, M. (2015). Value of voices, voice of values: Participatory and value representation in networked governance. In J. M. Bryson, B. C. Crosby, & L. Bloomberg (Eds.), *Creating public value in practice: Advancing the common good in a multi-sector, shared-power, no-one-wholly-in-charge world* (pp. 67–86). Routledge.

Hall, P. D. (2013). Philanthropy, the nonprofit sector, & the democratic dilemma. *Daedalus*, *142*(2), 139–158. https://doi.org/10.1162/DAED_a_00209

Hammack, D. C. (Ed.). (1998). *Making the nonprofit sector in the United States: A reader*. Indiana University Press.

IRS. (2022). *Describing exempt purpose in* Part III, *Form 990*. www.irs.gov/charities-non-profits/political-organizations/political-organization-annual-reporting-requirements-describing-exempt-purpose-in-part-iii-form-990

Jenkins, J. C. (2006). Nonprofit organizations and political advocacy. In W. W. Powell & R. Steinberg (Eds.), *The nonprofit sector: A research handbook* (2nd ed.) (pp. 307–332). Yale University Press.

Kennedy, B. (2022, June 11). "Enough is enough" is message at March for Our Lives rally in Washington, D.C. *Local 10 News*. www.local10.com/news/politics/2022/06/11/survivor-parents-of-murdered-teen-at-parkland-at-gun-reform-rally-in-dc/

Kramer, M., & Harlan, J. (2019, February 13). Parkland shooting: Where gun control and school safety stand today. *New York Times*. www.nytimes.com/2019/02/13/us/school-shootings-parkland.html

La Pira, T. M. (2016). Lobbying the shadows: How private interests hide from public scrutiny and why that matters. In A. J. Cigler, B. A. Loomis, & A. J. Nownes (Eds.), *Interest group politics* (9th ed.) (pp. 224–248). CQ Press.

Loomis, B. A., & Cigler, A. J. (2016). Introduction: The changing nature of interest group politics. In A. J. Cigler, B. A. Loomis, & A. J. Nownes (Eds.), *Interest group politics* (9th ed.) (pp. 1–33). CQ Press.

Madison, J. (1985). *Notes of debates in the federal convention of 1787 reported by James Madison*. Ohio University Press. (Original work published 1840.)

Madison, J. (2001). Federalist no. 10. In A. Hamilton, J. Jay, & J. Madison, *The federalist* (pp. 42–49). Liberty Fund. (Original work published 1787.)

Mandeville, J. (2007). Public policy grant making: Building organizational capacity among nonprofit grantees. *Nonprofit and Voluntary Sector Quarterly*, *36*(2), 282–298. https://doi.org/10.1177/0899764006297668

March for Our Lives. (2022). *Mission & story*. https://marchforourlives.com/mission-story/

Mason, D. E. (1996). *Leading and managing the expressive dimension: Harnessing the hidden power source of the nonprofit sector*. Jossey-Bass.

Mason, L. (2018). *Uncivil agreement: How politics became our identity*. University of Chicago Press.

Morris, A. D. (1984). *The origins of the Civil Rights Movement: Black communities organizing for change*. Free Press.

National Council of Nonprofits. (2019, September). *Nonprofit impact matters: How America's charitable nonprofits strengthen communities and improve lives*. www.nonprofitimpactmatters.org/site/assets/files/1/nonprofit-impact-matters-sept-2019–1.pdf

Olen, H. (2021, September 18). Opinion: Occupy Wall Street won the future. *The Washington Post*. www.washingtonpost.com/opinions/2021/09/18/occupy-wall-street-won-future/

Pitkin, H. F. (1967). *The concept of representation*. University of California Press.

Putnam, R. D. (2000). *Bowling alone: The collapse and revival of American community*. Simon & Schuster.

Putnam, R. D., & Garrett, S. R. (2020). *The upswing: How American came together a century ago and how we can do it again*. Simon & Schuster.

Reed, B. (2011, October 4). The nation: Are Wall St. protests demanding enough? *NPR*. www.npr.org/2011/10/04/141034728/the-nation-are-wall-st-protests-demanding-enough

Renz, D. O. (2016). The future of nonprofit leadership and management. In D. O. Renz & Associates (Eds.), *The Jossey-Bass handbook of nonprofit leadership and management* (4th ed.) (pp. 734–745). John Wiley & Sons. https://doi.org/10.1002/9781119176558

The Salvation Army. (2022). *Red kettle history.* www.salvationarmyusa.org/usn/red-kettle-history/

Schuck, P. H. (1997). Against (and for) Madison: An essay in praise of factions. *Yale Law & Policy Review*, *15*(2), 553–598.

Stewart, E. (2019, April 30). We are (still) the 99 percent. *Vox*. www.vox.com/the-highlight/2019/4/23/18284303/occupy-wall-street-bernie-sanders-dsa-socialism

Susan G. Komen Race for the Cure. (2022). *Find a race or walk.* www.komen.org/how-to-help/attend-events/race-for-the-cure/

Tocqueville, A. D. (2000). *Democracy in America.* H. C. Mansfield & D. Winthrop, Ed. & Trans. University of Chicago Press. (Original work published 1835, 1840.)

Unidos US. (2022). *Immigration.* www.unidosus.org/issues/immigration/#our-work

Weber, P. C. (2015). The paradoxical modernity of civil society: The Weimar Republic, democracy, and social homogeneity. *Voluntas*, *26*(2), 629–648. https://doi.org/10.1007/s11266-014-9448-z

Wilson, J. Q., DiIulio, J. J., Bose, M., & Levendusky, M. S. (2022). *American government: Institutions and policies* (17th ed.). Cengage.

Zunz, O. (2012). *Philanthropy in America: A history.* Princeton University Press.

14 Nonprofits as Facilitators of National Self-development

ADA ORDOR

This chapter explores the African continental context for themes and patterns in nonprofit law that can expand global views of nonprofit theory. It challenges the prevailing views of nonprofits in the context of developing economies, suggesting that sustainable nonprofit and civil-society institutions must emerge from within developing economies rather than through external aid. This contribution is made from the perspective of law, with a specific concern for the legal systems in developing and transitioning countries. The argument is both descriptive and normative. Descriptively, it offers a view of the role of nonprofit organizations in developing and transitioning states, which is that nonprofits are a critical component of economic *self*-development. Normatively, it suggests that the law should be used to support nonprofits in that role.

The chapter thus applies an alternative development theory focused on self-development to the nonprofit sector, emphasizing the importance of creating a legal framework that allows people to participate in the improvement of their own lives and communities through self-development.[1] With an appropriate legal framework in place, individuals have greater economic and social incentive to work within their own communities to create organizations that help individuals, families, and communities to meet their own needs. This paradigm stands in contrast to views of nonprofit organizations as facilitators of rescuing behavior, in which one group of people – often a group that views themselves as advantaged – seeks to uplift another. I will use cases from Nigeria and South Africa to illustrate the role and importance of nonprofits in facilitating improvement of individuals, institutions, and communities from within, drawing out nuanced aspects of nonprofit sector activity in the developing world – and by extension, the world at large.

[1] This subject was earlier explored in Ordor (2014a), drawing on the theory of alternative development within law and development contexts as articulated by Paul and Dias (1992a, 1992b).

Nonprofit theory and policy have been developed largely in the Global North, and their application to the Global South and developing economies has been most relevant to the international nongovernmental entities that have entered the spaces of the Global South with an intent to provide development aid. Nonetheless, the understanding of the nonprofit organization as the legal and structural form of associational life is generally applicable. So is the fact that civil society associations serve a variety of empowering, supporting, and supplemental roles in the conceptualization and delivery of development programs. Strategically, they serve as an information bridge or channel, articulating and transmitting government policies and programs to target recipients. In transition processes in new democracies in Africa, they maintain a necessary countervailing position to political power. In these capacities, the nonprofit sector plays a major role in keeping the government accountable to citizens by urging and monitoring government performance. Perhaps most importantly, and often overlooked, development programs contribute to individuals working on their own self-development, thereby enabling and fostering community longevity and sustainability.

In conventional practice, international intergovernmental organizations carry out the deflected mission of governments through local nongovernmental organizations (NGOs) in the areas where they operate. Thus, rather than support self-development, the situation for developing nations caught up in this model is often one of complex international intervention with little room for accountability and a stifled sense of community, self-empowerment, and internally driven development. The result is internationally organized activity that aims to address the problems of state-managed development. The premise, and often the reality, is that only by organizing to access the support of external groups can the prime targets of development – that is, the poor and underserved – hope to secure the benefits of governance, even within an autonomous democracy (Paul & Dias, 1992b, p. 296). Citizens must often act through actors external to their own community and state to affect change in their own communities rather than being able to organize directly to pressure for remedy directly from their own state actors.

Western nonprofit theory and law presume certain types of stable state structures. For example, there is an expectation that whatever the specific mechanisms, legal rules can be enacted by a central authority and enforced by police, the judiciary, and other specialized agencies and regulatory bodies. In turn, disputes can be resolved by appeals to some type of court system or private arbitration, though each of these state operations can be organized, staffed, and run in many different ways (Gray, 1999, p. 63).

The operant assumption in the international community seems to be that legal processes and institutions in developing countries are weak in the kind of functional efficiency described here, and consequently they need external, nonstate support, which a network of international NGOs provides. The consequence of this thinking, where it remains unqualified and absolute, is that the role of NGOs is confined to legitimizing the actions of the strong, centralized actors, reducing much of the nonprofit sector to a vehicle for the exercise of authority by the government more than an instrument of accountability and grassroots action (Webb, 1999, p. 35). Rather than the development of a nonprofit sector that influences, shapes, and holds the state and other institutions accountable from within, unilaterally defined international intervention weakens civil society, legitimizes struggling government and legal institutions, and reduces the citizens to people who are to be acted upon rather than agents of their own development.

14.1 A Theory of Self-development

In this section, a theory of self-development is outlined, including the laws that make it possible and the role that nonprofits can and do play in that theory. The discussion commences with a focus on the African context, since understanding this originating context is crucial to making sense of the alternative theory of development and applying it to any other situation.

14.1.1 Background on Foreign NGOs in Africa

Understanding the background of the nonprofit sector environments found in Africa is necessary to understand the theory, given that the African context challenges some general theoretical assumptions about the nonprofit sector. That is, nonprofit theories constructed around a particular political and socioeconomic reality (i.e., Western democracies) may not satisfactorily explain the origins of nonprofit organizations in a different environment. For example, dissatisfaction with public and private provision of public goods is understood to contribute to the demand for the more values-based provision by the nonprofit sector in developed societies, which significantly accounts for their growth (James, 1990, p. 23; Salamon, 1999, p. 12). However, in relation to the nonprofit sector in Africa and other parts of the developing world, the concept of competition between public and private provision does not appropriately capture a situation where the overwhelming majority of communities are underserved with public goods.

A second illustration of the incongruency between theory and reality shows up in what has been described as the narrow ahistorical focus of theory, which tends to see the presence of voluntary organizations in Africa as a *recent* development that has arisen in response to the socioeconomic malfunction of African countries rather than as a phenomenon predating the modern African state (Anheier, 1990, pp. 367–368). For instance, the genesis of African civil society can be traced to kinship values, particularly at the community level, captured by the well-known *ubuntu* philosophy. African civil society is found within traditional ethnolinguistic and communal organizations that have long promoted civic values as distinct from the "elite-controlled cosmopolitan groups that enjoyed communication links and proximity with foreign donor agencies" (Onwudiwe, 1998, p. 14).

It must be noted, however, that the distinction between indigenous African civil society and modern nonprofit organizations is not binary but rather a space that hosts a spectrum of evolving nonprofit activity, reflecting the pluralism in which life in Africa is embedded. The modern cosmopolitan nonprofits gained prominence with the post-Cold War shift of African governments from centralized large-scale planning, often monopolized by the state, to a more decentralized system of development. This shift led to the rechanneling of development finance to voluntary organizations, which in turn, induced growth in the roles of nonprofit development organizations as intermediaries (Anheier, 1990, pp. 362–363). However, while this trend may have altered the configuration of nonstate actors, it cannot be taken as the origin of the African nonprofit sector.

Third, studies on the growth of indigenous human rights organizations in Africa in the 1990s linked this growth to an increased respect for the rule of law (Ibhawoh, 2001, p. 30; Welch, 2004, pp. 201–202). The findings demonstrated how opening up political spaces created an impetus for rights-promotion activities in ways that necessitated setting up dedicated human rights organizations. This distinct political factor, which is quite common to the nonprofit sector in the developing world, is not emphasized in traditional political theories on the origins and growth of the nonprofit sector (Ordor, 2014b, p. 51).

Fourth, many contemporary nonprofit organizations in Africa have emerged primarily as an expression of the employment needs of people or "the result of local entrepreneurship that, for one reason or another, cannot be realized in other sectors of the economy" (Anheier, 1990, p. 364). This dynamic is succinctly captured in the following observation:

> The sharp increase in resources directed to the NGO world has directly spawned many new organizations in Southern countries, and a new concept of "opportunistic NGOs" has entered the language. Many of these new organizations are driven by the hunt for money and employment before anything else; they are often started by unemployed professionals, increasingly casualties of the brutal reduction of the state sector. They will operate as subcontractors for any job, and have little inherent commitment to, or experience in, working with grassroots communities. ... They feed particularly off the increasing demand for international NGOs to take over areas of basic service provision. They are a logical response to the presence of resources in a climate of increasing structural middle-class unemployment. But they bring in very different qualities and relational aspects to the sector, and they are particularly vulnerable to donor pressures and agendas. (Harding, 1994, p. 23)

Furthermore, it is quite often the case in African contexts that local communities benefit more from the presence of external nonprofit agencies in indirect and incidental ways than from the direct and deliberate activities of those agencies. As Anheier (1990) wrote, "the majority of economic benefits seemed to derive from the NGO presence in the village as such ... employment, construction ... and only secondarily because of project results" (p. 365).

The analysis thus far establishes the context for a discussion on people-centered development models based on the rights of participation through various forms of organized associational life. Invariably, for development policy to achieve its goal of generating development, it is necessary to deploy tailored social, economic, and political analyses to create the foundation for a suitable legal framework or an "appropriate legal regime" (Kennedy, 2003, p. 19).

14.1.2 *The Alternative Development Approach*

The central contention of the alternative approach to development is that people have the right to participate in their own development. The descriptive observation of this chapter is that nonprofits can and do facilitate this right to self-development, and the normative argument is that laws *should* provide institutional support for the efforts of nonprofits in that regard. The resulting civic and economic structures that result – whether formal nonprofit organizations or not – demonstrate the role of self-development as an anchoring and definitional factor that should be accounted for in nonprofit theory. In alternative development theory, development must be *by* people, not only *for* them. Therefore, people must participate fully in the decisions and processes that shape their lives (De Feyter, 2001, p. 4). Much attention has focused on the ways in which law, in its various forms and sources, impacts development processes. Although law has the potential to promote self-reliance and a more equitable allocation of resources, it has often worked to entrench disempowering cycles.

Government near-monopolization of the development process is antithetical to core concepts of participatory development. To start with, a multiplicity of actors, not just government officials, is essential for the process of participatory development to be successful; it is unrealistic to rely on the state to meet needs connected with the deployment of organizational resources on behalf of civil society (Paul & Dias, 1992a, p. 309). This observation in law and development scholarship corresponds to economic theories of government failure as a reason for the growth of the nonprofit sector. Thus, nonprofit agencies are seen as better positioned for the task of providing organizational resources to grassroots organizations.

The principle of alternative development is anchored to the need to facilitate formal organization at the local level. The alternative development approach resonates with the principle that it is not merely the framework of government but rather the *people* involved who must create and participate in the development of processes that affect their lives. In this respect, the rights of people to participate in their own development may be formulated around a variety of legal obligations. Proponents of alternative development acknowledge, however, that "promises of participation – legal and otherwise – will do little to help the very people who are supposed to be empowered unless they enjoy rights to participate through organizations" (Paul & Dias, 1992b, p. 284).

Therefore, in the alternative development paradigm, the tasks of development efforts are (a) helping people form their own organizations and (b) helping those organizations play a much more pervasive and dynamic role in the design and administration of development. In this regard, people must be mobilized and helped by support groups to use new legal rules and resources, as neither the legislature nor the judicial process will activate these resources on their behalf (Paul & Dias, 1992b, p. 296).

The corollary in this approach is that "legal processes will normally succeed to the extent that they are not complex or arbitrary, are based on a system of consultation with the people affected by them and are realistic in their reliance on existing institutions" (Shihata, 1999, p. xx). The picture that emerges is one that reflects the rights of people to form their own nonstate organizations through which to engage in different dimensions of development as well as reflects the rights of groups to participate in the design and administration of development programs and processes. This concept is supported by Muchlinski (1987), who describes an approach to development that is rooted in the theory of basic needs in which "if development occurred within a politically accountable, pluralistic and decentralized form of state, a free-market economy could be controlled for the gain of the poor" (p. 239).

Clearly, the major obstacle in developing contexts is the challenge of establishing politically accountable governments in a balanced system of devolved state power within pluralistic societies. The international solution to this problem has been to introduce accountability from above and outside – with international policy, international intervention, and international NGOs exercising external oversight. However, a more appropriate and effective approach would be to generate accountability from below through grassroots civic organizing by the people that government institutions and policies should be accountable to. The international approach to nonprofit organizing in the developing context tends to displace or distort such internal development, reducing the ability of the governed to organize effectively for their own benefit. In the face of large, wealthy, powerful organizations from outside, how audibly can the voice of local civic formations speak into the important process of establishing law and governance? This displacement of the internal nonprofit sector by international change agents, where it occurs, renders developing nations severely destabilized by a lack of effective internal civic institutions, dependent on foreign structures and aid, and unable to create their own internal accountability mechanisms that would address corruption and enhance democratic oversight.

14.1.3 Why Nonprofits?

The chapter thus far has highlighted the role of nonprofit organizations in the alternative theory of development. The aim in this section is to show how the alternative theory of development also informs a nonprofit sector theory. As indicated in Chapter 1 of this volume, one way of conceptualizing sector theory is as an answer to the question, Why nonprofits? In other words, Why do, or why *should*, nonprofits exist? Some answers are historical, but some are also descriptive; their answers pertain to the role that nonprofits play in society. Still other answers are normative theories, responding to the question of why we might want nonprofits in society, regardless of why they are historically present.

In the African contexts described in this chapter, one of the roles that nonprofits play is to facilitate self-development. The term "nonprofits" is used here to refer to community-based nonprofits, populated by members of the community in question. From a normative perspective, nonprofits thus play a critical role in development. Nonprofits can aid alternative development only if they are populated and managed by local people interested in addressing their own challenges, and law and regulation should promote the development and formalization of these locally organized efforts.

In the area of women's rights, for example, nonprofits in Africa have been active in a variety of roles. These include activating legal provisions to overturn arbitrary death sentences imposed under religious law in Nigeria, challenging discriminatory inheritance laws in Uganda, providing a suite of support for mental health care for emotional trauma, legal and medical aid in Cote D'Ivoire, and advancing gender law reform through strategic impact litigation in Namibia (Asiimwe, 2014, p. 77; Bahi, 2014, p. 150; Hubbard, 2014; p. 19; Ordor, 2014a, pp. 216–217).

Associations of civil society such as town unions, village meetings, age-grade groups, women's networks, and other peer-group formations, by default, constitute locally recognized authority structures in many rural and peri-urban towns. Optimizing the role of these nonprofits for the self-development of nation states will require an understanding of how to navigate and maximize synergies between plural forms of nonprofits, ranging from grassroots organizations to intermediary NGOs.

Any given component of African society features an assortment of expressions and associations of civil society. Some of these associations are clustered around kinship, ethnolinguistic, and other cultural lines. Others reflect vocational, life-cycle, livelihood, and other forms of solidarity. The argument here is therefore not for the creation of new superficial legal entities but for the recognition, integration, inclusion, and deployment of these "organic" nonprofit formations in development design and implementation. Their potential for impact is demonstrated in how effectively they are mobilized for political campaigns along ethnic, linguistic, religious, and other loyalties. Those same "fault lines" can be realigned to developmental ends. In other words, these grassroots nonprofits provide associational leverage for alternative development.

14.2 Self-development: An Application

A compelling case for the self-propelling capacity of local civil society to respond to its environment is repeatedly demonstrated by examples in political transition in Africa. In this regard, the military-to-civilian governance transition in Nigeria and the apartheid-to-democracy transition in South Africa present comparative insights.

In Nigeria, successive military interventions post-independence were ostensibly predicated on poor governance. The result was a dual crisis of militarization and state failure in service provision, both of which fueled people's self-reliant efforts to solve common problems. Urban-based civil-society agencies soon became the voice for grassroots organizations meeting community needs. The strategic importance of civil-society organizations was reinforced when it became obvious that government employees and government-affiliated institutions could not successfully champion the campaign for a democratic agenda without coming up against their military employers and overseers (Banwo, 1997, p. 48). On the other hand, the inefficiencies of military rule served to emphasize the relationship between the economic objectives of trade unions and the imperative of political reform (Akinyanju, 1997, p. 69). To a large extent therefore, today's assortment of nongovernmental agencies and civic-advocacy organizations is a legacy of the prodemocratic civil-society activism of the 1980s and 1990s.

As their activities increasingly came up against military autocracy, preexisting and historically strong civil-society formations, including professional bodies, student movements, women's associational networks, and trade unions, coalesced around a common agenda of ending military dictatorship. This consolidation of prodemocratic efforts by diverse nonprofit organizations crystallized into the Transition Monitoring Group (TMG). The TMG became the voice of civil society between 1998 and 2000, a critical period of time that ushered in Nigeria's return to democratic civilian rule.

The transition program that immediately followed the death of Nigeria's penultimate military head of state in 1998 was propelled forward internally by pressure from civil-society organizations and externally from the international community. The internal push was led by the TMG, which had a threefold mission of observing elections, fostering civic education, and promoting democratic norms. These goals positioned the TMG to work with the state, particularly through its electoral body in monitoring elections, and with various development agencies, including those operating through diplomatic missions, to train elected officials in federal and state legislatures.

The Nigerian case presents a clear example of civil-society solidarity demonstrated in the banding together of a wide variety of nonprofit organizations to overcome a common enemy. These diverse nonprofits, representing virtually all demographics of Nigerian society, experienced military rule in a sufficiently disempowering way to elicit a strong reaction, and their response is noteworthy. It signaled that the state cannot successfully govern for the long term in isolation of the very structures that give expression to peoples' citizenship rights – namely, the nonprofit sector.

With regard to South Africa, two distinct and clearly identifiable phases of civil-society history in South Africa coincide with key moments in the evolution of the political system. First was the liberalization phase of the early 1980s, which saw a phenomenal growth in associational life and a marked resurfacing of Black civil-society actors. Second was the democratization phase that began in 1994 and extends to the present day (Habib, 2004, p. 230). The liberalization of political and economic controls in South Africa in the 1980s and early 1990s resulted in the emergence and growth of large numbers of civil-society organizations that were critical of the government, which led to the creation of a nonprofit sector described as "politically centered" and "artificially large" (Smith, 2001, pp. 7, 11).

The years leading up to the 1994 elections were characterized by a "mushrooming of development forums," ascribed to the need to better equip local interest groups, represented by community-based organizations (CBOs), to compete in a globalized context – a situation which called for multiple interest forums and frameworks to coordinate and drive socioeconomic strategies (Pieterse, 1995, p. 19). All said, the cell-like multiplication of civil-society organizations during this period was perceived as a positive buildup to the democratic elections, on the rationale that the proliferation of CBOs that have an impact on a particular institution advances ownership of that institution by ordinary people and, thus, their capacity to transform it (Kaplan, 1994, p. 9).

The transition to a general democracy in South Africa was visited with a number of issues, all of which confirm the centrality of the nonprofit sector in self-development processes. These issues included the loss of key civil-society leaders after they were recruited by the new government, the need to develop skills and capacity for more constructive engagement with the state by organizations rooted in resistance, the loss of funding, and the necessity of redefining post-apartheid causes in a way that kept the nonprofit sector mobilized (Greenstein et al., 1998, p. 6; Kraak, 2001, p. 129; Marais, 1997, p. 116). Recognizing the importance of a friendly legal environment to address some of these concerns, a network of nonprofits immediately set to work on law reform, resulting in the enactment of a much more enabling legal framework by way of the Nonprofit Organisations Act (NPO Act) in 1997 (Dangor & The Development Resources Centre, 1997, p. 30; Ordor, 2010, pp. 120–122). Incidentally, the campaign for the act itself constituted a valuable immediate rallying point for the nonprofit sector following the 1994 general elections.

In respect of its substantive effect, the Nonprofit Organizations Act (NPO Act) provided less onerous registration processes for nonprofits, which assisted with access to funding. Given that registration was a requirement for nonprofits that became involved in service delivery, the new registration processes helped them receive government funding. Furthermore, having been quite lenient during the antiapartheid period, reporting requirements for funding from external donors became more rigorous; they now required more formal documentation from grant recipients (Smith, 2001, p. 11). Thus, ease of registration was an enabling development for nonprofit sector organizations and a necessary precursor to securing funding and technical support for capacity-building programs.

From the South African case, it is clear that the disenfranchised indigenous population was already connected in strong civil-society networks; these connections carried into formal workplaces by way of vigorous trade unions. Furthermore, the exclusionary and segregated nature of the apartheid system meant that nonprofits were inherently political in their modus operandi, representing, as they typically did, one race or another. It was these nonprofits who chipped away at formal apartheid structures until they finally gave way. Postapartheid transition processes were also brokered by a remarkable diversity of nonstate organizations on all sides, indicating the indispensability of the nonprofit sector in mobilization, bridge-building, and governance in transition contexts.

14.2.1 Similarities in Growth Factors

Although the histories differ, certain key similarities in the factors responsible for the growth of concerted nonprofit activity are shared by the two countries, principally government failure in the delivery of citizenship rights – civil-political and socioeconomic. In relation to Nigeria, the deterioration of public services led to an explosion in self-help activities by citizens, reflected in the growth of both informal associations and formal human rights organizations in response to the excesses of successive military juntas. Decisive elections in 1999 finally brought more than three decades of military rule to an end. In South Africa, government failure clearly unfolded in the apartheid policy which systematically excluded the majority of the population from political, educational, social, and economic opportunities. It was the sustained response and reaction to these respective manifestations of state failure that defined the dominant character of the modern nonprofit sector in both countries.

Another point of similarity in the development of the nonprofit sector in both Nigeria and South Africa has to do with the effect of international fiscal policy and globalization. The two countries experienced a departure from homegrown development models through

(a) favoring the neoliberal economic policies of the International Monetary Fund (IMF) and the World Bank and (b) pushing the state to withdraw from the economy, which in Nigeria has been referred to as "anti-statism" (Onimode, 1998, p. 12).

In the case of Nigeria, the sharp decline in the prices of agricultural and mineral exports in the 1970s, the cuts in government expenditure on social services in the 1980s, and the mismanagement of the 1980s and 1990s triggered a severe economic crisis. This crisis led to the replacement of the mixed economy development model, which had been adopted postindependence, with the neoliberal development models of the IMF and the World Bank as the condition for intervention by these multilateral bodies (Sunmonu, 1998, p. 7). In South Africa, the Reconstruction and Development Programme was replaced by the Growth Employment and Redistribution strategy in response to the imperative of entering into the global economy, even while growing the local economy.[2]

These developments, which saw the retreat of the state, expanded the roles of nonprofit organizations in the provision of social services in South Africa, as observed earlier. However, in Nigeria, the harsh effects of the implementation of a structural adjustment program (SAP) by military governments eroded standards of living and led to disenchantment and unrest among the citizenry. In turn, citizens found an outlet in many forms, including dedicating themselves to the campaigns of civil-society organizations (Gana, 2000, p. 267). Indeed, it has been suggested that the SAP, by its very nature, worked to validate the presence of the military in governance, the rationale being that "because SAP policies are so unpopular, unjust and oppressive, they require this authoritarian state to impose structural adjustment policies in most countries" (Onimode, 1998, p. 13).

In the period immediately following the transition, the focal point for civil-society activity crystallized around antipoverty engagement in South Africa and democracy consolidation in Nigeria – all self-propelled by local civil society. The focus has expanded over the years to a number of other issues, including state capture in South Africa and security concerns in Nigeria.

[2] See article 1.1 of the document "Growth, Employment and Redistribution: A Macroeconomic Strategy," constructed by the South African government in 1996; www.gov.za/reports/1996/macroeco.htm.

14.3 Conclusions

It is important to observe that many of the issues raised in this discourse are also applicable to developing countries outside Africa. The unique international context of foreign aid to developing economies creates a sharp contrast between an international community of nonprofit NGOs and "organic" internal development of civil society and self-development organizations, and such contrasts also exist in the nations of the Global North. A theory of self-development, applied to the nonprofit sector, suggests that a key role of the nonprofit sector is to facilitate the organizing of the governed to address the failings and incapacities of their own government. Filling in for government is, of course, not the *raison d'être* of many nonprofits, since civil-society activity primarily operates independently of the state. However, when the quality of associational life is reduced by government inefficiencies, local nonprofits are intrinsically constituted to respond to protect and restore the public sphere in which they operate.

Put differently, through associational life found in the nonprofit sector, the primary targets of development, including local constituencies of people, can secure the benefits of governance, much in the same way lobby groups secure benefits for their members within well-established democracies. A development-friendly legal system should therefore possess the key elements of (a) simplicity of procedures, (b) predictability and accessibility of legal processes, (c) participation of the affected people, and (d) accountability of public officials; each element enhances the legitimacy of the rules and contributes to the public's confidence in the legal framework as a whole.

Gray (1999, pp. 63–65) identified three steps to constructing a sound legal system in developing and transition countries: creating laws that clearly set out individual responsibility and incorporate market-friendly economic policies, establishing a broad set of implementing institutions, and putting in place incentives for individual market participants to take full advantage of their legal rights. Implementing institutions include formal agencies, such as the judiciary and the police, as well as complementary semiformal agencies, such as alternative dispute-resolution bodies, the press, and the private bar. Yet these agencies, although they operate in the public sphere, are not easily accessible to ordinary citizens, making it imperative for citizens to approach through associational networks of nonprofits.

Generally speaking, the right of association may be expressly stated in the constitution, or it may be inferred from other rights or from collective jurisprudence emerging from court cases or both. Africa's deep legal pluralism often means that a variety of sources need to be consulted to determine the law on any subject. This makes it attractive to try and promulgate a single law to capture legal provisions scattered in various locations. However, given that the nonprofit sector is in a real sense the custodian of the right to association, that role needs to be safeguarded even in the most benign attempts to regulate the sector for accountability and effectiveness (Ordor, 2014b, p. 68). In this regard, while a consolidation of applicable laws in a single framework legislation may be orderly and signal an alive-and-well nonprofit sector (Ferraro, 2000), it is ultimately how nonprofit sector actors experience the law that will determine which legal framework functions best in a particular country.

Nonetheless, some nonprofit stakeholders may find it useful to have a soft template for improving the nonprofit laws of a particular jurisdiction. In this regard, Ferraro (2000) proposes the concept of a framework legislation that brings together, in one place, various nonprofit sector-specific laws. A framework legislation does not operate as a single law, nor is it merely a receptacle for a variety of nonprofit laws; it is a compendium of laws crafted in a way that makes it easier for nonprofits to navigate their legal environment. A framework legislation should therefore be drafted with nonprofit sector-friendly principles and outcomes in mind, including certainty and simplicity of administration, openness to draw from other jurisdictions while being rooted in a particular local tradition, accountability channels, and a clear definition of tax benefits.

Be that as it may, even the best of framework legislation cannot stand alone, and a comprehensive nonprofit sector-friendly environment will have in place other measures that ensure that law is not wielded in the breach to counter the activities of nonprofits. Such an environment will be forward-thinking and conducive for sustainable innovation, in part by recognizing the value of inter-sectoral consultation. In a hospitable nonprofit sector ecosystem, it becomes easier for people to chart and advance their own alternative, supplemental, and complementary paths to development.

In summary, the concept of self-development is not new. Rather, it is a way of life in Africa's plural societies, expressed through associations of civil society, which are categorized in legal terms as nonprofit organizations. This chapter contributes to the discourse that demonstrates the pivotal role of the nonprofit sector, both as an indicator and a stimulator of self-development. The vibrancy of nonprofit activity in a society is often an indicator of the democratic health of that society. Conversely, poor vital signs of associational life are indicative of a self-development malady in a community. Often, a lack of associational life stems from governance deficits and political suppression, which ultimately trigger mass civil-society activism, as seen in the cases of Nigeria and South Africa.

References

Akinyanju, P. (1997). Trade unions and democratic struggle. In O. Olorode, W. Raji, J. Ogunye, & S. Jegede (Eds.), *Nigeria non-governmental organisations and democracy* (pp. 66–76). Committee for the Defence of Human Rights.

Anheier, H. K. (1990). Private voluntary organisations and the third world: The case of Africa. In H. K. Anheier & W. Seibel (Eds.), *The third sector: Comparative studies of nonprofit organizations* (pp. 361–374). Walter de Gruyter.

Asiimwe F. A. (2014). Constitutionalism and the law of inheritance: Recent experiences from Uganda. In S. Röhrs & D. Smythe (Eds.), *In search of equality, women, law and society in Africa* (pp. 64–89). University of Cape Town Press.

Bahi, M. A. (2014). The justice system and women's rights in Cote D'Ivoire. In S. Röhrs & D. Smythe (Eds.), *In search of equality, women, law and society in Africa* (pp. 148–170). University of Cape Town Press.

Banwo, A. (1997). Democracy and human rights in Nigeria: An overview. In O. Olorode, W. Raji, J. Ogunye, & S. Jegede (Eds.), *Nigeria non-governmental organisations and democracy* (pp. 4–51). Committee for the Defence of Human Rights.

Dangor, Z., & The Development Resources Centre. (1997). *The non-profit sector in South Africa.* Charities Aid Foundation.

De Feyter, K. (2001). *World development law: Sharing responsibility for development.* Intersentia.

Ferraro, P. (2000) *Legal and organizational practices in nonprofit management.* Kluwer Law International.

Gana, A. T. (2000). Civil society and the consolidation of democracy in Nigeria. In I. A. Ayua, D. A. Guobadia, & A. O. Adekunle (Eds.), *Nigeria: Issues in the 1999 constitution* (pp. 254–273). Nigerian Institute of Advanced Legal Studies.

Gray, C. W. (1999). Reforming legal systems in developing and transitional countries. In A. Seidman, R. B. Seidman, & T. W. Walde (Eds.), *Making development work: Legislative reform for institutional transformation and good governance* (pp. 61–66). Kluwer Law International.

Greenstein, R., Heinrich, V., & Naidoo, K. (1998). *The state of civil society in South Africa: Past legacies, present realities and future prospects*. The Community Agency for Social Enquiry (CASE).

Habib, A. (2004). State-civil society relations in post-apartheid South Africa. In J. Daniel, A. Habib and R. Southall (Eds.), *State of the nation: South Africa 2003–2004* (pp. 671–692). Cape Town: Human Sciences Research Council.

Harding, D. (1994). *From global to local: Issues and challenges facing NGOs*. Olive Information Service.

Hubbard, D. (2014). Challenges in litigation on gender issues in Namibia. In S. Röhrs & D. Smythe (Eds.), *In search of equality, women, law and society in Africa* (pp. 19–63). University of Cape Town Press.

Ibhawoh, B. (2001). *Human rights organisations in Nigeria*. The Danish Centre for Human Rights.

James, E. (1990). Economic theories of the nonprofit sector: A comparative perspective. *The third sector, comparative studies of non-profit organizations* (pp. 21–30). De Gruyter.

Kaplan, A. (1994). *NGOs, civil society and capacity building: Towards the development of strategy*. Community Development Resource Association. www.cdra.org.za/writings-by-cdra-practitioners.html

Kennedy, D. (2003). Laws and developments. In J. Hatchard & A. Perry-Kessaris (Eds.), *Law and development: Facing complexity in the 21st century* (pp. 17–26). Cavendish Publishing Ltd.

Kraak, G. (2001). The South African voluntary sector in 2001: A great variety of "morbid symptoms". *Development Update*, *3*(4), 129–150.

Marais, H. (1997). Annual review: The voluntary sector and development in South Africa 1996–97. Special issue of *Development Update 1*(3).

Muchlinski, P. T. (1987). Basic needs theory and development law. In F. Snyder & P. Slinn (Eds.), *International law of development: Comparative perspectives* (pp. 237–269). Professional Books.

Onimode, B. (1998). Structural adjustment, development and democracy – What options for Africa? In F. Adewunmi (Ed.), *Trade unions, national development and military rule* (pp. 11–32). Friedrich Ebert Foundation and the Organisation of African Trade Unity.

Onwudiwe, E. (1998). Civil society: A definition and an African perspective. In E. Onwudiwe (Ed.), *African perspectives on civil society* (pp. 1–15). Central State University.

Ordor, A. O. (2010). The South African nonprofit sector: Legal and policy environment. *Speculum Juris*, *24*(1), 118–135.

Ordor, A. O. (2014a). Associational life and women's constitutional rights in Africa. In S. Röhrs & D. Smythe (Eds.), *In search of equality, women, law and society in Africa* (pp. 208–242). University of Cape Town Press.

Ordor, A. O. (2014b). The nonprofit sector in the context of law in development in Africa. *Journal of African Law*, *58*(1), 45–70.

Paul, J. C. N., & Dias, C.J. (1992a). Alternative development: A legal prospectus. In A. Carty (Ed.), *The international library of essays in law and legal theory: Legal cultures; Vol. 2. Law and development* (pp. 303–331). Dartmouth Publishing Company.

Paul, J. C. N., & Dias, C. J. (1992b). State-managed development: A legal critique. In A. Carty (Ed.), *The international library of essays in law and legal theory: Legal cultures; Vol. 2. Law and development* (pp. 279–302). Dartmouth Publishing Company.

Pieterse, E. (1995). *Local activism in a global era: Emerging debates for CBOs and NGDOs*. Olive Organisation Development and Training.

Salamon, L. M. (1999). *America's nonprofit sector: A primer* (2nd ed.). The Foundation Centre.

Shihata, I. F. (1999). Good governance and the role of law in economic development. In A. Seidman, R. B. Seidman, & T. W. Walde (Eds.), *Making development work: Legislative reform for institutional transformation and good governance*. Kluwer Law International.

Smith, T. (2001). *Questioning the crisis: International donors and the reconfiguration of the South African NGO sector*. Olive Publications, AVOCADO Working Paper Series (Vol. 2).

Sunmonu, H. A. (1998). Democracy, development and trade unions. In F. Adewunmi (Ed.) *Trade unions, national development and military rule* (pp. 1–21). Friedrich Ebert Foundation and the Organisation of African Trade Unity.

Webb, D. (1999). Legal system reform and private sector development in developing countries. In A. Seidman, R. B. Seidman, & T. Walde (Eds.), *Making development work: Legislative reform for institutional transformation and good governance*. Kluwer Law International.

Welch, C. E. (2004). Human rights and development: NGOs. In P. Zeleza & P. McConnaughay (Eds.), *Human rights, the rule of law, and development in Africa* (pp. 198–208). University of Pennsylvania Press.

15 *Nonprofits as Part of an Engineered Social Economy*

MEEYOUNG LAMOTHE, JIWON SUH, MISUN LEE, HEE SOUN JANG, BOK GYO JEONG, AND SEONGHO AN

Much of Western theorizing about the emergence of nonprofit organizations focuses on the sector's unique role in society, rationalizing its existence as necessary to address market or government failures (Hansmann, 1980; Weisbrod, 1988) or as a conduit for facilitating democracy through civil society and social capital-building (Clemens, 2006). Common understandings of the nonprofit sector, especially in the United States, have developed largely around a notion of the sector's distinctiveness, resulting in the establishment of elaborate legal and tax guardrails along sectoral borders to keep the nonprofit sector from mingling excessively with the market or politics and to reduce entanglements across the sectors (Hemel, 2020).

We argue that this traditional Western, and particularly US, notion of nonprofit distinctiveness is not only rapidly eroding in the face of sector-bending activities but is also being fundamentally challenged by the global diffusion of social enterprise in places where the government has a far reach in shaping the social and economic sectors of society. This chapter therefore examines social enterprise, especially in the context of South Korea, in order to highlight how conventional notions of the nonprofit sector fall short in some non-Western settings. The case of South Korea suggests new ways of thinking about why nonprofits exists, including how the social economy evolves vis-à-vis government policy.

Social enterprise is commonly defined as the pursuit by private entities, regardless of organizational form, of social missions primarily through the use of business means in marketplaces to generate revenues (Kerlin, 2006). The conceptualization of social enterprise, however, has varied widely depending on region (Defourny & Nyssens, 2017; Kerlin, 2013) and schools of thought (Young & Lecy, 2014). The rise of social enterprise in recent decades, in both the nonprofit and for-profit spheres, has considerably disrupted the sectoral border between nonprofits and commercial businesses as these types of entities merge market tools seamlessly and aggressively into their pursuit of social missions; this in turn has sparked a sense of identity crisis among sectoral traditionalists over the marketization of the nonprofit sector (Eikenberry & Kluver, 2004).

Blurred boundaries have also emerged as a result of the nonprofit sector's relationship with government. Social enterprises' global reach has exposed the very different roles governments around the world play in shaping the contours of the economies and the civil societies within which these entities emerge (Coskun et al., 2019; Kerlin, 2013). Outside the US context, for example, some governments have actively promoted social enterprise as a policy tool, rather than exclusively as a voluntary phenomenon, to address hard-to-tackle socioeconomic problems. Other governments have taken further steps to nurture social enterprises with elaborate government-led assistance schemes as a way to solve policy problems in the absence of a vibrant civil-society sector.

Given the continuing convergence among the sectors, further refining the existing theories that focus on sectoral divisions will not provide satisfying answers to the central questions this volume poses (i.e., What is the nonprofit sector, and why do nonprofits exist?). Rather, addressing these questions hinges at least partly on a better understanding of what underlies the global diffusion of social enterprise and what the "social enterprise phenomenon" (Defourny & Kim, 2011, p. 90) means to the purpose of the nonprofit sector around the world. Many scholars have already explored the causes, organizational processes, and effects of nonprofit marketization through theoretical and empirical research on social enterprises and, more broadly, "business-like" nonprofit organizations (Maier et al., 2016, p. 73). What has remained mostly unexplored is the nature and extent of government intervention in the development of social enterprise, specifically government's role as a major facilitator in building and, to a degree, directing the social economy through the aggressive use of state power, capacity, and elaborate policy designs.

Focusing our inquiry mainly on the relationship between social enterprise and government, our answer to one of the central questions of this volume is that social organizations equipped with marketized operations sometimes exist because they serve as an effective policy tool that government can tap into from the civil society and voluntary sector to tackle critical societal problems. Past efforts made by governments to compensate for the failure of the administrative state in tackling tough policy issues, such as New Public Management-inspired reforms that primarily resorted to markets, had, at best, mixed results (Dunleavy & Hood, 1994). Likewise, the attempt to expand the welfare state by enlisting nonprofit partners has been cited as the reason behind the nonprofit sector's increasing dependence on the state (Heimovics et al., 1993; Mosley, 2012). Market-based but socially oriented entities may offer a better hope for policymakers when confronting and finding solutions for stubborn socioeconomic challenges. Curiously, the role of the social sector as a vital policy tool can also be observed in countries where the civil-society sector is historically and institutionally underdeveloped and has a low capacity to handle serious policy tasks. How does the social sector emerge and function effectively as the new partner of government under such circumstances? The purpose of this chapter is to explore this possibility under the auspice of what we call an *engineered social economy* framework.

15.1 A Theory of an Engineered Social Economy

In the theory of an engineered social economy, the government aggressively asserts itself as a policy innovator, leveraging both the market and civil-society sectors to solve challenging socioeconomic problems, but it does not become a major financier for the effort or control it through bureaucratic accountability mechanisms. The relationship between the nonprofit, or more broadly the social, sector and government in the engineered social economy is significantly different from Salamon's (1981, 1987) third-party government or Smith and Lipsky's (1993) contracting regime in which nonprofit social-service providers essentially serve as street-level bureaucrats for governments that fund them. The role of government in the engineered social economy is limited to actively nudging the social sector to marketize itself for self-sufficiency rather than relying on government resources to achieve social missions and deliver public services. The government helps these social organizations if they lack resources and expertise, but the goal is for government to assist them in eventually reaching independence and sustainability through market-based activities.

The theory of an engineered social economy also departs fundamentally from the traditional Tocquevillian approach to the nonprofit sector in which social organizations in the private sphere serve as major venues through which voluntary civic activities occur and social capital is built, which ultimately contributes to pluralism-based "democracy and good government" (Smith & Grønbjerg, 2006, p. 229). The civil-society theorists, while heavily borrowing from the Tocquevillian perspectives, take a less optimistic tone regarding the relationship between government and the civil-society sector, arguing that government represents a central authority that pushes for universal values and standards that threaten local values and cultural heritage (Berger & Neuhaus, 1977; Nisbet, 1953). For these theorists, civil society is mainly responsible for solving social problems, with nonprofits acting as intermediating institutions, but without government intervention, in order to preserve and encourage self-governing communities (Smith & Grønbjerg, 2006). While the civil-society model for the nonprofit sector has long served as one of the major pillars of the sector-based understanding of nonprofit organizations, we take a dramatic departure from this tradition in formulating the theory of an engineered social economy. The role of government in this model is that of a facilitator or even a creator of civil-society sector for the instrumental purposes of pursuing state policy goals regarding socioeconomic welfare.

This model is likely to emerge in countries where government is traditionally proactive in advancing economic development, welfare spending is low, and the civil-society sector has yet to be firmly established (with its own capacity and clear sectoral boundaries or identities). Under this system, the government may induce innovation, such as the use of social enterprise to address tough socioeconomic problems, rather than wait for innovation to arise spontaneously from the private sector. In other words, government may serve as the major catalyst not only for importing and imitating innovation from around the globe but also for nurturing the civil-society sector through government assistance to prop it up to function as viable partners in implementing public policies.

The real-world manifestation of an engineered social economy is observed in South Korea. Jeong (2015) traced the root of the government-led development of social enterprise to the developmental state that some Asian countries, such as South Korea and Japan, had pursued in the past. In a developmental state, government and its bureaucrats have clear intent and capacity to formulate and implement national economic development plans (Evans, 1989; Woo-Cumings, 1999). Close cooperation between businesses and government is essential. In this type of relationship, businesses are privately owned and managed. The state, however, exerts significant control over the private sector by setting economic policies that shape businesses and influence business decisions (Johnson, 1982). The state's prioritization of economic growth is consistent and continuous over time, providing a stable path to enduring economic growth (Johnson, 1982).

In an engineered social economy, government plays a similar role in terms of intentionally planning, designing, and implementing national-level policies that promote the social economy and rely on social enterprises to achieve its goals. Policies are strictly designed to steer social enterprises toward certain activities that align with policy goals, such as employing members of disadvantaged groups and providing equitable wages or contributing to community welfare. Policies are also designed to operate under democratic governance that involves several stakeholders representing communities, employees, and beneficiaries. In the extreme, government may adopt a strict control mechanism, such as the social enterprise certification system in South Korea, to dictate specific conditions social organizations must meet to be qualified as social enterprises and what specific economic and social outcomes they must achieve to maintain their social enterprise status. To help social enterprises become self-sufficient and competitive in marketplaces, the government provides not only wage support and tax benefits but also business-plan consultations, marketing, and other professional assistance (Kim, 2014). Government assistance for nurturing social enterprises is extensive but is intended to last for only a limited time, reducing long-term reliance on government.

It is important to note that while South Korea might currently be the only true prototype of the engineered social economy model, there are many variations of this model globally that share some of its key elements. The growth of social enterprises in Western Europe, for example, is directly connected with its public policy. Many European countries have historically had strong government-led welfare systems. During the 1980s, however, public finance crises combined with increasing structural unemployment problems motivated governments to look for new ways to address labor issues. Since much of the underlying conditions afflicting chronically unemployed populations intersect with social-service needs, involving nonprofit social-service organizations and cooperatives to implement active second labor market programs was an attractive labor policy tool (Defourny & Nyssens, 2008).

Several European governments also established legal frameworks and policy parameters to regulate social enterprises and steer them toward intended policy goals. The prohibition of profit distribution and the use of asset locks are common features of European social enterprises (Davister et al., 2004). In Italy, where social enterprises have a significant presence, social cooperatives, the most dominant organizational form, are allowed to distribute some portion of their profits to members and to convert themselves to regular commercial companies if they so choose (Triponel & Agapitova, 2016). If the social cooperative is dissolved, however, the remaining assets must be distributed to other cooperatives. In 2006, Italy adopted a more stringent legal definition of social enterprises, prohibiting both direct and indirect profit distribution to shareholders or members, regardless of their organizational form (e.g., nonprofits, cooperatives, and for-profit companies). Similarly, the United Kingdom enacted a new legal form of social enterprise (i.e., the community interest company) in 2004, which comprised a wide range of organizational forms (e.g., nonprofits, for-profits) that were uniformly subject to limitations on profit distribution during operations and asset locks in case of dissolution. These European organizational and legal frameworks, in fact, were largely influential in shaping the South Korean model of social enterprise, although the South Korean government expanded its efforts by aggressively pursuing a national plan to systematically nurture and grow social enterprises through extensive legal, organizational, financial, and technical support.

Surprisingly, the engineered social economy model championed by South Korea has so far not been fully replicated in the rest of the East Asian region. In Japan, for example, since the adoption of the new comprehensive legal system to establish the nonprofit sector in 1998, employment programs for the elderly and disabled have been administered by nonprofit entities, generating market-based incomes through product sales. The introduction of the Long-Term Care Insurance System in 2000 led to the expansion of social enterprises into the social and health-care industries in competitive marketplaces (Laratta et al., 2011). The extent of government policies to nurture social enterprises, however, was relatively measured since there was neither effort to provide separate legal definitions of social enterprises to guide their development nor special government assistance to stimulate their growth (Tsukamoto & Nishimura, 2009).

In China, the role of government in directly nurturing and promoting social enterprises has also been limited, although there are some tax-exemption benefits for social enterprises that participate in work integration for the disabled. Social enterprises are scattered across different sectors, and while some entities are government-led, others are initiated through private and international venture philanthropies and associations (Yu, 2011, 2013, 2016). As in Japan, there is no overarching law or administrative authority to guide or coordinate social enterprises in China.

In South Korea, the evolution of social enterprise development has taken a very different route. Unlike its neighboring countries, South Korea viewed social enterprises as a potentially effective labor policy instrument to address the acute unemployment issues it faced after the severe financial crisis of the late 1990s (Bidet & Eum, 2011; Crotty & Lee, 2002; Jeong, 2015). In the following section, we examine the South Korean case more closely to see how a government-engineered social economy is manifested in practice and discuss its implications.

15.2 The South Korean Case of an Engineered Social Economy

Bidet and Eum (2011) have argued that while the use of the term "social enterprise" did not appear in South Korea until 2002, the government initiatives to implement work integration programs started in 1999 as part of the adoption of a broader social welfare policy, the National Basic Livelihood System (NBLS), which provides a cash allowance to households under the absolute poverty line. For South Korea, which has long been known for its productivist welfare capitalism (Holliday, 2000; Jeong, 2015), the establishment of the NBLS signaled a fundamental shift in the country's social welfare policy (Kwon & Holliday, 2007). Nonetheless, requiring work for the able-bodied to get full welfare benefits was the underlying condition for this reform. As part of the NBLS, some of these work integration programs were implemented directly by the government, but civil-society organizations (*Jiyeok Jahwal* centers, or local self-sufficiency centers [LSSCs]), which were heavily subsidized by the government, were mainly responsible for operating most of the work programs (Bidet & Eum, 2011; Lee & Min, 2015). One of the main tasks of these civil-society organizations was to set up self-sufficiency enterprises (*Jahwalgongdongche* and *Jahwalgeunlo eobdan*). These entities were collectively owned, hired at least one-third of their employees from NBLS beneficiaries, and were supposedly self-sustaining through business activities in such industries as construction, cleaning services, agriculture, and manufacturing (Eum, 2008). When they were formally recognized (i.e., certified) by local authorities, these enterprises received government support for their economic activities. Bidet and Eum (2011) have contended that self-sufficiency enterprises became the "main basis for social enterprise creation in South Korea," reporting that as of 2010, approximately 20% of the certified social enterprises were NBLS-related entities (p. 80).

The clearest form of social enterprise in South Korea, however, is demonstrated in the organizations certified under the Social Enterprise Promotion Act (SEPA) that was passed in 2006. Interestingly, the bill was initially proposed by the conservative opposition party at the National Assembly and repackaged by the ruling liberal party as a "job-creation" program (Bidet & Eum, 2011, p. 77). The major political and socioeconomic backdrop at the time of the act's passage was the large-scale financial crisis of the 1990s that swept through East Asian countries, including South Korea; the sharp rise in unemployment, which was largely caused by structural changes resulting from globalization; and the increasing social issues tied to income inequality and poverty (Ha & Lee, 2001; Park & Wilding, 2013). In addition to the previously mentioned NBLS, which was a significant step toward enhancing basic social welfare, the South Korean government responded to these crises by aggressively searching for innovative policy solutions to both ease the labor problems and meet increasing social needs (Park & Wilding, 2013). Social enterprise captured South Korean policymakers' attention as a potentially critical policy instrument to achieve these twin goals but particularly to improve deteriorating labor market conditions for vulnerable populations (Choi & Choi, 2019; Kim & Jeon, 2013; Park & Wilding, 2013).

It is worth noting that, prior to establishing the SEPA and promoting social enterprises, the South Korean government had tried to alleviate unemployment through public initiatives. However, these attempts generated harsh criticism because most of the jobs were temporary and offered low wages. As a result, the government looked elsewhere to generate higher-quality, more stable jobs (Kim, 2011; Kim & Jeon, 2013), which resulted in government-driven initiatives and the promotion of social enterprises. The government's active role in this effort was evident from the inception of social enterprise in South Korea, when it dispatched a large number of civil servants and researchers to Western Europe to learn about various forms of social enterprise and related legal frameworks (Defourny & Kim, 2011). The implementation of the SEPA and its certification system was administered by the Ministry of Employment and Labor (MOEL) and later by the Korean Social Enterprise Promotion Agency created under the MOEL, signifying the program's focus on labor issues.

According to Article 2 of SEPA, a social enterprise is defined as "an enterprise engaging in business activities through the production and sales of goods and services, while pursuing social goals such as improving the quality of life for local residents [and] providing social services or employment opportunities to the disadvantaged" (The Korean Law Information Center, 2012). Article 8 of the SEPA lays out the explicit conditions that must be met for a social enterprise to be "certified." While we will not discuss the details of these conditions, the basic standards for certification are (Kang, 2014; Kim, 2020) that the organization must be an autonomous legal entity, regardless of the organizational form it takes (e.g., nonprofit organizations, for-profit corporations, and co-operatives); it must hire at least one paid employee (five paid employees in the case of work integration social enterprises); it must generate business-related income covering at least 50% of goods and services production costs; and its pursuit of a social mission must fall under certain focus areas, such as providing social services or employment to disadvantaged groups, improving the quality of life in local communities, or solving social problems in innovative ways (The Korean Law Information Center, 2012).

Additionally, social enterprises must have multi-stakeholder-based governance to be certified (Jang, 2007; J. Kim, 2014). Multi-stakeholders include not only the officers and board members of the social enterprise but also workers' representatives, representatives of beneficiaries and their guardians, local community leaders, major institutional or private donors, and so on. For-profit social enterprises must also reinvest two-thirds of their profit for social purposes. Importantly, for-profit social enterprises are not only mandated to explicitly include this profit constraint in their bylaws but are also expected to obtain formal agreements from their shareholders to ensure compliance. Similarly, if a for-profit social enterprise is dissolved, two-thirds of the remaining assets must be distributed to other social enterprises or public funds (the asset lock provision). These profit- and asset-related constraints also apply to member-based cooperatives that allow profit distribution to their members (The Korean Law Information Center, 2012).

Government support for certified social enterprises is extensive in this framework (see Table 15.1). Notably, various types of government assistance are designed to meet the needs that arise in the life cycle of social enterprise organizations and are based on the activities they engage in. For example, for social enterprises that create jobs in the social economy, government provides direct wage support of up to 50% for the first 50 employees. This support is designed to phase out within the first three years of certification, with diminishing amounts of cost coverage over those years. This wage/salary support includes hiring at least one professional employee who can assist the organization in strategic planning, accounting, or marketing. In recent years, the scope of government assistance has expanded to include consultation on social enterprise planning and the development of business models for social entrepreneurs (Ahn, 2021). Similar types of government support are also available at the regional and local levels. While a national agency oversees and manages the program, regional and local governments establish close relationships with the social enterprises in their jurisdictions and provide day-to-day assistance such as leasing facilities and helping to build community networks (Jung et al., 2016).

We speculate that this extensive government support has contributed to the considerable growth of social enterprises in South Korea (Kim et al., 2018). In 2007, when the certification system was established, the number of social enterprises in South Korea was 55 but increased to more than 3,000 by 2021 (see Figure 15.1). Figure 15.1 also shows that the employment type has been the dominant mode of social enterprise, compared to community benefit and innovation types. It is, therefore, not surprising that social enterprises in South Korea have adopted the for-profit organizational form rather than the nonprofit or cooperative organizational forms.[1]

[1] As of 2019, for example, the total number of certified social enterprises in South Korea was 2,435. Among these, 1,095 organizations voluntarily reported

Table 15.1 *Government support for certified social enterprises*

Financial support	Wage/salary expenses
	Wage/salary expenses for expert hiring
	Research and development expenses
	Insurance coverage
	Tax exemption: corporate tax, income tax, acquisition tax, property tax, VAT (value added tax)
Startup support	Social venture competition
	Establishing a new social enterprise or cooperative
	Growth support center
	Social entrepreneur academy programs
	Social economy leadership course
	Social economy startup course
	Expertise course
	Social economy camp
	Training program for schoolteachers
	Development of standard lesson plans on the social economy
	Online curriculum
	Supporting certification
Growth support	Sales channels and public procurement
	Support with access to public and private buyers and expansion of sales outlets
	Integrated platform to support online sales
	Management consultation
	Linking resources
	Public and private resources
	Social finance (crowdfunding, monitoring policy funds and briefing)
Ecosystem-building support	Partnership network
	National (regional) network with communities
	Business network
	Building awareness
	Promoting the social economy
	International cooperation
	Policy development (policy development, business development, and realization of social values)
	Evaluation and monitoring
	Evaluation of social values
	Review of business reports and performance analysis
	Voluntary public disclosure of management performance
	Fact-finding survey on social enterprises

Source: The Korea Social Enterprise Promotion Agency website, retrieved and summarized in June 2022. In English: www.socialenterprise.or.kr/_engsocial/?m_cd=0202. In Korean: https://socialenterprise.or.kr/social/care/financeJob.do?m_cd=E034

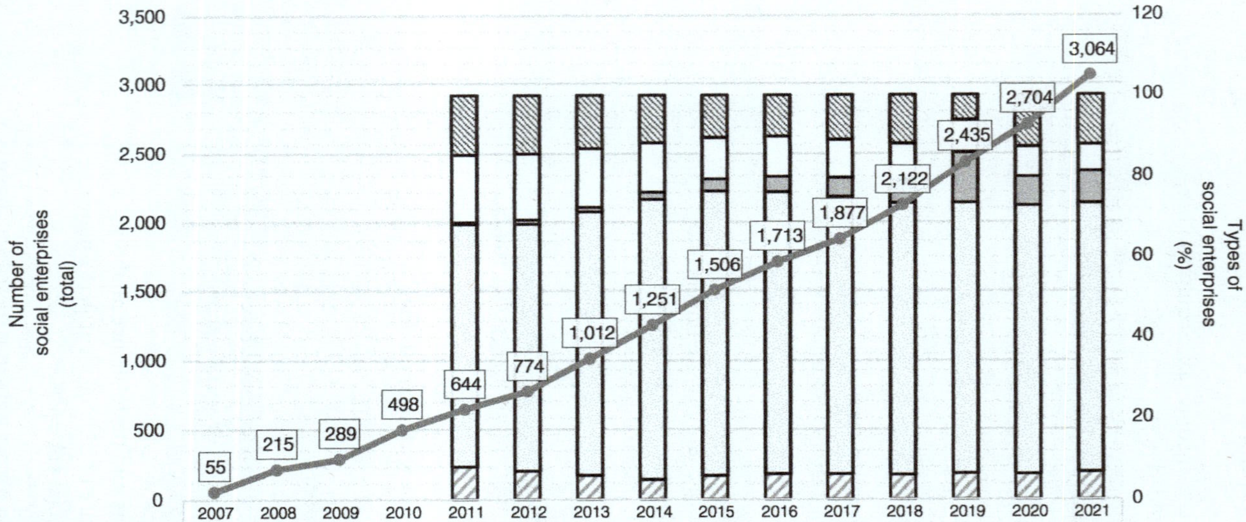

	2007	2008	2009	2010	2011	2012	2013	2014	2015	2016	2017	2018	2019	2020	2021
Creative/Innovative					14.6	14.34	13.04	11.67	10.42	10.16	10.97	11.97	6.16	12.76	12.21
Mixed					16.93	16.54	14.72	12.39	10.36	9.98	9.43	9.1	7.97	7.4	6.49
Community contribution					0.47	1.03	1.09	1.76	3.05	3.91	4.79	5.7	12.61	7.25	8.13
Employment					59.94	61.11	65.22	69.3	70.32	69.7	68.57	67.2	66.9	66.42	66.45
Social services					8.07	6.98	5.93	4.88	5.84	6.25	6.23	6.03	6.37	6.18	6.72
Total	55	215	289	498	644	774	1,012	1,251	1,506	1,713	1,877	2,122	2,435	2,704	3,064

Year

Figure 15.1 The growth of social enterprise in South Korea (2007–2021)

Note: The graphic shows the total number of social enterprises that are registered with and certified by the Korea Social Enterprise Promotion Agency. Five types of social enterprises are specified by the Social Enterprise Promotion Act: (1) social services to disadvantaged groups (social services); (2) employment to disadvantaged groups (employment); (3) quality-of-life improvement in local communities (community contribution); (4) both social service and employment to disadvantaged groups (mixed); and (5) innovative solutions to social problems (creative/innovative). The table was reconstructed based on the data from the Korea Social Enterprises Promotion Agency (2011 to 2021) and the Ministry of Employment and Labor (2007 to 2010).

As mentioned, by design, the generous and comprehensive financial and nonfinancial assistance provided by the government is intended to decrease over time to encourage self-sustainability. To examine the extent to which this policy goal has been achieved, we utilized the 2019 voluntary reporting data previously mentioned (see note 1) to explore two primary factors. First, we explored how the level of government assistance has changed since the organizations were certified and started receiving government assistance (see Figure 15.2), and second, we examined how organizations' reliance on market-based sales for self-sufficient incomes as well as private resources have also changed as they mature (see Figure 15.3). Figure 15.2 shows that the proportion of government assistance for certified social enterprises has dwindled over time, reaching below 10% on average by the fourth year of certification. Figure 15.3, on the other hand, shows steady increases in marketized and private revenues during the same examination period. Given the voluntary nature of this data, caution needs to be taken in interpreting these findings. Nonetheless, the implication is that direct and comprehensive government support does not necessarily lead to long-term dependency on public funds when policy is intentionally designed to promote self-sufficiency through marketization.

In recent years, social enterprise policy in South Korea has entered a new phase, as the existing system appears to be producing diminishing marginal returns. Despite the steady increase in certified social enterprises over the years, growth in South Korea does not match growth in other countries, for example, in Great Britain. Despite the strong policy initiatives and the intensive support provided by the South Korean government, the expansion of social enterprises was slower than expected, causing concern among policymakers and scholars who have debated the underlying rationales and ultimate goals of the highly controlled certification system (Kim et al., 2018). The system has particularly been criticized for prioritizing narrowly defined, employment-centered policy outcomes (Kim et al., 2018). Reformers contend that augmenting the existing program to accommodate a

information regarding various organizational characteristics to government (i.e., the Korea Social Enterprises Promotion Agency) through a social enterprise reporting system called the Voluntary Public Disclosure of Social Enterprise Management Performance. According to these data, among 1,095 organizations reporting, 65% were for-profits, 11% nonprofits, and 24% cooperatives.

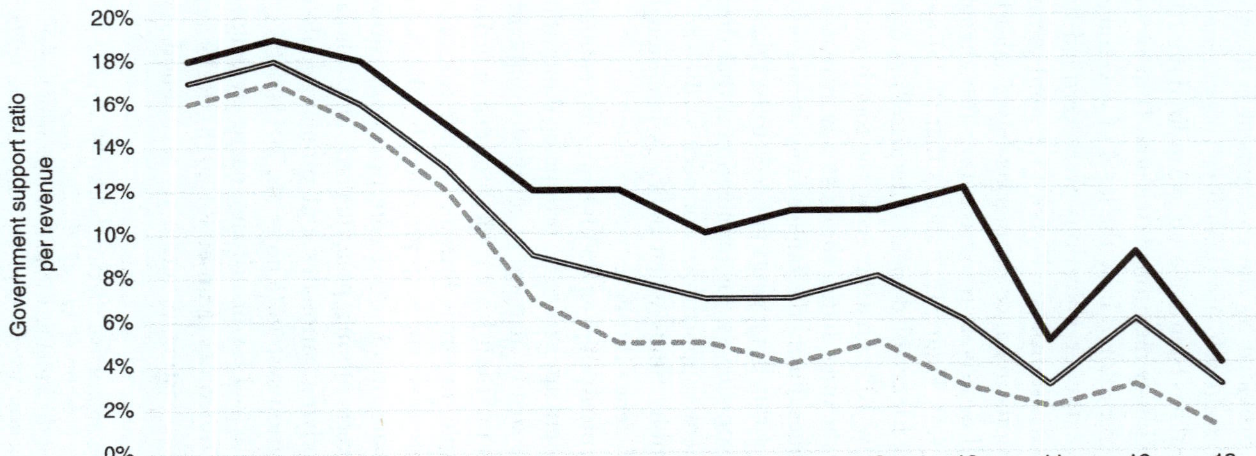

	1	2	3	4	5	6	7	8	9	10	11	12	13
Nonprofits	18%	19%	18%	15%	12%	12%	10%	11%	11%	12%	5%	9%	4%
Total	17%	18%	16%	13%	9%	8%	7%	7%	8%	6%	3%	6%	3%
For-profits	16%	17%	15%	12%	7%	5%	5%	4%	5%	3%	2%	3%	1%

Certification age

Figure 15.2 Government financial support ratio by certification age

Note: Government financial support is offered for (1) employment; (2) hiring professionals; (3) developing programs; (4) insurance; and (5) other funding. The analysis is limited to the organizations that submitted the 2019 Voluntary Public Disclosure of Management Performance Report to the Korea Social Enterprises Promotion Agency.

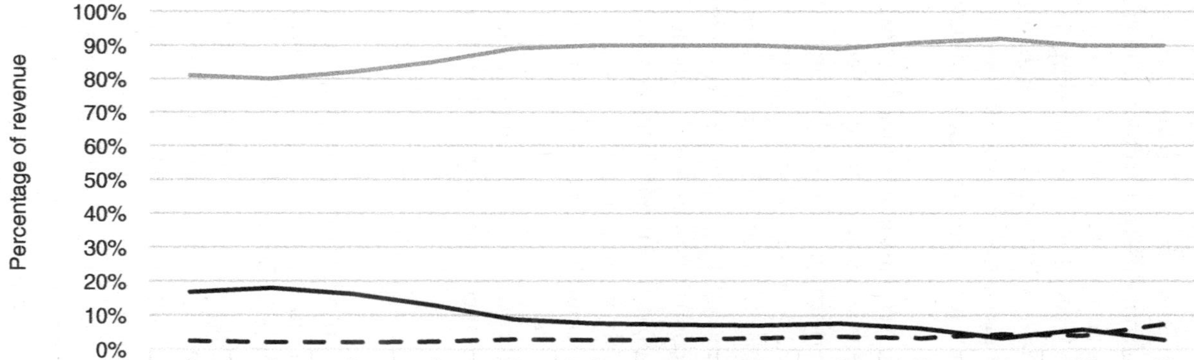

	1	2	3	4	5	6	7	8	9	10	11	12	13
Sales	81%	80%	82%	85%	89%	90%	90%	90%	89%	91%	92%	10%	90%
Govt. support	17%	18%	16%	13%	9%	8%	7%	7%	8%	6%	3%	6%	3%
Private support	2%	2%	2%	2%	3%	3%	3%	3%	4%	3%	4%	4%	7%

Certification age

Figure 15.3 Revenue sources of social enterprises by certification age

Note: Government support is the same measurement used in Figure 15.2. Private support includes (1) donation from business firms; (2) donation from headquarters that the social enterprise is associated with; (3) donation from individuals or other non-profits; (4) funds from business financial firms; and (5) others. The analysis is limited to the organizations that submitted the 2019 Voluntary Public Disclosure of Management Performance Report to the Korea Social Enterprises Promotion Agency.

wider variety of social enterprises through a less restrictive registration system will increase social innovation and attract a greater number of social entrepreneurial organizations from different sectors (Kim et al., 2018). One tricky aspect of implementing a new registration system will be determining the appropriate level of government support for the newly recruited organizations. How will the lack of a high degree of quality control, a likely scenario given the purpose of the reform to loosen requirements and oversight, affect the program's ability to achieve its intended policy goals?

In addition to the reform issues, scholars have raised questions about the effectiveness of government support on the certified social enterprises' economic and social performance in South Korea. Not surprisingly, the findings are mixed, with no definitive conclusions about the nature and magnitude of the effects and the many caveats of government support. Hwang and Jang (2017), for example, reported that government support may have contributed to social performance when the assistance was given to small, deficit-prone social enterprises, while it may have contributed to only economic performance when the support was directed to large, profitable social enterprises. Kang (2014), on the other hand, argued that government support tends to generate a U-shaped impact on social enterprise performance, suggesting that a certain level of public assistance is necessary to be effective.

15.3 Conclusions

In answering one of this volume's central questions – Why does the nonprofit sector exist? – we focused our inquiry on social enterprises and argued that they exist because these socially oriented, yet commercially viable organizations might provide a key to helping governments solve tough socioeconomic problems. The rapid, global diffusion of social enterprises highlights the possibility of this type of organization emerging and growing even in countries where the civil-society sector is traditionally underdeveloped. To better explain this phenomenon, we have proposed the theory of an engineered social economy. This theory argues that social enterprises (and perhaps other organizations in the social sector) can be actively nurtured by government as an effective policy instrument and carefully steered through intensive yet time-limited government assistance resulting in clearly defined state-sanctioned outcomes.

For scholars who uphold the idea that the civil-society sector is spontaneous, voluntary, authentic, and citizen-led, embracing a theory that suggests a state-engineered or government-nurtured civil society might be difficult. We contend, however, that the past sector theories are deeply steeped in the Western civil-society perspective, and we assert that their universal appeal should be reexamined in the context of the state's emerging role in the Global East in the development and growth of social enterprises and their integration into the social economy. The South Korean case may best illustrate how the engineered social economy model might work. Can this theory be applicable beyond one unique case? The possibility arises in some Asian countries in which a strong state role exists in the private economy and the civil-society sector has either substantial influence or potential to grow. The existence of vibrant market environments, alongside extensive government support, appears to be critical to success. The engineered social economy model might also work in Europe, as some elements of the model, such as robust government policy intervention, have already been manifested in the development of social enterprises. For example, in the UK, government policies at the national and local levels fostered the emergence and growth of social enterprises, as evidenced in the adoption of the Public Services Act in 2012 and the creation of community interest companies under the Companies Act in 2004 (Choi et al., 2020; Nicholls, 2010). The difference between the South Korean model and the UK model is that the South Korean model is driven by strong government control through a highly structured certificate system and direct government support, while the British model utilizes social impact investments to nurture a higher level of market competitiveness for social enterprises (Choi et al., 2020).

We conclude our chapter by posing a question regarding the future of the existing sector theory that has defined the nature of the relationship between nonprofits and government in certain ways. The past literature, for example, has largely focused on either the civil-society view of the sector or a particular type of state–nonprofit collaboration in which nonprofits instrumentally serve government for the expansion of the welfare state (Salamon, 1987). These characterizations have led scholars to explore the extent of nonprofits' dependency on the state and concerns regarding their autonomy and community-based identity. While these have certainly been worthy and relevant topics to study, we call for a broadened scope of inquiry to deepen our understanding of the nonprofit sector and its relationship with the state. Such an expanded scope of inquiry would be beneficial, for example, in the study of countries and societies that share the same historical paths of strong government control over the private sector, as implied in the developmental state theory (Jeong, 2015). Additionally, incorporating a diverse group of theories may offer a useful comparative lens to better understand the nonprofit sector and social economy that is rooted in the contextual understanding of the macro-level inter-sectoral relationships.

References

Ahn, B. J. (2021). [Live 중소기업] 한국경제 새 활력 "소셜비즈니스"... 디자인으로 혁신하다. *MK News*. www.mk.co.kr/news/business/view/2021/01/33442/

Berger, P. L., & Neuhaus, R. J. (1977). *To empower people: The role of mediating institutions in public policy*. American Enterprise Institute for Public Policy Research.

Bidet, E., & Eum, H. (2011). Social enterprise in South Korea: History and diversity. *Social Enterprise Journal*, 7(1), 69–85. https://doi.org/10.1108/17508611111130167

Choi, D., Berry, F. S., & Ghadimi, A. (2020). Policy design and achieving social outcomes: A comparative analysis of social enterprise policy. *Public Administration Review*, *80*(3), 494–505. https://doi.org/10.1111/puar.13111

Choi, J. E., & Choi, Y. J. (2019). How local governments influence the growth of social economy. *Journal of Korean Social Welfare Administration*, *21*(1), 225–251. https://doi.org/10.22944/kswa.2019.21.1.009

Clemens, E. S. (2006). The constitution of citizens: Political theories of nonprofit organizations. In W. W. Powell & R. Steinberg (Eds.), *The nonprofit sector: A research handbook* (2nd ed.) (pp. 207–220). Yale University Press.

Coskun, M. E., Monroe-White, T., & Kerlin, J. (2019). An updated quantitative analysis of Kerlin's macro-institutional social enterprise framework. *Social Enterprise Journal*, *15*(1), 111–130. https://doi.org/10.1108/SEJ-03-2018-0032

Crotty, J., & Lee, K. K. (2002). A political-economic analysis of the failure of neo-liberal restructuring in post-crisis Korea. *Cambridge Journal of Economics*, 26(5), 667–678.

Davister, C., Defourny, J., & Gregoire, O. (2004). *Work integration social enterprises in the European Union: An overview of existing models. European Research Network*. EMES Working Papers no. 04/04.

Defourny, J., & Kim, S. (2011). Emerging models of social enterprise in Eastern Asia: A cross-country analysis. *Social Enterprise Journal*, *7*(1), 86–111. https://doi.org/10.1108/17508611111130176

Defourny, J., & Nyssens, M. (2008). Social enterprise in Europe: Recent trends and developments. *Social Enterprise Journal*, *4*(3), 202–228. https://doi.org/10.1108/17508610810922703

Defourny, J., & Nyssens, M. (2017). Fundamentals for an international typology of social enterprise models. *Voluntas*, *28*(6), 2469–2497. https://doi.org/10.1007/s11266-017-9884-7

Dunleavy, P., & Hood, C. (1994). From old public administration to new public management. *Public Money and Management*, *14*(3), 9–16. https://doi.org/10.1080/09540969409387823

Eikenberry, A. M., & Kluver, J. D. (2004). The marketization of the nonprofit sector: Civil society at risk? *Public Administration Review*, *64*(2), 132–140. https://doi.org/10.1111/j.1540-6210.2004.00355.x

Eum, H. (2008). *Social economy and social enterprise in South Korea*. Working Together Foundation.

Evans, P. B. (1989). The future of the developmental state. *The Korean Journal of Policy Studies*, *4*, 129–146.

Ha, S.-K., & Lee, S.-W. (2001). IMF and the crisis of the marginalized urban sector in Korea. *Journal of Contemporary Asia*, *31*(2), 196–213.

Hansmann, H. B. (1980). The role of nonprofit enterprise. *The Yale Law Journal*, *89*(5), 835–901. https://doi.org/10.2307/796089

Heimovics, R. D., Herman, R. D., & Coughlin, C. L. J. (1993). Executive leadership and resource dependence in nonprofit organizations: A frame analysis. *Public Administration Review*, *53*(5), 419–427. https://doi.org/10.2307/976342

Hemel, D. J. (2020). Tangled up in tax: The nonprofit sector and the federal tax system. In W. W. Powell & P. Bromley (Eds.), *The nonprofit sector: A research handbook* (3rd ed.). Stanford University Press.

Holliday, I. (2000). Productivist welfare capitalism: Social policy in East Asia. *Political Studies*, *48*(4), 706–723. https://doi.org/10.1111/1467-9248.00279

Hwang, J., & Jang, Y. (2017). Government funding as a double-edged sword: Governmental support and the performance of social enterprises in Korea. *The Korea Association for Policy Studies*, *26*(2), 225–258.

Jang, W. B. (2007). 특집 논문 : 사회적 경제와 한국시민사회의 과제; 사회적 경제(Social Economy)의 대안적 개념화: 쟁점과 과제. *Civil Society and NGO*, *5*(2), 11–43.

Jeong, B. (2015). The developmental state and social enterprise in South Korea. *Social Enterprise Journal*, *11*(2), 116–137. https://doi.org/10.1108/sej-01-2014-0005

Johnson, C. (1982). *MITI and the Japanese miracle : The growth of industrial policy, 1925–1975*. Stanford University Press.

Jung, K., Jang, H. S., & Seo, I. (2016). The government-driven social enterprises in South Korea: Lessons from the social enterprise promotion program in the Seoul metropolitan city. *International Review of Administrative Sciences*, *82*(3), 598–616.

Kang, S.-M. (2014). An empirical study on the effect of government support on social enterprise performance. *Social Enterprise Studies*, *7*(2), 3–19.

Kerlin, J. A. (2006). Social enterprise in the United States and Europe: Understanding and learning from the differences. *Voluntas*, *17*(3), 246–262. https://doi.org/10.1007/s11266-006-9016-2

Kerlin, J. A. (2013). Defining social enterprise across different contexts: A conceptual framework based on institutional factors. *Nonprofit and Voluntary Sector Quarterly*, *42*(1), 84–108. https://doi.org/10.1177/0899764011433040

Kim, D.-H., & Jeon, I.-S. (2013). Over the examinations of the historical development of enterprises based on reflections on social enterprise. *The Review of Business History*, *28*(3), 5–24.

Kim, H., Kim, S., Kang, D., Park, H., Byun, H., & Yang, D. (2018). A research on introduction of registration system for social enterprise in Korea. *Journal of Social Value and Enterprise*, *11*(3), 95–124.

Kim, J. (2014). A legal arguments of corporate governance on the social enterprise. *Law & Policy Review*, *2*, 95–126.

Kim, S. Y. (2020). A study on the sustainability of social enterprise by support of governmental subsidies. *Cooperative Economics and Management Review*, *53*, 1–15.

Kim, Y.-J. (2011). The comparative law study concerning to social enterprises. *Public Law Journal*, *12*(2), 295–318.

Kwon, S., & Holliday, I. (2007). The Korean welfare state: A paradox of expansion in an era of globalisation and economic crisis. *International Journal of Social Welfare*, *16*(3), 242–248. https://doi.org/10.1111/j.1468-2397.2006.00457.x

Laratta, R., Nakagawa, S., & Sakurai, M. (2011). Japanese social enterprises: Major contemporary issues and key challenges. *Social Enterprise Journal*, *7*(1), 50–68. https://doi.org/10.1108/17508611111130158

Lee, H., & Min, Y. (2015). A study on institutional isomorphism experience in social enterprise: Focused on the cases of Chungbuk self-sufficient enterprises. *Health and Social Welfare Review*, *35*(3), 515–552.

Maier, F., Meyer, M., & Steinbereithner, M. (2016). Nonprofit organizations becoming business-like: A systematic review. *Nonprofit and Voluntary Sector Quarterly*, *45*(1), 64–86. https://doi.org/10.1177/0899764014561796

Mosley, J. E. (2012). Keeping the lights on: How government funding concerns drive the advocacy agendas of nonprofit homeless service providers. *Journal of Public Administration Research and Theory*, *22*(4), 841–866. https://doi.org/10.1093/jopart/mus003

Nicholls, A. (2010). Institutionalizing social entrepreneurship in regulatory space: Reporting and disclosure by community interest companies. *Accounting, Organizations and Society*, *35*(4), 394–415. https://doi.org/10.1016/j.aos.2009.08.001

Nisbet, R. (1953). *The quest for community: A study in the ethics of order and freedom*. Oxford University Press.

Park, C., & Wilding, M. (2013). Social enterprise policy design: Constructing social enterprise in the UK and Korea. *International Journal of Social Welfare*, *22*(3), 236–247. https://doi.org/10.1111/j.1468-2397.2012.00900.x

Salamon, L. M. (1981). Rethinking public management 3rd party government and the changing forms of government action. *Public Policy*, *29*(3), 255–275.

Salamon, L. M. (1987). Of market failure, voluntary failure, and third-party government: Toward a theory of government-nonprofit relations in the modern welfare state. *Nonprofit and Voluntary Sector Quarterly*, *16*(1–2), 29–49.

Smith, S. R., & Grønbjerg, K. A. (2006). Scope and theory of government–nonprofit relations. In W. W. Powell & R. Steinberg (Eds.), *The nonprofit sector: A research handbook* (2nd ed.) (pp. 221–242). Yale University Press.

Smith, S. R., & Lipsky, M. (1993). *Nonprofits for hire: The welfare state in the age of contracting*. Harvard University Press.

The Korean Law Information Center. (2012). *Social Enterprise Promotion Act*. www.law.go.kr/engLsSc.do?menuId=1&subMenuId=21&tabMenuId=117&query=사회적기업육성법#

Triponel, A., & Agapitova, N. (2016). *Legal frameworks for social enterprise*. World Bank Group.

Tsukamoto, I., & Nishimura, M. (2009). Social enterprises in Japan. In J. A. Kerlin (Ed.), *Social enterprise: A global comparison* (pp. 163–183). Tufts University Press.

Weisbrod, B. A. (1988). *The nonprofit economy*. Harvard University Press.

Woo-Cumings, M. (1999). *The developmental state*. Cornell University Press.

Young, D. R., & Lecy, J. D. (2014). Defining the universe of social enterprise: Competing metaphors. *Voluntas*, *25*(5), 1307–1332. https://doi.org/10.1007/s11266-013-9396-z

Yu, X. (2011). Social enterprise in China: Driving forces, development patterns and legal framework. *Social Enterprise Journal*, *7*(1), 9–32. https://doi.org/10.1108/17508611111130130

Yu, X. (2013). The governance of social enterprises in China. *Social Enterprise Journal*, *9*(3), 225–246. https://doi.org/10.1108/sej-08-2012-0034

Yu, X. (2016). Social entrepreneurship in China's non-profit sector: The case of innovative participation of civil society in post-disaster reconstruction. *China Perspectives*, *2016*(3), 53–61. https://doi.org/10.4000/chinaperspectives.7051

16 *Nonprofits as Shaped by the Ruling Party*

MING HU AND YUNG-PIN LU

Following Western mainstream theory on government–nonprofit relationships, scholarship on nonprofit organizations in developing countries usually overlooks the influence of political parties. However, political parties, particularly the ruling party, often determine the nature of the nonprofit sector in those societies. This chapter proposes a tripartite model to explicate relationships between the party, state, and nonprofit organizations in countries with a sole ruling party. The model is applied to the one-party state of China, demonstrating how the ruling Chinese Communist Party has fundamentally shaped the emergence and development of the nonprofit sector.

In the extant literature, the role of the political party is generally under-researched, if not totally neglected. The inadequate attention to the relationship between political parties and nonprofit organizations is understandable in liberal democracies, in which political participation by nonprofit organizations is restricted and their association with political parties is minimized to the noninstitutional and insubstantial level (Jenkins, 2006). Accordingly, nonprofit researchers typically focus on the relationships between nonprofit organizations and governments (not nonprofit organizations and parties; Smith & Gronberg, 2006) that rule on behalf of the state.

However, nonprofit organizations in nondemocratic countries, or in countries without mature democratic institutions, cannot operate independently of political parties. Rather, their operations are often deeply entangled (Clarke, 1998; Fisher, 1997). Nonprofit organizations may build close connections with political parties to seek sponsorship or to pursue their missions by means of political participation. Political parties in turn collaborate with nonprofit organizations to widen and strengthen their political bases. This dynamic can result in rather complex state–nonprofit relationships, which vary with the configuration of the political regime and the development of the rule of law (Clarke, 1998; Heurlin, 2010). The purpose of this volume is to address what the nonprofit sector is and why nonprofits exist. In this chapter, we explore how the ruling party, together with the government, shapes the nonprofit sector in states with a permanent ruling party.

A one-party state (also called a *party-state*) is defined as a state in which "only one party exists and is allowed to exist" (Sartori, 1976, p. 197). A one-party state often emerges from political crisis and prioritizes the cohesion of the state over the rights of opposing bodies. The permanent ruling party identifies itself with the state, exercising exclusive power and illegitimating opposition parties, if there are any (Sartori, 1976). Unlike in liberal democracies, the generation of state agencies in a one-party state is noncompetitive and completely under the control of the ruling party. This dynamic inevitably affects the creation and implementation of public policies relevant to nonprofit organizations, which are manipulated to benefit the party. At the same time, nonprofit organizations often have missions outside of primary party interests. Indeed, one critical source of the legitimacy of nonprofit organizations is their distinct values, such as voluntarism and solidarity (Atack, 1999), which by nature conflict with the dominant ideology and centralized power a single ruling party seeks to establish. These contradictory pressures naturally result in nonprofit organizations being involved in politics, willingly or unwillingly.

Despite the complex and consequential relationship between nonprofit and party, most scholarship scarcely examines the role of the ruling party in the state–nonprofit relationship. The exact mechanisms of the state–nonprofit relationship in the one-party state, especially the role of the ruling party in creating and shaping the nonprofit sector, remain little understood. Additionally, the conflation of the ruling party and state in prior work has led to theoretical and practical confusion; it has blurred rather than revealed the structure and dynamics of political power in regard to the nonprofit sector, as if the party and the state were always on the same page (Snape & Wang, 2020). While a few studies have begun to explore the influence of the ruling party on nonprofit organizations in the one-party state context (e.g., Shen et al., 2020; Thornton, 2013), a holistic model that integrates the three elements and explains the political settings for nonprofit organizations is still absent.

In response, we have developed a sectoral theory that illuminates the relationship between party, state, and nonprofits in the context of one-party states and apply the theory to the case of the nonprofit sector in China. We argue that in the one-party state, the nonprofit sector exists to serve the party and state in two ways: First, the state makes and implements public policies concerning nonprofit organizations that serve the interest of the ruling party. Second, the ruling party exerts its political domination over nonprofit organizations by manipulating public policies or directly subjugating nonprofit organizations by means of top-down political mobilization. The two sometimes-conflicting mechanisms create a highly unstable and restrictive nonprofit sector, as is often seen in one party regimes like China.

The chapter continues as follows. We first present a tripartite model of nonprofit organizations in the one-party state and explain the model's connection with sector theory in nonprofit research. Then, we give a historical account of the nonprofit sector in China and apply the model to analyze the development of the nonprofit sector. We conclude by discussing the benefits and limitations of the tripartite model.

16.1 A Theory of Nonprofit Organizations in the One-Party State

The term "state" generally refers to "a nation or territory considered as an organized political community under one government" (Oxford Learners' Dictionaries). The most familiar academic conceptualization equates the state with a bureaucratic apparatus of control (Bealey & Johnson, 1999), which is often exchangeable with government, the agent of the state. For example, Skocpol (1979) defined a state as "a set of administrative, policing, and military organizations headed, and more or less well coordinated by, an executive authority" (p. 29).

Modern states feature the operations of political parties, the "intermediary institutions located somewhere between society and the state" (van Biezen, 2008, p. 339). Political parties are organized to represent key constituencies and interests within society and seek to acquire political power in order to implement their agendas. Unlike state agencies, which are based on bureaucratic institutions, political parties derive their legitimacy (and power) from their ability to represent their constituency (Sartori, 1976).

But the relationship between state (or government) and political party varies depending on the nature of the state and the development of state-building. In some regimes, the state dominates political parties by funding them and regulating their activities, like public utilities, as seen in European democracies (van Biezen, 2008). By contrast, in other regimes, political parties, usually a dominant ruling party, occupy the state and perpetuate its rule by excluding oppositional political groups (Sartori, 1976). To avoid confusion when analyzing the relationship between the state and the nonprofit sector, it is necessary to single out the party from the general state–nonprofit relationship (Snape & Wang, 2020).

In a one-party state, nonprofit organizations are subject to two types of state power: the state (or government) and the ruling party, which are distinct yet intertwined. Nonprofit organizations, as characterized by being organized, private, self-governing, non-profit-distributing, and voluntary (Anheier, 2005), are established to enhance the interests of their members or the public. At their best, nonprofits enhance social capital and self-organization in society and increase social-service provision, which can supplement public services and increase government capacity (Brinkerhoff, 2002). The government in turn regulates nonprofits' activities and sometimes funds them to improve their ability to provide public goods. Nonprofit organizations are also subject to the ruling party, which seeks to strengthen its power by representing, substantially or rhetorically, more interest groups, including nonprofit organizations. Any social organizations with values distinct from the ruling party may be seen as a threat because they provide an alternative to the party's agenda (Sartori, 1976). The ruling party may directly extend its system to nonprofit organizations to control them politically or indirectly manipulate their existence and operations to serve the party's interest by making laws and policies through the state (or government). Sometimes nonprofits are subject to both state (or government) power and party power. Figure 16.1 presents the tripartite model of the three sectors.

Under party-state power, nonprofits face a dual predicament of legitimacy. Unlike their counterparts in liberal democracies, nonprofits operating in a party-state cannot acquire adequate legitimacy by merely meeting the government's institutional requirements. If nonprofits distance themselves from the party organizations, they receive no political protection or connection, which potentially costs them legal or financial support from the government, since the party controls the government. But ingratiating themselves with the party to acquire political support is only a partial solution for nonprofits, because by doing so, they might lose the legitimacy that results from

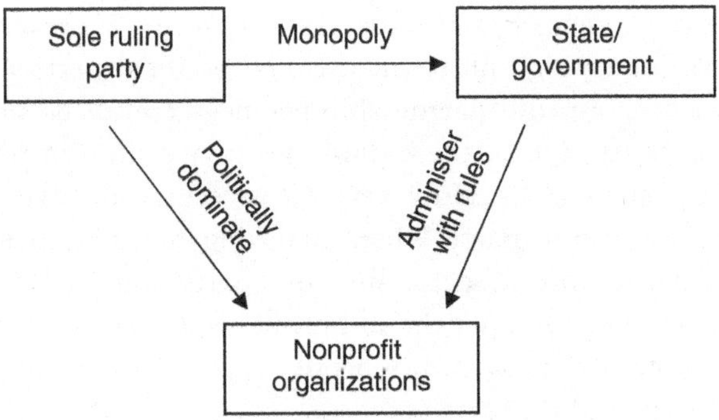

Figure 16.1 Nonprofit organizations in the one-party state

representing particular societal interests, which are exclusively represented by the ruling party.[1]

This predicament often creates a severely restricted nonprofit sector in party-states. Nonprofit organizations must follow the ruling party (sometimes through a state agency), which compromises their organizational autonomy and pursuit of their values. Nonprofit organizations that choose to maintain their autonomy and further their values and mission may have few resources to sustain their operations, especially when those values are not compatible with party interests.

The tripartite model provides a political-party perspective that allows exploration of the existence and development of the nonprofit sector in nondemocratic countries. From an institutionalist perspective, nonprofit researchers have well noted that the state can play a critical role in shaping the nonprofit sector (e.g., Smith & Gronberg, 2006). However, most mainstream theories on nonprofits were developed in the context of liberal democracies, in which the rule of law and electoral parties prevail (e.g., Brinkerhoff, 2002; Jenkins, 2006). In these environments, political parties usually have temporal, contingent, and loose linkage with the state and are subject to interparty competition and regular elections (van Biezen, 2008). The state dominates political parties, laying a solid foundation for the separation between party

[1] Admittedly, such extrapolation may simplify the complex relationships between the ruling party and nonprofit organizations in a one-party state. Their specific forms may vary with the party's organizational capacity and ruling strategy (Heurlin, 2010; Sartori, 1976). But the simplified model is useful to highlight the major traits of nonprofit organizations in a one-party state.

organizations and state agencies and thus restricting state power over nonprofit and voluntary organizations through political parties. Though the government–nonprofit partnership has been embraced in recent decades (Brinkerhoff, 2002), the boundaries between political parties and nonprofits remain clear. However, it is necessary and even desirable to consider the ruling party when analyzing the existence and development of the nonprofit sector in a one-party state. Also, examining the party's role in shaping the nonprofit sector can better explain the organizational behavior of nonprofit organizations when interfacing with the party and the state.

16.2 The Chinese Case

In this section, we demonstrate how the ruling Chinese Communist Party (CCP), together with the state, has influenced the development of the nonprofit sector in contemporary China. In short, we document how the nonprofit sector arose in China and, importantly, how its creation and subsequent development was deeply tied to the ruling party, for better or worse. We first introduce the configuration of the Chinese party-state and then provide a history of the evolution of nonprofit organizations since the mid-twentieth century.

16.2.1 The Configuration and Dynamics of the Chinese Party-State

The state in contemporary China was established after the collapse of the imperial regime that had ruled ancient China for more than 2,000 years. The CCP, a mass-based revolutionary party, won the civil war against another revolutionary party, the Nationalist Party (also called Kuomingtang), and founded the People's Republic of China (PRC) in 1949. Following the Leninist doctrine that views the state as an instrument of class rule and calls for proletarian dictatorship, the CCP sought to establish a new state under its exclusive and permanent leadership, with the state eventually withering away and all people becoming members of a communist society (Zheng, 1997).

Three organizational devices have served the CCP's domination over the state: CCP core groups serving as state institutions (e.g., the party committees established at each jurisdictional level), CCP work departments built alongside government departments at the same level, and directives jointly issued by the CCP and the government (Zheng, 1997). Consequently, a dual ruling system is currently in place in China, in which the government agencies at various levels report vertically to their superiors in the government system and horizontally to the party committees at the same level. It is in this manner that the CCP has become a central part of the state apparatus and directly controls the government.

The party–state relationship in China is replete with tensions (Feng, 2011; Zheng, 1997; Zhou, 2012). Since the founding of the PRC, the CCP has had a long-term goal of establishing a strong, modern nation-state. But the CCP's organizational features are in fact the greatest obstacle to developing state institutions. For instance, the CCP's revolutionary ideology has served as a hotbed for class struggle that threatens social stability. Additionally, the Leninist organizational principle of democratic centralism often prioritizes political loyalty over administrative capacity and performance, and the way social and public resources are mobilized tends to foster political campaigns against state bureaucracy and public policy continuance (Zheng, 1997; Zhou, 2012). This tension has remained despite the fact that in the early 1980s the CCP declared its intent to shift its focus from class struggle to economic development, and in the early 2000s declared its transformation from a revolutionary party to a ruling party by building the rule of law and institutionalizing its leadership (Liu, 2011; Zheng, 1997).

In addition to having direct control over the government, the CCP must also maintain and consolidate the basis of its power: its representation and leadership of "the masses" (*qunzhong*). In party-political discourse, the masses are the embodiment of the abstract concept "the people" (*renmin*). In contrast to the CCP's self-described progressiveness, the masses are considered backward, passive, and disorganized and are therefore unqualified to constitute the state sovereignty independently, necessitating leadership by – and only by – the CCP (Cong, 2005).

To strengthen its self-claimed "flesh and blood" linkage with the masses, during the wartime 1940s, the CCP popularized the slogan, "All for the masses, all depend on the masses, from the masses and among the masses" (Frenkiel & Shpakovskaya, 2019, p. 211). As a broad guideline for dealing with the masses, this so-called "mass line" has not been fully enacted by the CCP, except for the establishment of the People's Congress and the Peoples' Consultative Conference, which are controlled by CCP elite. Often, building CCP branches alongside mass organizations (including nonprofit organizations) replaces the practice of the mass line. Meanwhile, other political forces that seek to represent the masses are banned and punished, an action that poses a particular challenge to nonprofit organizations.

16.2.2 The Party, State, and Nonprofit Sector in China: A Historical-Institutional Account

Nonprofit organizations in China are usually called "social organizations" (*shehui zuzhi*), a term that conveys their nature and status in the sociopolitical system (Luo, 2020). When the CCP-dominated state was established in 1949 to enact the idea of proletarian dictatorship, a state-versus-society mentality developed in which the CCP and other state organs under the CCP's control constituted the state and everyone else belonged to "society." *Society* in this sense refers broadly to the aggregate of all the individuals who do not work in party or state agencies, since any form of organization independent of the state was not allowed. However, the emergence of a market economy beginning in the early 1980s created space for the development of voluntary organizations, first in the market sector and then in the sphere of social life (Luo, 2020). The definition of *social organization*, and of its early version, *mass organization*, has varied across the decades, reflecting how the party and state have perceived and treated voluntary associations in a one-party regime.

The evolution of the nonprofit sector vis-à-vis the party and state has occurred in four phases since 1949 (see Table 16.1).

16.2.2.1 Phase 1: Mass Organizations in the Totalitarian Era (1949–1978)

Shortly after its victory in the civil war, the CCP, with the backing of its ideological and military power, established a totalitarian state in which the party-state directly controlled nearly every aspect of society. Though a government system was founded at national, provincial, and county levels, it was under the close supervision of, and sometimes directly replaced by, CCP organizations at the same levels. The state also implemented a planned economy in which private ownership was abolished. The state controlled all the means of production and directly managed the production and allocation of products.

Table 16.1 *Evolution of CCP–State–nonprofit organization relationships in China (1949–present)*

	Mass organizations (1949–1978)	Emergence of nonprofit organizations (1979–1997)	Institutional development for nonprofit organizations (1998–2012)	Institutional absorption of nonprofit organizations (2013–present)
Sources of state legitimacy	Ideology	Performance	Performance	Performance weakened, and ideology to be rebuilt
CCP's principal ruling strategy	Class struggle	Economic construction	Economic construction with rule by law	Social governance
CCP–government relationships	CCP replaced the government	Tentative separation between CCP and government	Institutional development of division of labor between CCP and government, yet under CCP leadership	CCP power over government recentralized and strengthened
CCP strategies for nonprofits	Mass organizations incorporated into state apparatus	Nearly nonexistent	CCP organizations built into nonprofits	All nonprofit organizations required to build a CCP group; CCP members asked to volunteer and build volunteer organizations
Government policies for nonprofits	Nearly nonexistent	Nearly nonexistent; numerous nonprofits affiliated with government organizations	Reinforced institutional development for nonprofits; sponsored service-oriented nonprofits but restricted rights-based nonprofits	More government procurement for service-oriented nonprofits; rights-based organizations severely punished; more restrictive measures
Development of nonprofits	Independent nonprofits banned; mass organizations established from the top down	Independent nonprofits emerged in economic domains and expanded to other fields	Striking rise of nonprofit organizations; numerous nonprofits affiliated with government or mass organizations established	Increase in number of nonprofit organizations; rights-based nonprofits disappeared; international nonprofits became inactive

Consequently, any public life outside the party-state lost its sociopolitical and economic base.

To defend the new regime and pursue the mission of building a modern state, the CCP launched a series of political, economic, and sociocultural mobilizational movements. In the name of "class struggle" (*jieji douzheng*), political policies were enacted with militant measures to eradicate the landlord and capitalist classes and subdue the intellectual class. Based on new economic policies, the CCP undertook many large-scale public works projects, such as irrigation systems, highways and railways, and public facilities, and created new forms of economy, such as cooperatives and state-owned production units. Sociocultural policies destroyed numerous traditional cultural institutions and places and promoted Marxist and Maoist ideology and cultural institutions. These movements gained traction because of the CCP's absolute leadership over the state and because the masses enacted them.

Before its revolutionary victory, the CCP had stressed the importance of leading the masses by founding and overseeing mass organizations, such as peasants' associations, women's federations, youth clubs, and small producers' associations (Wang, 2020). In doing so, the party created associations that in other contexts might be organized by or in the nonprofit sector. By effectively practicing the mass line, the CCP gathered popular support, strengthened its organizational foundation, and finally toppled the Nationalist Party's regime. After the birth of the PRC, some mass organizations were incorporated into some levels of the CCP-led People's Consultative Conference. The party-state also created new industrial associations, cooperatives, cultural and artistic institutions, and so forth to organize the masses from the top down and to facilitate social control by placing the mass organizations directly under state power (Luo, 2020). At the same time, previously formed private associations and charities were regarded as conservative and reactionary forces and were dismissed (Zhou & Zeng, 2006). Such measures led to the dissolution of nonprofit and voluntary associations outside of the party and state system.

16.2.2.2 Phase 2: The Emergence of Modern Nonprofit Organizations (1978–1997)

The totalitarian regime created by the CCP resulted in economic and political disaster: millions of people died from violence, natural and technological disasters, and economic difficulties; state institutions remained weak and unstable; and the CCP's leadership was seriously undermined as the masses became frustrated that the promise of a prosperous and strong country was still unrealized (Zheng, 1997). Circumstances changed, however, in 1978, when the CCP leadership shifted its fundamental focus from "class struggle" to economic development. Accordingly, the CCP attempted to separate itself from the state to some degree to support the institutional development of the state apparatus. The introduction of the market economy in China freed people from their work units and communes and transformed them into autonomous individuals in the economy and in their private lives. The market economy also enhanced institutional development in the government, which fostered economic growth and improved social order. Economic development in turn rejuvenated the CCP's leadership of the state and consolidated the government's capacity.

The first voluntary nonprofit organizations in China were primarily industrial associations, technological organizations, and economy-related research institutes. These organizations emerged after the economy opened up, as autonomous market players, such as business owners and enterprise managers and their supporters in academia and industry, came together to pursue their common interests (Wei & Chen, 2019). Voluntary organizations soon expanded to the cultural and private spheres. At the end of the 1990s, there were roughly 170,000 legally registered nonprofits in China (Luo, 2020). Interestingly, the state intervened very little in these nonprofits partly due to its own lack of administrative capacity and partly due to its general support for nonprofits. As a result, many nonprofits were not registered with the state but were loosely affiliated with a variety of state agencies. In addition, the collapse of the planned economy led to dysfunction in numerous grassroots CCP organizations, which further weakened the CCP's control over these new nonprofit organizations. However, the mass organizations that had been institutionalized and incorporated into the state apparatus were retained after China enacted its "Reform and Open-Up" policy in the 1980s.

16.2.2.3 Phase 3: Institutional Development for Nonprofit Organizations (1998–2012)

The gradual establishment of the state-controlled market economy and China's entry into the World Trade Organization soon transformed China into the world's workshop. The country's unprecedented economic success aligned with the CCP's core strategy to "take economic construction as the central task" (CCP, 1987), which further enhanced the institutional development of the state agencies to pursue long-term economic prosperity. Economy-centered development, however, caused social conflict, corruption, environmental degeneration, and an increasing income gap. To maintain and reinforce state legitimacy, the CCP made social stability a top priority. In 1997, the Report of the 15th CCP National Congress (Jiang, 1997) proposed that the Party "should rule the nation by law." During this period, the principle of division of labor between the CCP and the government was retained and further institutionalized to ensure that the government could work more efficiently as the hub of executive authority but still remain under the CCP's leadership.

In this phase, the number of nonprofit organizations rose sharply and included charitable foundations, voluntary associations, independent charitable organizations, and advocacy organizations dedicated to labor rights, environmental rights, women's rights, LGBT issues, and others (Luo, 2020). Around 500,000 nonprofits were legally registered with the government (Luo, 2020). This increase resulted from factors such as the rapidly accumulated personal and corporate wealth during the economic bloom, the relatively relaxed government policies for nonprofit and voluntary organizations, and the rising awareness of citizen rights. Trade, commerce, and industrial associations also multiplied but were largely absorbed into the state apparatus by affiliating with state agencies.

Facing increasing social conflict as well as the formidable task of fighting poverty, the government chose to support the growth of nonprofit organizations, especially service-oriented nonprofits. Some government departments and "mass organizations" that were converted into state agencies established nonprofit organizations to assist in their efforts. Overseas nonprofits dedicated to development issues were also welcomed in China. Even so, the government reinforced regulations on nonprofits, especially rights-based nonprofits, partly due to typical authoritarian concerns about organized social forces outside the party and partly due to its fear of the spread of the Color Revolutions, the series of peaceful uprisings throughout postcommunist Eurasia between 1996 and 2005. A notorious "dual management" (*shuangchong guanli*) system was established in the late 1990s, in which even lawful nonprofit organizations were required to receive endorsements from both the civil affairs authorities and a supervisory agency, usually a state agency (Luo, 2020; Wei & Chen, 2019). Because of this policy, numerous grassroots nonprofit organizations could not be legally registered and risked being charged as illegal organizations.

Interestingly, the CCP's stance toward nonprofits was not clear in this period. Aware of the decline of the legitimacy of Marxist ideology, the CCP began to rely more on economic and social prosperity to maintain and consolidate the party-state's legitimacy (Zhao, 2009). The CCP seldom intervened in the operation of nonprofits, partly due to its disengagement of the mass line: When party organizations were increasingly institutionalized to serve the economy-centered grand strategy, the mass line that often featured irregular and mobilizational policymaking was put aside (Feng, 2011). In addition, the party did not yet consider the nonprofit organizations that developed outside the traditional societal sphere after the 1980s reform to be part of "the masses" (Chu, 2020). However, the Color Revolutions in Central and Eastern Europe raised concerns about nonprofit organizations, which were perceived as a potential threat to state power. The CCP rigorously constrained nonprofits, particularly rights-based nonprofits, through domestic security authorities and propaganda agencies. The CCP also suggested that all nonprofit organizations build a party cell to directly follow the CCP's leadership (Chu, 2020; Shen & Yu, 2019).

16.2.2.4 Part 4: Institutional Absorption of Nonprofit Organizations (2013–Present)

China's high-speed economic growth slowed in the early 2010s, a phenomenon that challenged the party-state's performance-based legitimacy. However, uneven socioeconomic development and social conflicts increased to an unprecedented level. Rampant corruption in the CCP and the government weakened people's trust in the party and state. Feeling the threat to its legitimacy, the CCP responded in two ways: first, by reinforcing the party's control over the government and society, and second by enhancing its commitment to social welfare. The CCP reasserted control by putting ideological hegemony and centralized leadership at the focus of party organizations and government departments. Unruly officials were prosecuted, disciplined, and purged. The newly amended constitution confirmed the CCP's status as the permanent ruling party, and the powerful Central National Security Commission was established to monitor and address any potential threat to the party and state. Additionally, the media and Internet were actively censored. These changes have resulted in the reemergence of a neo-totalitarian regime in contemporary China (Béja, 2019). At the same time, however, the CCP emphasized its commitment to social welfare. Under the banner of fostering people's livelihood (also called *minsheng politics*), the CCP launched a series of anti-poverty movements and tried to improve social-security institutions in an attempt to rebuild its support among working-class Chinese, including the peasantry.

With respect to nonprofit organizations, the party and state (Hu, 2012) proposed a new framework that was "CCP-led, government-managed, society-coopted, the public engaged, and guaranteed by the rule by law" (section 7) to provide social services, alleviate social conflicts, and strengthen social control under the "social governance" (*shehui zhili*) banner. Compared to the previous social control pattern that was managed exclusively by the party and state, the new pattern was more open to other types of organizations, including nonprofits, corporations, and state-sponsored political organizations. The party and state have since developed large-scale public procurement projects for social-service providers, including nonprofit organizations. Additionally, nonprofit organizations have been formally incorporated into the mass organization sector to help the CCP continue "practicing [the] mass line in the new situation" in order to strengthen its claimed representation of the people (Wang, 2020). This new pattern has resulted in another wave of rapid growth of nonprofit organizations, a large proportion of which are in fact established and managed by party and government agencies.

The roles of nonprofit organizations, however, are at best accessory and executory – and far from decision-making (Teets, 2013). All legally registered nonprofit organizations are required to build a CCP party cell that participates in decision-making but reports only to a higher-level CCP committee established inside the party-state. Thus, the CCP exercises organizational control over all nonprofit organizations. And while the CCP calls on all of its members to volunteer and encourages all party- and state-affiliated organizations to create volunteer organizations, the government has imposed laws and policies to further regulate nonprofits. Foreign funding sources for Chinese nonprofits have mostly been cut off, and international nonprofits are actively restricted. Rights-based organizations and human rights activists have been punished harshly. Consequently, the unprecedented party-state absorption of nonprofits has diminished the Chinese nonprofit sector that reemerged in the 1980s.

16.2.3 Assessment of the Tripartite Model in China

As discussed, the CCP has been at the root of the ever-changing state–nonprofit relationship in contemporary China and is central to the existence and development of the nonprofit sector; it is impossible to comprehend one without the other. To maintain the legitimacy of the CCP-dominated state, the CCP has used different ruling strategies (e.g., "class struggle," economy-centered development, and "social governance") in different periods, which has shaped CCP-government relations and determined policies for nonprofit organizations.

The government is an important part of the story too, even if the CCP and the government have approached nonprofits differently. The CCP sought to consolidate its representative power by developing its ideological hegemony and organizational control. For its part, the government emphasized institution-based and utilitarian management of nonprofit organizations in order to manipulate them to provide social services and alleviate social conflicts on the government's behalf. Which logic prevailed depended largely on CCP–government relations. When the CCP reinforced its direct control over the government and strengthened its ideological practice, policies for nonprofits became restrictive and detrimental. But when the CCP allowed for more governmental autonomy, policies for nonprofits became relatively tolerant and even supportive by focusing on social issues rather than political concerns. Due to a weak or absent rule of law, the CCP's preoccupation with legitimacy fundamentally influenced public policies for nonprofit organizations. Consequently, state–nonprofit relationships in China have been complex and highly fluid in the past decades (Snape & Wang, 2020; Zhang & Guo, 2020).

The relationships between government, party, and nonprofits in China have created an unfavorable environment for nonprofit organizations. In response, nonprofit organizations either yield to collaborations with the state or attempt to cling to their values and mission. If the latter, they are often marginalized or suppressed. Reconciling party needs, government requirements, and organizational mission has proven to be challenging, if not impossible (Shen & Yu, 2019), and it has resulted in a divided yet generally state-dependent nonprofit sector (Zhang & Guo, 2020).

16.3 Conclusions

Analyzing the development of nonprofits in the one-party state reveals the political aspect of the nature of nonprofit organizations (Clarke, 1998; Fisher, 1997). As voluntary associations, nonprofits are established to bring autonomous individuals together to pursue common interests. In other words, nonprofits take a bottom-up approach to organizing society, which may serve as an alternative to the top-down social-control approach used by one-party states like China (Lin, 2007). For this reason, one-party states usually perceive nonprofits as potential threats to their rule and, therefore, try to suppress or destroy them. With no legally binding separation between political parties and nonprofit organizations, even nonprofits in two-party or multiparty regimes can be used as political forces by the state or political parties, as seen in some African and South Asian countries (Clarke, 1998).

While nonprofits are often co-opted by the ruling party and are affected by party–government relations, it is possible for nonprofit organizations to escape politicization and pursue their missions with autonomy. When the ruling power is confident that the political environment is relatively stable, it reduces its efforts of consolidating its top-down representativeness through political mobilization and organizational control. This creates space for the party and the government to develop bureaucratic organizations and institutions. Under these circumstances, nonprofits can earn some degree of autonomy by meeting the institutional requirements even when they are organizationally absorbed into the party and state.

More likely, however, the state management of nonprofits will create a divided nonprofit sector in which a large proportion of nonprofits are organizationally and financially dependent on the party and state, which compromises their capacity to represent particular interests. Other nonprofits will likely be marginalized or suppressed. Under these circumstances, a nonprofit sector can hardly foster voluntary associations, enhance civic engagement, and encourage active citizens.

This chapter contributes to the extant literature in two ways. First, it adds a political-party perspective to the mainstream theories of the state–nonprofit relationships and thus more clearly explains the existence and dynamics of the nonprofit sector in one-party-state contexts. The tripartite model may also apply to other regimes that share the characteristics of the one-party state, such as Vietnam (Wells-Dang, 2014), Russia under the Putin administration (Salamon et al., 2015), and even Singapore (Tang, 2022). We call for more inquiry into the role of political parties in shaping the nonprofit sector in different social contexts, particularly those with a monopolistic ruling party, to gain a more complete picture of the relationship between the party, the state, and nonprofit organizations. On the other hand, inquiry into the interplay between nonprofit organizations, particularly rights-based organizations, and the ruling party can reveal how the landscape of political representation is currently being reshaped by the nonprofit sector.

Second, in the case study of the tripartite relationships between the party, the state, and nonprofit organizations in China, we uncover how the CCP fundamentally shaped the emergence and development of the nonprofit sector. In the existing literature on state–nonprofit relationships in China, the role of the CCP has been underestimated, if not neglected (Snape & Wang, 2020). Too often, researchers have combined the CCP and the government in their analyses. By examining the distinct functions of the CCP and the government in relation to nonprofit organizations, this study more clearly unveils the relationship between the three sectors in contemporary China.

References

Anheier, H. K. (2005). *Nonprofit organizations: Theory, management, policy*. Routledge.

Atack, I. (1999). Four criteria of development NGO legitimacy. *World Development*, *27*(5), 855–864.

Bealey, F., & Johnson, A.G. (1999). *The Blackwell dictionary of political science: A user's guide to its terms*. Wiley-Blackwell.

Béja, J. P. (2019). Xi Jinping's China: On the road to neo-totalitarianism. *Social Research: An International Quarterly*, *86*(1), 203–230.

Brinkerhoff, J. M. (2002). Government–nonprofit partnership: A defining framework. *Public Administration and Development: The International Journal of Management Research and Practice*, 22(1), 19–30.

CCP. (1987). 中国共产党第十三次全国代表大会关于十二届中央委员会报告的决议 [The resolution of the 13th CCP National Congress on the 12th CCP Central Committee's report]. https://china.huanqiu.com/article/9CaKrnK5jyF

Chu, S. (2020). 改革开放以来社会组织党建政策的演进及其逻辑 [Party-building policies for social organizations since China's Open-Up and Reform: Their evolution and logic]. *Tansuo*, *4*, 99–110.

Clarke, G. (1998). Non-governmental organizations (NGOs) and politics in the developing world. *Political Studies*, *46*(1), 36–52.

Cong, R. (2005). 当代中国政治语境中的"群众"概念分析 [Analyzing the concept "masses" in the political discourse in contemporary China]. *Tribune of Political Science and Law*, *23*(2), 15–24.

Feng, S. (2011). 中国国家运动的形成与变异：基于政体的整体性解释 [The formation and transformation of state movement in China: A policy-based systematic explanation]. *Kaifang Shidai*, *1*, 73–97.

Fisher, W. F. (1997). Doing good? The politics and antipolitics of NGO practices. *Annual Review of Anthropology*, *26*(1), 439–464.

Frenkiel, E., & Shpakovskaya, A. (2019). The evolution of representative claim-making by the Chinese Communist Party: From Mao to Xi (1949–2019). *Politics and Governance*, *7*(3), 208–219.

Heurlin, C. (2010). Governing civil society: The political logic of NGO–state relations under dictatorship. *VOLUNTAS: International Journal of Voluntary and Nonprofit Organizations*, *21*(2), 220–239.

Hu, J. (2012). 胡锦涛在中国共产党第十八次全国代表大会上的报告 [President Hu Jintao's report at the 18th CCP National Congress]. http://cpc.people.com.cn/n/2012/1118/c64094-19612151.html

Jenkins, J. C. (2006). Nonprofit organizations and political advocacy. In W. Powell & R. Steinberg (Eds.), *The nonprofit sector: A research handbook*, 307–331. Yale University Press.

Jiang, Z. (1997). 江泽民在中国共产党第十五次全国代表大会上的报告[Jiang Zemin's Report at the 15th National Congress of the Communist Party of China]. https://fuwu.12371.cn/2012/09/27/ARTI1348726215537612.shtml

Lin, S. (2007). 两种社会建构：中国共产党与非政府组织 [Two types of social construction: CCP and nongovernmental organizations]. *China Nonprofit Review*, *1*, 1–13.

Liu, J. (2011). 党政关系的历史变迁与国家治理逻辑的变革 [The history of the CCP–government relationship and the change of the state governance logic]. *Shehui Kexue*, *12*, 4–11.

Luo, Q. (2020). 从团结型社会组织、行政型社会组织到治理型社会组织 [From solidarity social organization and administrative social organization to the governance social organization]. *Tsinghua University Journal*, *3*, 191–206.

Oxford Learners' Dictionaries. (2021, December 1). Oxford University Press. www.oxfordlearnersdictionaries.com

Salamon, L. M., Benevolenski, V. B., & Jakobson, L. I. (2015). Penetrating the dual realities of government–nonprofit relations in Russia. *Voluntas: International Journal of Voluntary and Nonprofit Organizations*, 26(6), 2178–2214.

Sartori, G. (1976). *Parties and party systems: A framework for analysis*. Cambridge University Press.

Shen, Y. D., & Yu, Z. H. (2019). 社会组织党建动力机制问题：制度契合与资源拓展 [The issue on the promoting mechanism of social organizations' party building: Institutional coincidence and resource development]. *Journal of Beijing Institution of Administration*, 6, 13–21.

Shen, Y. D., Yu, J., & Zhou, J. (2020). The administration's retreat and the party's advance in the new era of Xi Jinping: The politics of the ruling party, the government, and associations in China. *Journal of Chinese Political Science*, 25(1), 71–88.

Skocpol, T. (1979). *States and social revolutions: A comparative analysis of France, Russia and China*. Cambridge University Press.

Smith, S. R., & Grønbjerg, K. A. (2006). Scope and theory of government–nonprofit relations. In W. Powell & R. Steinberg (Eds.), *The nonprofit sector: A research handbook* (pp. 221–242). Yale University Press.

Snape, H., & Wang, W. (2020). Finding a place for the party: Debunking the "party-state" and rethinking the state–society relationship in Chin's one-party system. *Journal of Chinese Governance*, 5(4), 477–502.

Tang, H. W. (2022, January). Charitable organizations in Singapore: From clan based to state facilitated endeavors. *Nonprofit Policy Forum*. www.degruyter.com/document/doi/10.1515/npf-2021-0032/html

Teets, J. C. (2013). Let many civil societies bloom: The rise of consultative authoritarianism in China. *The China Quarterly*, *213*, 19–38.

Thornton, P. M. (2013). The advance of the party: Transformation or takeover of urban grassroots society? *The China Quarterly*, *213*, 1–18.

van Biezen, I. (2008). State intervention in party politics: The public funding and regulation of political parties. *European Review*, *16*(3), 337–353.

Wang, S. K. (2020). 新群众"和"老传统":新时代中国共产党治国理政中的群众路线 ["New masses" and "old tradition": The mass line of the Communist Party of China in the new era]. *Tansuo*, 2, 107–118.

Wei, K., & Chen, J. (2019). 新中国70年社会组织发展的历程、成就和经验 [The process, achievements and experience of social organizations development in the 70 years of New China]. *Xueshu Yanjiu*, *11*, 46–54.

Wells-Dang, A. (2014). The political influence of civil society in Vietnam. In J. D. London (Ed.), *Politics in contemporary Vietnam* (pp. 162–183). Palgrave Macmillan.

Zhang, Z., & Guo, C. (2020). Nonprofit-government relations in authoritarian China: A review and synthesis of the Chinese literature. *Administration & Society, 53(1)*, 64–96.

Zhao, D. (2009). The mandate of heaven and performance legitimation in historical and contemporary China. *American Behavioral Scientist*, *53*(3), 416–433.

Zheng, S. (1997). *Party vs. state in post-1949 China: The institutional dilemma*. Cambridge University Press.

Zhou, Q., & Zeng, G. (2006). 中国慈善简史 [A brief history of Chinese charity]. Renmin chubanshe.

Zhou, X. (2012). 运动型治理机制：中国国家治理的制度逻辑再思考 [Movement-based governance: Rethinking the institutional logic of state governance in China]. *Kaifang Shidai*, 9, 105–125.

17 Nonprofits as Sources of Authoritarian Regime Stability

YULIA SKOKOVA AND IRINA KRASNOPOLSKAYA

Civil society and democracy have traditionally been perceived as inseparable, with the former having an ability to democratize different parts of the world (White, 1994). Following Tocqueville's (2004) and Putnam's (2000; Putnam et al. 1992) logic, the normative understanding of civil society as a "good society" that promotes equality and tolerance, builds social capital, and contributes to democratization has dominated for a long time. In this framework, civil society and its organizations make contributions to the democratic process by being a "school of democracy" in which people learn political skills and develop civic virtues, by pluralizing the institutional arena, by giving voice and representation to different actors, and, finally, by checking state power, specifically its potential abuses and violations (Fung, 2003; Mercer, 2002).

In fact, in the 1990s, the prevailing position was that democracy and an open, free civil society were "the end of history" (Fukuyama, 1992). However, subsequent global processes of increasing authoritarianism and the emergence of new forms of hybrid political regimes (Levitsky & Way, 2010) raise the question of whether and how civil society is possible in such a contested and dividing context (Cavatorta, 2015). Recently scholars have claimed that civil society has a limited ability to restrain modern forms of "updated" and consolidated authoritarianism (Kalandadze & Orenstein, 2009). Moreover, both in authoritarian regimes and in countries undergoing democracy backsliding, the number of right-wing movements, pro-government rallies, and GONGOs (governmental-organized nongovernmental organizations) is growing (Atalay, 2018; Cianetti et al., 2018; Hasmath et al., 2019; Hellmeier & Weidmann, 2020; Hemment, 2012; Matchanka, 2014; Strachwitz & Toepler, 2022; Zhao & Lilly, 2021). From a normative perspective, these can hardly be considered "good" developments. If civil society is not a contribution to democratization, then what other functions does it perform in nondemocratic contexts?

In this chapter, we shift from the normative approach and adhere to the organizational understanding of civil society as a set of formal and informal/nonstate nonprofit organizations that pursue a social mission. We do not associate civil society and nonprofits exclusively with the democratic values of inclusion and equality. As Cavatora (2015) has written, "Neutrality of values ensures that one should analyze the component parts of civil society (groups and organizations) by highlighting their ethos, their activities and their commitment, or lack of, to democratic practices" (p. 5). Framing things in this way allows us to take a positivist look at ongoing processes and to analyze the societal functions of civil society in authoritarian regimes, in which the accepted logic about contributions to democratization might not work.

Authoritarian regimes do not simply repress all nonprofits as one might expect. Instead they seek to take advantage of what nonprofit organizations are doing and, more obviously, restrain nonprofits that undermine regime resilience. They accomplish this mainly through two methods: first, by supporting organizations that provide social services to the population, and second, by restricting advocacy of rights-based nonprofit organizations (Daucé, 2014; Hu & Guo, 2016; Jing, 2015; Njoku, 2022; Popplewell, 2018; Skokova et al., 2018; Toepler et al., 2020). By ascribing service results to their own success and limiting competition for securing political dominance, authoritarian regimes enhance their legitimacy in the eyes of society. In this sense, we claim that authoritarian regimes do not use only traditional political institutions like legislatures, elections, and political parties for stabilization as the classical political science literature postulates (Gerschewski, 2013). They also use the nonprofit sector.

Scholars have observed that authoritarian regimes rely on three pillars to maintain regime stability: repression, co-optation, and legitimation (Gerschewski, 2013). These pillars are relevant for understanding why and how the nonprofit sector exists in the authoritarian context. However, this framework has rarely, if ever, been considered in conjunction with the role of the nonprofit sector. A significant amount of research has been devoted to the question of how an authoritarian state shrinks the civic space and uses repression and restrictive legislation to keep politically critical parts of civil society at a safe distance (Dupuy et al., 2015; Flikke, 2018; Gilbert, 2020). At the same time, scholars have noted the growing number of ways in which authoritarian states financially support social welfare nonprofits.

By providing this financial support, the state replaces illegitimate foreign funding and co-opts nonprofits (Enjuto Martinez et al., 2022; Fröhlich & Skokova, 2020; Jing, 2015; Krasnopolskaya et al., 2015; Spires, 2020). Also, scholars have shown that nondemocracies use civil society to strengthen regime legitimization by presenting nonprofits as a façade of democracy, using civil society as a feedback mechanism, and ascribing their output to state success, among other things (Lorch & Bunk, 2017).

In this chapter, we bring together the literature on the three pillars (repression, co-optation, legitimation) of authoritarian regime stability (Gerschewski, 2013) and patterns of regime legitimation (Lorch & Bunk, 2017), emphasizing the role of nonprofits in these processes. Our main contributions relate to a different perspective on nonprofit organizations in an authoritarian context. We claim that nonprofits are not limited to being objects of governmental policy but also play a significant role in regime stabilization, which is the core function of nonprofits operating under an authoritarian regime. We briefly reassess and summarize the current literature and then apply the framework to the case of Russia, which serves as an example of a post-Soviet state with a strong Soviet legacy where democratization processes have failed (Evans, 2011), authoritarianism has consolidated over the years (Gel'man, 2015), and the question of the nonprofit sector has become strategic for the regime's stability.

17.1 A Theory of Nonprofits as a Source of Authoritarian Regime Stability

Civil society and the nonprofit sector have a wide range of functions. They mobilize for collective action and advocate for social change, provide social services, represent and empower diverse social groups, attract public interest to social problems, and monitor state agencies. What are the ultimate societal consequences of these functions? The traditional answer is that they enhance democracy, suggesting that a strong civil society leads to strong democracy, and vice versa. But what happens in authoritarian regimes when civil society exists in a contested environment with limited opportunities for effecting change and challenging the state? Based on the literature on state–civil society relations under nondemocratic regimes and our own research on Russia, we claim that the core societal function of civil society and the nonprofit sector in an authoritarian context is maintaining regime stability.

Our argument rests on the observation that power relations between the state and civil society are unequal because the former maintains absolute control over decision-making. Nondemocratic regimes provide far fewer opportunities for nonstate actors to advocate for and enact social change. This puts civil society in a truly secondary position and limits the range of functions it is able to perform. Using both co-optive and repressive methods, authoritarian regimes have the power to regulate the strength and structure of civil society and strategically use civil society for their own purposes of gaining and maintaining regime stability. We claim that authoritarian regimes use civil society as another political institution to prolong their stay in power and do so through repression, co-optation, and legitimation (Gerschewski, 2013).

Repression is the most common and the most studied tactic used by authoritarian regimes. To maintain regime stability, authoritarian states limit the power of oppositional political forces and, generally, anyone who can undermine and question their legitimacy. Nonprofits, especially those that work in the contested fields of human rights, civic education, and electoral monitoring, are the first to be limited. After the "color revolutions," post-Soviet and other nondemocratic countries turned their attention to the political role of nonprofits, viewing them as an important driving force in mobilizing the protest movement and as a threat to regime stability (Gilbert, 2020). Since then, legal regulation has become the main tactic for keeping claim-making nonprofits under control (Spires, 2020). This legal regulation includes not only constructing formal barriers to nonprofit registration and requiring extensive reporting but also restricting foreign funding and labeling nonprofits that continue to rely on foreign funding as illegitimate "foreign agents" (Flikke, 2018).

Restricting foreign funding is a commonly used tactic by many types of regimes. According to Dupuy et al. (2015), by 2012, "44% of countries (86 of 195) [had] adopted legislation that specifically restrict[ed] foreign NPOs [nonprofit organizations] and/or foreign funding flows" (p. 423). Among them are not only the well-known cases of Russia (Flikke, 2018) and Egypt (Herrold, 2016); Israel, Canada, Australia, and India (Bromley et al., 2020; Carothers & Brechenmacher, 2014) also implemented measures to limit foreign funding for nonprofits for the same reason: to preserve "national security" (Katz & Gidron, 2022, p. 239) and to abolish the "threat of foreign interference undermining democratic processes" (Matejova et al., 2018, pp. 9–10).

However, authoritarian regimes cannot rely only on the repressive pillar for their longevity. Indeed, the state also needs to cooperate with nonprofit organizations that can work for it and stay in the depoliticized line of state welfare functions. Co-optation, meaning "the capacity to tie strategically-relevant actors (or a group of actors) to the regime elite" (Gerschewski, 2013, p. 22), is the second pillar of authoritarian regime stability. The state is strategically interested in nonprofits and their leaders. Nonprofits provide social services and solve numerous social problems that the government has failed to solve. State support of "politically inactive and professionally capable" nonprofits (Jing, 2015, p. 589) guarantees that civil-society actors continue social welfare activities without challenging the status quo.

Authoritarian states use a rich variety of co-optation tactics, such as providing financial support to socially oriented nonprofits (Bederson & Semenov, 2021; Enjuto Martinez et al., 2022; Jing, 2015; Krasnopolskaya et al., 2015; Spires, 2020; Zhang, 2015) and involving nonprofits in consultative bodies (Ljubownikow & Crotty, 2016; Owen, 2020; Pape & Skokova, 2022; Teets, 2013; Zhang, 2018). They even support politically neutral research on nonprofits (Ma, 2022), which gives them data about the sector that can then be used for better control over the nonprofit sector and its development.

In sum, while restricting claim-making nonprofits and nonprofits that support social welfare, the authoritarian state uses "regulation as political control" (Spires, 2020) that restructures civil society (Skokova et al., 2018), makes it more manageable (Ljubownikow & Crotty, 2017; Plantan, 2022), and shrinks the space for advocacy and activism (Toepler et al., 2020).

The third pillar of authoritarian regime stability is legitimation. Following the Weberian tradition, achieving political legitimacy is understood as a process of gaining support that is justified and accepted by society. Lorch and Bunk (2017), studying Algeria and Mozambique, suggested five ways authoritarian regimes strategically use civil society for legitimation purposes. This framework was later used for studying other authoritarian countries such as Vietnam (Wischermann et al., 2018), Venezuela, and Bolivia (Reaves, 2018), with many similarities among them.

The first way authoritarian regimes use legitimation is by holding up civil society as a facade of democracy. For both domestic and international audiences, the growth of volunteering and social welfare nonprofits is portrayed as a sign of functioning democracy. Authoritarian states use GONGOs (Hasmath et al., 2019; Hemment, 2012; Hsu, 2010; Hsu & Jiang, 2015; Matchanka, 2014), state-mobilized volunteering (Zhao & Lilly, 2021), and pro-government rallies (Hellmeier & Weidmann, 2020) to show support from below and demonstrate regime legitimacy. By allowing nonprofit registration, authoritarian states also signal to the international audience that they are "conforming to a global discourse on civil society" (Lorch & Bunk, 2017, p. 990) and liberalization.

The second way authoritarian governments use civil society for legitimation purposes is by "making civil society play by the rules." Doing so relies on nonprofits being embedded into bureaucratic networks. To do their work, nonprofit organizations need to cooperate with the state and follow its rules (Lorch & Bunk, 2017; Reaves, 2018). Whatever restrictive legal amendments are applied, nonprofits are compelled to follow them in order to secure their social mission and realize the interests of their beneficiaries. For instance, in the authoritarian context of China, "compliance with state norms becomes synonymous with organizational competence" (Tian & Chuang, 2022, p. 509). Where the skill of organizational survival requires a highly developed sense of the permitted and prohibited and the ability to maneuver in a complicated context, this compliance can be perceived as a sign of professionalism.

Next, authoritarian regimes use civil society as a mechanism of limited participation and as a feedback mechanism. Nonprofits participate in various councils and advisory boards, which helps the state stay informed about social grievances and harness professional expertise in social policy. Although nonprofit organizations can successfully use these opportunities as "limited indirect advocacy tactics" (Ljubownikow & Crotty, 2016), their designed role in pseudo-democratic institutions is to legitimize the decision-making process (Lorch & Bunk, 2017; Reaves, 2018; Toepler et al., 2020). Sharing responsibility with nonprofits makes outcome decisions seem more legitimate (Wischermann et al., 2016, 2018).

Fourth, rulers provide core social services and guarantee an appropriate quality of life in exchange for the loyalty of the ruled (Geddes &

Zaller, 1989). Lorch and Bunk (2017) have argued that authoritarian regimes are interested in utilizing nonprofit outputs to demonstrate their own achievements. Where nonprofits enhance the delivery of social services or support the implementation of official policies, they increase the authoritarian regime's legitimacy.

Finally, nonprofits strengthen the state's official discourse. As Lewis (2013) showed, authoritarian regimes tend to rely on conservative, traditionalist, and fundamentalist values, and local civil society plays an important role in reproducing this discourse. They can support patriarchal gender norms (Wischermann et al., 2016), fundamentalist religious values (Atalay, 2018), and militarism (Alava, 2021; Fröhlich & Skokova, 2020). In addition, nonprofits in authoritarian contexts avoid using alternative discourses and self-censor to minimize potential conflict with officials (Lorch & Bunk, 2017).

This review shows that authoritarian regimes are quite inventive in finding effective sources and tools for maintaining long-term stability. Civil society and the nonprofit sector play an important role in this process. On the one hand, claims-making nonprofits can challenge the status quo, shaking political stability. In this case, the regime's reaction would be repressive, aimed at limiting the power of critical civil society. On the other hand, as nonprofits support authoritarian regimes in the implementation of the welfare function, they can be an active pro-government voice and enhance the legitimacy of the state in the eyes of the population. The three pillars of authoritarian regime stability work together, making their cumulative effect stronger. Long-standing authoritarianism relies on all three pillars of stability simultaneously. Based on the case of Russia, we show how these pillars are applied in practice and how they affect and divide the nonprofit sector.

17.2 The Russian Case

The case of Russia is useful for understanding how the nonprofit sector operates in a contested context. After the collapse of the Soviet Union in the 1990s, nonprofits were supported by international donors while local government was ambivalent about the demand for nonprofit sector development (Skokova et al., 2018). When Putin came into power, the notion of domestic civil society became a more relevant policy field. During the 2000s, the Russian government began drafting an institutional framework to "manage" civil society (Ljubownikow & Crotty,

2017) that become more visible in the years that followed (Stuvøy, 2014). Today, the Russian case represents the most prominent example of how an "updated" authoritarian regime or hybrid regime strategically uses civil society as a source of stabilization. After discussing the theory of nonprofits as a source of regime stability, we answer the question of how and why nonprofit organizations operate in Russia.

17.2.1 Classics of Repression and Co-optation

Authoritarian regimes manage nonprofits through repression and co-optation. The Russian government has a history of enacting restrictive initiatives intended to limit financial and institutional opportunities for nonprofits working in the contested areas of human rights and advocacy (Crotty et al., 2014; Flikke, 2018). The nonprofit sector is clearly divided about how or whether to challenge the state; nonprofits that do challenge the state face significant restrictions.

In Russia, the legislation on foreign agents (2012), the subsequent law on "undesirable organizations" (2015), and recent legislative additions (2022) allow the state to grant foreign agent status to an individual. This status is assigned to nonprofit organizations and individuals who receive foreign funding and are involved in very loosely defined political activity or information distribution. Being assigned foreign agent status entails significant bureaucratic and financial restrictions as well as fines. If an agent does not meet all the restrictions, they might be subject to additional fines or criminal prosecution. Through these laws, the state and the Ministry of Justice have developed a lever of influence over the work of nonprofits and individuals. The difficulties of withdrawing the status in court as well as the threat of criminal prosecution prevent nonprofits from challenging the law, which maintains the image of legitimacy of governmental repression.

Another recent example of restrictions relates to eligibility criteria for governmental support (TASS, 2022). The 2022 Russian–Ukrainian conflict has led to multiple free-speech restrictions on nonprofits. Nonprofits that speak against the conflict face restrictions in government support allocation, a decree initiated by the Deputy Chairman of the State Duma Committee on the Development of Civil Society and supported by the Ministry of Economic Development. These institutions act as gatekeepers to exclude nonprofits that undermine regime legitimacy from a range of nonprofits eligible for state support.

Apart from repression, the government co-opts nonprofit efforts, thereby depoliticizing them and eliminating their protest mobilization against the authoritarian nature of the state. Some scholars claim that the regime balances the suppression of civil society by allocating funds to nonprofit organizations, thus buying their loyalty (Bederson & Semenov, 2021, p. 544). Indeed, the Russian government provides substantial financial support to nonprofits in the form of grants and contracts for social services (Fröhlich & Skokova, 2020; Krasnopolskaya et al., 2015) and creates various participation and expression mechanisms, such as the Public Chamber or advisory boards (Ljubownikow & Crotty, 2016). Nonprofits are highly welcomed in these consultative bodies, but actual participation is limited to technical rather than principal decisions (Pape & Skokova, 2022; Stuvøy, 2014), and the government is not obligated to follow nonprofit organizations' recommendations or make institutional changes. Less than 20% of nonprofits believe their expertise is taken into account by the government (Pulsngo, 2022).

The marginalization of advocacy inevitably follows co-optation processes. Pape and Skokova (2022) demonstrated the mostly apolitical character of advocacy among Russian nonprofits. Advocacy for sensitive environmental or human rights issues is not perceived as an appropriate behavior either by the government or by the majority of the nonprofit sector. Nonprofits admit and accept a power-imbalance role in their relationship with the state, with only about 10% of Russian nonprofits declaring that the state sees nonprofit organizations as equal partners (Pulsngo, 2022).

17.2.2 Five Patterns of Legitimation

Here we provide illustrations of how nonprofits contribute to the legitimation of the current regime according to the five patterns of legitimation explained earlier.

17.2.2.1 Civil Society as a Façade of Democracy

Civil society helps the Russian state create the appearance of a functioning democracy. Until the mid-2010s, the facade of Russian civil society was remarkably vivid: human rights organizations enjoyed some degree of freedom, and nonprofits did not face massive legal restrictions on their operations. This dynamic allowed Russia to be portrayed as conforming to a global discourse on civil society with international legitimacy. Even recently, in 2021, the Russian government gave awards to human rights nonprofits to maintain the appearance of supporting democracy and providing a space for civil society.

More recently, the question of legitimacy for domestic audiences has become more relevant, and the state has put enormous efforts into building a democracy-like picture of support for civil society at home. The government has accomplished this by maintaining open procedures to register a nonprofit, unlike China (Heurlin, 2010); financially supporting nonprofits (Skokova et al., 2018); and creating GONGOs. GONGOs act in various areas of civic engagement, volunteering, and election observation. They aim to demonstrate civic engagement as a form of democracy to strengthen the legitimacy of the regime (Alava, 2021; Hemment, 2012). They also mobilize citizens for rallies with pro-government agendas. For instance, the All-Russia People's Front regularly holds mass street campaigns to support various state decisions (Hellmeier & Weidmann, 2020). By promoting public activity, GONGOs crowd out independent nonprofit organizations and replace bottom-up civic engagement.

The Russian government actively promotes volunteering as the most apolitical form of civic participation to demonstrate democracy and the growth of bottom-up initiatives (Malinova, 2022). The state actively shapes organizations to promote a volunteering agenda at home and abroad. One example is the Association of Volunteer Centers (AVC), established in 2014. The largest of the volunteering GONGOs, the AVC boasts more than two million volunteers across Russia. The AVC, together with government authorities, created an infrastructure that tends to have a monopoly on volunteering. It includes volunteering centers all across the country, involves youth at schools and universities, and has a huge network of volunteers among the elderly.

State-run nonprofits exemplify and substitute civic engagement as the fabric of the community and portray a façade of meaningful civic engagement with the public and unprivileged groups that are missing from the conversation.

17.2.2.2 Making Civil Society Play by the Rules

Nonprofit organizations contribute to reaffirming the existence of the state and therefore contribute to the legitimacy of authoritarian rule. The most striking example in Russia is the way nonprofits acquiesce to the restrictions of the "foreign agents" law. For instance, after the law was enacted, only a few nonprofits went to court and withdrew their foreign agent status; the majority of organizations conformed to the restrictions and discontinued operation, gave up foreign funding, or ceased to be politically active. According to the Russian Ministry of Justice, 137 nonprofits out of 244 conformed to the restrictions with the foreign agent status for the period of 2012–2022. Nonprofit organizations generally follow the state's adaptation and compliance strategies (Skokova et al., 2018) and by doing so reaffirm the power balance and legitimacy of the regime that established those rules.

Russian nonprofit organizations that follow the rules and fall in line with the political status quo utilize an output-maximization strategy. They assess the risks of challenging the state and give up an open confrontation to reaffirm organizational stability and secure opportunities to operate. Similarly, Tian and Chuang (2022) and Vu (2019) have noted that for nonprofits in China, compliance with state norms has become synonymous with organizational competence and capacity. This balance between nonprofits' autonomy to pursue a social mission and the maintenance of a depoliticized neutrality in relation to the state (Jing, 2015; Tian & Chuang, 2022) secures the established organizational networks that allow the nonprofits to continue their work. Bederson and Semenov (2021) similarly concluded that the principal survival of nonprofit organizations depends on access to resources and that the state manipulates the rules of access in Russia and in authoritarian regimes generally.

17.2.2.3 Civil Society as a Mechanism of Limited Participation and Feedback

Governments collaborate and consult with nonprofits on policies and legislation in relevant areas. However, this collaboration is "often just window dressing, used by the regime to legitimize its decisions" (Lorch & Bunk, 2017, p. 7), which is partially true for Russia.

There are broad formal opportunities for nonprofits to be involved in government consultation and agenda-setting in Russia (Pape & Skokova, 2022). The state and the president generally recognize nonprofits' expertise and call for taking it into account. Public Chambers and advisory boards are official consultative bodies for the government, aimed at providing expertise on laws, consulting, and critically evaluating government operations. The Public Chamber (est. 2005) consists of members selected by the president, representatives of regional Chambers, and representatives of nonprofit organizations (mainly GONGOs). Federal and regional authorities are obliged to work with advisory boards that include civil-society representatives (Federal Law No. 212, 2014). However, their feedback is rarely taken into account, and their participation is limited to the sphere of social issues (Ljubownikow & Crotty, 2016; Stuvøy, 2014).

Despite the lack of official feedback mechanisms, there are examples of effective participation. Nonprofit organizations significantly contributed to the creation of governmental orders promoting philanthropy and volunteering. Furthermore, nonprofits were consulted during the COVID-19 pandemic, proposed and led the execution of the philanthropy tax deduction for businesses (2020), developed federal standards for volunteer support, and offered input on several other initiatives (Agentstvo strategicheskikh initsiativ, 2017).

Regardless, despite some positive cases of bottom-up feedback and consultation, when nonprofits provide feedback and share responsibility in the decision-making process, the overall outcome is legitimizing the state (Heurlin, 2010; Wischermann et al., 2018).

17.2.2.4 Civil Society as a Strategy to Increase Output Legitimation

Nondemocratic regimes rest their legitimation efforts on a reciprocal social contract in which the state maintains social guarantees in exchange for citizens' loyalty. The overall output legitimacy is achieved through a discourse of support and the appropriation of joint work with nonprofits (Toepler et al., 2020). Russian nonprofit organizations deliver social services, create partnership projects with authorities, and participate in government programs in health, social welfare, education, sports, and other areas. These initiatives are covered in the media for the benefit of the general public, and the state claims credit for the services provided. Nonprofits also create publicity out of these joint initiatives and thereby reinforce the contract between citizens and the authoritarian regime to deliver social services and maintain the regime (Brass, 2022).

The regime attracts nonprofits to governmental social welfare programs and creates publicity about nonprofits' participation. For instance, nonprofit organizations have helped to implement seven out of 12 Russian national projects (Topoleva-Soldunova, 2019). The largest nonprofits initiated and implemented federal projects with authorities, as is the case with the Vera Foundation. The Vera Foundation initiated the development of a palliative care system in Russia and, with the

Ministry of Health, runs several large-scale projects aimed at modifying the country's neuropsychiatric boarding school system. These projects started in 2019 after Putin's instructions to develop and improve palliative care in the country (ONF, 2022). Another example is the federal Concept of Active Longevity, initiated by the nonprofit "Old Age to Joy" and run with the Ministry of Labor and Social Protection.

The government uses media to broadcast and absorb the achievements of nonprofit organizations and inform Russians about its increasing financial and infrastructural support to nonprofits. The official discourse excludes the ideas of human rights protection and is largely equated with social services, charity, and volunteering (Belokurova, 2010). For example, federal state-owned TV channels regularly highlight the role of social service nonprofits, showing real cases of their help to people in need. Many Russians do not distinguish what social services are provided by nonprofit organizations and what come from state institutions. Showing the success of nonprofits on TV helps to strength the image of the state as socially responsible and caring for citizens. Moreover, the role of social nonprofits and volunteering is a common point in annual presidential addresses to the Federal Assembly, which is widely broadcast in the media. To maintain regime legitimation and stability, the Russian government needs nonprofit organizations to carry out social services and thus supports them in doing so, with the state taking credit for the service and the nonprofits having little voice in the matter.

17.2.2.5 Civil Society and Regime Discourse

The fifth way nonprofits strengthen the legitimacy of an authoritarian regime is by supporting and reproducing regime discourse. The Russian government actively uses the discourse of traditional values, nationalism, patriotism, and Russian Orthodoxy, as well as military strength and social welfare (Malinova, 2022). The Russian government supports organizations that support the regime's priorities. As Frohlich and Skokova (2020, p. 698) have shown, projects that conform to state-led conservative public discourse are privileged by the Presidential Grant Foundation, the state's major funding program.

In Russia, about 12% of all nonprofit organizations work in the areas of patriotism and historic memory (Rosstat, 2020). These include the largest GONGOs, such as Russia's Young Army (Unarmia), which has over 200,000 members, and the Russian Union of Veterans of

Afghanistan, which has about 500,000 members. The Unarmia promotes military-patriotic education in Russia that aligns with state discourse about traditional values, heroism, and masculinity (Alava, 2021).

In line with military and imperial discourse, more than 6,000 nonprofits signed a letter in support of the so-called military operation in Ukraine: "We, the leaders of public organizations, civil activists, support the course of our President and call for the unification of all public forces" (Yandex, 2022). Regional nonprofit organizations, including resource centers for nonprofits, signed similar letters in their regions. For comparison, a little more than 500 nonprofits signed a letter against the conflict.

17.3 Conclusions

Political context, namely the type of political regime, determines the hierarchy of societal functions that civil society performs. In a democracy, the key function of civil society is to monitor and challenge the state, and advocacy is often perceived as a main activity of nonprofit organizations, even those that deal with social welfare. This dynamic is possible because of the open nature of the political context and the ability to solve many social problems through the functioning channels of political communication. In an authoritarian context, there is no such openness, and the state controls associational life and a discourse of power to a much greater extent. We claim that the core societal function of nonprofits in authoritarian settings is regime stabilization obtained by repression, co-optation, and legitimation applied by the state to civil society.

In Russia, all three pillars of regime stability are in place. The state represses claims-making nonprofits that aim to challenge the state while supporting and co-opting social welfare nonprofits. The policy results in the optimal strength and structure of civil society for maintaining and securing the authoritarian regime. By using nonprofit organizations as a facade of democracy and as a feedback mechanism, by establishing GONGOs, and by appropriating nonprofits' outcomes, the authoritarian regime enhances its legitimacy and secures stability.

Governmental funding and co-optation does not automatically make nonprofits regime supporters. As objects of tight political regulation and control, nonprofit organizations are compelled to work in existing circumstances in which they must weigh the risks of political confrontation and rationally choose their social mission as a priority. They can achieve their mission only in a game of balance between autonomous work with their beneficiaries and the maintenance of a depoliticized neutrality in relation to the state. This balance is key to organizational success and survival in an authoritarian context. Nonprofit organizations play the game by the regime's rules.

Concluding that nonprofits contribute to regime stability, we go further than conclusions about the undermining of political activism, the loss of autonomy, and the displacement of advocacy in nondemocratic regimes as consequences of government interactions or interventions. We go beyond the sectoral analysis and consider the interaction between the state and nonprofits in a broader social system.

References

Agentstvo strategicheskikh initsiativ. (2017). Standart podderzhki dobrovol'chestva (volonterstva) v regionakh Rossiyskoy Federatsii. https://edu.dobro.ru /upload/uf/394/39486b5504fcc7bf61053fc966ce815a.pdf

Alava, J. (2021). Russia's young army: Raising new generations into militarized patriots. *Nexus of patriotism and militarism in Russia: A quest for internal cohesion*. Helsinki University Press. https://helda.helsinki.fi/handle/10138/333718

Atalay, Z. (2018). Authoritarian neoliberalism and Islamist civil society in Turkey. In P. Kamruzzaman (Ed.), *Civil society in the Global South* (pp. 176–192). Routledge.

Bederson, V., & Semenov, A. (2021). Political foundations of state support for civil society: Analysis of the distribution of presidential grants in Russia. *Post-Soviet Affairs*, *37*(6), 544–558. https://doi.org/10.1080/1060586X.2021.1976575

Belokurova, E. (2010). Civil society discourses in Russia: The influence of the European Union and the role of EU–Russia cooperation. *Journal of European Integration*, *32*(5), 457–474. https://doi.org/10.1080/07036337.2010.498630

Brass, J. N. (2022). Do service provision NGOs perform civil society functions? Evidence of NGOs' relationship with democratic participation. *Nonprofit and Voluntary Sector Quarterly*, *51*(1), 148–169. https://doi.org/10.1177/0899764021991671

Bromley, P., Schofer, E., & Longhofer, W. (2020). Contentions over world culture: The rise of legal restrictions on foreign funding to NGOs, 1994–2015. *Social Forces*, *99*(1), 281–304. https://doi.org/10.1093/sf/soz138

Carothers, T., & Brechenmacher, S. (2014). *Closing space: Democracy and human rights support under fire*. Carnegie Endowment for International Peace.

Cavatorta, F. (2015). *Civil society activism under authoritarian rule: A comparative perspective*. Routledge.

Cianetti, L., Dawson, J., & Hanley, S. (2018). Rethinking "democratic backsliding" in Central and Eastern Europe – Looking beyond Hungary and Poland. *East European Politics*, *34*(3), 243–256. https://doi.org/10.1080/21599165.2018.1491401

Crotty, J., Hall, S. M., & Ljubownikow, S. (2014). Post-Soviet civil society development in the Russian Federation: The impact of the NGO law. *Europe-Asia Studies*, *66*(8), 1253–1269. https://doi.org/10.1080/09668136.2014.941697

Daucé, F. (2014). The government and human rights groups in Russia: Civilized oppression? *Journal of Civil Society*, *10*(3), 239–254. https://doi.org/10.1080/17448689.2014.941087

Dupuy, K. E., Ron, J., & Prakash, A. (2015). Who survived? Ethiopia's regulatory crackdown on foreign-funded NGOs. *Review of International Political Economy*, 22(2), 419–456. https://doi.org/10.1080/09692290.2014.903854

Enjuto Martinez, R., Qu, Y., & Howell, J. (2022). Effects of government contracting of services on NGOs in China: Convergence and divergence with international experience. *VOLUNTAS: International Journal of Voluntary and Nonprofit Organizations*, *33*(4), 685–695. https://doi.org/10.1007/s11266-021-00383-1

Evans, A. B. (2011). The failure of democratization in Russia: A comparative perspective. *Journal of Eurasian Studies*, *2*(1), 40–51. https://doi.org/10.1016/j.euras.2010.10.001

Federal Law No.212-FZ "On basic principles of public control in the Russian Federation." July 21, 2014.

Flikke, G. (2018). Conflicting opportunities or patronal politics? Restrictive NGO legislation in Russia 2012–2015. *Europe-Asia Studies*, *70*(4), 564–590. https://doi.org/10.1080/09668136.2018.1455806

Fröhlich, C., & Skokova, Y. (2020). Two for one: Public welfare and regime legitimacy through state funding for CSOs in Russia. *VOLUNTAS: International Journal of Voluntary and Nonprofit Organizations*, *31*(4), 698–709. https://doi.org/10.1007/s11266-020-00203-y

Fukuyama, F. (1992). *The end of history and the last man*. Free Press.

Fung, A. (2003). Associations and democracy: Between theories, hopes, and realities. *Annual Review of Sociology*, *29*, 515–539. https://doi.org/10.1146/annurev.soc.29.010202.100134

Geddes, B., & Zaller, J. (1989). Sources of popular support for authoritarian regimes. *American Journal of Political Science*, *33*(2), 319–347. https://doi.org/10.2307/2111150

Gel'man, V. (2015). *Authoritarian Russia: Analyzing post-Soviet regime changes*. University of Pittsburgh Press.

Gerschewski, J. (2013). The three pillars of stability: Legitimation, repression, and co-optation in autocratic regimes. *Democratization*, *20*(1), 13–38. https://doi.org/10.1080/13510347.2013.738860

Gilbert, L. (2020). Regulating society after the color revolutions: A comparative analysis of NGO laws in Belarus, Russia, and Armenia. *Demokratizatsiya: The Journal of Post-Soviet Democratization*, *28*(2), 305–332. www.muse.jhu.edu/article/754564

Hasmath, R., Hildebrandt, T., & Hsu, J. Y. J. (2019). Conceptualizing government-organized non-governmental organizations. *Journal of Civil Society*, *15*(3), 267–284. https://doi.org/10.1080/17448689.2019.1632549

Hellmeier, S., & Weidmann, N. B. (2020). Pulling the strings? The strategic use of pro-government mobilization in authoritarian regimes. *Comparative Political Studies*, *53*(1), 71–108. https://doi.org/10.1177/0010414019843559

Hemment, J. (2012). Nashi, youth voluntarism, and Potemkin NGOs: Making sense of civil society in post-Soviet Russia. *Slavic Review*, *71*(2), 234–260. https://doi.org/10.5612/slavicreview.71.2.0234

Herrold, C. E. (2016). NGO policy in pre- and post-Mubarak Egypt: Effects on NGOs' roles in democracy promotion. *Nonprofit Policy Forum*, *7*(2), 189–212. https://doi.org/10.1515/npf-2014-0034

Heurlin, C. (2010). Governing civil society: The political logic of NGO–state relations under dictatorship. *VOLUNTAS: International Journal of Voluntary and Nonprofit Organizations*, *21*(2), 220–239. https://doi.org/10.1007/s11266-009-9103-2

Hsu, C. L. (2010). Beyond civil society: An organizational perspective on state–NGO relations in the People's Republic of China. *Journal of Civil Society*, *6*(3), 259–277. https://doi.org/10.1080/17448689.2010.528949

Hsu, C. L., & Jiang, Y. (2015). An institutional approach to Chinese NGOs: State alliance versus state avoidance resource strategies. *The China Quarterly*, *221*, 100–122. https://doi.org/10.1017/S0305741014001568

Hu, M., & Guo, C. (2016). Fundraising policy reform and its impact on nonprofits in China: A view from the trenches. *Nonprofit Policy Forum*, *7*(2), 213–236. https://doi.org/10.1515/npf-2016-0003

Jing, Y. (2015). Between control and empowerment: Governmental strategies towards the development of the non-profit sector in China. *Asian Studies Review*, *39*(4), 589–608. https://doi.org/10.1080/10357823.2015.1090394

Kalandadze, K., & Orenstein, M. A. (2009). Electoral protests and democratization beyond the color revolutions. *Comparative Political Studies*, *42*(11), 1403–1425. https://doi.org/10.1177/0010414009332131

Katz, H., & Gidron, B. (2022). Encroachment and reaction of civil society in non-liberal democracies: The case of Israel and the New Israel Fund. *Nonprofit Policy Forum*, *13*(3), 229–250. https://doi.org/10.1515/npf-2020-0043

Krasnopolskaya, I., Skokova, Y., & Pape, U. (2015). Government–nonprofit relations in Russia's regions: An exploratory analysis. *VOLUNTAS: International Journal of Voluntary and Nonprofit Organizations*, *26*(6), 2238–2266. https://doi.org/10.1007/s11266-015-9654-3

Levitsky, S., & Way, L. A. (2010). *Competitive authoritarianism: Hybrid regimes after the Cold War*. Cambridge University Press.

Lewis, D. (2013). Civil society and the authoritarian state: Cooperation, contestation and discourse. *Journal of Civil Society*, *9*(3), 325–340. https://doi.org/10.1080/17448689.2013.818767

Ljubownikow, S., & Crotty, J. (2016). Nonprofit influence on public policy: Exploring nonprofit advocacy in Russia. *Nonprofit and Voluntary Sector Quarterly*, *45*(2), 314–332. https://doi.org/10.1177/0899764015583121

Ljubownikow, S., & Crotty, J. (2017). Managing boundaries: The role of non-profit organisations in Russia's managed democracy. *Sociology*, *51*(5), 940–956. https://doi.org/10.1177/0038038515608111

Lorch, J., & Bunk, B. (2017). Using civil society as an authoritarian legitimation strategy: Algeria and Mozambique in comparative perspective. *Democratization*, *24*(6), 987–1005. https://doi.org/10.1080/13510347.2016.1256285

Ma, J. (2022). How does an authoritarian state co-opt its social scientists studying civil society? *VOLUNTAS: International Journal of Voluntary and Nonprofit Organizations*. https://doi.org/10.1007/s11266-022-00510-6

Malinova, O. (2022). Legitimizing Putin's regime: The transformations of the narrative of Russia's post-Soviet transition. *Communist and Post-Communist Studies*, *55*(1), 52–75. https://doi.org/10.1525/j.postcomstud.2022.55.1.52

Matchanka, A. (2014). Substitution of civil society in Belarus: Government-organised non-governmental organisations. *Journal of Belarusian Studies*, *7*(2), 67–94. https://doi.org/10.30965/20526512-00702004

Matejova, M., Parker, S., & Dauvergne, P. (2018). The politics of repressing environmentalists as agents of foreign influence. *Australian Journal of International Affairs*, *72*(2), 145–162. https://doi.org/10.1080/10357718.2017.1421141

Mercer, C. (2002). NGOs, civil society and democratization: A critical review of the literature. *Progress in Development Studies*, *2*(1), 5–22. https://doi.org/10.1191/1464993402ps027ra

Njoku, E. T. (2022). Strategic exclusion, co-option and containment: Towards an integrative theory of state–CSOs relations. *Critical Studies on Terrorism*, *15*(4), 917–944. https://doi.org/10.1080/17539153.2022.2111776

ONF. (2022). Region zaboty. https://onf.ru/region-zaboty

Owen, C. (2020). Participatory authoritarianism: From bureaucratic transformation to civic participation in Russia and China. *Review of International Studies*, *46*(4), 415–434. https://doi.org/10.1017/S0260210520000248

Pape, U., & Skokova, Y. (2022). Nonprofit advocacy in Russia's regions. *Journal of Civil Society*, *18*(1), 1–22. https://doi.org/10.1080/17448689.2022.2061545

Plantan, E. (2022). Not all NGOs are treated equally: Selectivity in civil society management in China and Russia. *Comparative Politics*, *54*(3), 501–524. https://doi.org/10.5129/001041522X16258376563887

Popplewell, R. (2018). Civil society, legitimacy and political space: Why some organisations are more vulnerable to restrictions than others in violent and divided contexts. *VOLUNTAS: International Journal of Voluntary and Nonprofit Organizations*, *29*(2), 388–403. https://doi.org/10.1007/s11266-018-9949-2

Pulsngo. (2022). Doing NPOs: Assessment of organizational environment. https://pulsngo.ru/results

Putnam, R. D. (2000). *Bowling alone: The collapse and revival of American community*. Simon & Schuster.

Putnam, R. D., Leonardi, R., & Nanetti, R. Y. (1992). *Making democracy work: Civic traditions in modern Italy*. Princeton University Press.

Reaves, A. (2018). *The role of civil society in competitive authoritarian legitimation strategies: An analysis of Venezuela and Bolivia*. University of North Carolina at Chapel Hill Graduate School. https://cdr.lib.unc.edu/concern/dissertations/sq87bz928

Rosstat. (2020). Itogi vyborochnogo obsledovaniya sotsial'no oriyentirovannykh nekommercheskikh organizatsiy na osnove formy № 1-SONKO. Rosstat, 2020. rosstat.gov.ru›storage/mediabank/1-sonko2020.doc

Skokova, Y., Pape, U., & Krasnopolskaya, I. (2018). The non-profit sector in today's Russia: Between confrontation and co-optation. *Europe-Asia Studies*, *70*(4), 531–563. https://doi.org/10.1080/09668136.2018.1447089

Spires, A. J. (2020). Regulation as political control: China's first charity law and its implications for civil society. *Nonprofit and Voluntary Sector Quarterly*, *49*(3), 571–588. https://doi.org/10.1177/0899764019883939

Strachwitz, R. G., & Toepler, S. (2022). Contested civic spaces in liberal democracies. *Nonprofit Policy Forum*, *13*(3), 179–193. https://doi.org/10.1515/npf-2022-0026

Stuvøy, K. (2014). Power and public chambers in the development of civil society in Russia. *Communist and Post-Communist Studies*, *47*(3–4), 409–419. https://doi.org/10.1016/j.postcomstud.2014.10.002

TASS. (2022). MER odobrilo kriterii dlya isklyucheniya sotsial'nykh NKO iz svoyego reyestra. https://tass.ru/ekonomika/14881933

Teets, J. C. (2013). Let many civil societies bloom: The rise of consultative authoritarianism in China. *The China Quarterly*, *213*, 19–38. https://doi.org/10.1017/S0305741012001269

Tian, F., & Chuang, J. (2022). Depoliticizing China's grassroots NGOs: State and civil society as an institutional field of Power. *The China Quarterly*, *250*, 509–530. https://doi.org/10.1017/S0305741022000157

Tocqueville, A. de (2004). *Democracy in America* (A. Goldhammer, Trans.). Library of America.

Toepler, S., Zimmer, A., Fröhlich, C., & Obuch, K. (2020). The changing space for NGOs: Civil society in authoritarian and hybrid regimes. *VOLUNTAS: International Journal of Voluntary and Nonprofit Organizations*, *31*(4), 649–662. https://doi.org/10.1007/s11266-020-00240-7

Topoleva-Soldunova, Y. A., et al. (2019). Uchastiye NKO v okazanii uslug v sotsial'noy sfere. https://opuo.ru/wp-content/uploads/2020/02/doklad_uchastie_NKO_socuslugi05112019.pdf

Vu, A. N. (2019). NGO-led activism under authoritarian rule of Vietnam: Between cooperation and contestation. *Community Development*, *50*(4), 422–439. https://doi.org/10.1080/15575330.2019.1642925

White, G. (1994). Civil society, democratization and development (I): Clearing the analytical ground. *Democratization*, *1*(2), 375–390. https://doi.org/10.1080/13510349408403399

Wischermann, J., Bunk, B., Köllner, P., & Lorch, J. (2018). Do associations support authoritarian rule? Evidence from Algeria, Mozambique, and Vietnam. *Journal of Civil Society*, *14*(2), 95–115. https://doi.org/10.1080/17448689.2018.1464707

Wischermann, J., Cuong, B. T., & Phuong, D. T. V. (2016). Vietnamese civic organisations: Supporters of or obstacles to further democratisation? Results from an empirical survey. *Journal of Current Southeast Asian Affairs*, *35*(2), 57–88. https://doi.org/10.1177/186810341603500203

Yandex. (2022). *Otkrytoye obrashcheniye liderov i aktivistov rossiyskikh NKO*. https://forms.yandex.ru/u/621bac4b3fbbe6feb2610093/

Zhang, C. (2018). Nongovernmental organizations' policy advocacy and government responsiveness in China. *Nonprofit and Voluntary Sector Quarterly*, *47*(4), 723–744. https://doi.org/10.1177/0899764017705735

Zhang, Y. (2015). Dependent interdependence: The complicated dance of government–nonprofit relations in China. *VOLUNTAS: International Journal of Voluntary and Nonprofit Organizations*, *26*(6), 2395–2423. https://doi.org/10.1007/s11266-015-9645-4

Zhao, R., & Lilly, A. G. (2021). The role of state mobilization for volunteerism in China. *Nonprofit and Voluntary Sector Quarterly*. https://doi.org/10.1177/08997640211057458

18 *Nonprofits as Creators of Transformative Symbolic Reality*

ROBERT W. RESSLER

This chapter introduces Transformative Symbolic Reality, a new sociological theory that emphasizes the unseen and systemic influences that connect nonprofit organizational work to improvements in the human condition. Transformative Symbolic Reality highlights the importance of social reality in human development and demonstrates how transformative social realties influence both the way we imagine ourselves and important life outcomes. Besides explaining Transformative Symbolic Reality, I provide an application of the theory that illuminates a specific, but often overlooked, impact of the nonprofit sector: positive changes in social reality. Transformative Symbolic Reality is therefore applied as a normative sector theory, or an account of the benefits nonprofits can provide to society. Drawing on sociological theory, I argue that a key mechanism through which society reproduces or changes is the combination of physically and temporally bounded social contexts. By extension, manipulating certain social realities, or facilitating some social realities and inhibiting others, can directly improve the quality of life for minoritized individuals and social groups as they exist within society and over time. Central to the influence of social reality, organizations – including nonprofit organizations – help produce these culturally based socio-ecological factors that create and shape lived experience.

I use the following terms throughout the chapter:

Social reality: Our perceptions and experiences are influenced by the physical world, and, in society, are also the result of other peoples' beliefs and biases that have been incorporated into social systems. This "social reality" (alternatively "symbolic reality") is the reality people experience – the basis from which they form their own opinions, make decisions, and take actions.

Social systems: Communities, organizations, institutions, and bureaucracies that form the structure that communicates and reinforces social realities to individuals and thereby constrains or allows individual agency.

Transformative Symbolic Reality (capitalized): A theoretical approach characterized by attention to how individuals in groups and organizations manipulate social reality to bring about positive social change.

Transformative symbolic reality (no capitalization): A social reality characterized by challenging the dominant forces that advantage the lives and developmental outcomes of one group over others and instead structures experiences that promote equity and development of the human condition.

Through the lens of Transformative Symbolic Reality, this chapter introduces the notion of the nonprofit sector as a potential wellspring of transformative symbolic realities or social realities that result in positive social change. Positive social change means improving the objective and subjective well-being of members of a society, especially those marginalized and excluded by current social systems. Importantly, transformative symbolic realities directly confront and sometimes overcome the limitations that systemic biases place on individuals because of categorical discrimination, such as discrimination based on race or ethnicity, geography, gender, or social class. Using examples from my own and other scholars' research, the rest of the chapter explores how the nonprofit organizational form, in contrast to organizations in the public or private sector, is particularly suited to the creation of transformative symbolic reality (Ressler et al., 2021; Sharkey et al., 2017). Incorporating critiques that nonprofit organizations do not always create transformative symbolic realities, I explore the ways that we can leverage this understanding of the nonprofit sector to help organizations wrestle out of the grips of the Nonprofit Industrial Complex, allowing them to instead contribute more successfully to lasting social change (INCITE!, 2007).

18.1 A Theory of Transformative Symbolic Reality

18.1.1 Social Reality and Social Change

In sociology, George Herbert Mead is the founder of *symbolic interaction*, a rich and expansive theoretical framework that centers the influence of everyday interactions between people in the construction of social life (Charon, 2010). Importantly, according to symbolic interaction, individuals make decisions and navigate their lives based on their unique present circumstances (Herman-Kinney & Reynolds, 2003). The symbolic interactionist perspective supports the common notion that there exists a distinct reality apart from the natural, biological, or physical world and that this symbolic world has a direct and powerful influence on how all individuals experience themselves in it. Alternatively labeled the "social world," "social reality," or "symbolic reality," examples include the importance of money, beauty standards, and spirituality – all things that have some basis in the objective world but that nevertheless are defined *socially*.

The main contribution of Transformative Symbolic Reality is to draw a distinction between social realities that reproduce the status quo and those that change it. Using a Gramscian (1891–1937) understanding of hegemony, I argue that groups of individuals, organizations, and institutions are able to reproduce *or manipulate* the content of social realities and that we can use sociological ideas to discern the qualities that would make such manipulations transformative for society.

As society has become more complex, and our scientific observations of the social world more precise, it is increasingly difficult to deny the fact that society influences who we are and who we become (Collins, 1990, 2010). Society influences our lives by manipulating our social reality, or the range of ideas and opportunities available to us throughout our life course (Mills, 2000). As a whole, the social reality we experience forms our understanding and perception of the world and our place within it.

Social realities, however, are different for different groups of people (e.g., the social reality of a Wampanoag tribal member visiting Congress is not the same as the social reality of the Muslim politician who invited them). But how did this variation come to be? Sociologists often frame the variation in social realities as inequities, or structurally determined opportunities for some individuals over others based on socio-economic circumstances that are largely outside of any individual person's control. Age, sex, gender, race, ethnicity, class, ability, identity, personality, capital: all of these categories represent multiple and intersecting dimensions upon which some individuals receive societal benefits and others encounter barriers.

Transformative Symbolic Reality draws a distinction between the social realities individuals experience that reproduce inequities and those that alleviate them. Together, the social realities that promote positive social change form transformative symbolic realities. Much like virtual reality, these symbolic spaces are simultaneously "real" and "not real" as they represent a combination of purposefully designed components that may not necessarily reflect the structure or order of the outside world. But like a cultural holodeck, they nonetheless influence in-the-moment interactions. Another way to think of transformative symbolic realities is as the metaphysical spaces constructed by individuals and organizations that are oriented toward promoting positive and equitable human development. Such spaces expand the realm of possibilities to counter oppressive forces such as racism, classism, and xenophobia. Transformative symbolic realities, in other words, are the laboratories in which we synthesize a social reality oriented toward equitable social change.

By contrast, the social reality of most socio-ecological contexts is the product of social systems that *reproduce* dominant cultural or systemic norms. The pull of this status quo-reinforcing symbolic reality is strong, leading, for example, to even well-meaning international aid organizations supporting Western colonial hegemony (Girei, 2016). In an inequitable, violent, and stratified world, transformative symbolic realities counter those that constrain or undermine the quality of the experience by one group for the benefit of another. In contrast to reproducing society, transformative symbolic realities promote equitable social change.

These three statements summarize the theory of Transformative Symbolic Reality, including its potential for social change:

1. Organizations of people, through their own agency, can manipulate social reality to either reproduce or change social systems.
2. Transformative symbolic realities are social realities manipulated to directly confront systems of exploitation and oppression.
3. Transformative symbolic realities engender social change through enhancing the imagination and realization of changes in the universal social reality shared among individuals and groups.

Transformative Symbolic Reality as a social theory contributes to our understanding of the organizational mechanisms underlying social change (Ray, 2019). It does so by drawing attention to the cumulative nature of individual experiences within organized social contexts. Social change therefore happens through repeated exposure to transformative symbolic realities, or socially constructed ecological contexts that invite the enactment of counterhegemonic norms, values, or cultures that directly challenge the power of inequitable structural systems. Transformative symbolic realities permit individuals to experience a more equitable social reality, which facilitates further imagining of positive social change. Transformative social spaces help people experience locally what that change in social reality might be like before it happens globally. In colloquial terms, social spaces characterized by transformative symbolic realities allow people to "see it" before they can "be it."

18.1.2 Nonprofits' Role in Creating Transformative Symbolic Realities

For some, the nonprofit organizations represent a response to the failure of governments or markets to produce socially desirable but difficult-to-commodify goods such as free education, undeveloped natural spaces, or social cohesion (Anheier, 2014; Salamon, 1987; Weisbrod, 1988). For others, nonprofits are the expression of their founder's personal identity, such as their unique values regarding meaningful work, or their access to information or resources (Frumkin, 2009). Still others view charitable giving, and the nonprofit work that it supports, as an attempt to protect the capitalistic concentration of large quantities of wealth by surveilling, marketing, and monetizing individual misfortune (INCITE!, 2007). These pressures and constraints have resulted in a unique type of organization that receives a favorable tax status in exchange for at least claiming to provide services that are beneficial to communities (Clotfelter & Ehrlich, 1999).

Common perspectives such as these conceptualize nonprofits as components of existing political or social processes, but this view obscures or denies their role as potential agents of social change. Several scholars and activists who investigate lasting change in the nonprofit sector conclude that nonprofits do not contribute to social change but rather serve as a vehicle through which social change energy is co-opted by the dominant systems (Arena, 2012; INCITE!, 2007; Kivel, 2007). These critiques, as well as growing public desire for accountability and continued government divestment in public life, call for a theoretical roadmap that will help scholars understand the importance of the nonprofit sector and its contributions to long-term public good (Flynn & Hodgkinson, 2013).

Transformative Symbolic Reality helps to bridge the gap between these critiques of the nonprofit sector and the demonstrated, empirical evidence that communities with more nonprofit social services experience positive social outcomes such as reduced crime, higher levels of subjective well-being, increased access to resources and information, and better health (Andrews & Withey, 2012; Currie et al., 2009; Deza et al., 2020; Ressler et al., 2021; Sharkey et al., 2017; Small, 2009; Taylor et al., 2016). Indeed, in her article "Why Afterschool Matters," Nelson (2017) called the resources provided by a particular college preparatory program "transformative" for the students who are experiencing the most barriers to academic success.

Given the clear immediate and long-term benefits of nonprofit organizations, is there a theoretically grounded and real-world articulation for how nonprofit organizations can create systemic change while still largely operating within traditional capitalist structures? Is it possible that nonprofit organizations are uniquely positioned, comparatively to government and private services, to create the potential for transformative social change?

I argue that the key to answering these questions lies in conceptualizing the nonprofit sector as positioned to change the social reality that influences the lived experiences of individuals and that leads to positive social change over time. Nonprofits are unique in this way because they do not suffer the constraints of the profit motive of private organizations, nor do they have the need for widespread public consensus of the public sector in their engagement with social realities (Weisbrod, 1988). Private and public organizations necessarily bound their symbolic realities in ways that limit their potential to achieve positive social change. Private organizations maintain an orientation toward profit, reproducing unfair and limiting notions of individuals as proletariat consumers and bourgeoisie owners of production. Public organizations are predominantly concerned with maintaining the stability of political and economic systems, which themselves rely on existing power structures and benefit groups with existing power and influence over others. Transformative Symbolic Reality suggests, by contrast, that nonprofit organizations are uniquely positioned to create transformative symbolic realities or symbolic realities that directly challenge "common sense" or the "status quo" (Barman, 2016; Nelson & Gazley, 2014; Ray, 2019).

The constraints experienced by actors in the private and public sectors means that the social realities they produce are more in line with dominant hegemonic systems, which results in reproducing society as is. The reproduction of society makes it difficult for them to produce the social change necessary to confront "big" environmental and social problems. While all organizations can be said to operate according to some form of "common sense," or the social realities that reproduce the status quo, constraints on organizations in the private and public sector limit their ability to operate according to principles that actively challenge or confront aspects of common sense (such as racial/ethnic bias and gender discrimination) that restrict universal positive social change. Nonprofit organizations, which instead are mission-driven, are not necessarily beholden to solely market or state funding streams and often subsist on local, individual, and governmental support in the form of grants. They are then positioned to challenge the status quo and purposefully construct a particular kind of social reality in which novel relationships can be formed, novel opportunities can be shared, and diverse resources can be marshalled toward alleviating social ills and promoting social change.

Attention to transformative symbolic realities shifts the focus from the nonprofit production of goods that are hard to obtain but socially desirable (e.g., social capital, health, trust, empathy, and civic engagement) to the production of the prerequisite socio-ecological contexts in which those goods *can be* manifest. In other words, in addition to the production of social goods, nonprofits must first create the contexts that facilitate the production of those goods in the first place.

Transformative symbolic reality is especially possible in the nonprofit sector precisely because these are organizations that have a mission oriented toward fulfilling otherwise unfulfilled social needs. Nonprofit theory suggests that community organizations are special because they are oriented toward social ends rather than private benefit (Weisbrod, 1988). Similarly, these organizations are often formed as a response to perceived community need and are theorized to innovate at higher rates than other organizations (Bornstein, 2007; Fleishman, 2007; Katre & Salipante, 2012; Smith, 1974). Transformative Symbolic Reality reformulates these propositions to focus on the specific contexts that nonprofit organizations create in response to current social structures and processes. Traditional nonprofit theory would frame professional organizations for underrepresented minoritized scholars, for example, as providing services that help to counter the effects of racism, classism, and inequality. Transformative Symbolic Reality instead views these organizations as an instrument in creating literal and figurative spaces where social norms of racism and classism are temporarily relaxed, allowing individuals in those spaces to mentally and physically experience what a world would be like in which these negative social forces are no longer present. Importantly, for the many communities actively traumatized by misogynist, racist, and exploitative cultures, these transformative spaces can represent an *organizational* manifestation of the transformative symbolic realities already present in their homes and among families.

If some social realities are indeed transformative – that is, if they enact contexts that counter dominant systems of stratification, alienation, and inequality – then they should result in individuals and communities developing new perspectives and understandings regarding their ability to leverage their position in the world to create social change (Collins, 2010). Community organizations are already theorized to have the exact conditions under which important social goods, such as trust and empathy, can be built (Paxton & Ressler, 2018). To be transformative, such experiences should also broadly influence a community's ability to enact change in the lives of its members and across society.

Theorizing nonprofits through the lens of Transformative Symbolic Reality focuses our attention on the symbolic spaces created by nonprofit organizations. It is therefore a theory that can help us construct hypotheses regarding how and why some organizations or movements are more effective than others. Transformative Symbolic Reality can also be used to understand why cultural sensitivity is so important to successful interventions, or how having just one positive experience in a community organization can totally change how individuals navigate their lives (Nelson, 2014; Small, 2009). Such a perspective may also help illuminate why certain organizations appear to make some progress in reducing systemic inequalities while others seem so easily co-opted into oppressive institutions. In an era of globalization and rising inequalities, such processes have direct implications for the role of governments and private or nonprofit enterprises in improving quality of life.

18.2 An Illustration of Transformative Symbolic Reality

To illustrate the importance of transformative symbolic reality in the manifestation of social change, I provide here some examples of how nonprofit organizations can be involved in creating new social realities.

One simple and familiar focus in nonprofit studies, mission statements, illustrates how nonprofit organizations construct transformative symbolic realities. Nonprofit mission statements are "legitimizing myths" that hold an organization together but also signal organizational features and values (Koch et al., 2015; Morphew & Hartley, 2006). The language they use, for example, such as "educational opportunity," "equality," or "community support," can be understood as responses to perceived community need. Transformative Symbolic Reality posits that having a mission that promotes equity represents a distinct effort toward creating a social reality that produces social change. Mission statements are more than promises; they are visions of a different world.

Consider, for example, how applying Transformative Symbolic Reality can be a useful tool to understand why public mental health advocacy and positive representation of individuals from marginalized populations by leaders of community organizations is so beneficial for others within the community (Campbell & Wolbrecht, 2006; Hatzenbuehler et al., 2010). Similarly, nonprofits involved in the work of creating transformative symbolic reality are also evident in the education sector within the United States. The creation of the United States public education system was initially justified and supported because of its function in producing a well-trained populace ready for the modern workforce (a hegemonic symbolic reality of people as proletariat). As Transformative Symbolic Reality theory would suggest, abundant evidence indicates that this approach to education has created systemic gaps that reproduce inequality and undermine education's promise for equity (Alexander et al., 2014). Some organizations, with nonprofits making up a large portion of these, have stepped in to fill this gap while simultaneously creating transformative symbolic realities within educational spaces; this in turn promotes the representation and well-being of children underserved by current educational policy (Nelson & Gazley, 2014). Such services not only provide children from Black, Hispanic, and immigrant families with quality educational opportunities but also offer the socio-ecological support they need to challenge and overcome biased and unfair educational policies and norms (Duncan & Magnuson, 2013; Ellington & Frederick, 2010; Nelson & Gazley, 2014; Rosenbaum, 1978).

Data gathered through observing nonprofits in after-school and summer camps, outlined in the following paragraphs, illustrate how mission-oriented organizations can be critical in creating transformative symbolic realities. During the school year and summer of 2017, I studied the social reality surrounding three partnerships among a large city's network of community organizations and three public elementary schools. In addition to observing these educational programs, I interviewed 30 parents of participants, asking questions about their role as parents in their children's educational lives, as well as how having these programs influenced how they navigated pursuing educational opportunities for their children.

Interviews were conducted in the communal spaces frequently available in elementary schools, including libraries, cafeterias, hallways, and teacher break rooms. It was in one such break room that I interviewed Sandra, a mother of two. After thanking her for her time, getting her permission to record our conversation, and asking a few preliminary warm-up questions, our conversation turned toward what she appreciated about the free after-school program her oldest child was currently enrolled in:

> Sandra: My son comes home, and he has all these stories of what they did. He has fun. He dreams stuff that he did, or stuff that he learned. Sometimes, "What did you learn?" "I'm learning about sea animals." "Is it with [school teacher]?" "No, it's with the after-school." He also has knowledge from school, but he's also gaining more information in after-school. That's what I like about it.

Consider here and in the following quotes the language these parents chose to describe their observations. Sandra used the word "dreaming," while other parents used words like "imagining" and "expressing." Such language reflects the symbolic and transformative nature of the after-school program in the lives of individual families. It is well documented that budget and cultural constraints limit the social realities supported by public school curricula, into which teachers are generally forced to fit narrow topics and standardized knowledge (Duncan & Murnane, 2011). The symbolic spaces created by nonprofits are transformative when they allow individuals (in this instance, children and families) to "dream" or imagine new possibilities for themselves that are not constrained by their current circumstances or lack of the "regular" opportunities provided by the public or private sectors.

Evidence from these interviews suggests that nonprofit organizations create transformative symbolic realities through a two-step process. The first step involves creating a literal space or opportunity for the manipulation of social reality to occur where one would not otherwise exist. The second is to ensure that the manipulation follows principles that are socially transformative.

Similar to Sandra, other interviewees noted growth or change in their students and attributed those changes to the after-school program. Importantly, many of these mothers attributed their children's growth to the novel and supportive context of the after-school program, saying their children felt "safe" or "happy" in after-school. For individuals who, because of systemic racism and bias, do not experience ubiquitously "safe" and "happy" spaces, such experiences are the first step in a process of creating a transformative symbolic reality: creating the space within which to manipulate the social reality of individuals.

I interviewed two Spanish-speaking mothers with children in elementary school who appreciated the new things their children are learning, and they connected this learning directly to their ability to become more expressive individuals:

Araceli: "Qué beneficios hay" En que mis hijos están aprendiendo cosas nuevas y diferentes, como hacer películas, el niño dice, "Hoy aprendí esto" y yo, "Ah, qué bueno" y son cosas que a mí me da gusto, porque son cosas que uno ni siquiera por la mente lo tenía, y digo yo, "Que bueno que ellos se estén preparando mucho más que uno, para que no se queden como nosotros, que no sabemos a veces ni expresarnos" y ellos ya el día de mañana, estudiando mucho y aprendiendo cosas, ya van a saber expresar sus sentimientos, ya no se van a quedar como nosotros, de que te preguntan algo y no sabes cómo explicarlo, cómo expresarte.

Araceli: What benefits are there? In my children they are learning new and different things, like how to make movies, and my son says, "Today I learned this," and I say, "Ah, qué bueno," and they are things that I like because they are things that I wouldn't have ever even thought about. And I say, "How great that the program is preparing them so much more than I could alone, so that way they don't stay stuck like us, not knowing how to express ourselves." So, they're already learning a lot during the day, but now they'll also know how to express their feelings, so they won't be stuck like us who when you ask us something we don't know how to explain or express ourselves.

Jasmine: Sí, de hecho, ya dibuja más todo, hace muchos dibujos para expresar lo que él siente, dice, "Esta es mi familia," "Aquí está mi papá haciendo esto," todo con sus dibujos, cosas que antes no lo hacía.

Jasmine: Yes, actually, now he draws more than ever; he makes more drawings to express what he feels and says, "This is my family," "Here is my dad doing this thing," and everything with his art, things that before he never did.

Nonprofit theory suggests that nonprofit organizations exist to fill the gap left between scarce government services and for-profit private enterprises (Cheng, 2019). Indeed, many parents speculated about what their children would be doing if not for the free after-school program, often reporting that their children would do far fewer activities and instead just watch TV:

Monica: Sí. Porque siento que aquí les van a enseñar un poquito más, porque ellos llegan a la casa cuando no se quedan después de escuela llegan hacen su tarea, comen y se bañan, ya después lo que les queda es mirar televisión o videojuegos y aquí yo sé que su cuerpo está activándose porque los ponen a correr, a caminar y cosas así.

Monica: Yes, because I feel like in after-school they are going to teach my children a little more, because they just come right home when they don't stay in after-school, and do their homework, eat, clean up, and then they just watch TV or play video games.

Rosa: La diferencias es con ella. Lo que a mí me gusta – porque a veces ella se queda después de la escuela porque en la casa lo que llega es a puro ver televisión, y aquí en la escuela hacen otras cosas, como ella dice bailar, a ella le gusta cantar, después se metió en el coro y el ballet.

Rosa: The difference with her that I like the most – why she stays after school – because at home what ends up happening is just pure television and here at school they do other things, like she likes to dance and likes to sing, and after, she joined a choir and the ballet.

A nonprofit organization acknowledging this gap is, in a way, acknowledging the limitations of most social realities to uplift all communities and therefore creates the space for a transformative symbolic reality to arise. As suggested by the words of Rosa, who enrolled her daughter in choir and ballet *after* her experiences in the after-school program, transformative symbolic realities are dependent upon having this space. Individuals must first be able to imagine changes in their own lives and in the lives of others before they can manifest those changes.

Clearly, there remains an important step between merely creating the space in which a transformative symbolic reality *can* occur and one in which it *does* occur. This represents the second phase in the creation of transformative symbolic realities: challenging hegemonic forces. Here again, nonprofit theory that positions nonprofits as emotive or altruistic suggests that nonprofit organizations are particularly oriented toward achieving this phase because they are mission-driven. In contrast to the public and private sectors, which are constrained in the kinds of symbolic spaces they can create because of their reliance on consensus and profit, nonprofit organizations can create spaces that open the door for transformative symbolic realities to occur by directly challenging dominant market or political forces. Indeed, popular critiques of the nonprofit industrial complex center around nonprofits not fulfilling this role efficiently enough because they have shifted toward adopting the motives of public or private services and away from creating the contexts necessary for systemic change.

In addition to the guiding transformative symbolic reality of nonprofit after-school programs more generally – that children should be enveloped in educational environments not provided by our current public/private education system – nonprofits with a more transformative mission should also create more transformative symbolic realities. In this instance, the coordinating foundation that supports the after-school program claims to want to create a world in which there are "endless opportunities" for children and in which communities "thrive." In supplemental interviews conducted with staff and organizers of the program, a desire to create a sense of "community" and "family" was pervasive. Whether or not these kinds of transformative symbolic realities are possible in public educational settings, the nonprofit organizations in these partnerships were the ones given the flexibility and had the independent motivation to manipulate the social reality of family participants toward reducing inequitable access to opportunities and educational child care.

The purposefully transformative context created by the program resulted in real changes in interviewees' social realities. These mothers could observe new futures unfolding for their children that they did not previously consider, acknowledging retrospectively that because of systemic barriers, they would have been unable to create these opportunities for themselves. Neveah, an energetic Black woman with one child in after-school, credits the program with igniting in her daughter an entirely new passion that has connected their family to different communities in culturally meaningful ways and has positively influenced her daughter's well-being:

> She found out about dance [in after-school], showing them different dance moves and calling her out to make up dance routines for songs that they created. It just sparked an interest in her, and so now she dances for church. She does hip-hop dancing, she does lyrical dancing, she does reggae and African dancing. She does any kind of dancing that there is, just about, and she loves it. It keeps her busy, four to five days a week, if not a little less. She's always in a competition. She's busy, and she loves it. It makes her happy; it keeps her on the straight and narrow as well.

18.3 Conclusions

The way that Transformative Symbolic Reality reframes common debates within the nonprofit sector can contribute to the difficult work of reconciling the nonprofit sector's intimate connections to capitalism and its sincerely held beliefs about creating social change. The most insightful critiques of the nonprofit sector portray the Nonprofit Industrial Complex as an extension of capitalism that serves to monitor and neutralize the threats grassroots organizers pose to the social reproduction of inequality (INCITE!, 2007). It is hard to argue that the history of nonprofits, and indeed of charitable giving more broadly, is *not* deeply connected to the wealthy and privileged sharing a small portion of their enormous amounts of capital, and allocating it according to their own wants and desires, in order to keep the public from demanding the government collect it in taxes for transformative purposes instead.

The lens of Transformative Symbolic Reality can be used to distinguish between nonprofit organizations that are creating the transformative contexts that lead to social change and those that merely perpetuate unjust social systems. But what would an organization that is enacting a transformative symbolic reality look like? A key component of a transformative symbolic reality is the ability for individuals to imagine new positive social realities through experiencing the alleviation of oppressive social forces. Sociologists often focus on how these forces fall along dimensions of race, gender, and class. Transformative spaces would therefore be ones that actively try to counter dominant forces that oppress people because of their biological sex, skin color, or economic background. A transformative symbolic reality for a Latinx researcher, for example, could be one in which they attend a conference given by community organizers all with a high school education, or one in which the same Latinx researcher attends a conference for trans and nonbinary scholars. Transformative Symbolic Reality pivots away from questioning what services are being provided or how many people are receiving them toward analyzing these dimensions of power and cultural exchange. Future research could explore quantifying these differences in more robust and representative ways.

Indeed, even within the educational field, which is perhaps more oriented toward transformative symbolic realities than other social service domains, there is a clear indication that not all nonprofits provide ecological contexts that challenge oppressive capitalist systems. One single mother whose busy college schedule prompted her to enroll her child in a nonprofit after-school program that had adapted a for-profit fee structure told me, "I just felt like it would be a good learning experience [for my daughter] and a good breaking-out-of-her-shell experience." But because of a perceived lack of care from the organization about her desire for educationally and socially stimulating programming, this mother struggled with her decision: "I'm starting to not feel like that so much now. I'm starting to feel like maybe this was a really bad idea, and I already started my semester, and I can't wait to get out of school now." Even though a nonprofit organization offered the program at below-market costs, it was enacting a social reality more aligned with market logics and based on bare-minimum childcare – not a transformative one in which each child would receive the investments they need to learn and thrive. In short, this after-school care provider failed to realize the second phase in the formation of transformative symbolic realities and ended up being judged as less adequate by parents because of it. Further research could investigate the necessary and sufficient conditions that must align to ensure the creation of transformative symbolic realities in these organizational spaces.

Many questions remain regarding the application of Transformative Symbolic Reality to the nonprofit sector and beyond. Conceptually, applying Transformative Symbolic Reality in a globalized context may further clarify its usefulness. Is there any one social reality that could be said to result from a set of global symbolic principles we all share? In a globalizing world, through what avenues can individuals and organizations in one country manipulate social realities in contrast to the mechanisms at play for individuals from other national and cultural contexts? If governmental or international systems are interested in regulating and defining the nonprofit sector, are they capable of also managing, controlling, or directing the kinds of social realities that organizations can enact? There is considerable evidence for the fact that the closer organizations become to their private or public counterparts, the less transformative and more hegemonic their social realities are (Arena, 2012; Girei, 2016; King, 2006). We can therefore investigate and evaluate governmental policies, and individual organizations, according to how they navigate the line between creating truly transformative symbolic spaces and conducting business-as-usual, from both a local and global perspective.

Methodologically, a logical next step is constructing measures of transformative symbolic reality that could be used to empirically observe and evaluate social spaces. Such measures are already being developed for the systematic social observation of civic or equitable activity within and outside of the classroom (Baggetta & Bredenkamp, 2019). I would also consider exploring what measures of ecological contexts exist within educational studies or in neighborhood research. In qualitative data collection efforts on the ground, I would encourage techniques like ripple-effect mapping that are well suited to capturing down-stream effects of community interventions (Emery et al., 2015).

Theoretically, however, is where we find the more perplexing questions. How would we conceptualize and classify social realities that actively attempt to marginalize or create inequities? Is the apparent connection between professionalization and incorporation into the Nonprofit Industrial Complex a result of declining transformative symbolic reality within an organization over time, or was it never there to begin with? If the ability for the nonprofit sector to create transformative symbolic realities is dependent on creating novel and meaningful social connections and experiences, are evaluations of the sector that reflect dominant hegemonic concerns, such as test scores or financial efficiencies, missing the mark? Are some organizational fields more inclined to transformative symbolic realities than others? What are the implications for Transformative Symbolic Reality in other interesting domains such as psychology, public administration, and social work?

In this chapter, I introduced the theory of Transformative Symbolic Reality and applied it to the nonprofit sector. I provided some observational evidence of the importance of transformative symbolic reality in setting the stage for individual and collective social change. In so doing, I hope to redirect efforts away from positioning the nonprofit sector as either necessary services or capitalist tools toward a better understanding of how nonprofit organizations can effectively participate in long-term transformative social processes.

References

Alexander, K. L., Entwisle, D. R., & Olson, L. S. (2014). *The long shadow: Family background, disadvantaged urban youth, and the transition to adulthood. Rose Series in Sociology*. Russell Sage Foundation.

Andrews, F. M., & Withey, S. B. (2012). *Social indicators of well-being: Americans' perceptions of life quality*. Springer Science & Business Media.

Anheier, H. K. (2014). *Nonprofit organizations: Theory, management, policy* (2nd ed.). Routledge.

Arena, J. (2012). *Driven from New Orleans: How nonprofits betray public housing and promote privatization*. University of Minnesota Press.

Baggetta, M., & Bredenkamp, D. M. (2019). Systematic social observation in the study of civil society organizations. *Sociological Methods & Research*, *50*(4), 1694–1724. doi.org/10.1177/0049124119826148

Barman, E. (2016). *Caring capitalism: The meaning and measure of social value*. Cambridge University Press.

Bornstein, D. (2007). *How to change the world: Social entrepreneurs and the power of new ideas*. Oxford University Press.

Campbell, D. E., & Wolbrecht, C. (2006). See Jane run: Women politicians as role models for adolescents. *The Journal of Politics*, *68*(2), 233–247.

Charon, J. M. (2010). *Symbolic interactionism: An introduction, an interpretation, an integration*. Pearson College Division.

Cheng, Y. (2019). Exploring the role of nonprofits in public service provision: Moving from coproduction to cogovernance. *Public Administration Review*, *79*(2), 203–214.

Clotfelter, C. T., & Ehrlich, T. (Eds.). (1999). *Philanthropy and the nonprofit sector in a changing America*. Indiana University Press.

Collins, P. H. (1990). Black feminist thought in the matrix of domination. *Black Feminist Thought: Knowledge, Consciousness, and the Politics of Empowerment*, *138*(1990), 221–238.

Collins, P. H. (2010). The new politics of community. *American Sociological Review*, *75*(1), 7–30. doi.org/10.1177/0003122410363293

Currie, J., Neidell, M., & Schmieder, J. F. (2009). Air pollution and infant health: Lessons from New Jersey. *Journal of Health Economics*, *28*(3), 688–703.

Deza, M., Maclean, J. C., & Solomon, K. T. (2020). Local access to mental healthcare and crime. National Bureau of Economic Research Working Paper Series, www.nber.org/papers/w27619.pdf

Duncan, G. J., & Magnuson, K. (2013). Investing in preschool programs. *The Journal of Economic Perspectives*, *27*(2), 109–131. doi.org/10.1257/jep.27.2.109

Duncan, G. J., & Murnane, R. J. (2011). *Whither opportunity? Rising inequality, schools, and children's life chances*. Russell Sage Foundation.

Ellington, R. M., & Frederick, R. (2010). Black high achieving undergraduate mathematics majors discuss success and persistence in mathematics. *Negro Educational Review*, *61*(1–4), 61–84.

Emery, M., Higgins, L., Chazdon, S., & Hansen, D. (2015). Using ripple effect mapping to evaluate program impact: Choosing or combining the methods that work best for you. *Journal of Extension*, *53*(2). Article 28. https://tigerprints.clemson.edu/joe/vol53/iss2/28

Fleishman, J. L. (2007). *The foundation: A great American secret; How private wealth is changing the world* (1st ed.). Public Affairs.

Flynn, P., & Hodgkinson, V. A. (2013). *Measuring the impact of the nonprofit sector*. Springer Science & Business Media.

Frumkin, P. (2009). *On being Nonprofit: A conceptual and policy primer*. Harvard University Press.

Girei, E. (2016). NGOs, management and development: Harnessing counter-hegemonic possibilities. *Organization Studies*, *37*(2), 193–212. doi.org/10.1177/0170840615604504

Hatzenbuehler, M. L., McLaughlin, K. A., Keyes, K. M., & Hasin, D. S. (2010). The impact of institutional discrimination on psychiatric disorders in lesbian, gay, and bisexual populations: A prospective study. *American Journal of Public Health*, *100*(3), 452–459.

Herman-Kinney, N. J., & Reynolds, L. T. (2003). *Handbook of symbolic interactionism*. AltaMira.

INCITE! Women of Color Against Violence. (2007). *The revolution will not be funded: Beyond the non-profit industrial complex*. South End Press.

Katre, A., & Salipante, P. (2012). Start-up social ventures: Blending fine-grained behaviors from two institutions for entrepreneurial success. *Entrepreneurship Theory and Practice*, *36*(5), 967–994. doi.org/10.1111/j.1540-6520.2012.00536.x

King, S. (2006). *Pink ribbons, Inc: Breast cancer and the politics of philanthropy*. University of Minnesota Press.

Kivel, P. (2007). Social service or social change. In INCITE! (Ed.), *The revolution will not be funded: Beyond the non-profit industrial complex* (pp. 121–149). Duke University Press.
Koch, B. J., Galaskiewicz, J., & Pierson, A. (2015). The effect of networks on organizational missions. *Nonprofit and Voluntary Sector Quarterly*, *44*(3), 510–538.
Mills, C. W. (2000). *The sociological imagination*. Oxford University Press.
Morphew, C. C., & Hartley, M. (2006). Mission statements: A thematic analysis of rhetoric across institutional type. *The Journal of Higher Education*, *77*(3), 456–471.
Nelson, A. A., & Gazley, B. (2014). The rise of school-supporting nonprofits. *Education Finance and Policy*, *9*(4), 541–566. doi.org/10.1162/EDFP_a_00146
Nelson, I. A. (2017). *Why afterschool matters*. Rutgers Series in Childhood Studies. Rutgers University Press.
Paxton, P., & Ressler, R. W. (2018). Trust and participation in associations. In E. M. Uslaner (Ed.), *The Oxford handbook of social and political trust* (pp. 149–171). Oxford University Press.
Ray, V. (2019). A theory of racialized organizations. *American Sociological Review*, *84*(1), 26–53. doi.org/10.1177/0003122418822335
Ressler, R. W., Paxton, P., Velasco, K., Pivnick, L., Weiss, I., & Eichstaedt, J. C. (2021). Nonprofits: A public policy tool for the promotion of community subjective well-being. *Journal of Public Administration Research and Theory*, *31*(4), 822–838. doi.org/10.1093/jopart/muab010
Rosenbaum, J. E. (1978). The structure of opportunity in school. *Social Forces*, *57*(1), 236–256.
Salamon, L. M. (1987). Of market failure, voluntary failure, and third-party government: Toward a theory of government–nonprofit relations in the modern welfare state. *Journal of Voluntary Action Research*, *16*(1–2), 29–49.
Sharkey, P., Torrats-Espinosa, G., & Takyar, D. (2017). Community and the crime decline: The causal effect of local nonprofits on violent crime. *American Sociological Review*, *82*(6), 1214–1240. doi.org/10.1177/0003122417736289
Small, M. L. (2009). *Unanticipated gains: Origins of network inequality in everyday life*. Oxford University Press.
Smith, D. H. (1974). *Voluntary action research: 1974*. Voluntary Action Research Series. Lexington Books.
Taylor, L., Tan, A. X., Coyle, C. E., Ndumele, C., Rogan, E., Canavan, M., Curry, L. A., & Bradley, E. H. (2016). Leveraging the social determinants of health: What works? *PLOS ONE*, *11*(8), 1–20. doi.org/10.1371/journal.pone.0160217
Weisbrod, B. A. (1988). *The nonprofit economy*. Harvard University Press.

19 *Nonprofits as Distributors of Toll Goods*

EVA WITESMAN

Nonprofit organizations have long been identified in the United States as legal entities that meet certain requirements and provisions set forth in section 501 of the US tax code.[1] Though a formal nonprofit sector does not exist in many nations in the same legal form as it does in the United States, scholars have adopted "structural/operational" definitions of the nonprofit sector that capture the relevant characteristics of the US tax code when defining nonprofits for international comparisons (Abzug, 1999; Salamon & Anheier, 1992a, 1992b). The Johns Hopkins Comparative Nonprofit Sector Project was among the first to define the nonprofit sector as an international concept, and this definition has been one of the most ubiquitous since: "the non-profit sector is a set of organizations that are formally constituted; non-governmental in basic structure; self-governing; non-profit-distributing; and voluntary to some meaningful extent" (Salamon & Anheier, 1992b, p. 268).

While this definition is described by its authors as relying on sector characteristics rather than legal rules (which vary substantially internationally), it is nonetheless compatible with US tax law and defines a sector that largely shares those characteristics recognized by it (Salamon & Anheier, 1998). The most obvious references to US tax code are the requirement that nonprofits be "self-governing," referring to the legal requirement that nonprofit organizations be governed by boards, and that they be "non-profit-distributing," which refers to the non-distribution clause in US tax law that prevents nonprofits from distributing profits for the benefit of one or more private shareholders.

[1] This chapter and Figure 19.1 are adapted from a paper originally published in *Nonprofit and Voluntary Sector Quarterly* entitled "An Institutional Theory of the Nonprofit: Toll Goods and Voluntary Action." It is reprinted here (with adaptation) with permission from the publisher, SAGE. The input of Brenda Bushouse was essential in bringing this chapter to fruition.

Despite a coalescence around definitions of the nonprofit sector that identify and strengthen legalistic sectoral boundaries, individual firms and organizations within all three sectors (public, private, and nonprofit) seem to be evolving toward one another in a phenomenon known as the "blurring of the sectors" (Brody, 2003; Bromley & Meyer, 2014; Dees & Anderson, 2003; Eikenberry & Kluver, 2004; Ferris & Graddy, 1999). Where pursuit of the public interest and tackling of pervasive public challenges were once decidedly outside the purview of markets, public, private, and nonprofit organizations now appear to simultaneously value at least some of the same types of social objectives (Ben-Ner, 2002; Steen, 2008). At the same time, some nonprofit organizations have adopted revenue models that deeply tie them to government (Gazley, 2008; Guo, 2007; Lipsky & Smith, 1989; Saidel, 1991; Salamon, 1987; 2003), while others engage in social enterprise activities and fee-for-service models that resemble those in for-profit firms (Eikenberry & Kluver, 2004; Froelich, 1999; Weisbrod, 1997, 2000). This has led some economists to question the utility of nonprofit status as a legal distinction separate from private business or government or to promote additional legal designations (B-corps, S-corps and L3C's) that identify socially beneficial activities that occur outside the nonprofit sector (Ben-Ner, 2002; Grimm, 1999; Mayer & Ganahl, 2014; Weisbrod, 1997). New legal forms and changing sector boundaries raise questions about the necessity of the non-distribution constraint and board governance in identifying "nonprofit-type" socially oriented organizations.

In this chapter, I explore the role of the nonprofit sector in distributing toll goods, remedying a market failure often overlooked in the literature: the underconsumption of goods for which there is little cost to producers for allowing additional people to benefit, but for which the natural state of the good is exclusion. In this view, nonprofits serve a role in providing needed services to people who may otherwise not receive them, even though the goods are socially beneficial and create little marginal cost.

Various theories have evolved to justify the role and status of the nonprofit sector. The most prevalent of these is market failure/government failure theory. Market failure theory suggests specific circumstances in which markets do not operate efficiently, thus giving rise to government (Bator, 1958; Stiglitz, 1989; Weimer & Vining, 2005; Weisbrod, 1977). Government failure theory, in turn, suggests particular limitations of government action that lead to the rise of the nonprofit sector (Brinkerhoff & Brinkerhoff, 2002; Douglas, 1983, 2003; Weisbrod, 1977). Other nonprofit theories, notably voluntary failure theory (Salamon, 1987, 2003) and contract failure theory (Hansmann, 1980; Young, 2016), have supplemented, rather than supplanted, the traditional and ubiquitous market failure/government failure couplet.

The legalistic orientation of theories of nonprofit activity places constraints on the evolution of thought about the history, role, and potential of nonprofit-type activities in society. By focusing primarily on those characteristics of nonprofit activity that have been formalized in legal institutions, the development of theory has overlooked underlying sector-crossing, extralegal institutional characteristics that are both more descriptive of nonprofit-type activities and more theoretically useful (Abzug, 1999; DiMaggio & Anheier, 1990). In particular, sector-based theories of the nonprofit have had limited ability to describe, predict, and explain the following phenomena:

- **Informal organizations** and interactions among members of society when not part of formally recognized groups or legal entities (Abzug, 1999; Ferris & Graddy, 1999; Gronbjerg et al., 2010; Smith, 1975, 1997; Van Til, 2000).
- **International contexts** where nonprofit status does not formally exist as part of the legal structure so organizations may not meet definitional requirements based on characteristics derived from the US tax code (Salamon & Anheier, 1998; Seibel, 1990).
- **Sector-blurring** (Brody, 2003; Bromley & Meyer, 2014; Child, 2015; Dees & Anderson, 2003; Eikenberry & Kluver, 2004; Ferris & Graddy, 1999) in which activities carried out in the public and private (for-profit) sectors seem to better cohere with the nature and culture of nonprofit activity (i.e., social business, social entrepreneurship, corporate social responsibility, corporate philanthropy, government grant making, etc.) and vice versa.
- **The origin of nonprofit-type activity.** Current nonprofit theory does not explain the origin of the nonprofit sector in a manner that is consistent with the development and role of actual organizations and social interactions in history (Brody, 1996b; Morris, 2000; Salamon, 1987). Likewise, they do not provide meaningful predictions if and when nonprofit-type activity would be expected to spontaneously occur.

- **The role of nonprofit-type activity,** particularly in being used to solve pervasive social problems and make goods and services available to populations that have been underserved by public and private institutions (Amendola et al., 2011; Lipsky & Smith, 1989; Steinberg & Weisbrod, 1998, 2005).

19.1 An Institutional Perspective on Nonprofits

This chapter proposes a theory of the nonprofit based on a definition of nonprofit-type activity that is institutional rather than sectoral or legalistic. Nonprofit-type institutions may usefully be defined as involving (1) voluntary (as opposed to coercive) exchanges between parties, and (2) separation of the roles of payer and consumer, making them redistributive (as opposed to consumptive) in nature. It is further proposed that such an institutional arrangement is particularly suited to distributing goods that are excludable and non-subtractable – toll goods. In answer to the questions raised in this volume (i.e., what is the nonprofit sector and why does it exist), I posit that the nonprofit sector includes institutions in which the interactions are voluntary and the consumer is not the same as the payer (redistributive). I suggest that such institutions ought to exist (i.e., we should expect to see them with greater frequency *and* prefer them to be present) in situations where a desirable good is both inexhaustible (is not exhausted when it is consumed) and excludable (has one or more characteristics preventing additional people from consuming it).

This approach to defining nonprofit-type activity allows for the examination of institutionally similar activities regardless of sector in order to refine our preexisting theories of nonprofit-type activity to better reflect the full range and history of such activity and to identify situations in which we might expect nonprofit-type activity to evolve in response to distributional problems encountered in society. In particular, this theory suggests reasons we might expect nonprofit activity to evolve even in the absence of market and government institutions in response to the need to distribute a particular class of goods, suggesting a parallel – not serial – evolution of the sectors.

This chapter views sectors and institutions as two different types of organizing principles. In the sector view, the nonprofit sector is therefore usefully and predominantly defined according to characteristics identical or similar to the legal requirements set forth in section 501 of the US tax code. Under this sector-based approach, social enterprises that are incorporated as private, for-profit businesses are not considered part of the nonprofit sector no matter how much their activities may resemble those of nonprofit sector organizations. Likewise, such a definition does not include the so-called nonprofit "dark matter" that includes both informal voluntary activity and formal activity that occurs without registration with a government entity (Gronbjerg et al., 2010; Smith, 1997; Van Til, 2000).

Alternatively, Elinor Ostrom defines institutions as "the prescriptions that humans use to organize all forms of repetitive and structured interactions including those within families, neighborhoods, markets, firms, sports leagues, churches, private associations, and governments at all scales" (Ostrom, 2005, p. 3). These prescriptions are comprised of rules, norms, and strategies employed by individuals and organizations to achieve a wide variety of individual and group objectives. To observe nonprofit institutions, therefore, we are interested in what types of interactions are repetitively employed in what we would collectively identify as "nonprofit-type" activities, and when such interactions might be prescribed.

This distinction between sectors and institutions is not trivial. Though the institutional lens has been previously used to examine individual nonprofit organizations or service areas (Bushouse, 1999; Cooney, 2006; Feeney, 1997; Newhouse, 1970), only a very few nonprofit theorists suggest origins of nonprofit organization as a whole based on principles of institutional theory outside of the traditional economic market failure/government failure couplet (notable exceptions include Kramer, 2000, Ben-Ner, 2002, and Amendola et al., 2011). This means that while current sector theory may provide powerful narratives for the protections, restrictions, and incentives legally associated with nonprofit status, it does little to explain how and why people voluntarily organize themselves to carry out nonprofit-type activities even when no such legal protections, restrictions, and incentives exist (Brody, 1996a). Without institutions, nonprofits are a mere figment of our legal imagination.

Empirically, sector alone appears largely insufficient to make meaningful distinctions between organizations. In many cases, research has demonstrated that even on social outcome dimensions, sector does not predict important differences in performance (Heinrich, 2003;

Leviten-Reid, 2010; Luksetich et al., 2000; Rosenau & Linder, 2003; Witesman & Fernandez, 2013), management (Moore, 2000), purpose (Child et al., 2014), or even public perception (Handy et al., 2010). Organizational form appears to be more an artifact of tax regulations than truly descriptive of unique organizational characteristics, motivations, functions, or even history (Brody, 1996a, 1996b). Given their failure to identify unique characteristics of nonprofits in the present, legalistic and sector-based definitions of economic activity seem inadequate to provide clear hypotheses about how nonprofits may evolve in the future.

New institutional economic theory – closely related to political economy and the public choice movement – focuses largely on the rules, norms, and strategies that human beings use to deal with the presence of certain biophysical characteristics of the world in which we live (Ostrom, 2005). In particular, these rules, norms, and strategies generally provide some mechanism for distributing goods within and/or across groups. It is from this perspective that this chapter seeks to enhance our understanding of nonprofit-type activity through propositions about the nature of nonprofit institutions – independent of sector.

19.1.1 Institutional Characteristics of Nonprofit-Type Activity

This chapter proposes a pair of criteria for defining nonprofit-type institutions. These criteria are not entirely novel; in fact, both have been made in various forms previously by nonprofit theorists (Ben-Zion & Spiegel, 1983; Hansmann, 1980; Salamon, 1999; Sefton & Steinberg, 1996; Sen, 1993; Steinberg, 1987). The contribution of this chapter is to identify these criteria as the two *central* characteristics of nonprofit-type activity, to justify their utility in defining the nature of nonprofit institutions, and to expand on their implications for the nature and role of nonprofit-type activity for distributing goods in society irrespective of sector.

19.1.1.1 Coercion vs. Voluntary Action

The ability of governments to levy sanctions and thus coerce citizens to pay for goods is one of the key institutional differences between both governments and nonprofits (Baumol, 1952; Salamon, 1999), and governments and private-market institutions (Friedman & Friedman, 1980). Whereas government relies heavily on its coercive power to levy taxes for the funding of its programs, nonprofits and private organizations rely on voluntary exchanges (Friedman & Friedman, 1980; Frumkin, 2002; Sen, 1993). When distinguishing between types of institutions, we should be particularly interested in whether or not a central authority (frequently – but not necessarily – government) has the coercive power to assign the roles of payer (the individual who pays for the good) and consumer (the person who derives direct value from the good) in a given exchange.

An institution is said to include the trait of coercion if an authority is responsible for determining (a) who will pay for goods or services and (b) who may receive goods or services. As a condition of this coercive power, the central authority should have the ability to levy sanctions on payers who do not pay, and on individuals who consume more or less than their allotted share. If a central authority does not have the power or authority to assign and enforce the roles of payer and consumer, or if such coercion is unnecessary, then the institutional type is said to be "voluntary." In a voluntary exchange, individuals determine for themselves whether they will assume the role(s) of payer and/or consumer. This leads to our first definitional criterion for nonprofit institutions, the *voluntary criterion*. Nonprofit-type institutions involve voluntary exchanges in which neither payers nor consumers are coerced by an authority to participate. Individuals determine for themselves whether they will assume the role(s) of payer and/or consumer.

Clearly, the voluntary criterion is insufficient by itself to define nonprofit-type institutions, particularly because it does not distinguish nonprofit activity from other exchanges that occur voluntarily in private markets (i.e., for-profit institutional arrangements). Thus, an additional condition must be met to adequately distinguish nonprofit institutions from their for-profit counterparts.

19.1.1.2 Consumption vs. Redistribution

Among the core activities carried out by institutional actors are payment for the production/provision of the good and consumption of the good (Ostrom, 2005). In typical private-market exchanges, the individuals who pay for the good are also generally the consumers of the good. We will call such arrangements "consumptive." There are two distinct types of consumptive arrangements. The first is when all citizens are both payers and consumers (e.g., all citizens pay taxes for a certain benefit and all receive that benefit), and the second is when citizens are payers if and only if they are also the consumers (i.e., private-market exchanges). In either case, consumers "get what they pay for" in such institutional arrangements.

In contrast, however, some institutions are arranged such that the payer relinquishes consumption of the good to another party, separating the roles of payer and consumer. Such an arrangement is termed redistributive. Separation of the roles of payer and consumer is central to both redistributive public policy (Lowi, 1979; Sefton, 2008) and the practice of donative redistribution (Hansmann, 1980; Salamon, 1999). In governments, taxpayers must frequently pay for public services under threat of sanction even if they are not beneficiaries of those services (Sefton, 2008). In nonprofit-type activities, donors frequently pay for services voluntarily in order to promote the availability of services to others and to express their own social preferences and values (Ben-Zion & Spiegel, 1983; Sefton & Steinberg, 1996; Steinberg, 1987).

Redistribution can take any of three forms. Either (1) the person who pays for the good never consumes it but allows one or more others to consume the good; (2) the person who pays for the good consumes the good and then relinquishes his or her ownership of the good to one or more others so that they may derive value from the good; or (3) the person who pays for the good consumes the good in conjunction with others who simultaneously draw value from it. In each of these cases, the individual who pays for the good is not the sole beneficiary of the good (or may not be a beneficiary of the good at all), and in each case, someone other than the payer derives value from the good. This redistribution of goods distinguishes nonprofit-type activities both from consumptive government regimes and also from pure private interactions, in which the purchaser of the good is the sole beneficiary.

Thus, in addition to the voluntary criterion, we define nonprofit institutions as those containing some form of redistribution from payer to consumer: the *redistributive criterion*. Nonprofit-type institutions involve redistribution, meaning that the individual who pays for the good is not the (sole) beneficiary of the good.

These two dimensions – coercion vs. voluntary action and consumption vs. redistribution – can be used to define key differences between the primary macro-institutions of society using a two-by-two matrix as represented by the top and left elements in Figure 19.1.

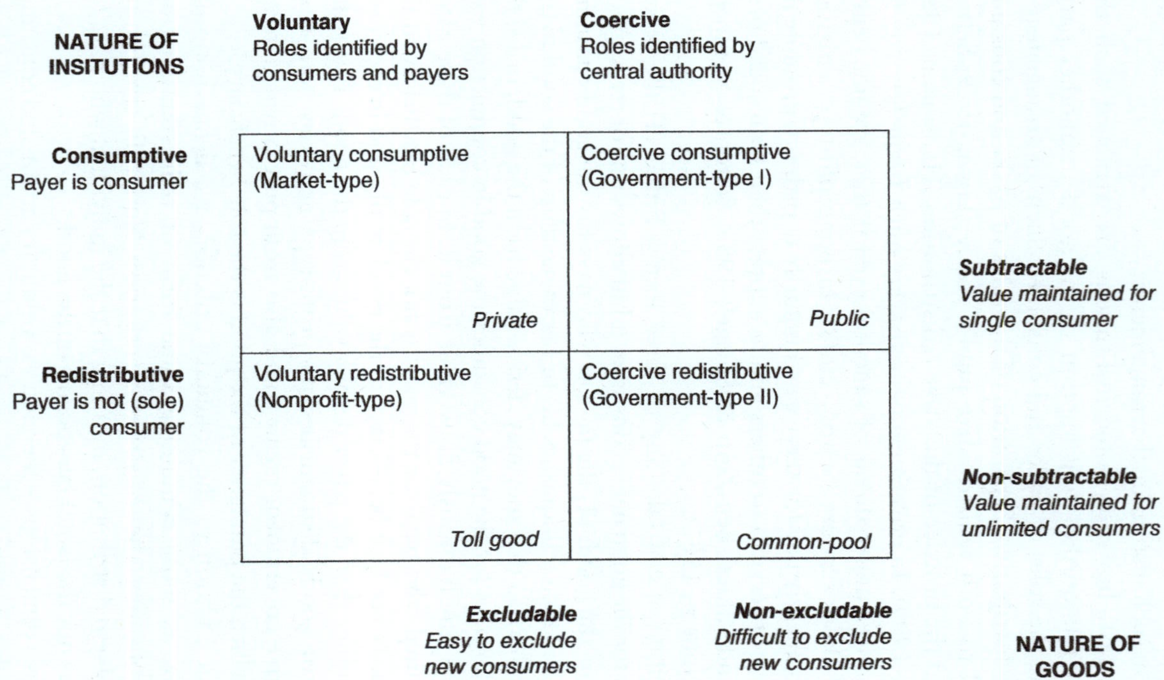

Figure 19.1 Nature of goods and nature of institutions

Exchanges that are both voluntary and consumptive in nature are identified as "market-type" arrangements, and are consistent with a free market economy in which individuals maximize personal utility. The use of a central authority to coerce either payment for goods or consumption (or nonconsumption) of goods is viewed as a "government-type" interaction. Government-type interactions are further divided into two types: those that do not involve redistribution (government-type I) and those that do (government-type II). Finally, voluntary and redistributive exchanges are identified as nonprofit-type activities.

Invoking these two criteria for nonprofit institutions will create different boundaries around nonprofit-type activity than do legalistic sector criteria. A legally recognized nonprofit organization or government agency could sell services using a fee-for-service model, in which consumers choose to purchase them and no redistribution would occur (e.g., museum souvenir shops, nonprofit sale of fairly traded goods, sale of postal products and services). Such a model would involve a voluntary consumptive institutional arrangement, or market-type exchange. Likewise, a government agency or for-profit organization could solicit donations to support a service it wanted to provide (e.g., donations to support a public park of for-profit hospital). Because donors voluntarily provide funding for benefits that accrue to others, this would describe a nonprofit-type or voluntary redistributive institutional arrangement, even though the organizations involved would be considered outside the formal "nonprofit sector."

Institutional rules, norms and strategies do not develop in a vacuum. Instead, they generally evolve in response to specific challenges posed by the biophysical world (Bromley & Meyer, 2014; Ostrom, 2003, 2005). Several scholars (Ben-Ner, 2002; Billis & Glennerster, 1998; Bushouse, 1999; Ferris & Graddy, 1999; Kingma, 2003; Weisbrod, 1977) have noted the need for distributing specific types of goods as a defining reason for the presence of the nonprofit sector.

One useful approach to understanding the nature of goods and their inherent relationship to the development of distribution mechanisms is a matrix describing their subtractability and excludability. Ostrom and Ostrom proposed this framework in 1977 based on the work of Samuelson (1954) and Olson (1965). Excludability is characterized by a situation in which it is "costly to exclude individuals from enjoying benefits" (Ostrom, 2005, p. 24). This chapter will employ the following operational test for "costly" vs. "not costly" exclusion: If the *default position* of a good is exclusion – that is, a proprietor must take some form of positive action in order to make the good available to others – then it is said to be "excludable" because the positive action required to share the good with others would impose a cost.

For excludable goods, this cost associated with inclusion may create a barrier to the distribution of some goods even though this might otherwise be desirable. This excludability problem is a hallmark of some persistent issues in society: There are goods that we want to make available to more people, but there are high associated costs. Such goods include intangibles such as health, education, job skills, and well-being; they also include tangible goods such as housing and vaccines.

According to the nature of goods framework, subtractability is "when the use of a flow of [goods or] services by one individual subtracts from what is available to others" (Ostrom, 2005, p. 25). A good is subtractable if consumption of that good by one person substantively diminishes the value of the good either for other simultaneous consumers or for subsequent consumers. This concept is not perfectly binary, but rather exists on a scale from perfectly subtractable to perfectly non-subtractable. A good is perfectly subtractable if consumption of the good completely precludes any value from being derived by any other potential consumer. On the other hand, a good is perfectly non-subtractable when an unlimited number of consumers can derive the whole value of the good either simultaneously or serially. Between these extremes lie cases in which use of a good by one consumer diminishes – but does not preclude – the value that can be derived by others.

The lower and right elements of Figure 19.1 create a two-by-two matrix describing the excludability and subtractability of goods. Excludable and subtractable goods are "private" goods, non-excludable and non-subtractable goods are "public" goods, excludable and non-subtractable goods are "toll goods," and non-excludable and subtractable goods are "common-pool resources." Each type of good is associated with its own distributional challenges. These include challenges in encouraging payment for public goods (the "free-rider" problem), preventing over-consumption of common-pool resources (the "tragedy of the commons"), and, in the case of publicly desirable toll goods, the problem of exclusion.

19.2 Nature of Goods and Nature of Institutions

There is a logic to the association of institutional arrangements with specific types of goods. Because each type of good may be associated with its own unique distributional challenges, the evolution of institutions surrounding the distribution of each type of good is likely to aim at ameliorating those challenges (Ostrom, 2005). In general, non-excludability of goods provides a potential justification for coercive institutional regimes, excludable goods are suited to distribution through voluntary regimes, subtractable goods can be logically associated with consumptive regimes, and non-subtractable goods are naturally suited to redistributive regimes.

Where goods are non-excludable, a free-rider problem may exist that markets and other voluntary arrangements are ill-equipped to manage. Because it is difficult for proprietors of non-excludable goods to prevent others from consuming them (creating a free-rider problem for public goods and over-consumption for common-pool resources), use of a central authority with coercive power may be valuable for assigning the roles of payer and consumer (Brennan & Buchanan, 1980; Stoker, 1998). This "failure" of market-type institutions to usefully distribute non-excludable goods is one common justification for the presence of government-type institutions (Bator, 1958; Stiglitz, 1989; Weimer & Vining, 2005; Weisbrod, 1977). Where goods are non-excludable, we can expect the evolution of coercive institutions to identify and enforce the roles of payer and consumer in order to protect against free-riding and over-consumption.

When goods are excludable, a central authority is not necessary for identifying the roles of payer and consumer because such roles are self-enforceable. In other words, if a good is excludable, it is possible for the proprietor of the good to prevent others from consuming it – or to require payment for it in the case of exchange – so a central authority is not as necessary (Bushouse, 1999). For excludable goods, voluntary institutional arrangements allow individuals to identify for themselves how much they value a good and to make exchanges accordingly.

Subtractable goods are naturally suited to consumptive institutional regimes. Because the value of subtractable goods decreases or disappears upon consumption, regimes in which the people who pay for the good also consume the good are logical because basic economic theories of the rational actor assume that a person will only pay for a good if they derive some value from it. While exceptions to this "self-interested, rational actor" hypothesis will be discussed later, traditional market theory presumes that consumptive regimes evolve in response to the distribution of subtractable goods on the basis that it is both logical and equitable that people who value a good should be able to consume it upon payment in an appropriate formal exchange (Weimer & Vining, 2005).

When a good is non-subtractable, a proprietor may consume the good without diminishing its value. Once the good is paid for, therefore, additional consumers may consume the good without detracting from the proprietor's ability to derive value from the good. The proprietor may derive as much value as she prefers, and because the good is non-subtractable, a Pareto-improving solution would be to allow others to benefit from the good as well. Thus, non-subtractable goods are naturally suited to redistributive regimes, since adding more beneficiaries without detracting value from the proprietor is Pareto-improving. In the words of Powell and Steinberg, allowing additional consumers access to such goods would "help them, hurt no one, and consume no additional scarce resources" (2006, p. 121).

We can extend the logic of the preceding paragraphs to determine the institutional characteristics we might expect to evolve in response to each of the four types of goods identified by the nature-of-goods framework. Namely, we would expect market-type regimes to evolve in response to the distributional characteristics of private goods, government-type regimes to evolve in response to the distributional characteristics of both public goods and common-pool resources, and voluntary redistributive (nonprofit-type) regimes to evolve in response to the distributional characteristics associated with toll goods. To demonstrate these "institutional matches," the nature-of-goods framework and institutional characteristics are overlaid into the same matrix in Figure 19.1.

This set of proposed matches between the nature-of-goods and institutional regimes suggests the possibility that the primary macro-institutions of society – governments, markets, and nonprofit-type institutions – evolved in parallel rather than in sequence, each in response to the distributional characteristics and constraints of a different set of goods. While this observation in no way negates the contributions of market failure, government failure, and other major theories contributing to our conception of nonprofit theory, it does suggest a paradigmatic shift in how these theories can and should be understood. Centrally, markets are not appropriately viewed as the dominant, original, or primary distributional mechanism for all goods. Neither are government or nonprofit institutions secondary institutions in any sense. Each type of institution has its own independent rationale for existence.

These observations suggest explanations for the significant role of churches and other nonprofit-type organizations throughout the history of society, and their largely parallel development with both market institutions and the state (Morris, 2000). They also suggest predictions about the circumstances in which nonprofit-type activity (voluntary redistributive exchange) would be both predicted and prescribed: such would be the case whenever the good to be distributed could be appropriately described as both excludable and non-subtractable – a toll good.

Perhaps the most common formulation and cohesive expression of toll goods theory is "club theory," including research that has examined aspects of the nonprofit sector from this perspective (Bushouse, 1999, 2011; Kushner & King, 1994). Club theory and the more general notion of toll goods differ in that for many toll goods, exclusion is the problem associated with the distribution of goods rather than a purported solution (Bushouse, 1999, 2011; Kennedy, 1990; Schweik at al., 2011). While traditional club theory suggests that the primary problem associated with clubs is congestion or crowding (Reiter & Weichenrieder, 1999; Sandler & Tschirhart, 1997), new club theory turns this idea on its head. Potoski and Prakash suggest that, rather than making other members of clubs worse off, "one firm's membership can often *enhance* the value that other members receive" (Potoski & Prakash, 2009, pp. 2–3, emphasis added). This suggests that, for beneficial toll goods, the natural distributional problem is that, because of their excludability, they are by default inaccessible to members of the relevant public who might benefit from them. Powell and Steinberg (2006) term this distributional inefficiency an "overexclusion market failure."

If we recognize that the main problem with distributing toll goods is the need to overcome their de facto state of exclusion, we can work to devise institutional mechanisms to overcome the barriers to inclusion (Bushouse, 1999). Among these mechanisms may be the employment of voluntary redistributive institutions. Rather than central institutions with coercive power being the primary distributors of such goods, efficiencies may be found in decentralizing the responsibility for the distribution of goods, allowing individuals and firms to voluntarily disseminate or redistribute toll goods.

19.3 Conclusions

In this chapter, it has been proposed that toll goods are naturally suited to distribution through voluntary redistributive (nonprofit-type) institutions. But clearly, it is not the case that *all* toll goods are distributed through nonprofit-type activity, or that toll goods are the only type of good that can be distributed in this way. In other words, the biconditional logic that *only* toll goods should be distributed by nonprofits and that nonprofits should *only* distribute toll goods is false. There are two primary reasons this is the case.

The first is that the approach of identifying "natural" matches between the nature of goods and specific characteristics of institutions relies heavily on an assumption of economic self-interest. In other words, we assume that actors will only pay for and value a good if they themselves can consume it. We know that this is not always the case

Second, institutions are dynamic, subject to sociological forces that allow for complex and unpredictable learning processes. People and organizations tasked with the distribution of specific goods may seek models and ideas from other organizations or sectors, and may innovate to identify new solutions to old distributional problems.

Though a main objective of this chapter is to suggest a natural match between toll goods and voluntary redistributive institutions, this is not to say that voluntary redistribution is without its problems. For example, voluntary regimes are subject to the idiosyncratic preferences of donors and consumers, and redistributive regimes are subject to significant information asymmetries.

The theory presented here suggests that nonprofit-type activity may be viewed as an institutional response to the existence of non-consumable goods for which exclusion is easy (and is possibly the default state) but not socially beneficial. This proposition suggests important revisions to our view of the relationships between government, markets, and the voluntary sector. Market failure theory, government failure theory, contract failure theory, and voluntary failure theory each contribute elements to the understanding presented here, but the present theory suggests revisions to – and connections between – each of these preceding theories.

One important theoretical contribution suggested by the institutional theory of nonprofits is that markets, government, and voluntary institutions are parallel rather than hierarchical, in contrast to the market-failure-leads-to-government-failure-leads-to-nonprofits narrative that has been so prevalent in the literature. Markets should only be considered the default institution when private goods are the subject of discussion. By extension, "market failure" suggests specific problems associated with the assumptions central to the distribution of private goods through market institutions, and "government failure" refers to problems associated with coercive regimes in distributing non-excludable goods. If these assumptions are broken – including assumptions about the nature of the good – inefficiencies may result.

Voluntary failure, then, should be extended to suggest the consequences inherent in relaxing the assumptions necessary to result in efficient distribution of toll goods through voluntary redistribution. This is a marked difference from its current construction, but potentially compatible with the intent of its author to correct both the "gross neglect of the nonprofit sector in most assessments of American social welfare policy" and to "acknowledge the significant and inherent shortcomings of voluntary organizations" (Salamon, 2003, p. 183).

A second major contribution of the institutional theory of nonprofits is that it suggests a rationale for the role of the nonprofit and voluntary sector even in informal settings or when markets and government institutions might be underdeveloped or in a significant state of flux, where other traditional theories of nonprofit and voluntary action have fallen short (Salamon & Anheier, 1998). Whereas market, government, and contract failure theories suggest that other key social institutions precede nonprofit and voluntary action, this institutional theory suggests circumstances in which we might expect to see the emergence of institutions that are characterized by voluntary redistribution. Where we see toll goods with marked overexclusion failures, we would expect to see voluntary redistributive regimes evolve in response.

Finally, perhaps the most important result from the theory presented here is the idea that the core problem associated with the distribution of desirable toll goods is overexclusion. This insight may provide greater traction in understanding what types of distributional solutions – including voluntary redistributive regimes – may work to overcome the exclusion barrier in order to raise the quality of life for all members of society.

References

Abzug, R. (1999). The nonprofit sector and the informal sector: A theoretical perspective. *Voluntas: International Journal of Voluntary and Nonprofit Organizations*, *10*(2), 131–149.

Amendola, A., Garofalo, M. R., & Nese, A. (2011). Is the third sector an emerging economic institution? Social preferences versus poverty traps. *Nonprofit and Voluntary Sector Quarterly*, *40*(5), 850–872.

Bator, F. M. (1958). The anatomy of market failure. *The Quarterly Journal of Economics*, *72*(3), 351–379.

Baumol, W. J. (1952). *Welfare economics and the theory of the state*. Harvard University Press.

Ben-Ner, A. (2002). The shifting boundaries of the mixed economy and the future of the nonprofit sector. *Annals of Public and Cooperative Economics*, *73*(1), 5–40.

Ben-Zion, U., & Spiegel, U. (1983). Philanthropic motives and contribution policy. *Public Choice*, *40*(2), 117–133.

Billis, D., & Glennerster, H. (1998). Human services and the voluntary sector: Towards a theory of comparative advantage. *Journal of Social policy*, *27*(01), 79–98.

Brennan, G., & Buchanan, J. M. (1980). *The power to tax: Analytic foundations of a fiscal constitution*. Cambridge University Press.

Brinkerhoff, J. M., & Brinkerhoff, D. W. (2002). Government–nonprofit relations in comparative perspective: Evolution, themes and new directions. *Public Administration and Development*, *22*(1), 3–18.

Brody, E. (1996a). Agents without principals: The economic convergence of the nonprofit and for-profit organizational forms. *New York Law School Law Review*, *40*(3), 547–536.

Brody, E. (1996b). Institutional dissonance in the nonprofit sector. *Villanova Law Review*, *41*(2), 433.

Brody, E. (2003). Are nonprofit organizations different? In H. K. Anheier & A. Ben-Ner (Eds.), *The study of the nonprofit enterprise* (pp. 239–244). Kluwer Academic/Plenum Publishers.

Bromley, P., & Meyer, J. W. (2014). "They are all organizations": The cultural roots of blurring between the nonprofit, business, and government sectors. *Administration & Society*, 0095399714548268.

Bushouse, B. K. (1999). *The mixed economy of child care: An institutional analysis of nonprofit, for-profit, and public enterprises* [Doctoral dissertation]. Retrieved from http://search.proquest.com/docview/304532864?accountid=4488.

Bushouse, B. K. (2011). Governance structures: Using IAD to understand variation in service delivery for club goods with information asymmetry. *Policy Studies Journal*, *39*(1), 105–119.

Child, C. (2015). Tip of the iceberg the nonprofit underpinnings of for-profit social enterprise. *Nonprofit and Voluntary Sector Quarterly*, 0899764015572901.
Child, C., Witesman, E. M., & Braudt, D. B. (2014). Sector choice: How fair trade entrepreneurs choose between nonprofit and for-profit forms. *Nonprofit and Voluntary Sector Quarterly*, 0899764014542688.
Cooney, K. (2006). The institutional and technical structuring of nonprofit ventures: Case study of a US hybrid organization caught between two fields. *Voluntas: International Journal of Voluntary and Nonprofit Organizations*, *17*(2), 137–155.
Dees, J. G., & Anderson, B. B. (2003). Sector-bending: Blurring lines between nonprofit and for-profit. *Society*, *40*(4), 16–27.
Douglas, J. A. (1983). *Why charity? The case for a third sector*. Sage Publications.
Douglas, J. A. (2003). Political theories of nonprofit organization. In W. W. Powell & R. Steinberg (Eds.), *The nonprofit sector: A research handbook* (pp. 43–54). Yale University Press.
Eikenberry, A. M., & Kluver, J. D. (2004). The marketization of the nonprofit sector: Civil society at risk? *Public Administration Review*, *64*(2), 132–140.
Feeney, S. (1997). Shifting the prism: Case explications of institutional analysis in nonprofit organizations. *Nonprofit and Voluntary Sector Quarterly*, *26*(4), 489–508.
Ferris, J. M., & Graddy, E. (1999). The role of the nonprofit sector in a self-governing society: A view from the United States. *Voluntas: International Journal of Voluntary and Nonprofit Organizations*, *9*(2), 137–151.
Friedman, M., & Friedman, R. (1980). *Free to choose*. Secker and Warburg.
Froelich, K. A. (1999). Diversification of revenue strategies: Evolving resource dependence in nonprofit organizations. *Nonprofit and Voluntary Sector Quarterly*, *28*(3), 246–268.
Frumkin, P. (2002). *On being nonprofit: A conceptual and policy primer*. Harvard University Press.
Gazley, B. (2008). Beyond the contract: The scope and nature of informal government–nonprofit partnerships. *Public Administration Review*, *68*(1), 141–154.
Grimm, Jr., R. T. (1999). Reforming property tax exemption policy in the nonprofit sector: Commercialism, collective goods, and the donative theory. *Nonprofit Management and Leadership*, *9*(3), 241–259.
Grønbjerg, K. A., Liu, H. K., & Pollak, T. H. (2010). Incorporated but not IRS-registered: Exploring the (dark) grey fringes of the nonprofit universe. *Nonprofit and Voluntary Sector Quarterly*, *39*(5), 925–945.
Guo, C. (2007). When government becomes the principal philanthropist: The effects of public funding on patterns of nonprofit governance. *Public Administration Review*, *67*(3), 458–473.

Handy, F., Seto, S., Wakaruk, A., Mersey, B. A., Mejia, A., & Copeland, L. (2010). The discerning consumer: Is nonprofit status a factor? *Nonprofit and Voluntary Sector Quarterly*, *39*(5), 866–883.

Hansmann, H. B. (1980). The role of nonprofit enterprise. *The Yale Law Journal*, *89*(5), 835–901.

Heinrich, C. J. (2003). Organizational form and performance: An empirical investigation of nonprofit and for-profit job-training service providers. *Journal of Policy Analysis and Management*, *19*(2), 233–261.

Kennedy, P. W. (1990). The market provision of club goods in the presence of scale economies. *Economica*, *57*(228), 515–524.

Kingma, B. R. (2003). Public good theories of the nonprofit sector. In H. K. Anheier & A. Ben-Ner (Eds.), *The study of the nonprofit enterprise* (pp. 53–65). Kluwer Academic/Plenum Publishers.

Kramer, R. M. (2000). A third sector in the third millennium? *Voluntas: International Journal of Voluntary and Nonprofit Organizations*, *11*(1), 1–23.

Kushner, R., & King, A. E. (1994). Performing arts as a club good: Evidence from a nonprofit organization. *Journal of Cultural Economics*, *18*(1), 15–28.

Leviten-Reid, E. (2010). Organizational form, parental involvement, and quality of care in child day care centers. *Nonprofit and Voluntary Sector Quarterly, 41*(1), *36–57*.

Lipsky, M., & Smith, S. R. (1989). Nonprofit organizations, government, and the welfare state. *Political Science Quarterly*, *104*(4), 625–648.

Lowi, T. J. (1979). *The end of liberalism*. Norton.

Luksetich, W., Edwards, M., & Carroll, T. (2000). Organizational form and nursing home behavior. *Nonprofit and Voluntary Sector Quarterly*, *29*(2), 255–279.

Mayer, L. H., & Ganahl, J. R. (2014). Taxing social enterprise. *Stanford Law Review*, *66*, 387.

Moore, M. H. (2000). Managing for value: Organizational strategy in for-profit, nonprofit, and governmental organizations. *Nonprofit and Voluntary Sector Quarterly*, *29*(suppl 1), 183–208.

Morris, S. (2000). Defining the nonprofit sector: Some lessons from history. *Voluntas: International Journal of Voluntary and Nonprofit Organizations*, *11*(1), 25–43.

Newhouse, J. P. (1970). Toward a theory of nonprofit institutions: An economic model of a hospital. *The American Economic Review*, *62*(1/2), 64–74.

Olson, M. (1965). *The logic of collective action*. Harvard University Press.

Ostrom, E. (2003). How types of goods and property rights jointly affect collective action. *Journal of Theoretical Politics, 15*(3), 239–270.

Ostrom, E. (2005). *Understanding institutional diversity*. Princeton University Press.
Ostrom, V., & Ostrom, E. (1977). Public goods and public choices. In E. S. Savas (Ed.), *Alternatives for delivering public services: Towards improved performance* (pp. 7–49). Westview Press.
Potoski, M., & Prakash, A. (2009). *Voluntary programs: A club theory perspective*. MIT Press.
Powell, W. W., & Steinberg, R. (Eds.) (2006). *The nonprofit sector: A research handbook*. Yale University Press.
Reiter, M., & Weichenrieder, A. J. (1999). Public goods, club goods and the measurement of crowding. *Journal of Urban Economics*, *46*(1), 69–79.
Rosenau, P., & Linder, S. (2003). Two decades of research comparing for-profit and nonprofit health provider performance in the United States. *Social Science Quarterly*, *84*(2), 219–241.
Saidel, J. R. (1991). Resource interdependence: The relationship between state agencies and nonprofit organizations. *Public Administration Review*, *51*(6), 543–553.
Salamon, L. M. (1987). Of market failure, voluntary failure, and third-party government: Toward a theory of government–nonprofit relations in the modern welfare state. *Nonprofit and Voluntary Sector Quarterly*, *16*(1–2), 29–49.
Salamon, L. M. (1999). *The nonprofit sector: A primer*. The Foundation Center.
Salamon, L. M. (2003). Voluntary failure theory correctly viewed. In H. K. Anheier & A. Ben-Ner (Eds.), *The study of the nonprofit enterprise* (pp. 183–186). Kluwer Academic/Plenum Publishers.
Salamon, L. M., & Anheier, H. K. (1992a). In search of the non-profit sector. I: The question of definitions. *Voluntas: International Journal of Voluntary and Nonprofit Organizations*, *3*(2), 125–151.
Salamon, L. M., & Anheier, H. K. (1992b). In search of the non-profit sector II: The problem of classification. *Voluntas: International Journal of Voluntary and Nonprofit Organizations*, *3*(3), 267–309.
Salamon, L. M., & Anheier, H. K. (1998). Social origins of civil society: Explaining the nonprofit sector cross-nationally. *Voluntas: International Journal of Voluntary and Nonprofit Organizations*, *9*(3), 213–248.
Samuelson, P. (1954). The pure theory of public expenditure. *The Review of Economics and Statistics*, *36*(4), 387–389.
Sandler, T., & Tschirhart, J. (1997). Club theory: Thirty years later. *Public Choice*, *93*(3), 335–355.
Schweik, C. M., Mergel, I., Sandfort, J. R., & Zhao, Z. J. (2011). Toward open public administration scholarship. *Journal of Public Administration Research and Theory*, *21*(suppl. 1), 175–198.

Sefton, M., & Steinberg, R. (1996). Reward structures in public good experiments. *Journal of Public Economics*, *61*(2), 263–287.

Sefton, T. (2008). Distributive and redistributive policy. In R. E. Goodin, M. Moran, & M. Rein (Eds.), *The Oxford handbook of public policy* (pp. 607–623). Oxford University Press.

Seibel, W. (1990). Government/third sector relationships in a comparative perspective: The cases of France and West Germany. *Voluntas: International Journal of Voluntary and Nonprofit Organizations*, *1*(1), 42–61.

Sen, A. (1993). Markets and freedom: Achievements and limitations of the market mechanism in promoting individual freedoms. *Oxford Economic Papers*, *45* (4), 519–541.

Smith, D. H. (1975). Voluntary action and voluntary groups. *Annual Review of Sociology*, *1*(1), 247–270.

Smith, D. H. (1997). The rest of the nonprofit sector: Grassroots associations as the dark matter ignored in prevailing "flat earth" maps of the sector. *Nonprofit and Voluntary Sector Quarterly*, 26(2), 114–131.

Steen, T. (2008). Not a government monopoly: The private, nonprofit, and voluntary sectors. In J. Perry & A. Hondeghem (Eds.), *Motivation in public management: The call of public service* (pp. 203–222). Oxford University Press.

Steinberg, R. (1987). Voluntary donations and public expenditures in a federalist system. *The American Economic Review*, *72*(1), 24–36.

Steinberg, R., & Weisbrod, B. A. (1998). Pricing and rationing by nonprofit organizations with distributional objectives. In B. A. Weisbrod (Ed.), *To profit or not to profit: The commercial transformation of the nonprofit sector* (pp. 64–82). Cambridge University Press.

Steinberg, R., & Weisbrod, B. A. (2005). Nonprofits with distributional objectives: Price discrimination and corner solutions. *Journal of Public Economics*, 89(11), 2205–2230.

Stiglitz, J. E. (1989). Markets, market failures, and development. *American Economic Review*, *79*(2), 197–203.

Stoker, G. (1998). Governance as theory: Five propositions. *International Social Science Journal*, *50*(155), 17–28.

Van Til, J. (2000). *Growing civil society: From nonprofit sector to third space*. Indiana University Press.

Weimer, D. L., & Vining, A. R. (2005). *Policy analysis: Concepts and practice* (4th ed.). Prentice Hall.

Weisbrod, B. A. (Ed.) (1977). *The voluntary nonprofit sector: An economic analysis*. Lexington Books.

Weisbrod, B. A. (1997). The future of the nonprofit sector: Its entwining with private enterprise and government. *Journal of Policy Analysis and Management*, *16*(4), 541–555.

Weisbrod, B. A. (2000). *To profit or not to profit: The commercial transformation of the nonprofit sector*. Cambridge University Press.
Witesman, E. M., & Fernandez, S. (2013). Government contracts with private organizations: Are there differences between nonprofits and for-profits? *Nonprofit and Voluntary Sector Quarterly*, 0899764012442592.
Young, D. R. (2016). Contract failure theory. In J. S. Ott & L. A. Dicke (Eds.), *The nature of the nonprofit sector* (3rd ed.) (pp. 193–196). Westview.

20 *Nonprofits as Agents of Moral Authority*

ROBBIE WATERS ROBICHAU AND KANDYCE FERNANDEZ

The nonprofit sector has pushed and been pushed by the boundaries of public and private endeavors, blurring distinctions among the sectors. Once relying solely on charitable donations, nonprofit organizations now, out of necessity, generate resources through enterprising efforts (Kerlin, 2013). Following the managerial trends implicit in neoliberalism, full-time, trained staff replaced dedicated volunteer leaders, and when outside accountability pressures forced nonprofits to justify their expenses, nonprofits were quick to minimize their overhead costs (Lecy & Searing, 2015). Market, professional, and corporate logics each played a role in stretching nonprofit action beyond the commonly expected behaviors of civil-society organizations (Jönsson, 2019; Maier et al., 2014).

These trends raise questions about what it means to be nonprofit and, normatively, what the value of nonprofit organizations is. Along with other chapters in this book, we investigate the *what* and *why* of nonprofit organizations, examining what is distinctive about nonprofit organizations and why we might want them to thrive. As others have argued (see Chapter 2 of this volume), we agree that nonprofits are needed to maintain healthy democracies (Dodge & Ospina, 2016; Mosely, 2014). Our unique contribution is to advance a theoretical framework of *nonprofitness*, grounded in nonprofits' moral authority, that examines nonprofit distinctiveness vis-à-vis other organizational forms and actions.

Drawing upon the integrated publicness literature, this chapter also explains why nonprofits are uniquely able to offer a moral counter to other types of organizations. By placing nonprofits on equal footing with public or private agencies in an "open systems" approach, all organizations influence and are influenced by their environment by *degrees* of moral, political, and market authorities (Robichau et al., 2015). Our "Nonprofitness Framework" accounts for the sector's distinction that is grounded in care for others while making a difference through mission and philanthropy (Choi & Mirabella, 2020; Grabowski et al., 2015), and it provides a rationale for why we should also consider charitable organizations in terms of degrees and dimensions rather than categories.

We define nonprofitness as the extent to which organizations are conditioned by a moral authority rooted in the ethos of the nonprofit sector that manifests in a strong value orientation, justifying their service, advocacy, or ability to correct a wrongdoing or deficit in society. Such organizations shape and are shaped by their history and the surrounding organizational environment (Sandberg, 2019). Here, we understand moral authority as "the potential to influence the morality of others through the use of power and platform granted to an entity based on the perception of its stakeholders that the entity is moral" (Hoppner & Vadakkepatt, 2019, p. 418). The organizations in question are both conditioned by and possess a moral authority. Where nonprofits are conditioned by moral authority, external pressures endow and constrain them as they carry out their mission, generate donors, attract volunteers, and assert themselves within their communities.

A Nonprofitness Framework helps us evaluate the breadth of organizations. Rather than viewing the world of organizations in binary terms (e.g., as being populated by businesses or not, nonprofits or not), our framework mirrors the complexity of the nonprofit sector, in which organizations may be more or less nonprofit-like. A great diversity of organizations are typically referred to as nonprofit. The Nonprofitness Framework provides a unique lens with which to understand this diversity, allowing organizations to be more or less nonprofit, private, and public entities rather than categorically nonprofit, business, or government entities.

For instance, while many advocacy nonprofits adhere to a strong value orientation and a moral authority based on sectoral ideals and values (e.g., caring for others, promoting philanthropy, or fostering collective action in their community), others may represent very narrow interests with a limited desire to produce public benefits and may be considered less trustworthy. Both types might technically be considered nonprofit organizations, but they are actually very different kinds of entities. Without a characterization of organizations that recognizes this difference, we fail to capture important contours of the organizational landscape. Along with publicness and privateness, nonprofitness, then, becomes a helpful tool for mapping organizations in modern society.

This chapter proceeds in the following way: We first account for what distinguishes nonprofit organizations from public- and private-sector ones. We then lay out a nonprofitness rationale and discuss how this characterization is distinct from publicness and privateness. Finally, we provide examples of how a Nonprofitness Framework can help us differentiate among nonprofit types to better understand the scope of the sector. In the Conclusion, we discuss the future of a Nonprofitness Framework and suggest areas in which research can further enhance our understanding of the institutional reality of the nonprofit sector.

20.1 A Theory of Nonprofitness: Exploring Moral Authority

20.1.1 Expanding the Publicness–Privateness Continuum

Civil-society organizations have provided goods and services in the US for hundreds of years (e.g., child welfare, religious associations, education) (Hall, 2006). However, a combination of government reinvention and the global wave of New Public Management shifted attention to a private, market-oriented delivery of public services through businesses and nonprofits (Kettl, 2005). In an effort to account for the shifts in service delivery by "public" providers, and their respective roles and responsibilities, empirical studies compared management within public and private organizations across an array of behaviors, outcomes, and managerial strategies (e.g., Andrews et al., 2011; Boyne, 2002). Underlying this line of research was the argument that all organizations are to some degree public, meaning that they are variably subject to public funding, control, and ownership (Bozeman, 1987).

In the theory of dimensional publicness, public and private organizations are contrasted. Public organizations are said to be funded by tax dollars, owned by citizens, and controlled by laws, elected officials, and regulatory agencies; they are influenced by political authority. Private organizations are funded by customers or investors, owned by one or many stakeholders, and controlled by competitive forces in the market. In practice, then, public organizations are constrained by political authority, including elected officials, public policy, and voting, which can affect their resources and operations. Private organizations, while also affected by public policy, are more readily influenced by the market's authority, as customers and executives can endow or constrain organizational outcomes. Publicness thus forms one end of an organizational continuum, while privateness occupies the other, with most organizations falling somewhere in the middle. All organizations from this view are thought to be more or less public or private depending on the *degrees* of *political* and *market authority* that shape them (Bozeman & Moulton, 2011).

Within the publicness literature, nonprofit organizations and the sector as a whole are not given much consideration, and the specific and unique ways nonprofits contribute to democratic values are largely underestimated. Nonprofits are conceptualized as having a unique role in meeting the demands of an expanding welfare state, and they are viewed as more akin to private for-profit actors than public ones (for exceptions, see Isett & Provan, 2005; Nutt & Backoff, 1993; Xu & Li, 2022). Given that government agencies are expected to meet the demands for public goods to satisfy the "median voter," and due to market failure or the unwillingness of businesses to provide certain goods and services, nonprofits are passively conceptualized as filling in the gap left for unmet demand for public goods and services (Weisbrod, 1975).

We contend that the public–private continuum suggested in the publicness scholarship does not fully capture the diversity of the organized world. Specifically, nonprofits actively create public value through their instrumental and expressive roles (Frumkin, 2005), including advocacy, service delivery, innovation, individual expression, social capital, and citizen engagement (Moulton and Eckerd, 2012). They do so from a different place than do public organizations, as they are conditioned by a moral authority, and in providing a counter to the other sectors, they exert a moral authority. This is why we suggest a third dimension: nonprofitness.

20.1.2 Characterizing the Moral Authority of Nonprofits

What makes nonprofits different – in theory, if not also in practice – from public or private organizations? We suggest it is their origins as specific types of organizations in society, the conditioning of moral authority, and the ways these are expressed in their mission-driven work. Unlike entities in the public and private sector, nonprofits are "relatively free to define their own missions, values, and purposes" in creating social impact (Schultz, 2004, p. 286), and many often do so based on religious traditions and values (i.e., compassion, trust, generosity, care, social justice, philanthropy). Nevertheless, nonprofits are conditioned differently by their environment given the contemporary structural manifestations of how society shapes and regulates such organizations (e.g., fundraising practices and support, IRS and state rules, board governance and oversight, etc.). Further, nonprofits do not all have the same normative orientation or operate over time in the same ways due to these external influences. Many nonprofits have to consider how the ongoing struggle between the head and the heart of the nonprofit sector in general affects their actions; particularly, the "kinds of values that *ought* to inform their functions and roles in democratic and civic life" (Choi & Mirabella, 2020, p. 166). Taking these influences into account, nonprofitness proposes charitable organizations by degrees of moral authority and their expression of nonprofit ideals, in which some nonprofit organizations move closer to public or private organizational ideals depending on factors like mission/purpose, funding, broader public or narrow private interests, and commitment to sectoral values (e.g., care, collective action, equity, representation).

A moral authority in nonprofit work manifests through entities' missions and the overall practice and promotion of a "value-based self-sustaining mechanism" in their operations (Knutsen, 2012, p. 993). These values, including trust, equity, stewardship, representation, care, and charity, endow nonprofits with resources (funding, volunteers), legitimacy (recognition of their collective work and accountability to stakeholders), and credibility (social capital) in carrying out their role in society. Research supports the view that nonprofits carry out and are grounded in moral work. For example, the delivery of nonprofit services and goods frequently relies on "moral frames" that shape nonprofits' approach to clients and influence how workers perceive the value of their work as it contributes to clients, communities, and beyond (Child et al., 2016; Garrow & Hasenfeld, 2014).

Similarly, other scholars have suggested that a nonprofit orientation shapes the work of organizations through managerial priorities (Robichau & Fernandez, 2017) by establishing a civic footprint (Handy et al., 2014) and fostering collective civic action (Fernandez et al., 2022). Cunningham (2010) referred to these orientations as constituting a "voluntary sector ethos" in which employees' commitment to social change and their community is based on philosophical and religious goals. Evidence also suggests that nonprofit employees, and the overall public, tend to view the nonprofit sphere as more trustworthy, warm, distinctive, and, at times, more competent in comparison to public and private agencies (Becker et al., 2020; Langer, 2022; Lapworth et al., 2018; Luo & Kaul, 2019; Park et al., 2018; Xu, 2020). Adherence to a moral authority as a guiding mechanism in their work therefore enables nonprofits to combine collective action and advocacy with charitableness and care and still be deliverers of services (Eikenberry & Kluver, 2004; Hall, 2006).

The perception that nonprofits hold a certain degree of moral authority justifies why some nonprofits are allowed and continue to take positions on difficult social challenges in a broader public governance system. To do so, the goals of any nonprofit organization to advance its work or respond to its environment may involve moving among the dimensions of publicness–nonprofitness–privateness, in which nonprofits are also subject to market and political authority and the creation of public and private values. Nevertheless, nonprofits are expected to balance their movement among the different dimensions, as nonadherence to a moral authority and violation of trust can constrain resources and reputation (Hornsey et al., 2021), calling into question the legal and institutional status of a nonprofit organization.

The moral authority manifested through nonprofit work does not presume that nonprofit actors pursue the best interests of society and beneficiaries at all times. Like business and government agencies, nonprofits experience dysfunction, with fraud and unethical behaviors occurring at staff and executive levels (e.g., see Gillespie et al., 2019; Lamothe et al., 2022). However, the response to nonprofit scandals is often especially negative, signaling a perceived betrayal of the public's trust and a challenge to the public's perception of what it means to be a nonprofit, because nonprofits are expected to take the moral high ground and be worthy institutions regardless of their mission.

20.2 A Nonprofitness Framework and the Span of the Sector's Moral Authority

Nonprofitness describes the degree to which organizations are conditioned by a moral authority and infused with a strong value orientation that justifies their actions to serve, advocate, or correct a wrongdoing or deficit in society. Our central contribution is thus to advocate for a nonprofitness perspective. That is, in answer to the question, What is the nonprofit sector?, our response is that it is a collection of organizations that possess a high degree of nonprofitness. But just as importantly, we prefer to view most organizations – regardless of sector distinctions – as possessing some level of nonprofitness. This means that we are not enamored with the idea of sector as an orienting concept. The nonprofitness conceptualization draws our attention away from boundaries and toward the qualities of organizations that make them more or less nonprofit (or public or private).

Nonprofit organizations are thought to be high in nonprofitness to the extent that their funding, ownership, and control fall under the influence of and commitment to a moral authority (Choi & Mirabella, 2020; Pynes, 2012; Wagner, 2014). We observe several ways nonprofits adhere to a moral authority and a values-based orientation. Internally, organizations establish and promote their values and ethics among staff, and those values shape the issues or needs of the organization and the ability to attract donors and volunteers. They also frame the nature of services to clients or other outputs in society. Externally, nonprofits reflect their moral authority in that they can foster public trust in society, focus on a multitude of causes, and support democracy through association, representation, and civic/political engagement.

Both internal and external dimensions of nonprofitness influence the different fields (e.g., health care, education, animals, etc.) and functions of organization (e.g., human service, membership association, B Corps, foundation, etc.) in diverse ways. While we can attribute some dimensions of the nonprofit sector to a more outward or inward orientation, the most salient argument is that these organizations still elect nonprofit forms and missions regardless. This choice provides nonprofits the flexibility to assert greater degrees of moral authority in society. We explore this dimensionality in the context of the publicness (political authority) and privateness (market authority) dimensions that influence organizations. In Figure 20.1, we characterize common nonprofit forms.

Nonprofitness is discernible through funding, ownership, control, mission/purpose, and commitment to broader sectoral values (collective action, representation, civic engagement, human well-being, philanthropy). The diagram in Figure 20.1 reflects the notion that some organizations fall closer to what we may consider a "pure charity" – an organization high in nonprofitness – that persists exclusively on

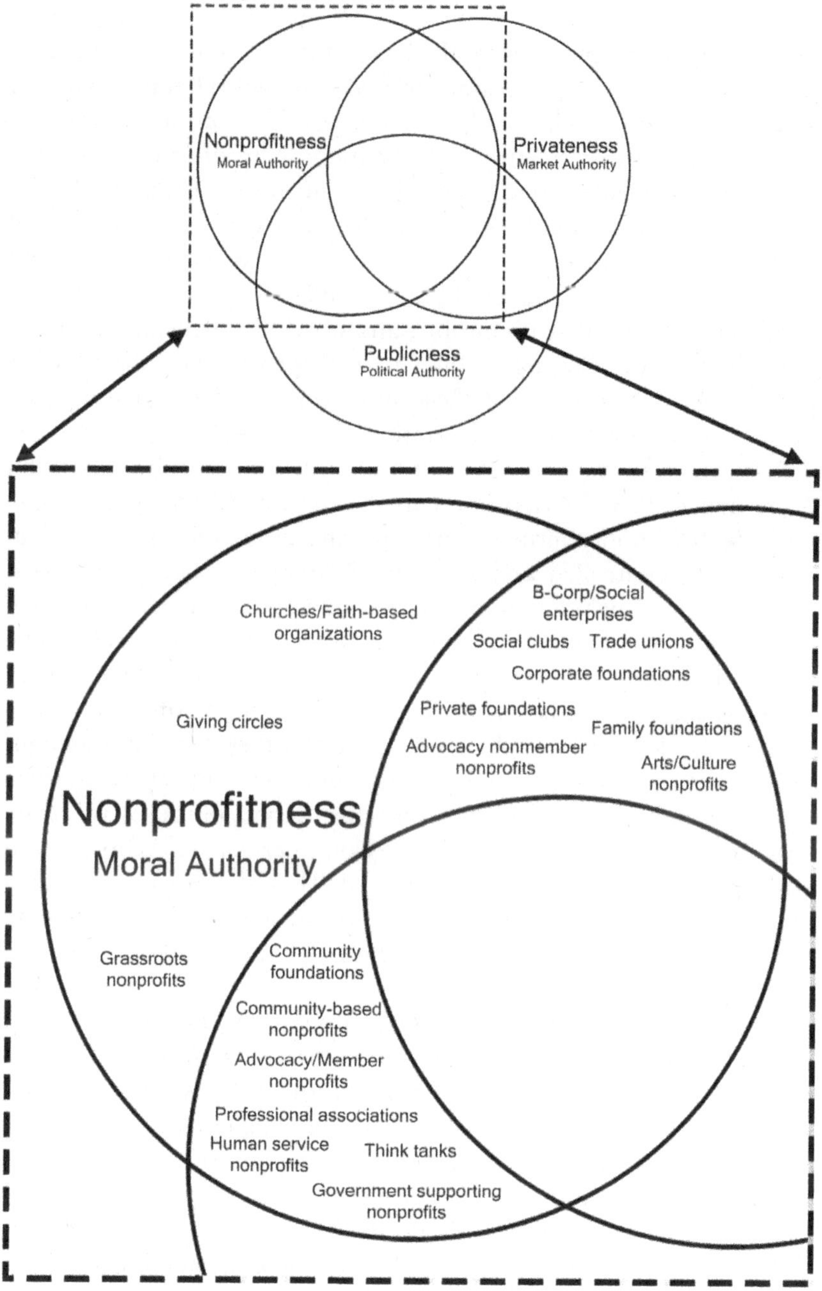

Figure 20.1 A nonprofitness framework

donations and for which funding comes from donor support, the mission is to serve people in need, the basis of the work is caring for others, and volunteers are necessary to make the work happen. Moving away from a narrow charitable function, some organizations draw on their moral authority to attract diverse funds in an effort to engage the community, provide services, or support members. These nonprofits also align with the public sector in their outward orientation. Still other nonprofits hover closer to the private sector in their form and function, drawing on generated funding and a moral orientation to do good, supporting other nonprofits, and providing association among individuals associating based on a narrower focus (i.e., social clubs, private foundations). Thus, these nonprofits tend to have a more inward- or narrow-focused orientation.

Religious charitable organizations, such as Catholic Charities, Ascension DePaul Services, or Latter-day Saint Charities, are especially high in nonprofitness. These organizations rely on individual donors; are controlled and accountable to their religious affiliates; care for others, including nonmembers; and operate in areas in which government and business tend to be absent. Other nonprofits, like grassroots groups, are also high in nonprofitness. These groups may begin as social movements, such as #MeToo, Stop American Asian Pacific Islander Hate, or climate justice, and then formalize as nonprofit organizations when they attain sufficient support. Grassroots groups mobilize volunteers for collective action purposes to create social change for their community-seeking participants who are and who are not affected by the issue at hand. They also rely on individual donors and operate in areas in which government or business often do not. We would assume a strong influence of a moral authority on their work and how they act in society.

Other common nonprofit types lean closer to the other sectors given their orientation towards more public-sector values/forms (i.e., government) or more private-sector values/forms (i.e., business). So, for example, organizations in the lower overlapping circles of nonprofitness/publicness have community as a primary dimension and tend to operate in more traditional nonprofit fields that align with the focus of the public sector. QueensCare Health Centers provides numerous types of health services to underserved and uninsured individuals throughout Los Angeles regardless of their ability to pay. Alternatively, a child welfare organization like Arizona's Hope & A Future derives its motivation from a religious basis to serve and equip youth in foster care as they age out of the child welfare system. A substance abuse program within the Salvation Army incorporates spirituality into its approach, believing that individuals recover more effectively when spirituality is part of their journey. These organizations serve in the human services role and are conditioned by moral authority.

Moving closer to publicness, professional associations like the Academy of Nutrition and Dietetics, the National Association for Black Public Administrators, and the International Lactation Consultant Association all maintain and serve members of their organizations. While these organizations are still subject to a moral authority in society in which values direct their organizations and missions, their nonprofitness – regardless of whether they are in fact classified as nonprofit organizations – is constrained by their focus on member interests and protection of a specific field rather than a community. They balance between nonprofit and public spaces as they are affected by political authority.

In the upper overlapping circles of nonprofitness and privateness, nonprofits support members involved in all manner of associational activities (e.g., social/sports clubs, trade unions), or they support other nonprofits (e.g., private and family foundations) or causes. Herein we expect some level of moral authority from organizations that aligns to member and mission interests, with a more or less private orientation depending on the purpose. We consider foundations and social enterprises, whose legitimacy is cultivated by how the organization chooses to engage in society and for what purpose. For example, private foundations intend to make society better according to a specific mission or vision of society, typically established by a founder who designates the purpose and provides the resources to carry out the work. The same is also true for family foundations that have a founder and primary donor but operate with much less transparency in their work, as the family oversees the giving process and does so according to its specific interests in helping in society. While moral authority shapes foundations in their establishment as philanthropic organizations, these foundations are largely shaped by the orientation and vision of their founders, including their private interests. As an example, Babo Botanicals is a B Corporation, or social enterprise, designed to "use markets to solve a social problem." The company responsibly sources its line of baby products and utilizes best hiring practices to "leave the world a better place than [they] found it." Babo Botanicals' nonprofitness is based in its commitment to improve society, and they do so by selling products to generate a profit, arguably a more privately oriented moral authority.

We may also consider organizations focused on a specific cause for advocacy or correction in society, a more public rather than charitable role. Again in the lower overlapping circles of public and nonprofit organizations, nonprofits like Mothers against Drunk Driving or the World Wildlife Fund have a specific mission to create awareness for a cause and generate support through donations. These organizations work in the policy arena to support changes in legislation or programs that impact their mission. We would expect these organizations to be driven by values that are laser focused on the issues encapsulated in their mission of bringing awareness to an issue in society that furthers systematic change, a narrow but public orientation.

In many cases, however, nonprofits operate where government and markets are unwilling or incapable of sufficiently serving the public demand (e.g., serving children in foster care, immigrants, veterans, neighborhoods, youth, disabled individuals), and we anticipate that they will comply with a moral authority shaped by the values of their mission. We also acknowledge that some organizations adhere to a moral authority in their expressive activities within civil society. These activities include advocating for clients and community needs or seeking to gain resources, change, or support from institutions that are underserving individuals with a specific need or issue. Nonprofits can also foster civic engagement with clients and the community when they encourage client engagement in community meetings, inform clients of issues in the community, and provide ways for clients and community to interact. If we examine a nonprofit like the National Association for the Advancement of Colored People (NAACP), we observe an organization engaging Black voters in our democracy but also tackling broader issues affecting People of Color, such as racial, educational, or health inequalities. Nonprofits like the NAACP utilize multiple strategies to address wrongdoings that disproportionately affect their stakeholders in an effort to improve public institutions and policies.

The Nonprofitness Framework allows for movement within the main nonprofitness circle (see Figure 20.1) by recognizing that organizational variations exist among nonprofits. Any nonprofit may move throughout the circle over time and for numerous reasons.

20.3 Conclusions

Research on nonprofits and the nonprofit sector needs to focus on systematically understanding the "perceived sector differences ... by tracing the moral and cultural origin of 'nonprofitness'" (Xu, 2020, p. 1306), the identity and legitimacy of the "in-between space" of the market and the state (Knutsen & Brock, 2014), public perceptions of how nonprofit charitable work is carried out (Child & Witesman, 2022), and how organizational and managerial operations influence the immediate and external work of nonprofit organizations (Fernandez et al., 2022; Robichau et al., 2015). In this chapter, we have argued that the nonprofit field will continue to shape society; therefore, conceptual clarity concerning the dimensionality of nonprofit work will only grow in importance to research and practice.

We have proposed furthering the theory of nonprofitness as a more comprehensive framing of the breadth and depth of nonprofit organizations that constitute the sector. A Nonprofitness Framework situates nonprofits on similar footing as government and for-profit organizations in shaping societal norms, values, and practices, but from a different orientation. Nonprofitness is the extent to which organizations are conditioned by a moral authority rooted in the ethos of the sector that manifests in a strong value orientation, justifying an organization's action to serve, advocate, or correct a wrongdoing or deficit in society. Acknowledging the work of past explanations on what the nonprofit sector is, we argue for an approach that expands upon the centrality of what nonprofits can do for society, culture, and democracy by providing a balance among a dominant private sector and an influential public sector.

The theoretical challenge set before us is how best to measure the variations within a Nonprofitness Framework of degrees and how to account for the richer differences between organizations in the sector. How can we study (and therefore discern) the value orientations and moral authority represented by different organizations in society? In some organizations, the value orientation may be clear. For example, in a member-based nonprofit, values and moral authority may be focused on prioritizing and advocating for the private interests of its members. In a human service organization, the mission may lead to an outward focus on delivering public goods and services, perhaps even with a religious inclination. Alternatively, some foundations may simultaneously prioritize public and private interests based on their founders' or major funders' preferences without need for other stakeholder input. This approach may become more prevalent as the sector becomes more individualized, targeting niche rather than broader issues in society. How do nonprofits with different orientations preserve their purposes of fostering democracy or charitableness while enhancing civil society more broadly? Another focus for research is exploring how the growth and influence of various nonprofit forms may limit nonprofit actions (e.g., B Corps versus government-supporting nonprofits) that change the trajectory of the sector at large. If nonprofit forms and structures continue to make subtle but relevant shifts from their origins, how do we reinforce the nonprofitness of the sector? This chapter raises questions for future theory that have considerable implications for practice. Most critically, we consider why a theoretical framework of nonprofitness, grounded in moral authority, is needed to explain individual and organizational behaviors.

References

Andrews, R., Boyne, G. A., & Walker, R. M. (2011). Dimensions of publicness and organizational performance: A review of the evidence. *Journal of Public Administration Research and Theory*, *21*(3), i301–i319.

Becker, A., Boenigk, S., & Willems, J. (2020). In nonprofits we trust? A large-scale study on the public's trust in nonprofit organizations. *Journal of Nonprofit & Public Sector Marketing*, *32*(2), 189–216.

Boyne, G. A. (2002). Public and private management: What's the difference? *Journal of Management Studies*, *39*(1), 97–122.

Bozeman, B. (1987). *All organizations are public: Bridging public and private organizational theories* (Vol. 1). Jossey-Bass.

Bozeman, B., & Moulton, S. (2011). Integrative publicness: A framework for public management strategy and performance. *Journal of Public Administration Research and Theory*, *21*(Supplement 3), i363–i380.

Child, C., & Witesman, E. (2022). The social meanings of the third sector: How action and purpose shape everyday understandings of "nonprofit." *Nonprofit and Voluntary Sector Quarterly*. https://doi.org/10.1177/08997640221081523

Child, C., Witesman, E., & Spencer, R. (2016). The blurring hypothesis reconsidered: How sector still matters to practitioners. *Voluntas: International Journal of Voluntary and Nonprofit Organizations*, *27*(4), 1831–1852.

Choi, K. J., & Mirabella, R. (2020). Beyond codes: Values, virtues, and nonprofit ethics. In H. K. Anheier & S. Toepler (Eds.), *The Routledge companion to nonprofit management* (pp. 165–176). Routledge.

Cunningham, I. (2010). Drawing from a bottomless well? Exploring the resilience of value-based psychological contracts in voluntary organizations. *The International Journal of Human Resource Management*, *21*(5), 699–719.

Dodge, J., & Ospina, S. (2016) Nonprofits as "schools of democracy": A comparative case study of two environmental organizations. *Nonprofit and Volunteer Sector Quarterly*, *45*(3), 478–499.

Eikenberry, A. M., & Kluver, J. D. (2004). The marketization of the nonprofit sector: Civil society at risk? *Public Administration Review*, *64*(2), 132–140.

Fernandez, K., Robichau, R. W., Alexander, J. K., Mackenzie, W. I., & Scherer, R. F. (2022). How a nonprofitness orientation influences collective civic action: The effects of civic engagement and political participation. *Voluntas: International Journal of Voluntary and Nonprofit Organizations*, *33*, 1051–1063.

Frumkin, P. (2005). *On being nonprofit: A conceptual and policy primer.* Harvard University Press.

Garrow, E. E., & Hasenfeld, Y. (2014). Institutional logics, moral frames, and advocacy: Explaining the purpose of advocacy among nonprofit human-service organizations. *Nonprofit and Voluntary Sector Quarterly*, *43*(1), 80–98.

Gillespie, E. M., Mirabella, R. M., & Eikenberry, A. M. (2019). #Metoo/#Aidtoo and creating an intersectional feminist NPO/NGO sector. *Nonprofit Policy Forum*, *10*(4), 1–9.

Grabowski, L., Neher, C., Crim, T., & Mathiassen, L. (2015). Competing values framework application to organizational effectiveness in voluntary organizations: A case study. *Nonprofit and Voluntary Sector Quarterly*, *44*(5), 908–923.

Hall, P. D. (2006). A historical overview of philanthropy, voluntary associations, and nonprofit organizations in the United States, 1600–2000. In W. W. Powell & R. Steinberg (Eds.), *The nonprofit sector: A research handbook* (2nd ed.) (pp. 32–65). Yale University Press.

Handy, F., Shier, M. L., & McDougle, L. M. (2014). Nonprofits and the promotion of civic engagement: A conceptual framework for understanding the "civic footprint" of nonprofits within local communities. *Canadian Journal of Nonprofit and Social Economy Research*, *5*(1), 57–75.

Hoppner, J. J., & Vadakkepatt, G. G. (2019). Examining moral authority in the marketplace: A conceptualization and framework. *Journal of Business Research*, *95*, 417–427.

Hornsey, M. J., Chapman, C. M., Mangan, H., La Macchia, S., & Gillespie, N. (2021). The moral disillusionment model of organizational transgressions: Ethical transgressions trigger more negative reactions from consumers when committed by nonprofits. *Journal of Business Ethics*, *172*(4), 653–671.

Isett, K. R., & Provan, K. G. (2005). The evolution of dyadic interorganizational relationships in a network of publicly funded nonprofit agencies. *Journal of Public Administration Research and Theory*, *15*(1), 149–165.

Jönsson, J. (2019). Logic salience in ideologically-torn nonprofit hybrids. *Nonprofit Policy Forum*, *10*(3), 1–18.

Kerlin, J. A. (2013). Defining social enterprise across different contexts: A conceptual framework based on institutional factors. *Nonprofit and Voluntary Sector Quarterly*, *42*, 84–108.

Kettl, D. F. (2005). *The global public management revolution*. Brookings Institution Press.

Knutsen, W. L. (2012). Adapted institutional logics of contemporary nonprofit organizations. *Administration & Society*, *44*(8), 985–1013.

Knutsen, W. L., & Brock, K. L. (2014). Introductory essay: From a closed system to an open system: A parallel critical review of the intellectual trajectories of publicness and nonprofitness. *Voluntas: International Journal of Voluntary and Nonprofit Organizations*, *25*, 1113–1131.

Lamothe, M., Ter-Mkrtchyan, A., Ruddle, T. B., & Kuyon, K. (2022). Examining the efficacy of accountability systems in preventing nonprofit misconduct: A look beyond financial fraud. *Nonprofit and Voluntary Sector Quarterly*. https://doi.org/10.1177/08997640211073750

Langer, J. (2022). Understanding the spirit of the sectors: Exploring identity in a new era of organizing. *Administration & Society*, *54*(5), 792–827.

Lapworth, L., James, P., & Wylie, N. (2018). Examining public service motivation in the voluntary sector: Implications for public management. *Public Management Review*, *20*(11), 1663–1682.

Lecy, J. D., & Searing, E. A. (2015). Anatomy of the nonprofit starvation cycle: An analysis of falling overhead ratios in the nonprofit sector. *Nonprofit and Voluntary Sector Quarterly*, *44*(3), 539–563.

Luo, J., & Kaul, A. (2019). Private action in public interest: The comparative governance of social issues. *Strategic Management Journal*, *40*(4), 476–502.

Maier, F., Meyer, M., & Steinbereithner, M. (2014). Nonprofit organizations becoming business-like: A systematic review. *Nonprofit and Voluntary Sector Quarterly*, *45*(1), 64–86.

Mosely, J. E. (2014). Collaboration, public-private intermediary organizations, and the transformation of advocacy in the field of homeless services. *The American Review of Public Administration*, *44*(3), 291–308.

Moulton, S., & Eckerd, A. (2012). Preserving the publicness of the nonprofit sector: Resources, roles, and public values. *Nonprofit and Voluntary Sector Quarterly*, *41*(4), 656–685.

Nutt, P. C., & Backoff, R. W. (1993). Organizational publicness and its implications for strategic management. *Journal of Public Administration Research and Theory*, *3*(2), 209–231.

Park, S., Mosley, J. E., & Grogan, C. M. (2018). Do residents of low-income communities trust organizations to speak on their behalf? Differences by organizational type. *Urban Affairs Review*, *54*(1), 137–164.

Pynes, J. E. (2012). Human resources management in nonprofit organizations. In N. M. Riccucci (Ed.), *Public personnel management: Current concerns, future challenges* (5th ed.) (pp. 196–212). Routledge.

Robichau, R. W., & Fernandez, K. (2017). Intersectoral experiences: Nonprofit managers and sector influences in child welfare agencies. *Human Service Organizations: Management, Leadership & Governance*, *41*(1), 76–93.

Robichau, R. W., Fernandez, K., & Kraeger, P. (2015). An integrated framework of inter-sectorality: Nonprofitness and its influence on society and public administration programs. *Journal of Public Affairs Education*, *21*(3), 315–336.

Sandberg, B. (2019). Critical perspectives on the history and development of the nonprofit sector. In A. Eikenberry, B. Sandberg, & R. Mirabella (Eds.), *Reframing nonprofit management: Democracy, inclusion, and social change* (pp. 26–37). Melvin & Leigh.

Schultz, D. (2004). Professional ethics in a postmodern society. *Public Integrity*, *6*(4), 279–297.

Wagner, A. (2014). Good governance: A radical and normative approach to nonprofit management. *Voluntas: International Journal of Voluntary and Nonprofit Organizations*, *25*(3), 797–817.

Weisbrod, B. A. (1975). Toward a theory of the voluntary nonprofit sector in a three sector Economy. In E. S. Phelps (Ed.), *Altruism, morality, and economic theory* (pp. 171–196). Russell Sage Foundation.

Xu, C. (2020). The perceived differences: The sector stereotype of social service providers. *Nonprofit and Voluntary Sector Quarterly*, *49*(6), 1293–1310.

Xu, C., & Li, H. (2022). Resource publicness matters in organizational perceptions. *Public Administration Review*, *82*(2), 338–353.

PART IV

Conclusion

21 Conclusions

EVA WITESMAN AND CURTIS CHILD

The objective of this volume has been to open new directions for thinking about the nonprofit sector – new directions that acknowledge the rich history of nonprofit sector theory while also forging new paths. To do this, we have sought to take an expansive view of theory that is inclusive of diverse ways of making sense of the world. Our collective work has been based on two presumptions: First, that understanding the rich world of interactions under the umbrella of the nonprofit and voluntary sector is important to the well-being of our world and the people in it. Second, that there is an opportunity to understand more of these interactions, and to understand them more deeply. Thus, we have invited critiques and refinements of the existing body of nonprofit sector theory and have sought to encourage new and diverse perspectives that question the very premises on which traditional nonprofit sector theory is based.

As Locke (2007) observed about scientific progress, "Progress is made (despite mistakes) in increments, some small, some large. The proper goal is not to pursue the hopeless grail of omniscience, but to constantly discover more" (p. 886). Our motivating concern has been that the innovative study of the nonprofit sector has slowed despite the growing need for imaginative, galvanizing efforts in society that have the hope of solving some of the greatest threats and challenges we have ever faced. As climate change amplifies natural disasters on the planet, millions of people are displaced by war, deep rifts plague communities, and trust in social institutions fades, there has never been a time more suited to the purposeful consideration of the institutions that bind us together and unite us in imagining a better world. These same circumstances also push us to question the institutions that have brought us to this point – and to challenge institutions that are not serving us.

In Chapter 1 of this volume, we laid out the purpose of the book and extended an invitation to rethink sector theory. Our collective work here has been a partial response, but the invitation remains open. We hope that this volume reinvigorates conversations about the *what* and *why* of the nonprofit sector so that we can more robustly explore questions that will not only help us to define, describe, explain, and predict the sector, but also to evaluate it and make prescriptions for the future.

We should consider theory not just in terms of creating generalizations, suggests Cunliffe (2002), but rather we should consider working toward *resonance* in theory: "resonance is far more powerful than theoretical generalization because it is provocative, personal, and allows us to interpret those insights in ways that are meaningful and significant to us and to our situation – in ways that ... are genuinely close to us" (p. 7). The truth is that the nonprofit sector matters deeply to the individuals whose lives are touched by it – either as a vehicle for personal values expression or as a means for meeting deep personal or societal needs.

In Chapter 2, we explored the various theories that have formed the bedrock of nonprofit theory to this point. These theories are already diverse; they explore political, economic, legal, sociological, organizational, and psychological approaches to nonprofit theory. As demonstrated by Megan LePere-Schloop and Rebecca Nesbit in Chapter 3, nonprofit scholarship has largely treated existing nonprofit theory in one of two ways – either using it as a touchstone for further discussion, or specifically to differentiate the nonprofit sector from other institutions. While this latter role suggests at least some attention to the *what* of the nonprofit sector (i.e., what is it vis-à-vis other institutions such as government and the market), it also suggests that many nonprofit scholars are building their scholarship on premises that, as we have demonstrated, may not be descriptive of our global reality. In addition to our call for deeper and more scholarship on the nonprofit sector, we propose deeper engagement with theory to more meaningfully inform nonprofit and voluntary sector scholarship.

We have also argued for diversity of methods and perspectives in theorizing, with the aim of creating a richer set of theory on which to draw for both research and practice in the sector globally (see Chapters 2, 3, and 4). In Chapter 11, Elizabeth A. Castillo pushes further our call for diverse perspectives and suggests that nonprofit sector studies could benefit from casting an even wider epistemological net, reaching not only to the soft sciences from whence most of our theories of the nonprofit sector emerge, but also to distant disciplines in the hard sciences, such as computer science and biology, to identify methodologies and frameworks that can challenge our thinking in ways that view human beings and our institutions and interactions as phenomena that can be informed, described, and explained by theories in the broader biophysical world.

Many of the authors in this volume suggest critiques or extensions of the theories we outlined in Chapter 2. From these authors, we see opportunities to build on existing theories and also reasons to shy away from traditional ways of thinking about the sector. Their critical examinations provide a roadmap to strengthening the broad set of perspectives that form the foundation of study of the nonprofit sector and the entities and actions that take place within it. Contributors to this volume also suggest new directions in nonprofit sector theorizing. These perspectives, rooted in the observation of practice and oriented in different cultures, national contexts, and methodologies, suggest new foundations on which alternative theories of the nonprofit sector could be built. Some of these new directions run parallel to existing theories, while others are philosophically opposed to prior views of the sector.

21.1 The What and Why of the Nonprofit Sector

We have found the nonprofit sector not to be a monolithic institution but rather as a set of intertwined and overlapping phenomena. The institutions described by some of our authors are antithetical to the institutions described by others. In a call for diverse perspectives, we have discovered a complexity of visions that, like in any pluralistic society, are sometimes at odds. Rather than creating a single definition and one path forward, then, we have succeeded instead in gathering a rich set of possible perspectives and paradigms, each of which has its own possibilities, limitations, and implications. Like the sector itself, our theories of the nonprofit sector are diverse and uniquely textured.

We also sought to explore the question of *why* the nonprofit sector exists. As we review our contributors' responses to this question, we discover that the question itself can be viewed divergently. Explaining the *why* of the sector considers the motivation and purposes for nonprofit organizing; however, it also encompasses questions of context and history that explain a more dispassionate view of the sector's origins.

In this volume the question of *what* is largely answered by providing the role of the nonprofit or its definition. In other words, our contributors either *defined* or *described* the nonprofit sector or some phenomenon deeply relevant to the sector. The question of *why* is largely answered with rationales for the nonprofit sector or for new constructs to replace the sector or sector theory, either by *explaining* why such constructs exist or prescribing why they *should* exist. It bears repeating that some of our contributors have focused on critiques or extensions of nonprofit theory, whereas others have sought to propose new directions for nonprofit theory. This collection of insights about the nonprofit sector demonstrates wide variation in author perspectives on the nonprofit sector, ranging from acceptance of "traditional" nonprofit sector or organization definitions to a rejection altogether of the premise that the nonprofit sector is the appropriate locus of prosocial activity. The rationales for nonprofit organizing presented in this volume suggest that there are many ways that we can conceive of nonprofit and voluntary action and organizing. Each of these suggests not only a possible way forward in developing nonprofit sector theory, but also for identifying questions about the ways in which the sector is formulated and interacts with individuals, organizations, and institutions in our global society.

21.2 Emergent Themes and Tensions

While each individual chapter in this volume provides a unique contribution to the study of the nonprofit sector, some themes emerge across different works and perspectives. These overarching themes suggest specific opportunities for future development in nonprofit sector theory. The first of these is the need for an internationalized perspective. Much important research and theory has been developed by scholars who have sought to apply the concept of the nonprofit sector internationally and to glean important lessons about the sector from this endeavor (e.g., notably, Anheier & Salamon, 2006; Young, 2000). Building on this prior work, our volume has identified voices from varied national, cultural, and political contexts. One theme that emerges is that our very conception of the nonprofit sector continues to need more scholarship from international, internationalized, and diverse perspectives. In addition to using traditional conceptions of the nonprofit sector and observing these phenomena in different countries (international), we need to rethink those very definitions and conceptions from an international perspective (internationalization).

Thus, rather than exclusively performing international research on the Western notion of the nonprofit sector, we should instead also internationalize our notion of the nonprofit sector itself.

The second overarching theme we have observed across works in this volume is the need to recognize and study the dark side of nonprofit organizing. Critical perspectives in this volume have suggested the need to avoid perpetuating views of the nonprofit sector and its legal and cultural assumptions in ways that may be harmful to people, groups, or society at large. Specifically, several chapters indicate that nonprofit formalization that is endorsed by the state may be a form of leveraging what appear to be prosocial efforts to, instead, subjugate certain people or perspectives and maintain and expand the coercive power of the state (Tilly, 1992). Still others suggest that even less formalized nonprofit organizing may ignore or exacerbate the very social problems they exist to address.

The third overarching theme we have observed is the astounding variation in nonprofit–state and nonprofit–politics interactions. While prior scholars of the sector have certainly described the intertwining of state and nonprofit institutions and diversity in this relationship across contexts, the extent to which this completely alters our very conception of the nonprofit sector is a key theme for scholars to consider. Several chapters in this volume suggest that the interactions between government and the nonprofit sector are diverse, heavily contextual, and vary in their consequences for the sector and for society. Our contributors' rich and international cases have only scratched the surface of the global variation in these phenomena. Deeper examination of the role of contextually unique nonprofit sectors in relation to equally contextually unique institutions of the state are needed.

The fourth overarching theme concerns the relationship of the nonprofit sector to other institutions. While the nonprofit sector has traditionally been defined through comparison and contrast to market and government institutions, authors in this volume suggest additional institutions, such as church and family, as major entities that should be considered in identifying the boundaries between institutions.

The fifth overarching theme addressed in this volume is the role of human need. Several authors in this volume have identified human needs (such as the need for human flourishing or the need for self-development) as central to the rationale for a nonprofit sector. Focusing on the needs of people and societies as the reason for the existence of the nonprofit sector may have been implicit in prior theories, but it is made even more explicit by contributors to this volume. Rather than viewing the sector as a failure of other institutions (such as markets or the state), they view the sector as meeting the fundamental needs of people.

The sixth theme is the role of nonprofit market characteristics in shaping the interactions between consumers and producers in the sector. Some authors in the volume focused on the goods being produced in the nonprofit marketplace (and the nature of those goods, such as whether they were public goods or toll goods), while others considered the information structures central to the structuring of interactions between consumers and producers. These approaches suggest that a focus on the market characteristics that give rise to nonprofit institutional forms may yet provide additional fruitful avenues of theory and study in the nonprofit sector.

Finally, many of our contributors emphasized the importance of subjective values and experiences in defining the role and nature of the nonprofit sector. The subjective, moral, and symbolic role of the sector was a common theme among several of our contributors. This suggests a psychological dimension to the nonprofit sector that cannot be fully observed without understanding the individual preferences, views, and experiences of individuals. This individual, personal perspective on the role and nature of the nonprofit sector suggests that people should be viewed not only as clients, donors, managers, or providers of goods and services in the nonprofit space, but also as forces whose values, perspectives, and preferences shape the space itself.

Our volume created some convergence around these themes, but it generated divergence as well. These tensions sometimes represent opposing views of the nonprofit sector and its role. For instance, while some authors celebrate and prescribe increased, state-sanctioned nonprofit formalization, others warn that it is precisely state-sanctioned nonprofit formalization that should be avoided. While one author suggests that nonprofit organizations exist to enhance representation for those who are underrepresented by political institutions, another suggests that political institutions can co-opt nonprofit organizations and undermine their representativeness. Where one author sees the innovation of the sector as being centered in organizing, another sees it largely in the creation of symbols. These tensions do not beg the question of whether side A or B is correct – because of course both are – but instead urges us to dig deeper to understand *under what circumstances* A is more accurate, and under which the answer is B. The opportunity to address these tensions is the gift of a diverse and globally inclusive nonprofit sector theory.

These themes and tensions gathered from across the chapters of this volume suggest a rich dialogue about the global nature of the nonprofit in all its diversity and complexity. Consideration of these themes and tensions also raises important questions that should be addressed in future research and theory on the nonprofit sector.

21.3 Big Questions in Nonprofit Sector Theory

In exploring the nature and purpose of the nonprofit sector, this volume raises many unanswered questions. Certainly, our originating questions of "*what* is the nonprofit sector?" and "*why* does the nonprofit sector exist?" remain open. So, too, does the call to develop nonprofit sector theory that can define and describe the sector, predict its future, explain the mechanisms by which the sector functions and interacts with other sectors, evaluate the results and effectiveness of the sector, and prescribe policy and practice.

In 2007, Lohmann wrote an essay in which he identified the "big questions of nonprofit management." While most of his questions focused on nonprofit management rather than sector theory, he also asked things like, "What exactly is the 'third sector' a sector of?" (p. 437) and "whether we have not yet gotten to the real nature of [nonprofit] organizations, sociologically, politically, or economically?" (p. 439). We build on this tradition of "big questions" and add our own questions specific to nonprofit sector theory.

Our work here suggests some overarching questions about the nonprofit sector that remain vital to our ability to comprehend the role of the nonprofit sector in society. These "big questions" form the basis of a research agenda for future work on the nonprofit sector.

1. *What are the other "sectors" to which the nonprofit sector should be compared?* Expanding on Lohmann's question about what the nonprofit sector is a sector *of*, an enduring question about the nature of the nonprofit sector is precisely what type of institution it is, and what other comparable institutions therefore must be.

The answers to this question are likely to exist in tension with one another. As demonstrated in this volume, the sector may simultaneously be a sector of the economy, social economy, polity, law, nation, culture, and more. The question therefore is less one of which approach is *correct* and more of how these sectoral perspectives can coexist in a shared framework.

2. *What is the nature of the relationship of the nonprofit sector to the state in a diverse, global context?* The role of the state is central to many of the formulations of the nonprofit sector. However, the role of the state varies from supporting nonprofit organizations, co-opting nonprofit institutions for its own aggrandizement, or needing nonprofit organizations to aid in representing the polity. Do these institutions exist in collaboration or contention? And do these institutions always develop in the same order (e.g., voluntary sector and then state, or state and then voluntary sector, or both at the same time), and what factors determine the nature of interaction between the two institutions?
3. *How does context shape the meaning and nature of the nonprofit sector?* We have discovered that the nonprofit sector is very different depending on where and when the phenomenon is observed. Are there patterns in the development of the sector and in the contextual factors that shape its characteristics? Are these predictable, or does the nonprofit sector emerge differently in every context, even when the contexts are somewhat alike?
4. *How should the many conceptions of the nonprofit sector be understood in a diverse global context?* In a diverse and pluralistic world, how should we structure our conversations about the nonprofit sector globally, to recognize and validate the many perspectives and contexts that exist within our global nonprofit fabric?
5. *Should society encourage or discourage the formalization of social organizing?* Bromley and Santos suggest that organizing is a defining feature of modernity. Under what circumstances does nonprofit formalization benefit or hinder the well-being of society and the people in it? To what extent does formalization favor one perspective or set of actors and disenfranchise others? Is formalization, at the organizational level or at the policy level, appropriate in the nonprofit sector? While Ordor advocates for increased support for organizational formalization and increased avenues for local organizing through legal structures, Rojas Durazo suggests

that formalization is precisely what has given rise to the nonprofit industrial complex, undermining the efficacy of social organizing. How is this tension to be resolved?

6. *What problems does the nonprofit sector exist to solve?* This question forms the basis for being able to perform evaluation on the sector as an institution, or to make valuable prescriptions about how to strengthen the sector or help it to evolve. Authors in this volume have suggested that nonprofits exist to address unmet need, to facilitate human flourishing, to aid in self-development, and to create a symbolic reality. Others suggest nonprofits as an aid to the state in representing the polity, while yet others suggest it is an arm of the state designed to subdue the public.
7. *How can theories of the nonprofit sector appropriately account for the role of the family in society?* How might this change across cultures, national contexts, and time?
8. *What is the appropriate role of politics in the nonprofit sector, and of the nonprofit sector in politics?* How does this change when ruling parties change, and what are the respective roles of nonprofits and political parties in representing the interests of the people? How does this role vary across international political contexts in which the relationship of political parties to the state may differ dramatically?
9. *How do theories of the nonprofit sector describe, predict, and explain sector blurring, social enterprise, and organizational hybridity*? Some definitions in this volume separate nonprofit organizations from for-profit social enterprise while others suggest constructs that could simultaneously account for formal, legally incorporated nonprofit organizations (or their global counterparts) and informal, unincorporated social organizing, as well as prosocial activity that generates and distributes profit. To what extent should theories of the nonprofit sector also provide useful theory for informal and/or for-profit social organizing?
10. *Is the nonprofit sector driven by altruism or self-interest?* To what extent do altruistic intentions limit the self-development capacity and personal agency of the people for whom we seek to improve circumstances? Would a view of the nonprofit sector as self-representation, self-development, and personally rewarding change our understanding of the institutions that comprise the sector?

11. *What is the relationship of the nonprofit sector to faith, belief, the expression of values, and organized religion?* To what extent is the sector focused on imposing values on others, to expressing values, and nurturing the expression of belief? Given the long history of the relationship between the nonprofit sector and churches, belief systems, and religions across the world, to what extent are these institutions distinct, and to what extent are they intertwined or even synonymous?

While not exhaustive, we suggest that this list of 11 questions is an important starting point for the further development of nonprofit sector theory. These build on the classic questions identified by Lohmann, the key tensions identified by our authors, and the themes observed through our international consideration of nonprofit prosocial organizing. We invite future scholars to explore these issues from diverse perspectives as we work toward a more representative body of nonprofit sector theories.

21.4 No Grand Theory of Nonprofit Institutions

While we observe many important themes in the manifestation of the nonprofit sector across global and ideological contexts, it is clear that pluralism exists in the ways people think about and interact with the sector as a construct, concept, and phenomenon. It is tempting to seek an approach to ordering this set of diverse and intertwined perspectives in a single unified whole – a grand theory of the nonprofit sector. The "grand theory" approach would arguably provide definitional clarity, suggest a shared language, and orient us to the nature and purpose of the nonprofit sector in a way that could provide a satisfactory and tidy answer to our inquiry about what the nonprofit sector is and why it exists.

However, no such grand theory can exist without first providing a space in the conversation for the astounding diversity of perspectives on the nonprofit sector and its many faces – including third sector, voluntary sector, civil society, social entrepreneurship, industrial complex, organizational expression, and transformative symbolic reality, to name just a few. Before we can hope to formulate a theory that accounts for these many manifestations of the nonprofit phenomenon globally, we must achieve some sense of saturation in the identification and explication of the qualitative experience of people, cultures, and nations with this phenomenon. That is, despite the rich diversity we have observed, we have observed too little to say we have seen enough and have gathered the universe of possible configurations of the nonprofit sector.

Perhaps legalistic and economic definitions of nonprofit institutions – and even the term "nonprofit sector" – has previously prevented us from answering questions about nonprofit organizing on a global scale. Despite some organizational characteristics that can be found globally, such as those identified by Anheier and Salamon (2006), there are a great many views from nations outside the West and from the voices of indigenous and minority communities in countries like the United States that suggest the importance of a much more diverse set of organizing forms, institutions, and perspectives that may fit the concept of "nonprofit" but not the formal definition of either "nonprofit organizations" or the "nonprofit sector." In considering the nature of nonprofit social association outside of formal organizations, we echo the call of Smith for the study of nonprofit "dark matter" (1997). Indeed, it may be that when it comes to the nonprofit sector the dark matter is the matter that matters most.

This volume suggests, if nothing else, a deep need to revisit the core assumptions of nonprofit sector theory. Despite laudable work in internationalizing the concept of the nonprofit sector, it is clear that there are many variables – natural, social, cultural, legal, political – that must yet be taken into account if we are to describe and explain the nonprofit sector in ways that also allow us to evaluate and predict it.

The insights provided by the authors in this volume suggest a rich opportunity for scholars to reimagine the nonprofit sector in a manner that extends the existing body of nonprofit sector theory and provides a more expansive view of the role of nonprofit activity in society. The contributors have revealed several important insights into the nonprofit sector and its place in society. They have shown that the conventional three-sector paradigm, which categorizes organizations into public, private, and nonprofit sectors, is limited and does not fully capture the dynamic interplay between people and organizations. Additionally, the contributors have illustrated that the standard theories of the nonprofit sector fail to account for the needs and viewpoints of the global majority. They have shown that the narrow Western and scientific understanding of the nonprofit sector limits our understanding of prosocial behavior in different cultural and religious contexts.

Theory and practice sometimes seem only distantly related – with theory focused on ideas and overarching concepts, whereas practice is rooted in the day-to-day details of operating nonprofit organizations. But the chapters in this volume demonstrate that theory has profound effects on the practice of nonprofit organization and management. The way we think about nonprofits affects the ways in which we regulate, structure, and operate them. The nonprofit space exists not only within organizations but also across organizations, creating a loose network of organizations that function similarly in society and influence one another like drops of water in an ocean. From the tide of nonprofit theory come ideas about the future of the sector – and of civil society generally – as well as riptides that pull us toward the past.

As we take stock of the purpose for which nonprofits – as a broad set of entities – exist, we must ask ourselves questions about the effectiveness of the overall nonprofit endeavor. Are nonprofits solving social problems? Are they improving the global quality of life for all people and for the planet? What is the effect of our institutions, writ large? And importantly, what harms or dependencies might we inadvertently be perpetuating? Moreover, how do our beliefs and assumptions about nonprofit work – codified in law, policy, and practice – prevent us from evolving into a more powerful state of affairs for our global civil society?

Taken as a whole, this work offers a broad and nuanced perspective on the nonprofit sector, its challenges and opportunities. The contributors have shown that the nonprofit sector is a complex and multifaceted phenomenon that is shaped by a variety of factors, including the political economy, cultural and religious traditions, and the needs and experiences of diverse populations. They have also demonstrated the importance of taking an interdisciplinary approach that draws on a range of perspectives and disciplines to better understand the nonprofit sector and its role in society. The authors hope that this work will inspire further research and dialogue in the field and contribute to a more inclusive and equitable society.

We opened this volume with a chapter inviting us to rethink nonprofit theory. The challenge of this volume, then, was to evaluate the current state of nonprofit theory by critiquing and extending existing theories and proposing new directions. Our hope has been to shake the nonprofit world out of the slumber of imagined convergence and awake us to the reality of a deep divergence of our conceptions and experiences of the nonprofit sector. We do so in hope of reinvigorating a lively discussion about the possibilities that await us in a diverse and global world of deep tradition and innovative solutions. In an ever-evolving world of rapidly changing wicked problems, the worst thing we can do is remain static in old ideas that no longer serve us.

References

Anheier, H. K., & Salamon, L. M. (2006). The nonprofit sector in comparative perspective. In W. W. Powell (Ed.), The nonprofit sector: A research handbook (2nd ed.) (pp. 89–116). Yale University Press.

Cunliffe, A. L. (2022). Must I grow a pair of balls to theorize about theory in organization and management studies? *Organization Theory*, *3*(3), 26317877221109277.

Locke, E. A. (2007). The case for inductive theory building. *Journal of Management*, *33*(6), 867–890.

Lohmann, R. A. (2007). Charity, philanthropy, public service, or enterprise: What are the big questions of nonprofit management today? *Public Administration Review*, *67*(3), 437–444.

Smith, D. H. (1997). The rest of the nonprofit sector: Grassroots associations as the dark matter ignored in prevailing "flat earth" maps of the sector. *Nonprofit and Voluntary Sector Quarterly*, 26(2), 114–131.

Tilly, C. (1992). *Coercion, capital, and European states, AD 990–1992*. Blackwell.

Weick, K. E. (2001). Sources of order in underorganized systems: Themes in recent organizational theory. In K. E. Weick (Ed.), *Making sense of the organization* (ch. 2). University of Michigan/ Blackwell Publishing.

Young, D. R. (2000). Alternative models of government–nonprofit sector relations: Theoretical and international perspectives. *Nonprofit and Voluntary Sector Quarterly*, *29*(1), 149–172.

Index

Printed by Integrated Books International,
United States of America